Modern Music-Makers

Modern MUSIC~MAKERS

Contemporary American Composers

By MADELEINE GOSS

We are the music makers,
And we are the dreamers of dreams . . .

ARTHUR O'SHAUGHNESSY

GREENWOOD PRESS, PUBLISHERS
WESTPORT, CONNECTICUT

ODE

By Arthur O'Shaughnessy

We are the music makers
 And we are the dreamers of dreams . . .
World losers and world forsakers.
 On whom the pale moon gleams:
Yet we are the movers and shakers
 Of the world for ever, it seems. . . .

But we with our dreaming and singing
 Ceaseless and sorrowless we!
The glory about us clinging
 Of the glorious futures we see,
Our souls with high music ringing:
 O men! It must ever be
That we dwell, in our dreaming and singing
 A little apart from ye.

FOREWORD

FEW people realize what a great deal of music is being written in the United States today. There are probably more composers now living than in all the years of our musical history before 1900.

Because of time and space it has been possible to deal with only a limited number in this book, and to make a more or less arbitrary selection. Although the list includes most of today's leading com-posers, many others necessarily had to be omitted.

Only American-born music writers have been included (with the exception of Lukas Foss, whose major training and work have been done in this country), and only those with whom the present writer has been able to talk personally. (Again with one exception—Charles Ives. He has been an invalid for a number of years, but his wife supplied the necessary information.)

The author wishes to express sincere appreciation to all the composers who have so generously co-operated in making this book possible. Their courtesy and helpfulness in the midst of exacting and absorbing work have lightened the labor of gathering the material, and have added considerably to its value.

CONTENTS

INDEX OF COMPOSERS

PHOTOGRAPHS

Modern Music-Makers

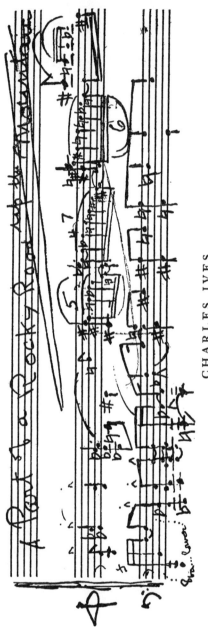

CHARLES IVES

CHARLES IVES

IN the late 1880's "modern" music, as we understand it today, was still unknown. Debussy, a young man in his twenties, had only recently begun to startle the world with his Impressionism—forerunner of the modern school, and as for atonality, polytonality, extreme dissonance (familiar fabric of today's music), these were considered musical aberrations beneath the notice of serious musicians. Yet even at this time the seeds of the new music had begun to sprout in a conservative New England village.

Charles Ives, born in 1874, started at an early age to explore untried musical territories. He was one of the first either here or abroad to write in the modern idiom; yet he has been one of the last to receive public recognition. During his years of work he composed mainly as a side line, in whatever moments he could spare from an exacting business career. And his music was so far ahead of his time that it is only in recent years that he has come to be acknowledged one of the foremost, and certainly the first, of America's new music composers. Even today Ives belongs in the advance-guard of the contemporary school.

Charles Ives' father, George Ives, was also a musician and an experimenter. He came of a long line of Yankee forbears, all of them from New England. There is no record of any special musical talent before his time, though in a distant branch of the family an Eli Ives had edited, in 1846, a "Musical Spelling Book" elaborately titled *A New Method of Instruction in the Rudiments of Music Together with Musical Recreations.*

George Ives organized his first band at the time of the Civil War, when he was only sixteen. (Abraham Lincoln mentioned this band with special praise.[1]) He had a prodigious curiosity for all things musical, and was forever trying out new sound effects and curious combinations of tones. Sometimes he would divide his band into groups and have them play from different levels—one on the village

[1] General Grant's apocryphal remark is said to have been made in connection with George Ives' band. When Lincoln praised it, Grant replied "They say it's the best band in the Army. But you couldn't prove it by me—I only know two tunes; one is *Yankee Doodle*—the other one isn't!"

15

green, another on the roof of a near-by building, and a third in the bell tower of the church. Bells in particular fascinated him—and so did echoes. There was a fine echo down by the Danbury Pond. Towards evening he would go down there and play on one of his musical instruments, then note the sound as it came back to him across the water. The echo, he discovered, was usually a half or a quarter of a tone lower than the original interval. . . .

He tried to make an instrument that would reproduce these quarter-tones, and manufactured a curious machine consisting of twenty-four violin strings stretched to a clothes-horse frame and held down by weights—primitive forerunner of the quarter-tone piano later perfected by Hans Barth.

George Ives' son Charles was born on October 20, 1874. At the age of four young Charlie began experimenting on the family's old square piano in the front parlor of their home in Danbury, Connecticut. Sometimes he played on the treble keys, imitating the cymbals that he heard in his father's band. Or he would thump vigorously on the piano's lower register—not with the indiscriminate banging that most children delight in, but with purposeful and unmistakable rhythm—attempting to reproduce the roll of the drums. These ventures into musical dynamics marked the beginning of a long line of experiments that later made Charles Ives known as the most original of all American composers.

Fortunately his father did not discourage these early efforts. He taught the boy everything he knew about music, and instilled in him a wholesome respect for the classics as well as interest in original research. Charlie learned to play the piano, violin, cornet and organ—not to mention his early enthusiasm, the drum—and rapidly absorbed the fundamentals of harmony and sight-reading.

His first piece was a *Dirge* for the family cat (who was named Chin-Chin after the Chinese laundryman). This doleful melody proved such a success with all who heard it that he kept on composing funeral music for defunct village pets. One, in passacaglia style, was appropriately based on the *Dead March* from Saul. At thirteen Charlie branched into livelier subjects and wrote a *Holiday Quick-Step* for his fathers' band. This piece was played at a local concert and received high praise.

Young Ives was already at that time a first-class organist. A pupil of

Charles Ives

Dudley Buck's, he began at the age of twelve to play in Danbury's churches—"the youngest organist in the state," as *The News* proudly reported. He earned his expenses while at Hopkins' Preparatory School, and later at Yale, by playing the organ. In his younger days, however, athletics interested him almost as much as music, and he was particularly good at baseball. About his musical achievements young Ives was always shy. If anyone asked him what he played, he was more apt to answer "short-stop" than "piano" or "organ."

At Yale Ives completed both academic and music courses, the latter under the direction of Horatio Parker. Mindful of his father's early precepts, he dutifully learned all the rules and regulations of formal composition, and stayed reasonably close to tradition in his music-writing of that period. While at college he wrote a number of fairly conventional songs, but on the side he kept on trying out unorthodox experiments with curious harmonies and frequent and abrupt changes of key and rhythm. Before the days of Schoenberg and Stravinsky, Ives—completely unaware of their existence—was making discoveries similar to their own. It was not until years later that he even heard of Debussy and Impressionism. . . .

On graduating from Yale, a musical career seemed indicated. But Ives knew that to make a success as a composer he would have to write in the conventional ways that had been drummed into him at college, and he was too much Georges Ives' son to follow such a program. He lost his father during his freshman year at Yale; but the latter left him as legacy an eager, questioning mind, and this he was never to lose.

Now, with typical independence, Ives decided to go into business. He wanted to learn more about human nature, and to put into practise some of his theories about service and relationships. The insurance business appealed to him as a good opportunity for this. Shortly after graduating from Yale he went to New York and took a job at five dollars a week with the Mutual Life Insurance Company. A few years later he and a fellow clerk set up their own firm. After some initial difficulties in getting established, the firm of Ives and Myrick grew into one of the largest and best of its kind in the country—a monument to Charles Ives' belief in democracy, with justice and liberty for all.

Business to him, however, was largely a means towards what he most desired—the opportunity to compose the kind of music that he wanted to write, without being obliged to conform to conventional standards.

In 1908, the year after he and Julian Myrick set up their own insurance firm, Charles Ives married Harmony Twitchell. (They have one daughter, now Mrs. George Grayson Tyler). Mrs. Ives' father, the Reverend Joseph Twitchell of Hartford, was an intimate friend of the literary celebrities of his day, including Whittier, William Dean Howells, and Mark Twain. Harmony Twitchell Ives, herself, has the sensitive awareness and understanding of a poet and her husband has set a number of her verses to music. She encouraged Ives to go on writing music in his own original way—even when most of his friends were urging him to "stick to 'geiger' music."

The years immediately following Charles Ives' marriage were the most productive of his entire career. He was always a very slow worker, partly because his business left him little leisure and partly because of the painstaking labor with which he developed his ideas. Yet in spite of this fact he worked so consistently that he managed, during the relatively short span of his productive years (illness put an end to his career in 1927) to turn out a prodigious amount of music.

His very first compositions were songs, and he continued to write them all through his career. There are several hundred in all, and for many of these he has written the words as well as the music. Ives composed his first song before he was fifteen, and the last in 1927 shortly before the break in his health made further work impossible. A collection of a hundred and fourteen songs was privately printed in 1921. In the preface he stated, with typical independence, that the collection "was thrown, so to speak, at the music fraternity, who for this reason will feel free to dodge it on its way—perhaps to the wastebasket." He goes on to say:

Various authors have various reasons for bringing out a book. . . . Some have written a book for money; I have not. Some for fame; I have not. Some for kindlings; I have not. I have not written a book for any of these reasons or for all of them together. In fact, gentle borrower, I have not written a book at all—I have merely cleaned house. All that is left is out on the clothes-line. . . . .

Charles Ives

Copland says of this collection of songs:[2] "There is no order here—either of chronology, style, or quality . . . . Almost every kind of song imaginable can be found. . . . Songs of every character and description, songs bristling with dissonances, tone clusters and "elbow chords" next to songs of the most elementary harmonic simplicity. All thrown together helter-skelter, displaying an amazing variety and fecundity of imagination. . . ."

Copland finds the songs written between 1919 and 1921 the best in the collection:

Taken as a whole, despite many and serious shortcomings, these songs are a unique and memorable contribution to the art of song writing in America . . . a contribution that, for richness and depth of emotional content, for broad range and strength of expression, for harmonic and rhythmic originality, will remain a challenge and an inspiration to future generations of American composers.[3]

Charles Ives wrote his *First Symphony* while he was still in college, and the *Second* soon after. There are four in all, and three other large orchestral works that might be called symphonies, though they are not so listed: *Holidays* (in four movements: "Washington's Birthday," "Decoration Day," "Fourth of July" and "Thanksgiving") and two *Orchestral Sets.*

In the earlier years, while he was acting as organist, Ives composed a number of choral and organ pieces; next choral works with accompaniments of various combinations of instruments; and finally three large works for unison chorus and full orchestra: *Lincoln, The Great Commoner* (to a poem by Edwin Markham), *An Election;* and *War March*—this last including full brass and drum corps. *War March* was written in 1917 during the First World War, and is "a kind of reflection . . . of the spirit . . . of days of storm and stress in this country's march on its road of liberty." The closing chorus sings of a theme dear to Ives's heart:

Then it's build a People's World Nation
Every honest country free to live its own Native life. . . .

[2] *Our New Music,* by Aaron Copland. Whittlesey House, 1941.
[3] *Ibid.*

19

Modern Music-Makers

In his political views as well as in his music Charles Ives was in advance of his time. He has expressed his ideas in various articles and pamphlets. The only hope of the world, he believes is in its people. Just as music expresses the experiences and emotions common to every man, so government should—in practice as well as theory—represent the views of all the people, and not only of the politicians, who too often seek personal power rather than the good of each. The people, in Ives' opinion, should have more opportunity to state their views. Some years ago he had printed and mailed out at his own expense, thousands of copies of a proposed "Twentieth Amendment," whereby Congress should consider plans sent in by the people and resubmit the best of these for popular vote.

War would be entirely eliminated, Ives feels, if all the inhabitants in every country were given the full truth and then the people themselves were allowed to make the final decision. In an article written during the First World War he suggested a plan:

A people's World Nation in which every honest country will be free to live its own native life with the help of its World Army Police will bring the greatest hope of the world today to its realization; a world where men can stand up as men and friends, and "do unto others as they would be done by."—a world in which the people will have more to say and the boss politicians less. . . .

New England, the home of Ives' ancestors and the center of his own interests, has been the theme of most of his works. *The First Orchestral Set,* subtitled "Three Places in New England," was begun in 1903 (though not completed until 1914). It describes three historic spots: "The Boston Common," "Putnam's Camp" and "The Housatonic at Stockbridge." Like most of Ives' scores, the *New England Symphony* (as it is sometimes called) is extremely difficult to play. When Nicolas Slonimsky conducted it he said that he had to invent "a new baton technique—never letting my right hand know what my left was doing, but letting my mind know what both were doing."

The *Second Orchestral Set* is also in three parts, likewise springing from a New England background: "Elegy," "The Rockstrewn Hills Join in the People's Outdoor Meeting," and "From Hanover Square North—at the End of a Tragic Day, the Voice of the People Again Arose." This is one of Ives' later works—finished in 1915. He began

Charles Ives

a *Third Orchestral Set* in 1919, but though he worked on it until 1926, only two movements were completed.

The early hymn tunes of New England have been a constant source of inspiration to Charles Ives. He has used them as themes for a number of his compositions—notably in the "Thanksgiving" section of *Holidays,* in some of the violin sonatas, in the third movement of the *Second String Quartet,* and in the Fourth Symphony, which contains a fugue built on the opening bars of the old hymn *From Greenland's Icy Mountains.*

In 1911 Ives began what was to have been his largest work, but only the "Prelude" and part of one movement were completed. He called it *The Universe Symphony,* and the underlying plan was "a presentation and contemplation in tones, rather than in music (as such), of the mysterious creation of the earth and firmament, the evolution of all life in nature, in humanity to the divine."

Ives feels that music has endless possibilities for helping to solve the problems of mankind:

> The future of music may not be entirely with music itself, but rather in the way it makes itself a part with—in the way it encourages and extends, rather than limits, the aspirations and ideals of the people—the finer things that humanity does and dreams of: and perhaps the time is coming, but not in our time, when it will develop possibilities inconceivable now—a language so transcendent that its heights and depths will be common to all mankind.[4]

The chamber-music works of Charles Ives reveal the amazing fertility of his imagination and the diversity of his interests. In addition to regular trios, string quartets etc., he has experimented with endless varieties and combination of instruments. One of his works, appropriately scored with triangle, bass drums and cymbals "ad lib.," recalls the excitement of local conflagrations. It is in two sections: *The Gong on the Hook and Ladder,* and *Fireman's Parade on Main Street.*

Another work, named *The Pond*—for strings, flute, voice or English horn, harp, bells or celesta—may have been suggested by his father's early experiments with echoes, down by the Danbury Pond. Others,

---

[4] Charles Ives in the prologue of his *Essays before a Sonata.*

still, such as *Incantation, The Innate, The Unanswered Question,* branch into mystical themes.

The experiences and memories of Ives' life have all been woven into his music.

All of the elements of back-country New England music were assimilated by Ives, on whom they made a deep impression. Having too good a musical ear and general perception to do as the others have done and remove in the cultivated version of his music all the characteristics and charming irregularities, Ives began early to build himself a music in which he could include all these mooted elements.[5]

Ives' preoccupation with quarter-tones, dating from his father's early ventures in that field, led him to do considerable experimenting along that line. He discovered that massed chords or "tone-clusters," that is, large numbers of notes held down simultaneously, would create overtones that progressed into quarter intervals. He even tried writing music with actual quarter-tones. A *Chorale for Strings* (transcribed for two pianos) was played at an Aeolian Hall concert in 1925, on two specially constructed quarter-tone pianos designed by Hans Barth. To the audience,however—whose ears were unaccustomed to such intervals— the music merely sounded out of tune. "The naked exhibition of quarter-tone effects . . . attracted many of the listeners to laughter," wrote the critic of the *New York Sun.* "But calmer consideration will, perhaps, bring to some of them a realization of the truly estimable character of the melodic sequences."

Ives, at that time, was not popular . . . The story is told of another concert, shortly after the Aeolian Hall venture, where his music was played on the same program with that of Debussy. A man in the audience remarked to his neighbor: "This Debussy, he's dead, isn't he? And what about Ives—is he dead too?"

"No—" answered the other "—but he ought to be!"

Ives' music was seldom heard in the earlier days—save for an occasional performance by such liberal-minded groups as Pro Musica, The League of American Composers, New Music Society, and a few others. The reason for this was due in no small measure to the complicated appearance of his scores. After one look at an Ives score

---

[5] *Henry Cowell in American Composers on American Music.*

Charles Ives

conductors and players alike would throw up their hands and declare it "too difficult to perform."

> Much more is clear to the ear than to the eye. And music which seemed completely impossible when viewed as ink on paper, turned out to be a combination of sounds which were startlingly beautiful. . . .One must first break down his own barriers to an art which may seem strange and relentlessly uncomprising, but once the approach has succeeded, a very large figure looms out of the melange of consonance and dissonance and rhythmical complexity.[6]

In some of his music Ives wrote without key or time signatures, without even measure divisions. These things, he felt, restricted the composer in setting down his music, and the performer who interpreted it as well. He tried to devise a more fluid medium, better able to express the rich variety of his ideas. Ives' unconventional scoring gives his music what one critic called "the flexibility of a tree-top swaying in the wind."

He also wanted the performers to feel free to interpret his works in whatever way the music or mood struck them. On some of his scores he has penciled notations as caustic and full of Yankee wit as his own personality. Occasionally he indicates alternate phrases to suit the performer's mood of the moment. "Use on Saturday nights," he wrote over a somewhat trite cadence, and added "This song was written to clear up the disputed point—which is worse, the words or the music?" On another score, with a fine contempt for discord-hating hearers, he scribbled "Don't mind the soft ears a-lolling around in the hall—knock 'em over the ropes! Make 'em work their ears like real men!" "Lily-pad ears" is what Ives calls "nice" people who can't stand modern music ("Nice" being his most damning adjective).

At a concert where his own works were booed and jeered, he sat quietly until a piece by his good friend Carl Ruggles—another strong American individualist—received the same treatment from someone sitting near him. Then Ives, always quick-tempered, jumped to his feet and cried: "Don't be such a damn sissy! When you hear strong music like this, get up and try to use your ears like a man. . . ."[7]

[6] Goddard Lieberson in *Musical America.*
[7] This and a number of other incidents are related in an unpublished article *A Connecticut Yankee in Music,* by Lucille Fletcher (Mrs. Bernard Hermann).

Modern Music-Makers

There are still today "lily-pad" ears unwilling to meet the challenge that underlies most of Ives's music and, for that matter, all modern music. Those who try to "use their ears like men," however, will find much to reward them in his compositions.

Early in 1939 John Kirkpatrick, distinguished pianist, played an amazing piece of music at New York's Town Hall: Charles Ives' *Second* or *Concord Sonata*. The work, monumental in scope, in four separate parts and as long as a symphony, had been written nearly a quarter of a century before, but it was still more "modern" than many a composition of current vintage.

In certain of the passages Kirkpatrick supplemented his ten fingers with a narrow padded board about fourteen inches long by which he held down whole groups of notes, thus creating what one critic called "softly blent sonorities of ghostly effect."

Kirkpatrick first heard the *Concord Sonata* in Paris, in 1927. A part of it, that is—the entire work was then considered too difficult to perform at one sitting. Long before Charles Ives received full recognition in his own country, he was highly considered abroad. "The most original and authentic of American composers," someone called him.

At that initial hearing in Paris Kirkpatrick could make nothing of the *Sonata*. In fact he admits that he thought the composer "stark staring mad" to have written such music. But as he studied the piece— it took him twelve years to memorize it—he began to realize that here was an extraordinary work; now he considers it one of the greatest sonatas ever written.

The *Concord Sonata* is perhaps Ives' greatest work. For it represents the height of his musical development, and is likewise an expression of his personal philosophy which springs from the transcendentalism of New England. Ives has discussed at length both the musical program of the *Sonata* and his philosophical beliefs in *Essays before a Sonata*. (Of this book William Lyon Phelps wrote, "It is brilliant but provocative, full of challenging ideas and marked by chronic cerebration.")

The four parts of the *Concord Sonata* are dedicated to Emerson, Hawthorne, The Alcotts, and Thoreau.

Charles Ives

Emerson is portrayed as:

standing on a summit, at the door of the infinite where many men do not dare to climb, peering into the mysteries of life, contemplating the eternities, hurling back whatever he discovers there—now thunderbolts for us to grasp, if we can, and translate—now placing quietly, even tenderly, in our hands, things that we may see without effort—if we don't use them, so much the worse for us.

Next *The Alcotts.*

As one walks down the broad-arched street. . . .he comes presently to the old elms overspreading the Alcott house. It seems to stand as a kind of homely but beautiful witness of Concord's common virtue. . . .Within the house, on every side, lie remembrances. . . .There sits the little old spinet piano. . . .on which Beth played the *Fifth Symphony*. . . .There is an "oracle" at the beginning of the *Fifth Symphony*—in those four notes lies one of Beethoven's greatest messages. . . .the soul of humanity knocking at the door of the Divine mysteries, radiant in the faith that it *will* be opened—and that the human will become the Divine!

The Third Movement, *Hawthorne,* (in scherzo form).

is but an "extended fragment" trying to suggest some of his (Hawthorne's) wilder, fantastic adventures into the half-childlike, half-fairylike phantasmal realms.

For the last section, called *Thoreau,* Ives has written: "And if there shall be a program let it follow his thought on an autumn day of Indian summer at Walden. . . ." The *Sonata* ends on a note of quiet grandeur as Thoreau goes through the moonlight to his cabin "with a strange liberty in Nature, a part of herself."

With Kirkpatrick's 1939 performance of the *Concord Sonata* the American public began at last to wake up to the fact that a unique artist had been living in their midst, practically unrecognized, for more than forty years. He was hailed as "one of the most vital, original, audacious . . . most individual and authentic of all United States composers . . . as American as Mark Twain. . . "

John Kirkpatrick has played the *Concord Sonata* many times since. After a performance at the American Music Festival in Washington's

Modern Music-Makers

National Gallery in March, 1946, the critic of the *Times Herald* wrote:

This is the most important work to be added to the literature of the piano since Liszt wrote the great *Sonata in B Minor.* Ives composed it between 1911 and 1915. It still is far in advance of the present. New sounds, new moods, new acoustic vistas are unfolded in this amazing score. As the title suggests, the composer has sought to express in tones the spiritual values of those literary figures, the Concord transcendentalists, Emerson, Hawthorne, the Alcotts, and Thoreau. There has been no music like it.[8]

It was not until 1946 that Charles Ives really began to come into his own. That year a number of concerts featured his music. The *First Violin Sonata* was heard in February on a program sponsored by the League of Composers. In April the *Third Symphony,* written while Ives was still in his twenties and which had been "lying around in a New England barn for close to forty years," received its first performance. On this occasion the critics, commenting on "the neglect that has been meted out to one of this country's most gifted composers," at last began to pay Charles Ives the tribute that he deserves. His *Third Symphony* was awarded the 1947 Pulitzer Prize for "a distinguished musical composition in the larger forms of chamber, orchestral or choral music."

There were several other performances that same year, the most important of which took place during Columbia University's May Festival of Contemporary American Music. At that time a concert devoted exclusively to Charles Ives' works was given—"a belated but welcome homage to that almost legendary figure among native musicians." Seven of his songs were sung by Mordecai Bauman, including *General William Booth Enters Heaven* and *Charlie Rutlage.* The *Second String Quartet*—"a kind of fantastic 'quodlibet' of the modern age" as one critic called it, now was given its first complete performance. On the score of this work Ives had put the following penciled notes:

The first movement suggests an outdoor meeting of men in the country whose converse leads to discussion. Second movement—arguments which

[8] *The Washington Times-Herald,* March 18, 1946.

Charles Ives

almost bring on a fight. Third movement—all men join hands and march up the mountain to view the firmament.

The second part of the Columbia Festival program was orchestral, ending with the *Third Symphony* and beginning with two shorter pieces: *The Unanswered Question (A Cosmic Landscape)* and *Central Park in the Dark (Some Forty Years Ago.)* For these last, two orchestras were required, one on the stage, the other in the wings to simulate the effect of music coming from a far distance.

Ives originally called these two "A Contemplation of a Serious Matter" and "A Contemplation of Nothing Serious." The first, "a philosophical research into the Perennial Question of existence" ends in "Undisturbed Solitude." The second, in lighter vein, "purports to be a picture in sounds of the sounds of nature and of happenings that men would hear some forty or so years ago . . . when sitting on a bench in Central Park on a hot summer night. . . ."

Each year sees an increasing number of performances of Charles Ives' music. In 1951 his *Second Symphony*, composed over sixty years years ago, was finally given its first performance by Leonard Bernstein and the New York Philharmonic-Symphony. It was written, Ives explains, to express the musical feelings of the 1890 Connecticut countryside. The opening movement, played by the strings, is serene and unhurried, while the last contains what the composer calls "a sort of bad joke" . . . a set of Yankee tunes—including *Columbia, the Gem of the Ocean, Campton Races,* and *Turkey-in-the-Straw* set in counterpoint with some Bach tunes. "Unquestionably an authentic work of art" said Virgil Thomson of this symphony in the *Herald Tribune.*

Charles Ives belongs first and last to America. He has always been a "hard-headed Yankee," quick-tempered and ready to fight for his convictions—full of humor yet with a deep sense of reverence towards the fundamental values of life.

This "rugged individualist of the first order," this "intrepid explorer of the sounds of nature," has been aptly called "The Walt Whitman of Music." Like the great American poet he has given voice to his own country and people and to the foundation of their existence: Liberty. One of his songs he has titled *The Things Our Fathers*

Modern Music-Makers

Loved (and the Greatest of These Was Liberty). The words are his
own:

> I think there must be a place in the soul
> All made of tunes, of tunes of long ago;
> I hear the organ on the Main Street corner,
> Aunt Sarah humming gospels;
> Summer evenings,
> The village cornet band, playing in the square.
> The Town's Red, White and Blue,
> All Red, White, and Blue —
> Now! Hear the songs!
> (Often the words not clearly heard
> But they sing in the soul of the things our Fathers loved!)

Charles Ives

The Music of Charles Ives

30

Charles Ives

War March—chorus, orchestra, brass and drum	1917
Serenity—Whittier, unison chorus with harps or piano	1919
An Election—chorus and orchestra 2 *	1920
Aeschylus and Socrates—chorus with string orchestra or quartet *	1922

Chamber Music

A Revival Service—string quartet	1896
Largo—violin, clarinet and piano	1901
From the Steeples and the Mountains—strings, brass and bells	1901
Allegro and Largo—violin and piano	1901-1902
Incantation—trumpet, flute, three violins, piano, drum, piccolo and trombones *	
Trio—violin, clarinet and piano	1902-1903
Scherzo—string quartet	1903
Hymn—string quartet and basso	1904
Trio—violin, cello and piano	1904
Autumn Landscapes from Pine Mountain—strings, woodwind and cornet	1904
The Pond—strings, flute, voice or English horn, harps, bells or celeste *	1906
First Violin and Piano Sonata	1903-1908
The Innate—string quartet and piano *	1908
In Re Con Moto et al—string quartet and piano *	1908
The Unanswered Question (A Cosmic Landscape)—trumpet, four flutes, treble woodwind, and string orchestra 4	1908
Like a Sick Eagle—English or basset horn, voice, strings, piano *	1909
First Piano Sonata	1902-1909
Second Violin and Piano Sonata	1903-1910
Hallowe'en—string quartet and piano *	1911
The Last Reader—English horn or clarinet, strings two flutes *	1911
The Indians—English basset horn or trumpet, bassoon, strings, piano and Indian drum *	1912
The New River—chorus and chamber orchestra *	1912
Over the Pavements—clarinet, bassoon, trumpet, piano, drum, piccolo and trombones *	1906-1913
String Quartet—with English horn or flute, piano	
All the Way Around and Back—piano, two players, violin, clarinet, bells or French horn	
Second String Quartet	1911-1913

Modern Music-Makers

December—male chorus, brass and woodwind °	1912-1913
The Seer—clarinet, trumpet, alto horn, piano and drum °	1913
Third Violin Sonata	1912-1914
Fourth Violin Sonata [3]	1914
The Rainbow—flute, basset or English horn, strings, piano °	1914
Luck and Work—English or basset horn, flute, violins, piano and drum °	1916
Premonitions (Johnson)—voice or chorus with flute, oboe, clarinet, horn, strings, piano and drums °	1917
Aeschylus and Socrates—piano, string orchestra or quartet	1922

Songs

A Book of 114 Songs	1888-1921
A Book of 50 Songs (from above Edition)	
Album of 34 Songs (also from above Edition) [2]	1889-1921
Seven Songs [5]	1902-1921
Album of 18 Songs [2]	1902-1921
Eleven Songs	1922-1927

Organ

A National Hymn	1891

Piano

First Piano Sonata	1902-1909
The Masses—piano arrangement	1915
Fantasy for Piano—The Celestial Railroad	
Second Piano Sonata "Concord" [3]	1904-1915

Quarter-Tone Music

Chorale for Strings—for two pianos	1902-1914
Largo and Allegro—for two pianos	1923-1924

° Arrangements for voice and piano are published in the Song Albums of New Music Edition.

[1] C. C. Birchard.
[2] New Music Edition.
[3] Arrow Music Press.
[4] *Pan American Bulletin of Music.*
[5] Cos Cob Press.

CHARLES IVES

JOHN ALDEN CARPENTER

JOHN ALDEN CARPENTER *

FROM the very beginning of his career, when the colorful imagery of his early songs delighted concert audiences, John Alden Carpenter was one of the most beloved of our contemporary composers. Successful in business as well as in music, his life until the latter years was divided between the two.

Carpenter found nothing particularly remarkable in such a combination. "Even composers have to eat," he explained with quiet humor. "The majority of serious composers are forced to seek a living outside of composition. They teach, they write, they lecture—each according to his individual skill and opportunity—and compose when they can. The composer in business is fundamentally in much the same case."

It was Carpenter's mother who first inspired his interest in music. Elizabeth Greene Carpenter had a remarkably fine voice. If she had lived in a later day, when women were less restricted, she would have been a concert artist or opera singer. As it was, her husband—unusual in that Victorian era — encouraged her talent and even allowed her to leave her family several times and go abroad to study. She had lessons in Paris with Mme. Marchesi, and in London with the English teacher William Shakespeare.

Elizabeth Carpenter passed on her love of music to all of her sons. John Alden was the most talented of the four; he would listen enthralled when his mother sang. She gave him his first piano lessons when he was five, and he began almost at once to to "fiddle around," as he puts it, "which in a young child amounts to improvising." By the time he was ten he knew enough about notation to write down tunes. From then on he composed more or less continuously.

John Alden inherited his name in direct line from Priscilla's John Alden of Pilgrim fame. He was born in Park Ridge, Illinois, on February 28, 1876, and has lived most of his life in Chicago—with fre-

* John Alden Carpenter died in February 1951, after this manuscript had been completed.

34

John Alden Carpenter

quent trips to Europe. His summers are spent in New England, at Beverly, Massachusetts.

One of Carpenter's first teachers in Chicago was Amy Fay, sister-in-law of the orchestra director Theodore Thomas (her book *Music Study in Germany* was widely read in the eighties). Carpenter also studied with W.C.E. Seeboeck. He graduated from Harvard in 1897, in the music course as well as in the academic. John Knowles Paine, head of the music department, was disappointed when his talented pupil elected to follow the family profession instead of making a career of music.

"Do you really think you have to go into that business?" he exclaimed, looking at him, as Carpenter relates, with a woeful expression.

Young Carpenter felt that he had no choice. His father was expecting him to come into the firm, for several generations his family had manufactured supplies for ships, and had built up an important chandlery firm in Chicago. Besides Carpenter was engaged to be married. So after his graduation he became junior partner in the George B. Carpenter firm, and married Rue Winterbotham. They had one daughter, Genevieve. Mrs. Carpenter died in 1931 and two years later he married Ellen Waller Borden.

Business and family responsibilities occupied most of Carpenter's time during those early years, but he still managed to continue his music writing. He felt, however, that he needed further instruction. He wrote to Sir Edward Elgar, whose music had always appealed to him, and asked if he might study with him. Elgar replied that he was not interested in teaching. When in 1906 the two met in Rome, the English composer finally agreed to give the young American some lessons. Carpenter did not gain as much from these lessons as he had hoped. He worked only a short time with Elgar. Three years later in Chicago he found a teacher better suited to his needs. Bernard Ziehn did more for him, he says, than anyone he has ever worked with.

Possibly because his introduction to music came through his mother's singing, Carpenter's first compositions were mainly songs. One of his earliest works was a group amusingly titled *Improving Songs for Anxious Children.* He and his wife Rue wrote the words together.

In 1912 a delightful song-cycle *Gitanjali*—inspired by the poems of

35

Modern Music-Makers

Rabindranath Tagore—made John Alden Carpenter's name widely known to the public. Two of the group *When I Bring to You Color'd Toys* and *The Sleep that Flits on Baby's Eyes* still remain perennial favorites of the concert stage. Another song-cycle *Water-Colors: Chinese Tone Poems* appeared two years later, and this became equally popular. Carpenter later arranged orchestral accompaniments for both of these cycles. Among his many other songs some of the best-loved are: *Green River, Silhouettes, May the Maiden, The Home Road* (written during the First World War), *Serenade,* and *Berceuse de Guerre.*

In 1914 John Alden Carpenter wrote his first important orchestral work: *Adventures in a Perambulator.* It made him as famous in the symphonic world as he already was on the concert stage.

What made him choose the subject, he himself was unable to say. "All artists are interested at one time or another in children," he explained with a twinkle, "—or in the sea. And most musicians have a weakness for the Spanish musical idiom." All three of these have furnished him with inspiration for his compositions.

In *Adventures in a Perambulator* Carpenter described, with extraordinary insight and a rare gift for the whimsical, the world as seen through a child's eyes. This charming suite tells of a baby's outing in the park, and perfectly interprets the child's varying moods and adventures.

The suite is in seven parts, each with an explanatory preface written by the composer:

> I *En voiture.* Every morning—after my second breakfast if the wind and the sun are favorable, I go out. . . .My nurse is appointed to take me. . . .While I wait for her, resigned, I hear the cheerful steps, always the same. . . .

> II *The Policeman.* Out is wonderful! . . . .Some sounds seem like smells. Some sights have echos. It is confusing, but it is Life! For instance, the Policeman. . . .Round like a ball; taller than my father . . . .He walks like doom. My Nurse feels it too. . .My perambulator hurries, hesitates and stops. They converse. When I feel that they have gone far enough, I signal my Nurse, a private signal, and the Policeman resumes his enormous Blue March.

36

John Alden Carpenter

III *The Hurdy-Gurdy:* Then suddenly there is something else. I think it is a sound. . . .I find that the absorbing noise comes from a box . . . .I have a wild idea of dancing with my Nurse and my perambulator. . . .Suddenly. . . .I feel the approach of a phenomenon that I remember. It is the Policeman. He has stopped the music. . . .He seeks the admiration of my Nurse for his act. . . .He walks away, his buttons shine, but far off I hear again the forbidden music.

IV *The Lake.* Seated with adventure, my nurse firmly pushes me on, and before I recover my balance I am face to face with a new excitement. The land comes to an end, and there at my feet is the Lake. . . .Waves and sunbeams! Blue Water—white clouds—dancing, swinging! . . . .That is *My Lake!*

V *Dogs.* We pass on. Probably there is nothing more in the World. If there is, it is superfluous. *There IS.* It is DOGS! . . . .Not one of them—all of them. First one by one; then in pairs; then in societies. Little dogs, with sisters; big dogs with aged parents. . . . It is tremendous!

VI *Dreams.* Those dogs have gone! It is confusing, but it is Life! My mind grows numb. My cup is too full. . . .I lie very still. . . .It is pleasant to live over again the adventures of the day. . . .How very large the world is!

With *Adventures in a Perambulator* Carpenter's interest in song writing "began to fade out," and orchestral composition to occupy the greater part of his attention. His next major work was a *Concertino* for piano and orchestra (first played by Percy Grainger with the Chicago Symphony in March, 1916). Some of the rhythms in the *Concertino* had a definite jazz-like flavor—a daring innovation in those early days. Carpenter was one of the first of the serious composers to use jazz in his compositions. This typically American idiom found appropriate expression in the last two of his ballets, while Spanish rhythms formed the background of the first: *The Birthday of the Infanta.*

Oscar Wilde's story about the princess and the dwarf has inspired

37

more than one composer. Carpenter turned it into a colorful ballet which was lavishly staged and produced in December, 1919, by the Chicago Opera Company. Adolf Bolm, who has appeared in most of the important ballets of modern times, did the choreography and took the leading part, while the famous Robert Edmond Jones designed the scenery and costumes.

The ballet's opening scene takes place in the palace gardens, where preparations are being made for the royal Infanta's birthday fiesta. Soon the little princess appears, followed by her nurses, and receives her birthday guests. Next comes a procession of servants headed by the major-domo — all of them bearing gifts. Then follow gypsy dancers, a mock bullfight, and finally a dance by the clumsy, misshapen dwarf Pedro. This dance so delights the Infanta that she throws her handkerchief to the dwarf. Now the cook arrives with a huge birthday cake, and they all go into the castle. Only Pedro remains outside, dazed with joy and still holding his lady's handkerchief.

In the second act the dwarf, believing that the princess must love him since she has given him her favor, enters the castle to find her. As he passes through the gloomy hall he sees a grotesque form advancing towards him. Suddenly he realizes that it is his own figure reflected in a large mirror. All his bright dreams are now shattered, and his heart breaking with the bitter knowledge of his ugliness, he begins once more to dance. Wilder and wilder grow his capers until finally, in a frenzied climax, he seizes a silver candelabra—hurls it at the mirror, and falls dead before it. At this moment the Infanta returns. She commands the dwarf to dance for her again. But for once her wishes are not obeyed.... Imperiously she stamps her foot. Pedro's grotesque little figure lies silent....

The Birthday of the Infanta was the first important ballet by an American composer to be produced in the United States. It proved such a success that Carpenter immediately began to make plans for another. This time he wanted an American subject. He had long been a "complete Herriman fan," as he puts it ("still am, for that matter!"); the latter's cartoon series about Krazy Kat and Ignatz Mouse delighted him particularly. Now he decided to put Krazy into a ballet, with Adolf Bolm again in the leading part, while Herriman himself agreed to design the set and costumes. These were done entirely in

John Alden Carpenter

black and white, to simulate the original cartoons, with a moveable screen in the center that furnished a changing background.

Bolm, with a group of his pupils, first performed *Krazy Kat* at Town Hall in New York, in 1920. Then a Broadway organization took it over. In 1924 Adolf Bolm put on a special performance for a Children's Hospital Benefit in Chicago.

Carpenter did *Krazy Kat* frankly as a caricature, in jazz spirit, trying to retain the flavor of the original drawings. Although the subject is essentially slapstick humor, he interpreted the philosophy that underlies Herriman's delightful characters as well as their surface absurdity. Krazy—"a quadruped with more than human emotions" is, according to Carpenter, "the world's greatest optimist . . . Don Quixote and Parsifal rolled into one."

The original character and engaging humor of *Krazy Kat* brought John Alden Carpenter fame both at home and abroad. When that summer in Europe he met the ballet director Diaghileff, the latter asked him if he would write a ballet for his company. At that time the Russian was trying to organize a second tour of the United States and he was anxious to include an American piece in the company's repertory. "Something typically American," he specified, "something that will describe the industrial atmosphere of your country." Diaghileff's idea of industrial America had mainly to do with strikes. "*Grèves*"—the French word for strikes—would, he felt make a fitting title. (Eventually the ballet was called "Skyscrapers") "Go back to your country and write the score," he suggested. "Then when you have finished it, bring it to me."

A year later Carpenter came to Venice—where Diaghileff always spent his vacations—with the music and the impresario said it was just what he wanted. Carpenter discussed the ballet's choreography with Nijinska (sister of the famous dancer) and all apparently was set for a production in Monte Carlo the following March. But, the projected second American tour having failed to materialize, that was the last Carpenter heard from the Russian. "I do not write letters—not even telegrams," Diaghileff had warned him. When all means of reaching the ballet director had been exhausted, Carpenter finally agreed to let Gatti-Casazza produce Skyscrapers at the Metropolitan in New York.

Robert Edmond Jones, who designed the production and assisted

Modern Music-Makers

Carpenter in staging the ballet, gives an idea of the work involved in combining the two arts: music and drama.

Carpenter would play the music, giving me an impression of the changing orchestration. He played each passage over and over again for hours. This would give me certain ideas of movement, for which I drew tentative designs, to be discussed with him. Countless patterns were made during six months of grueling, unremitting labor. From these we selected the final succession of designs, one growing from the other, parallel with the music.[2]

To the printed score of *Skyscrapers* Carpenter added this note:

Skyscrapers is a ballet which seeks to reflect some of the many rhythmic movements and sounds of modern American life. It has no story, in the usually accepted sense, but proceeds on the simple fact that American life reduces itself to violent alternations of work and play, each with its own peculiar and distinctive character. The action of the ballet is merely a series of moving decorations reflecting some of the obvious external features of this life.

Following the New York presentation of the ballet, it was put on in Munich, and played there for several seasons.

Felix Borowski, in an article written some years ago, called John Alden Carpenter "of all our composers the most typically American."

Carpenter's music reflects the life and character of his country from widely differing angles. *Skyscrapers*, for instance, depicts the industrial world, while *Krazy Kat* is an interpretation of American wit and humor. In *Song of Faith* Carpenters turns to still another side, and pays tribute to what he calls "The Great American Dream." Composed in the darkest days of the depression, this choral work was commissioned for the Bicentennial George Washington celebration in 1932. Carpenter said of it:

In the writing of this work I have come to a new realization of the priceless inheritance that has come down to us from George Washington. I have felt, more than ever before, that the enduring value of this inheri-

[2] *In the Christian Science Monitor,* December 10, 1927.

JOHN ALDEN CARPENTER

John Alden Carpenter

tance is based not primarily on his military genius, or his contribution to the arts of government, but on the selfless integrity of his character.

It is from that character that we inherit the Great American Dream—the dream which has sustained us through out storms and trials, and which at this very moment we must strive in deepest sincerity to recapture. For the whole world is beset by a dangerous psychology of defeat which for us is but the modern counterpart of the snows of Valley Forge. And it is for our country now to raise its eyes in the faith of its founders, and lead the way out.

And therefore, if my *Song of Faith* can succeed in lighting a single candle of reaffirmation, I shall be content.[3]

Lawrence Gilman called this piece, "music of faith, and love and elevation. . . ."He went on to say, "It is significant of Mr. Carpenter's characteristics as an artist—his taste, his tact, his distinction of feeling and of thought."

After the beginning of the second world conflict, and shortly before the United States entered the war, Carpenter again reiterated his faith in the ideals of his country in another choral work entitled *Song of Freedom.*

Walt Whitman once remarked that *Leaves of Grass* was intended "as much for the musicians as for anyone, and, if it was not defeated in its purpose would perhaps inspire them to some noble, contemporaneous utterance."

The great bard would have been gratified at the many "noble utterances" which his *Sea-Poems* have evoked. They have found musical interpretation in Vaughan Williams' *Sea Symphony,* in Delius' cantata *Sea-Drift,* and in a symphonic poem by John Alden Carpenter which he, too, called *Sea-Drift.*

Away back around 1915, I experienced my first acute Whitman excitement, (Carpenter told Lawrence Gilman) and for some time, then, I studied the problem of setting to music in vocal form excerpts from some of the *Sea-Drift* poems. These experiments I could not bring to any result that satisfied me, and I dropped the project. . . .

Under the influence of the blue Mediterranean at Eze village, I took up the old problem again, and abandoned any attempt to make a literal

[3] As quoted by Lawrence Gilman in the New York *Tribune,* May 1st, 1932.

setting of the Whitman verses in a vocal work. I tried to make a composite orchestral record of the imprint upon me of these poems. My hope is that the music makes sense, just as music, with perhaps a special meaning for those who love Whitman. My work represents an effort to transcribe my impressions derived from these magnificent poems.[4]

Sea-Drift was first performed in November, 1934, by the New York Philharmonic under the direction of Werner Janssen; later in Rochester, and again at the Hollywood Bowl. Some years after, Carpenter revised the work and it was first played in its new form in October, 1944, with Arthur Rodzinski conducting the New York Symphony.

Carpenter celebrated his sixtieth birthday, by retiring from the business world. At a period in life when most artists are letting up on their creative work, John Alden Carpenter began one of the most productive stages of his musical career.

During his long career he received many honors, the most recent of these (in 1947) the National Institute of Arts and Letters' Gold Medal. This, the Institute's highest award, goes only once every nine years to a composer "for distinguished services in the field of music, based upon the entire work of the recipient." Only three other composers have received the Institute's Gold Medal.

Carpenter's *Piano Quintet* was commissioned by the Elizabeth Sprague Coolidge Foundation for the 1935 Library of Congress program. In 1937 he completed a violin concerto, first played by Zlatko Balakovic with the Chicago Symphony Orchestra. When this last-named organization celebrated its fiftieth anniversary in 1940, ten leading contemporary musicians were invited to furnish compositions for a special program in honor of the event. Carpenter's contribution was a revised edition of his *First Symphony* (originally written for the 1917 Norfolk Festival).

A *Second Symphony* followed the revised *First* the following year, and Bruno Walter played it with the New York Philharmonic-Symphony. Carpenter next added two shorter orchestral works to his list. After that *The Seven Ages.*

The famous lines spoken by Jacques in the second act of Shake-

---

[4] Quoted in the *New York Herald Tribune,* November 4, 1934.

John Alden Carpenter

speare's *As You Like It* had long intrigued the imagination of John Alden Carpenter:

> All the world's a stage,
> And all the men and women merely players;
> They have their exits and their entrances;
> And one man in his time plays many parts,
> His acts being seven ages. . . .

Carpenter felt that a dramatic ballet could be built around the theme of Man's seven ages. Several times he tried, though without success, to work out his own scenario. He finally gave up the idea of a ballet and wrote instead a Symphonic Suite in seven parts:

I *Vivace*	"All the World's a Stage"
II *Animato giocoso*	"Then the Whining Schoolboy"
III *Andantino Sentimentale* . .	"And then the Lover, sighing like a furnace"
IV *Allegro Barbaro*	"Then a Soldier"
V *Buffo-Pomposo*	"And then the Justice, in fair Belly with good Capon lin'd"
VI *Lento Dolente*	"The Lean and Slippered Pantaloon"
VII *Adagio-Agitato-Placido* . .	"Sans Eyes, sans Taste, sans Everything"

The Seven Ages was first performed at Carnegie Hall, December 2, 1945, Artur Rodzinski conducting. Carpenter added the following program notes:

The composer feels that any attempt on his part to provide a detailed "musical analysis" of this work should be highly unrewarding. The score contains no themes or devices which should not be obvious to the listener who troubles to read the subtitles of the work and their characterizing musical designation, as printed in the program.

One of Carpenter's last compositions was a *Concerto for Orchestra*. He wrote it in 1948 while in Carmel, California, (where he spent most of his winters) and named it the *Carmel Concerto*. It was first played in November, 1949, by Stokowski and the New York Philharmonic-Symphony, and was broadcast over radio as well. The music—oriental in spirit but modern in orchestration—is not an attempt to describe the actual scenery of his Carmel Highlands home, but rather the mood which it inspired.

John Alden Carpenter's music is largely "programmatic"—inspired by some outside source. As he put it, "With only a few exceptions (notably the two symphonies and his chamber-music) everything that I have written has started from a non-musical basis."

When he composed, there had to be first a special mood which created the desire for musical expression. This may have been produced by a poem—an emotion—an idea. "All music that lives is based on a mood, whether directly or indirectly." He once said to Lawrence Gilman, "I have found that the germ of an idea may become implanted and then lie dormant for a long period, only to be called into active life, after perhaps a considerable interval, by influences outside myself and not always recognizable."

Alfred Einstein, in his book *Greatness in Music* takes a pessimistic view of today's music and seems to feel that since the beginning of the century it has been progressively destroying itself. Carpenter however believed that the composers and artists of today are making a definite contribution through their experiments and the developing of new technical resources. These, he was confident, will furnish material for coming generations of creative workers who will bring about a rebirth of the arts.

John Alden Carpenter has indeed, as Olin Downes once declared, "contributed indispensably to the erection of the great future edifice of a national music . . . [and] . . . has wrought beautifully, wisely, truthfully and well."

John Alden Carpenter

The Music of John Alden Carpenter

NOTE: With the exception of the song *May, the Maiden,* all of Carpenter's compositions since 1903, have been published by G. Schirmer, Inc.

ORCHESTRAL WORKS

Adventures in a Perambulator—suite	1915
Concertino for Piano and Orchestra	1917
Birthday of the Infanta—suite from ballet	1919
Krazy Kat—suite from ballet	1922
Skyscrapers—suite from ballet	1926
Patterns	1932
Sea-Drift—tone poem (revised 1944)	1933
Concerto, violin, orchestra	1937
First Symphony	1940
Second Symphony	1941
Dance Suite	1942
Anxious Bugler	1943
The Seven Ages	1945
Carmel Concerto	1948

CHORAL WORKS

Song of Faith—mixed voices, orchestra	1931
Song of Freedom	1941

CHAMBER MUSIC

Sonata—violin, piano	1912
Water-Colors—from Chinese songs—mezzo soprano and orchestra	1918
String Quartet	1928
Gitanjali—mezzo soprano and orchestra	1932
Piano Quintet—piano, string quartet	1934

BALLET

Birthday of the Infanta	1919
Krazy Kat	1922
Skyscrapers	1926

John Alden Carpenter

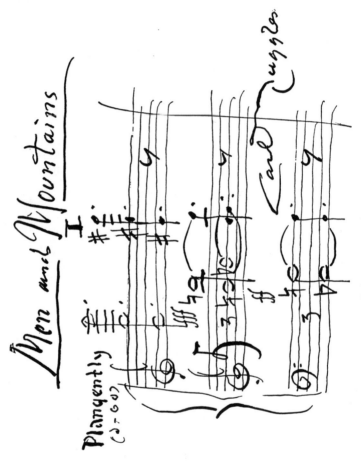

CARL RUGGLES

CARL RUGGLES has been called "the most delightful character in contemporary American musical life—the very quintessence of New Englandism."[1] Like Charles Ives, that other great New England individualist, Ruggles is one of the most original of our composers, and his music is equally modern in idiom.

Ruggles himself has no patience with those who speak of "modern music." "Music is music," he declares. " 'It is no better than it sounds'— as someone has said. The test is the quality that makes it last." His own music, most of it written twenty to thirty years ago, still sounds fresh and new.

"All art—music and painting especially," says Ruggles, "overlaps and continues from one artist to the next. It is a steady stream; each person is a part of all that has gone before. In his day Beethoven was a great modern. Wagner too was a great modern, and Bach perhaps the greatest 'innovator' of them all. I remember with what astonished joy I came upon a few passages in the middle of the great Bach cantata *Jesus Sleeps*. They were as dissonant as though they had been written yesterday. I spoke to Lawrence Gilman about it, and he went out and bought a score, then called me up to say: 'I can't find the part you spoke of!' We checked the edition that he had bought and found that the dissonant passages had been deleted by the publisher. When we looked at the older edition, there they were. . . ."

Carl Ruggles was born on Cape Cod March 11, 1876, in the town of Marion, Massachusetts, near Buzzard's Bay. As a child he lived for a time in the old Ruggles home built in 1640. (The present "Ruggles Street" marks the location of the old family property.) His mother was a singer with a trained voice, and music was a part of his earliest impressions. The sea, too, wove itself early into his heart and mind; but who shall say at what moment the future composer awoke within the child?

"You could write a great psychological novel on 'the awakenings' in life," he says. "If you look back at the things you remember . . .

---

[1] Charles Seeger in *The Musical Quarterly*, October, 1932.

the things that change your whole life. Sometimes it is no more than a gesture . . . the light breaking. . . ."

He recalls a lighthouse on Bird Island just across the bay from their home. The lighthouse keeper was his friend. One day when the man came to the mainland for provisions, and stopped by to see Carl, he found the boy busy at work trying to make a violin from a discarded cigar-box, so he could accompany his mother when she sang songs he loved so much to hear.

"You should have a real violin," the keeper exclaimed kindly. "I have one in the lighthouse—I'll bring it to you tomorrow."

The next day, however, it started to rain, and for three days the storm continued. Most of the time young Carl sat in the window with his nose pressed to the pane, his eyes fastened on the great light swinging through the mist and rain. Finally on the third day the weather cleared and, true to his promise, the lighthouse keeper brought him the violin. Carl played first by ear—his mother would sing and he would follow. Then he had lessons and soon played so well that he was often asked to entertain the summer visitors who came to Cape Cod. Among them were President and Mrs. Cleveland. Carl often played duets with Mrs. Cleveland.

Through all those early years flowed the spell of the sea. Its influence has colored both Ruggles' painting and his music (He sometimes wonders a bit wistfully why so much of his life since boyhood has been spent inland and in the mountains.) The sea was his first love. As a young man he thought of becoming a shipbuilder, and went to Boston to study the art of ship design. Soon after arriving there, however, he met a musician by the name of Joseph Klaus, at that time a teacher in the Boston Conservatory. Ruggles persuaded him to give him lessons in composition. Klaus—a great teacher in his estimation—gave him a thorough grounding, then told him to go to John Knowles Paine at Harvard.

"I have taught him all I can," Klaus wrote to Paine. "Now I am sending him to you. He will either dash his brains out against a wall, or he will jump over the wall. . . ."

Ruggles jumped over the wall. After a short time at Harvard he decided that he was getting nowhere in this new environment, and that a college degree was not for him. He wanted to give his full time to music, so now he went to Minnesota and founded an orchestra in

Carl Ruggles

Winona. There, through the inscrutable ways of Providence, he met the violinist Christian Timner, who had been Concertmaster of the Concertgebouw Orchestra in Amsterdam under Mengelberg ("the greatest orchestra in the world" according to Carl Ruggles), and who knew everything there was to know about an orchestra and conducting.

Ruggles had already embarked on his own highly original course of music-writing. For the next ten years, with Timner as his concertmaster, he toured through Minnesota, conducting the orchestra he had founded. This experience, with its study and performance of the world's greatest music, proved richly rewarding to Carl Ruggles.

The winter before he left Boston to go to Minnesota, he had attended a concert given by a young singer named Charlotte Snell. She was a New England girl from Lawrence, Massachusetts, and came from a Puritan line that went back to John Alden. She sang flawlessly a program of German lieder, and Ruggles was so attracted to the lovely singer that he went backstage after the performance to tell her how much he had enjoyed the concert. Soon after, Charlotte went on tour with the Minneapolis Symphony Orchestra, and in Minnesota he saw her again. Before long she and Carl were married. They made their home in Winona, and Ruggles' orchestra became the center of their existence. His wife often sang with the orchestra; she continued her career, and during the summers when they went East she was able to go on with her studies. (Their son, Micah, was born in Minnesota. A graduate of the University of Miami, he is now principal of the high school in Tampa, Florida.)

After eleven years in Minnesota, Ruggles moved back to New England. All during this time he had been composing. But he was never satisfied with his music. Highly self-critical, with painstaking effort he would write and rewrite his scores—and then destroy most of what he had written. For this reason, although he has continued through the years to devote a great part of his time to composing, his actual output has been small, and very little of his music has been available to the public. Many of his scores have been banished to the barn of his Arlington, Vermont, home. Among them is an unfinished opera to Hauptmann's *The Sunken Bell*.

Ruggles in his earlier days was closely associated with the International Composers Guild, and a number of his works were per-

Modern Music-Makers

formed at concerts given by this association. His great friends there were Edgar Varese, Charles Ives, and later Wallingford Riegger and Henry Cowell. "We played the greatest music in the world," he says. Bela Bartok, Schoenberg, Stravinsky, Hindemith, and the American moderns as well, were all represented.

One of the first works to survive Ruggles' pitiless self-criticism was *Angels* scored for seven muted brasses. *Angels* was revived a few years ago at a concert given in February, 1949, by the National Association for American Composers and Conductors. "Its revival," wrote Virgil Thomson in the *New York Herald Tribune*, "after more than twenty years was accompanied by the kind of intellectual excitement that has ever attended its performance, plus the deep joy of the young just making its discovery. . . ." He went on to say:

The dissonance-tension is uniform throughout, hence in the long run, harmonious, though that tension carries the maximum of dissonance possible to seven voices. Complete avoidance of the dramatic and the picturesque gives to the work a simplicity and a nobility of expression and the utter perfection of its workmanship place Ruggles as one of our century's masters, perhaps the one among all from whom the young have most to learn just now.

When *Angels* was first played, close to thirty years ago, at a concert of the International Composers Guild, the house broke into an uproar. "Terrible!" exclaimed a man sitting next to Ruggles. "What do they want to do a thing like that for?" At the same time a stout man whose wife was loudly expressing her disapproval said to her, "Be quiet, I like it. . . .As far as I can judge it's a great piece of music." (He was a French importer, and from that night became an ardent supporter to the Guild, contributing to it and always attending.)

Ruggles' audiences have always been divided in their reactions. At the conclusion of any performances of his music the house will break into both cheers and hisses. Once Eugene Goossens, after conducting *Portals* to the usual chorus of boos, hisses, and a smattering of enthusiastic applause, turned to the audience and said. "I am going to repeat this now, for I consider it a very important work." With that he played the piece all over again—this time to a more respectful audience.

Carl Ruggles

Ruggles has many amusing stories to tell about the early days when his music was first heard. On one occasion when a composition by Ruggles appeared on the program a man sitting next to the critic Gilbert Gabriel remarked, "I could write a better piece than that!" "Why don't you go home and do it, then?" Gabriel asked.

At the first performance of *Men and Mountains* by the New York Philharmonic-Symphony under Hans Langer, one woman in the audience kept muttering, "Terrible! Horrible! Terrible! . . ." A friend of Ruggles who was sitting near by whispered to her, "Madam, do be quiet—this is the piece I came expressly to hear." When the orchestra started the next number — Dvorak's *New World Symphony* — the the woman gave a sigh of relief. "*Now*—I can enjoy myself!" she said, and promptly fell asleep.

Men and Mountains, Ruggles' second important orchestral work, was originally written in 1924, but has since been revised. Following the performance by the New York Philharmonic-Symphony in 1936 he again revised it, and in this form it was presented in February, 1951, at WNYC's Music Festival. The title is taken from a line by Blake: "Great things are done when men and mountains meet. . . ." Suggestive of the stern New England countryside of his boyhood, *Men and Mountains* is "roughhewn, unrelentingly harsh and thoroughly inspired. . . .

Mr. Ruggles in revising his work has left untouched his original melodic line, but has substantially enlarged its expressive scope through formal modification and orchestral amplification. As it now stands, the work achieves the grandeur of the mountain of its title and combines with this a quality of warmth rarely present in music whose main concern is the exploitation of chordal sonority. And this is all, really, that *Men and Mountains* does; it gives us crag-like formations of sound, juxtaposes them, disintegrates them and builds them up anew. But every measure of the score reveals a Midas touch and a spirit which this reviewer takes to be truly generous and noble.[2]

Portals, for a small string orchestra of thirteen instruments, came next on Ruggles' list, and was first heard in 1926. With an augmented orchestra it was performed some years later by the remarkable "Con-

[2] J. S. H. in the *New York Herald Tribune,* February 13, 1951.

ductorless Orchestra" that played for six seasons at Carnegie Hall (at the same concert Zimbalist appeared in the Beethoven Concerto, playing from the string section, not standing as a soloist usually does, in the center of the stage.) *Portals* has been widely played both here and abroad.

Ruggles was six years writing *Sun Treader,* by some considered his major work. Its first performance was in Paris, in 1932, and it was also played at the Festival of the International Society for Contemporary Music in Barcelona, Paris and Berlin. Ruggles' *Angels* was included in a Festival concert at Venice, (at which time Toscanini is said to have walked out, but Malipieri, hearing that the piece needed more rehearsals and that money was running short, paid for the extra rehearsals out of his own pocket.)

Organum, a "short but very pungent piece" and the most recent work of Ruggles to be heard publicly, was the second of his compositions to be given its premiére by the New York Philharmonic-Symphony, in November, 1949. On this occasion Leopold Stokowski was the conductor. Ruggles considers Stokowski one of the most faithful friends of the American composer. (Once before playing a modern piece he said to the audience: "This is modern music. If you are sure before hearing it that you will not like it, please leave now. . . .") On his 1951 European tour Stokowski included *Organum* on his programs in London, Paris, Amsterdam, Munich, and Lucerne.

In reviewing the first performance of *Organum* Olin Downes wrote:

It is the matured and forceful expression of a composer who has been these many years a brave, original artist; one who never wrote music only to please and never hesitated to ride a conviction straight into the teeth of public disapproval or misunderstanding, with the inevitable consequences to his popularity and fortune. . . .

At a first hearing it had a fine musical logic, an emotional drive, with an appropriate bit of dissonance which is an organic development, and not an attempt to be queer. . . .We heard some say that they were glad the piece was only seventy-eight measures long. Various persons could be thus gratified, but for quite different reasons. It is an admirably compact work.[3]

[3] In the *New York Times.*

Carl Ruggles

Carl Ruggles has written many songs, but only a few have found their way to his permanent list. A group of these called *Vox Clamans in Deserto*, with small orchestra accompaniment, includes *Clear Midnight* (with text by Whitman), especially praised and often performed; several with words from Browning, and one to a delightful poem by the composer himself: *Toys*. The melodic line of this last song gradually mounts until it ends on a high B. When this was given at a concert of the International Composers' Guild, the singer instead of maintaining the line concluded on a note an octave lower than it was written. Ruggles intercepted her as she came down the stairs after the performance, and berated her roundly for daring to tamper with his music. . . . When she later recorded the song, he reports, she ended it on the high B. *Toys* was published by H. D. Gray. A friend of Ruggles', Mrs. Ernest Walton (loved and admired for all she has done for music and musicians) went in to buy the song. The clerk, however, warned her against it. "You won't like it," he said. "We have other songs more suitable for you." To the man's astonishment Mrs. Walton bought not one, but six copies.

In 1937 Ruggles was appointed to the music faculty of the University of Miami, and remained there until comparatively recently. He recalls that while teaching at U. M. one of the pupils in his class produced nothing whatever for two years. One day Ruggles decided to give his students an open assignment—he told them to write a song, choosing their own words, form, etc. To his surprise the silent boy brought in the best song of them all; it was the most outstanding work that had been done in the class. He had been quietly absorbing ideas, suddenly saw the light, and then was able to apply what he had learned. "You can't ask more than that," says Ruggles. "Creative work can't be taught—you can only provide the tools, the fundamentals. I promptly gave the boy an A plus for the two years. The school authorities were scandalized. . . . But the President saw it my way and the mark was allowed to stand."

"Great facility is dangerous," Ruggles insists. "Be glad of obstacles—if you don't run into them 'suspicion yourself.' Stumbling blocks should be steppingstones. . . ."

Today Carl Ruggles lives for the greater part of the year in sem retreat in Arlington, Vermont. There he has taken over an old school-house, transforming the forty-foot square classroom into a large music room. Ruggles likes bigness. When he composes he takes large sheets of paper of varying sizes—some as long as twenty feet (as when writing *Sun Treader*, so he could spread out a thirty-nine measure double-triple canon and view it all at once in developing a "cancrizan.") These sheets he rules with wide lines an inch or more apart, and fills them in with large fat notes, often made with crayons of different colors.

Ruggles is a born artist as well as a musician. About fifteen years ago, while he and his wife were on a vacation in Jamaica, they found themselves with a group of painters. For a while Ruggles watched the artists working, then one day he said:

"Give me a piece of that drawing paper and I'll show you what I can do. . . ." The result was such a good picture that he was encouraged to go on painting. Ruggles is intensely serious about his work. He has no hobbies (though he enjoys repairing antique furniture and is an adept storyteller). "There is only time in life for serious things," he declares. He has been very successful with his painting; his canvases sell for high prices and have been bought by a number of museums throughout the country, including the Whitney Museum, Anderson Galleries, Brooklyn, Williamstown, and Detroit Museums (the latter has five of his pictures.)

In the Vermont house where Ruggles spends spring, summer and autumn, he works at his music all morning and his painting every afternoon. He believes in discipline—self-imposed. "It is the only hope of accomplishing anything," he insists. His hours are sternly kept: breakfast at seven, luncheon at noon, dinner at six. Mrs. Ruggles, too, works all morning. She has a sign on the front door:

NO ADMITTANCE. DON'T KNOCK UNTIL ONE. . . .
THEN COME IN AND STAY AS LONG AS YOU LIKE.

Ruggles, like Ives, has a deep feeling for the vastness and mystery of the universe. "In all works there should be the quality we call mysticism," he says. "All the great composers have it. In Beethoven we find a transcendental love of nature, awe, mysticism . . . and in Bach, of course. . . ." When Ruggles was asked if his painting as well as

COURTESY OF JOHN ATHERTON

CARL RUGGLES

Carl Ruggles

his music had this mystic quality, he replied: "They say so. . . ."

There is in Ruggles' music a natural affinity with Blake's imaginative world. Lawrence Gilman calls him,

a rhapsodist and a mystic, a fabulous creature dreamed into being by some prankish fantasist with a savage sense of humor. . . . .the first unicorn to enter American music—a unicorn with a New England conscience. For half the intensity and power of Ruggles' music—and it is both powerful and intense—proceeds from the unabating struggle in Ruggles' soul between the unicorn and the New England ancestry. . . .

Side by side with the imaginative, mystical quality of Ruggles' music is another more hardy attribute. "There is a robustness about Mr. Ruggles' talent and a kind of forthright determination which abash the scoffer and exact respect in the face of an obstinate aesthetic skepticism," says Pitts Sanborn.[4]

Ruggles' music has often been compared to that of Arnold Schoenberg, but this is only a superficial estimate. Actually it is very much of an individual art. "Far from being an exponent of Schoenberg's technics and composition . . . he is a composer who stands closest to the highly individualized expressionistic method," says Nicolai Lopatnikoff.[5]

Charles Seeger in an article in the *Music Quarterly* (October, 1932) states:

There is one thing that can be said of him that can be said of very few indeed: his work is reminiscent of no other man, school or style. Small as the body of it is, it stands quite distinct and sui generis. . . . Ruggles' technique as a whole shows a curious ratio between organization and fantasy—though a vast preponderance of fantasy. . . .

If the materials of the art of music are ever assembled into a new style comparable to that of the great styles of the past—of Bach, Beethoven, of Palestrina—Ruggles will be among the men who will have contributed to its making.

Ruggles still continues to work daily at his composing and painting. To create—whether it be painting or music—is the main concern of Carl Ruggles' life.

[4] In *Modern Music*, January-February, 1927.
[5] *Ibid.*, 1930.

Carl Ruggles

CHRONOLOGICAL CHART OF MAIN EVENTS AND WORKS

Born March 11, Marion, Massachusetts	1876
Studies with Joseph Klaus in Boston	
Attends Harvard University	
Moves to Winona, Minnesota. Establishes orchestra there	
Marries Charlotte Snell	
Micah Ruggles born	1915
Moves back to New England	
Men and Angels	1920
Men and Mountains	1924
Portals	1926
Sun Treader	1933
Takes up painting in Jamaica	1935
Appointed to Music Faculty of University of Miami	1937
Moves to Arlington, Vermont	
Polyphonic Composition for Three Pianos	
Vox Clamans in Deserto—song suite	
Organum	1945
Evocations—four chants for piano	

The Music of Carl Ruggles

[1] Curwen.
[2] New Music.

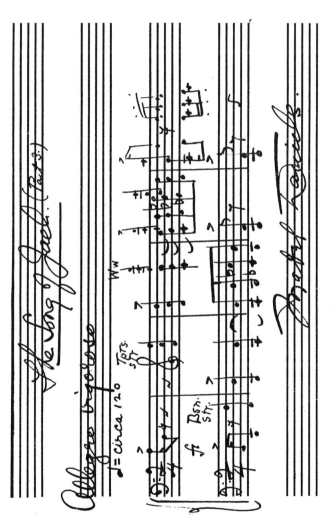

MABEL DANIELS

MABEL DANIELS

UNTIL comparatively recent years there have been only a few women composers, either in this country or abroad, and most of these have confined themselves to the smaller forms. They have written charming songs, chamber music, piano pieces, and choral works. But only a small number have composed for orchestra.

The reason for this, Mabel Daniels feels, does not necessarily lie in lack of talent. Women have imagination and great natural gifts, and they have achieved distinction in the other creative fields. But they have only recently begun to compose. Since music is the most intangible and the most exacting of the arts, infinite concentration, time, and actual physical labor are required in writing down the endless notes of an orchestral score. The general public has no conception of the work involved; the original inspiration is the least, if the most important, part.

Women with household cares and families to raise can rarely find the time and strength necessary for such work. But with the increasing leisure of today's world, more women will undoubtedly join the ranks of the composers. Mabel Daniels is so far one of the few who have composed for orchestra, and whose works have been played on important symphony programs.

During an intermission at one of the 1940 Worcester Music Festival concerts, a man walking through the corridors of the War Memorial Auditorium stopped to chat with Mabel Daniels. Albert Stoessel, directing the orchestra, a large chorus, and Rose Bampton soloist, had just finished a stirring performance of an important new choral work called *The Song of Jael.*

"I liked the piece they just played," the man confided. "That one about Jael. . . ."

Miss Daniels smiled and gave a slight bow. "Why on earth," he continued, "did they have that *woman* come up on the platform?"

"Perhaps—" Miss Daniels replied with a twinkle in her eyes, "she was the composer!"

"Composer?" the man looked bewildered. It hadn't occurred to him that such an ambitious work could have been written by a

Modern Music-Makers

woman—much less that he was at that very moment talking to the one who wrote it. His reaction, says Miss Daniels, is typical of most of the American public.

Although most of her life has been devoted exclusively to music Miss Daniels' first ambition was to write stories. Born in Swampscott, Massachusetts, she is a dyed-in-the-wool New Englander, and has spent most of her life in and around Boston. Music was a daily part of her early environment. One of her grandfathers played the organ, and the other directed a choir, while both her parents sang in Boston's Handel and Haydn Society chorus. (Mr. Daniels later became president of this society).

Mabel Daniel's earliest musical recollection has to do with a rehearsal of Verdi's *Requiem* which she attended, hand in hand with her mother. She was excited to discover her father in the chorus. The music fascinated her, but the *Dies Irae* so overpowered her by its terrifying force that she cried and begged her mother to take her home.

She was given piano lessons at an early age and often made up pieces to play. (When ten years old she wrote a *Fairy Charm Waltz*). She also had a fine soprano voice, and this was what really started her on a musical career. At Radcliffe she sang in the Glee Club and took leading parts in the college operettas. Soon she was made director of the Glee Club, and began writing music for the operettas. She composed two of these and conducted them herself. Miss Daniels graduated from Radcliffe *magna cum laude*—though she insists, with the charming sense of humor that is one of her main characteristics, that she received this honor only because the courses were elective and she chose the easiest ones.

By the time she had finished college Mabel Daniels knew that music, and more particularly composing, was to be her life's work. For a time she studied composition and orchestration with George W. Chadwick in Boston. Then she went to Germany to work with Ludwig Thuille.

When she tried to join the score-reading class at the Royal Conservatory in Munich, the director was frankly upset. No *woman* had ever before presumed to ask admittance. After long and weighty consideration, and "with an expression worthy of a crisis in the affairs of state," he finally gave his consent saying: "Of course, that a Fräulein

Mabel Daniels

has never before joined the class is no reason why a Fräulein never can!" When, after two winters spent in Germany Miss Daniels came back to the United States, she recorded this incident and many of her foreign experiences in an interesting book of memoirs.[1]

On her return to Boston she joined the Cecilia Society—a chorus of mixed voices. Since she could not play an instrument, the next best thing was to sing in a chorus giving works with orchestra, and since the Cecilia Society often performed modern works it offered her the chance to get at these scores "from the inside." The rehearsals with orchestra were especially valuable and stimulated her natural bent for choral writing.

Every creative artist, whether painter, sculptor, writer, or musician, dreams of a retreat where he can work undisturbed by noise or interruption. Edward MacDowell, America's first great composer, discovered such a retreat in the wooded hills of New Hampshire. There he found inspiration for his work, and refreshment for body, mind and spirit. These priceless gifts he longed to share with others.

At MacDowell's death his widow dedicated her life to the project they had planned together. The wooded acres of their New Hampshire farm were turned over to a Memorial Association, and largely through the personal efforts of Mrs. MacDowell, who toured the country giving concerts to raise the necessary funds, the colony gradually took shape: old farm houses were transformed into eating, sleeping and recreation buildings, and small studios were built—scattered through the woods—each one in that complete isolation that had meant so much to MacDowell himself. A group of working artists, recommended for their talent and promise and chosen by a special committee from a large number of applicants, gathers here each year, and many important works have sprung from this fruitful environment. It would be difficult to estimate the influence that the MacDowell Colony has had on the cultural development of America.

During the colony's early years a festival, or pageant, was put on each summer in the forest-encircled amphitheater. Mrs. MacDowell—always interested in promising young composers—learned of Mabel

---

[1] *An American Girl in Munich*, (Impressions of a Music Student). by Mabel Daniels—Little, Brown and Company.

Modern Music-Makers

Daniels's *The Desolate City* (an early choral work for baritone and orchestra) and was so struck by it that she asked her to direct a performance of *The Desolate City* at the pageant. This was Miss Daniels' first important composition. The following year she was invited to return as a colonist, and since then most of her music has been written at the colony. She is now a corporate member of the Edward MacDowell Association.

The lovely New Hampshire woods inspired one of her most widely played compositions. *Deep Forest*, a "delicately imaginative work," was originally written for chamber orchestra and first played by the Barrère Little Symphony. She later rewrote it for full orchestra and in that form it has been performed by Koussevitzky, Barbirolli, Kindler, and a number of other leading conductors throughout the country. At the Carnegie Hall Festival in 1939, under the sponsorship of ASCAP, Mabel Daniel's *Deep Forest* was the only work by an American woman composer to be played on the program of serious music. She is a member of the American Composers' Alliance, ASCAP, and the College Club of Boston; an honorary member of Phi Beta Kappa, Mu Phi Epsilon, and the Musical Guild; and an alumna trustee of Radcliffe College. In 1933 she was awarded an honorary M.A. degree from Tufts College, and in 1939 a Doctor of Music Degree from Boston University. She has also received a number of prizes for her compositions.

When Radcliffe College planned a special celebration for its fiftieth anniversary, in 1929, President Comstock invited Miss Daniels to compose a choral work in honor of the occasion. For this, she wrote *Exultate Deo,* for mixed chorus and orchestra. It was performed at the jubilee celebration by the combined Harvard Glee Club and Radcliffe Choral Society, and later by Koussevitzky with the Boston Symphony and the Cecilia Society, and the High School Choruses and Orchestra of Philadelphia. It has become Miss Daniel's best known work, and has been given all over the United States and as far west as Manila. Although it has been a good many years since this choral work was written it is still frequently performed on high school programs all over the country.

Among her other earlier compositions are *Peace and Liberty* (chorus and orchestra), and *Pirates' Island,* a humorous suite for orchestra alone. This last was played at summer concerts of the

MABEL DANIELS

Mabel Daniels

Cleveland Symphony under Rudolf Ringwell, and soon after Arthur Fiedler performed it with the Boston Pops Orchestra. It was just at this time that Ted Shawn, looking for new music for his ballet group, chanced to be in town. He heard Mabel Daniels' piece, and found it just suited his needs. The following summer *Pirates' Island* was given as a ballet at Robinhood Dell by Ted Shawn and his dancers, accompanied by the Philadelphia Orchestra. Another of Miss Daniels' more recent pieces has also been arranged for ballet: two movements from her *Three Observations for Three Woodwinds*.

Miss Daniels' most important work—*The Song of Jael*, scored for orchestra, chorus and soprano soli—is founded on a poem by Edwin Arlington Robinson. He was a close friend of Miss Daniels': shortly before his death in 1935 she discussed with him plans for the work. Although her earlier compositions are more conventional in style, *The Song of Jael* shows a definite use of modern idiom. The critic of the *Boston Post* called it:

A prolonged hymn of triumph that comes to a mighty climax. Few American composers have been so successful as Miss Daniels in choral writing and the outstanding feature of her *Jael* is the striking and frequent highly original handling of the chorus. There are, nevertheless, many effective moments in the orchestral score, while the long soprano solo is dramatic and impressive. This by no means conventional piece makes a valuable contribution to American choral literature.

The Song of Jael was Mabel Daniels' first venture into "modern" music writing. Since then she has written entirely in this style. Her later works include *Pastoral Ode* for flute and strings (1940) first played by members of the Boston Symphony Orchestra and by Dr. Frank Black over the National Broadcasting System; *Three Observations for Three Woodwinds,* a short satirical skit "not intended to be taken very seriously"—but always enjoyed by audiences; *Digressions for String Orchestra; Two Pieces for Violin and Piano: Diversion for Diana* and *Remembering Two Young Soldiers,* played by Oscar Bogerth, the brilliant Brazilian violinist, at his 1948 concert in Boston, and also by Ruth Posselt; and, in 1951, *Overture for Orchestra.*

Mabel Daniels has always taken a deep interest in music students. She has anonymously offered two prizes in composition to undergraduates in colleges for women. At Radcliffe she founded a loan fund for students majoring in music, and from this has sprung a "Mabel Daniels Beneficiary Fund" named by her class in her honor. This fund is used to buy symphony tickets and music, and to aid needy students. Shortly after she graduated she presented the college with a silver cup for the class singing competition, held annually in the spring in the college yard, which has since become a college tradition.

In her music Miss Daniels believes in retaining the best of the old, but she is constantly experimenting with new forms (as her later works show) selecting and choosing from modern counterpoint and harmony what seems to her to have the greatest value. Much of present day music, she feels, is immensely clever, but too often turns its back completely on the rich heritage of the past. In its effort to avoid the slightest taint of nineteenth century "lush sentimentality" it goes to the other extreme and becomes purely cerebral and mathematical.

"Real music should be more than a crossword puzzle," Mabel Daniels insists. "It must have something human in it." It is this human quality that makes her own work noteworthy.

Mabel Daniels

The Music of Mabel Daniels

ORCHESTRAL WORKS

Deep Forest—prelude [1]	1935
Pirate's Island [1]	1935
Digressions—for string orchestra	1947

CHORAL WORKS

Eastern Song, women's voices, 2 violins, piano (also with orchestral accompaniment) [2]	1911
The Voice of my Beloved, women's voices, 2 violins, piano	1911
Veni Creator Spiritus, women's voices, soprano solo [2]	1912
The Desolate City, baritone solo and orchestra [2]	1914
June Rhapsody, women's voices [2]	1914
Peace in Liberty (*Peace with a Sword*) mixed voices, orchestra [2]	1917
Songs of Elfland, women's voices, flute, harp and strings [2]	1924
The Ride, men's voices [2]	1926
Holiday Fantasy, mixed voices, orchestra [2]	1928
The Holy Star, mixed voices, orchestra [2]	1928
Through the Dark the Dreamers Came, mixed voices, also for women's voices [2]	1928
Exultate Deo, mixed voices, orchestra [2]	1929
The Christ Child, mixed voices	1931
The Song of Jael, mixed voices, soprano soli, orchestra — cantata [1]	1938
Salve Festa Dies, mixed voices[1]	1938
Dum Dianae Vitrea, women's voices [1]	1942
Flower Wagon, women's voices [1]	1946

CHAMBER MUSIC

Pastoral Ode, for flute and strings [1]	1940
Three Observations for Three Woodwinds (Oboe, clarinet, bassoon)	1945
Two pieces for Violin and Piano	1947
Diversion for Diana	
Remembering Two Young Soldiers	

68

Mabel Daniels

SONGS

In a Manger Lowly, soprano solo, violin obbligato [3]	1915
Cherry Flowers [2]	1925
The Tree and the Image [1]	1937
The Kilties Pass and many others [1]	1943

STAGE WORKS

Two operettas for women's voices	1900-1901
Operetta *Alice in Wonderland Continued*	1902
One-act operetta *The Legend of Marietta*	1909
Pirate's Island—ballet	1935
Two Movements from *Three Observations*—ballet	1945

PIANO WORKS

In the Greenwood Suite	1908
Fairy Scherzo	1914

[1] J. Fischer Bro.
[2] A. P. Schmidt.
[3] G. Schirmer, Inc.

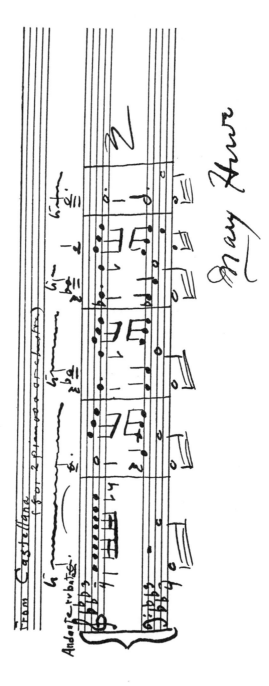

MARY HOWE

MARY HOWE

CHRONOLOGICALLY Mary Howe belongs to the earlier group of American composers; but her work actually places her in a later period, for it is definitely modern in style. She has the unique distinction of having begun her career as a composer at a time when, according to conventional ideas, she should have been too occupied with the care of her home and family to find time for outside creative work.

She had never thought, in her younger years, of becoming a composer. Her father, Calderon Carlisle, was an international lawyer of Scottish descent, and her mother—of Welsh ancestry—came from Virginia. Mary Carlisle Howe was born in Richmond at her grandmother's house, but her father was a Washingtonian and all of her life has been spent in Washington, D. C.

As a girl she traveled frequently abroad. She was an excellent pianist, and on one of her trips spent some time in Dresden studying with Richard Burmeister. Later she worked as a postgraduate piano student with Ernest Hutcheson and Harold Randolph at the Peabody Institute of Music in Baltimore. After her marriage to Walter Bruce Howe she began to play professionally, and for a number of years gave two-piano recitals with another gifted player, Anne Hull. The two soloed with several leading orchestras, including the Cleveland, Baltimore, National, and Russian Symphonies.

Mrs. Howe began to write music, she says, "simply because she felt like it"—which, after all, is the reason of most composers. But she soon discovered that she knew very little about composition. There was an excellent Music Conservatory in the neighboring city of Baltimore. There she enrolled at the Peabody Institute and was just beginning to do serious work in composing when she was interrupted by the First World War—and a new baby. Later she resumed her training at Peabody and continued her studies in composition with Gustav Strube.

To do this she had to go back and forth from Washington to Baltimore and at the same time care for her three children, home, and husband. A strenuous schedule! However, the children were by then in school and by sacrificing all social life and other outside activities, Mary Howe managed to complete her course at Peabody with flying colors. The examination required for her composition diploma, she confesses, was the first and only one she ever took in her life. Her education had always been at home, with tutors; she had never gone to a regular school.

Mary Howe's earliest compositions were for the piano. Next she did two choral works: *Catalina*, for mixed voices, and *Chain Gang Song*, the latter written especially for a choral group she was then conducting in Washington, D. C.

As a girl Mrs. Howe (then Mary Carlisle) often rode through the North Carolina mountains on horseback. One day on a lonely road by the edge of a mountain stone quarry, she came on a group of Negroes in prison-striped suits who, under the watchful eyes of armed guards, were driving wedges into the rocks to lay charges of dynamite. One of the ball-and-chain shackled convicts would hold the steel drill while two others alternately brought down their sledge hammers in crashing, rhythmical blows. As they worked they sang.

The curious rhythm of the singing fascinated Mary Carlisle, and the song's refrain, with its varying tempi of falling hammers, made a lasting impression on her musically-attured subconscious. *Chain Gang Song*, written many years later, proved so effective that Carl Engel (at that time head of the Library of Congress) suggested that she orchestrate the work. Elaborating it with interesting new harmonies, and reproducing the sound of falling sledge hammers by blows struck on a steel plate, Mrs. Howe arranged the song for male chorus with orchestral accompaniment.

The following autumn of 1925 *Chain Gang Song* was performed with great success at the Worcester Music Festival, Albert Stoessel conducting the orchestra and chorus. This was the first big public performance of Mary Howe's music. Emilie Bauer, music critic and sister of the eminent teacher and composer Marion Bauer, said *Chain Gang Song* was "a powerful piece of writing with no trace of femininity and astonishing skill in the handling of her resources." Miss Bauer added a prophetic sentence: "This work as well as its performance should make her known."[1]

[1] Emilie Bauer in *The Musical Leader*, Oct. 15, 1925.

MARY HOWE

Mary Howe

During the years that followed Mary Howe became widely known for her orchestral works, many of which have been played by leading symphony orchestras (among them the New York Philharmonic, the Philadelphia, Rochester, National, Baltimore, Indianapolis and Chicago Symphonies, the BBC Symphony in London, the Toronto Symphony in Canada, and several orchestras abroad and in South America.)

Dirge, one of Mrs. Howe's earliest orchestral works (written in 1931) was commended by the critics as "an impressive and noble work." *Sand*—called "crisply sparkling"—is a short piece with an intriguing staccato effect.

Castellana, for two pianos and orchestra, was written in 1935. It is one of Mrs. Howe's most popular works, and has been in the repertoire of such well-known duo-pianists as Luboschutz and Nemenoff and Bartlett and Robertson, and others both here and abroad. The critics spoke of *Castellana's* "fascinating rhythms" and "arresting and intriguing dissonances," and called it a valuable addition to two-piano literature.

"*Castellana,*" says Mrs. Howe, "is built on four authentic Spanish folk tunes which I have never seen in any collection but which I heard sung by some delightful Spanish cousins of my father.

"I have great musical sympathy with Spanish folk music—of ante bellum period—and feel I have a genuine traditional connection there through my family and my early days in Spain. Although the piece is in character a free tone poem, the four definite sections give it somewhat the air of a small, self-containing symphony. I wrote it first as a two-piano piece, and later amplified and developed it into the longer work for two pianos and orchestra."

Among other orchestral works of Mary Howe's that have been widely played is *Spring Pastoral* (1937), based on a poem by Elinor Wylie and written originally for women's chorus—then orchestrated. The *Washington Post* called it:

A wistful tone poem, adroitly scored with a keen sense of instrumental color, which embodies the timelessness and the bittersweet poignance of a drowsy reverie over a memory of long ago.[2]

[2] *The Washington Post,* March 15, 1937.

73

Modern Music-Makers

Her *American Piece,* was praised by Walter Damrosch for its "biting and original harmonies . . . alive and effective orchestration." *Stars,* an orchestral work depicting "the spreading immensity of the starry vault," won special praise from the critics. The *Post* said of it:

> Mrs. Howe's impressionistic *Stars* is the finest orchestral work that she has written thus far. The full sonorous ensemble of the strings opens the piece with the suggestion of the spreading immensity of the starry vault. As the music progresses one's imagination is carried into the contemplation of the awesome depths of space and into the sense of mystery with which man compares his insignificance with infinity. The close, fading into a lone tone vanishing on its way to another universe, brings the peace of complete abandonment to the spiritual force that guides the multitudinous suns.[3]

The work which all agree is Mrs. Howe's finest composition, and which she, herself, likes very much is the spirited *Paean* for full orchestra.

> Mary Howe's beautiful "Paean" is her finest writing for orchestra, opulently toned and dynamic in effect. Its passionate speech, surging spirit and broad outline expresses a sentiment that is gripping, while the freedom of style brings a rich variety of tonal color.[4]

One spring, while visiting the novelist, Katherine Dunlap, at her sixteenth century château in France, Mary Howe was particularly struck by the singing of the merles (French blackbirds), by a plaintive *bergerette* sung by a small French boy who didn't know where he had learnt it, and by an original love-song, or *plainte* of a pastoral character.

> *Ah! Qu'il revienne, (que la vie est amère)*
> *Ah! Qu'il revienne, celui qui m'est si cher.*
> *J'entends les merles qui chantent —*
>   *— Doux comme autrefois —*
> *Loin, loin de moi, la bas, que fait-il donc?*
> *Non! Ne me dites pas.*

---

[3] *The Washington Post,* December 19, 1940.
[4] *The Evening Star,* Washington, D.C., Feb. 15, 1943.

Mary Howe

Weaving together the various short melodies sung by the merles, together with the *bergerette* and the love-song, she wrote a charming orchestral work named after her friend's château, *Coulennes*.

During the war Mrs. Howe composed a moving tribute *To The Unknown Soldier*. This eloquent song with orchestral accompaniment was first performed by Emery Darcy, Metropolitan tenor, with the National Symphony, the late Hans Kindler conducting. Many of Mrs. Howe's orchestral works were first played by Dr. Kindler. He was one of our most progressive conductors—particularly sympathetic to the works of contemporary American composers. A number of orchestral pieces which have since been widely played by other symphonies (such as Piston's *Second Symphony*, Schuman's *Festival Overture*, Roy Harris' *Acceleration*, and many others) had their first performance under Hans Kindler and the National Symphony Orchestra.

Mrs. Howe's most recent orchestral work is *Agreeable Overture*, written in 1949. She has composed a long list of songs and piano pieces, and also a number of interesting chamber-music compositions. A *String Quartet* was played at Yaddo in 1940, and *G String Fugue* has been performed by the Pro Arte Quartet. Another string quartet she calls *Quatuor*, and a third, (1941) *Three Pieces after Emily Dickinson*.

Mary Howe passed on a love of music to all three of her children. Bruce and Molly sang, while Calderon—the eldest (named after his maternal grandfather) also learned to play the recorder, or "common flute" as it used to be called. In earlier days whole concerts were given on these instruments, using recorders of different pitches. This old-time wooden flute, played clarinet fashion, has recently become popular again. Mrs. Howe has written an *Interlude Between Two Pieces for Recorder and Harpsichord*, first played by her son Calderon Howe and Ralph Kirkpatrick. It has since been performed at other concerts with flute and piano substituting for the original instruments.

Mrs. Howe and her three children became famous for their madrigal singing. They were invited to appear in a number of different cities, and sang at Yale, Bryn Mawr, and the MacDowell Colony. The "Four Howes" as they came to be known professionally, were also engaged by Ralph Kirkpatrick to take part in one of the Williamsburg Festivals of old music given at the Governor's Palace in the reconstructed colonial town of Williamsburg, Virginia. Every detail of these musical programs—from candle-lighting to picturesque eighteenth century costumes—was planned to recreate the illusion of old colonial days. Even the programs were printed in the style of the period:

An Account of the Muſick for
Two Informal Series of

CONCERTS

TO BE PRESENTED IN THE

BALLROOM *of the* GOVERNOR'S PALACE
Williamſburg, Virginia,

by RALPH KIRKPATRICK, Eſq.,
Harpſichord,

ASSISTED BY

Ada MacLeiſh, *Soprano;* Orrea Pernel, *Violin;* Lois Porter, *Violin;* Aaron Bodenhorn, *Violoncello;* "The Four Howes," *Glees, Madrigals & Catches.*

(Mary Howe; Molly Howe; Bruce Howe;
Calderon Howe, *Common Flute.*)

Mary Howe

In addition to her important work as a composer, raising a family, and managing her household, Mary Howe has been actively connected with many of the city's artistic and philanthropic groups, and has served on the Boards of the Washington Chamber Music Society, the Friends of Music at the Library of Congress and the National Symphony. She was for four years National Chairman of Orchestras in the National Federation of Music Clubs, and is now on the International Music Committee. She is a member of ASCAP, the League of Composers, the National Association of American Composers and Conductors, and an honorary member of the American Composers Alliance. In 1950 she was elected honorary member of Sigma Alpha Iota.

Mary Howe is blessed with unbounded energy, an enthusiastic temperament, and a gracious personality—qualities that are evident in every department of her varied existence. Her music is written mainly during the summer months—often at the MacDowell Colony. (She has been for some years on the MacDowell Association's Board of Directors). Her long list of compositions and the frequent performances of her works both here and abroad have established Mary Howe as a composer of distinction.

Mary Howe

Born April 4, Richmond, Virginia	1882
Marries Walter Bruce Howe	1912
Debut as pianist "Ten Star Series" Washington D.C.	1915
Sonata in D for Violin and Piano	1922
Suite, String Quartet and Piano	1923
Catalina	1924
Debut duo-piano recital with Anne Hull	
Chain Gang Song	1925
Sand, for orchestra	1928
Studies at Peabody Institute with Ernest Hutcheson, Harold Randolph, Gustav Strube	1920-30
Dirge, for orchestra	1931
American Piece	1935
Castellana, two pianos, orchestra	1935
Spring Pastoral, for orchestra	1936
Coulennes, for orchestra	
Cards (ballet)	
Stars, Whimsy, for orchestra	1937
Quatuor, string quartet	1939
Land for Christmas, chorus	
Paean, for orchestra	1940
Potomac, suite for orchestra	
Three Pieces after Emily Dickinson	1941
Interlude Between Two Pieces, Flute and Piano	1942
Agreeable Overture, for orchestra	1949
Elected honorary member Sigma Alpha Iota	1950

The Music of Mary Howe

ORCHESTRAL WORKS

Fugue (for string orchestra)	1922
Poema	1925
Dirge [1]	1931
Sand (also for two pianos) [1]	1932
American Piece [1]	1935
Castellana (two pianos and orchestra) [1]	1935
Spring Pastoral (also for women's voices and piano) [1]	1936
Coulennes [2]	1936
Stars (also for piano) [3]	1937
Whimsy (also for piano) [3]	1937
Paean [2]	1940
Potomac (suite: *Prelude*, three sketches) [2]	1940
Polka, Waltz and Finale	1946
Agreeable Overture	1949

CHORAL WORKS

Drink to Me Only, mixed voices with piano [1]	1921
Catalina, mixed voices, piano [2]	1924
Chain Gang Song, male or mixed chorus with piano, orchestra or a cappella [1]	1925
Cavaliers, men's voices, piano	1933
Robin Hood's Heart, men's voices, piano	1936
Fiddler's Reel, mixed voices, piano or orchestra	1936
Land for Christmas, mixed voices, a cappella [1]	1936
Song of Palms, women's voices, piano or orchestra [2]	1939
Song of Ruth, mixed voices, organ [1]	1939
Williamsburg Sunday, mixed voices a cappella	1940
Six Songs for Children [4]	1941
Prophecy, men's voices with piano and brass or percussion	1943
A Devotion, men's voices a cappella	1944

CHAMBER MUSIC

Sonata for Violin and Piano	1922
Suite, String Quartet and Piano	1923
Three Spanish Folk Tunes, two pianos [5]	1926

79

Modern Music-Makers

Cancion Romanesca, string	1928
Ballade Fantasque, cello and piano	1930
Suite Melancolique, trio	1931
Cards: A ballet, two pianos	1936
Quatuor—string quartet	1939
Elegy, Organ [6]	1939
Three Pieces after Emily Dickinson, string quartet	1941
Interlude Between Two Pieces, harpsichord and recorder or flute and piano	1942

PIANO WORKS

Andante Douloureux [1]	Early Work
Prelude	1920
Berceuse (also for two pianos) [1]	1920
Nocturne	1920
Stars [3]	1934
Whimsy [3]	1934

SONGS

Cossack Cradle Song, piano or string quartet [7]	Early Work
Berceuse, piano or orchestra [1]	Early Work
"*O Mistress Mine,*" piano or string quartet [1]	1925
Ripe Apples, piano [1]	1931
The Little Rose, piano or string quartet [1]	1932
The Rag Picker	1932
Little Elegy, with piano or string quartet [1]	1934
Let Us Walk in the White Snow, piano or string quartet [2]	1935
When I Died in Berners Street, baritone piano or orchestra [1]	1936
Irish Lullaby, piano [2]	1939
Hymne	1943
To the Unknown Soldier, piano or orchestra [1]	1944
Mein Herz	1947
The Bailey and the Bell	1950
And many others	

[1] G. Schirmer.
[2] C. Fischer.
[3] Edition Musicus.
[4] Silver Burdett.
[5] Boston Music Co.
[6] H. W. Gray.
[7] Ditson & Co.

GENA BRANSCOMBE

GENA BRANSCOMBE

IT is chiefly through her choral music that Gena Branscombe has become known to the public at large. She has written close to fifty original choral works (many of them with full orchestral accompaniment) and has also made a large number of arrangements and transcriptions of other composers' music. Her works have been widely performed all over the United States and abroad, and have had a considerable influence throughout the country.

At the beginning of her career Miss Branscombe had no thought of becoming a conductor. It was necessity, she says, that "pushed her into conducting." Having composed a number of choral works, she found herself in constant demand to conduct her own music. So she enrolled in Dr. Warren Erb's class in conducting at New York University, and also studied with Dr. Frank Damrosch and with Chalmers Clifton as a member of the American Orchestral Society.

There are not many opportunities in this country for a woman conductor—aside from a few women's symphonies and Miss Branscombe has been guest conductor for most of these—but in choral directing she found a large field open to women, also in the writing of choral music. All through the country there are club, church and social organizations with choruses both large and small that are always looking for new music for their programs.

Miss Branscombe soon found herself with a heavy schedule as director of choral groups and women's orchestras. When the General Federation of Women's Clubs celebrated their jubilee in Atlantic City, some years ago, Gena Branscombe was chosen to direct the huge chorus at the final concert.

There were a thousand women on the stage for this climax of the Jubilee, and five thousand more in the audience—women who had gathered from every part of the United States to pay tribute to fifty years of women's achievements. The huge chorus was an inspiring sight. The singers, too, were inspired. Although they had never rehearsed as a combined unit, the individual groups had been so perfectly trained that when they came together they sang with the control and sensitivity of a small and intimate chorus. Their voices

Gena Branscombe

blended into an ensemble of rare quality—ethereal in the pianissimo parts.

This unique performance in Atlantic City was largely due to the planning and direction of the remarkable woman who had been chosen as leader of the great chorus. Long before the concert Gena Branscombe had sent out detailed instructions to the various groups that were to take part, so that all would have the same tempi, breath control, phrasing and interpretation of the pieces they were to sing. Fittingly, her program featured works by American women composers. It closed with a group by Haydn and Mozart, and a performance of Handel's *Hallelujah!* that literally swept the audience off its feet.

Gena Branscombe was born in Ontario, just across the Canadian border—though she comes of pioneer American stock, her people having landed in New York (then New Amsterdam) in 1640. Almost before she could read or write she began to make up pieces at the piano. When only five she invented a game of musical relationships which she called "cousins and aunts." This was a personal and highly original exploration into harmony. Before long she naturally began to combine the "cousins and aunts" into little pieces of her own.

Soon after she graduated from high school, at fifteen, she was sent to Chicago, to stay with her older brother who was a minister. Gena soon won a scholarship at the Chicago Musical College, and studied piano there with Rudolph Ganz, while Felix Borowski was for seven years her teacher in composition. Twice she won the gold medal for composition. After graduating, Miss Branscombe taught for a time at the Musical College, spent two years as head of the piano department at Whitman College, Washington, and then went to Berlin.

Music study in Germany, before the First World War was an exciting and rewarding experience, especially for those who wanted to follow a musician's career. All the leading artists visited Berlin; there were daily lieder and orchestral concerts, and the finest opera in all Europe (with the possible exception of Vienna). One of the most popular operas at that time was Humperdinck's *Hansel and Gretel*. Humperdinck was considered one of the best teachers in Berlin, and Miss Branscombe counted herself fortunate when he accepted her as a pupil. She studied orchestration and composition with him. At the end of a year, however, certain sentimental ties drew her homeward. She returned to the United States and married John Ferguson Tenney, a New York attorney.

The following years were very much taken up with the care of her home and three small daughters, though she still continued to write music. Her first important work was *Festival Prelude,* for orchestra, composed in 1913 for a summer pageant at the MacDowell Colony in New Hampshire, and later played in New York and San Francisco. *Quebec* is an orchestral suite written in 1928 which she has conducted with a number of groups including the Chicago Women's Symphony. *Elegie* was finished in 1937, and *Valse Joyeuse* in 1941, for full orchestra. She has done some pieces for chamber orchestra, among them *Maples, Baladine,* and *Procession,* and has also composed a few chamber-music works—notably *Carnival Fantasy* for strings, flute and harp and piano, *A Lute of Jade,* for woodwinds and soprano, *Sonata* for violin and piano, an arrangement of *Procession* for trumpet, organ and piano, and a very large number of songs. Over a hundred of the latter have been published, and they include the well-known *Hail Ye Tyme of Holie Days, The Morning Wind, At the Postern Gate, Happiness, Across the Blue Aegean Sea, Krishna,* and many others. Miss Branscombe has made scores of arrangements for chorus of the works of other composers, such as those of Bach, Mozart, Beethoven, Saint-Saëns, and Debussy, and for many of them has written her own original texts and translations.

Her first important choral work was a cantata for women's voices with soprano and alto solos, and orchestral accompaniment, for which she furnished the text as well as the music: *The Dancer of Fjaard.* A second followed that same year of 1926, for men's chorus and orchestra: *The Phantom Caravan,* with words by Kendall Banning.

Miss Branscombe had always had a special interest in history—particularly those dramatic moments which, through the ages, have revealed man's gallant spirit of courage and faith. Several of her most effective compositions interpret some of these historical incidents and dramatize them in musical form. She has been at work for several years on an opera based on such an incident and titled, *The Bells of Circumstance.* For this, as for so many of her choral works, songs and arrangements, she has written her own text. The orchestral suite *Quebec* is drawn from this opera. (In 1950 her Choral Society sang the finale from the second act at one of their Town Hall concerts).

Gena Branscombe

Pilgrims of Destiny, (one of Miss Branscombe's most ambitious works,) is also based on an historical incident. It is an hour and a quarter long work for solo voices, orchestra and chorus—a "poetic, melodious account of the voyage of the *Mayflower*, bubbling with tunefulness," as the *New York Times* put it. It describes life aboard the *Mayflower* during the last day and night before the sighting of the New World. This was first performed at Plymouth as the final event of the 1929 biennial convention of the National Federation of Music Clubs. It was awarded two prizes and brought the composer an honorary degree.

Melodious and rich in dramatic feeling, the score was shown to its best advantage at the hands of its composer, who elicited all the poetry and lyricism with which she had endowed it. *Pilgrims of Destiny* may well be said to be a stirring and eloquent bit of American history set to music.[1]

Youth of the World, another elaborate choral work written in 1932, is one of Miss Branscombe's most popular compositions. She has conducted it all over this country, and was invited to go to London and direct it there. *Youth of the World* stresses a theme particularly dear to her heart: world peace. The work has been called "a thrilling litany for everlasting peace."

During the last war Gena Branscombe was greatly moved on reading a poem by Violet Alvarez describing the bombing of ancient St. Michael's Cathedral, at Coventry in England. The church at the time of this disaster was entirely destroyed with the exception of the great Gothic tower, which remained untouched—a symbol of England's strength to endure, and a rallying point around which the bereaved townspeople gathered to sing and pray. Using the poem as text, Miss Branscombe apostrophized the event "in plain-spun style, tense with fervid feeling and grim, lyric defiance"[2] and called this vivid composition *Coventry's Choir* (for a four-part women's chorus and soprano solo). She wrote this, she says, as her tribute "to the indomitable courage of the English people during their darkest hours of trial." *Coventry's Choir* is the work she herself likes best of all her

[1] *Musical America.*
[2] Louis Biancolli in *The New York World Telegram,* May 3, 1944.

Modern Music-Makers

compositions. It was first performed at Town Hall on May 2, 1944, Miss Branscombe conducting her own choral group.

This chorus of women singers has made a name for itself in and around New York City. It began as a small group connected with the American Women's Association, under the auspices of Anne Morgan. When the association decided to disband the group, the members asked Gena Branscombe if they might continue under her leadership. So she herself took over the chorus, and since then it has steadily grown until it now numbers seventy-five women. Each year the Branscombe Choral Society, as it is now known, gives a series of concerts in Town Hall and also over the air. The first half of their season is usually devoted to liturgical works, from Palestrina to modern writers, and the latter half to secular music. Miss Branscombe always includes works by American composers on these programs. On December 20, 1946, she conducted her chorus in a Christmas program of "Carols from many lands" before the Secretariat of the United Nations in the Security Hall at Lake Success, New York. This was the first group to sing Christmas Music in that historic place, and the first occasion of its kind in the recorded history of the world.

At the conclusion of the May, 1949, concert of the Branscombe Choral Society, the American Mothers Committee of the Golden Rule Foundation presented Gena Branscombe with a special citation "in recognition of her outstanding contribution as a mother and a woman to the musical field."

Miss Branscombe's recent choral works include *Afar on the Purple Moor,* written in 1948 and based on eight measures of an old Norfolk air; *Murmur on, Sweet Harp,* from a recently discovered song by Stephen Foster; *Woodwinds,* for women's chorus. One of the most successful of her many arrangements of other composers' music is taken from the finale of Brahms' *First Symphony.* For this she wrote her own text and called it *The Lord Is Our Fortress.* It has had a number of performances, including an outstanding broadcast by the Salt Lake Tabernacle Choir in January, 1951.

Through all her professional career Gena Branscombe has remained a devoted wife and mother. Her three daughters have all distinguished themselves. Gena, the eldest and her mother's namesake, was awarded the Undergraduate Student Fellowship at Barnard College, and became the first American student to win the Foli

86

Gena Branscombe

scholarship in composition at the Royal College of Music in London; Vivian has a Doctor of Medicine degree from Cornell University, and Beatrice made a brilliant record while at Barnard.

"Having a home, a husband and children to love and serve brings enrichment of life to a woman," says Miss Branscombe. "But being a part of the world's work in humbly serving and loving the illumined force which is music brings fulfillment."

Gena Branscombe

Born November 4, Picton, Ontario, Canada	1881
Attends Chicago Musical College. Studies there with Rudolph Ganz and Felix Borowski	1897-1904
Teaches at Chicago Musical College	1904-1907
Heads piano department at Whitman College, Wash.	1907-1909
Summer months—study in Europe	1908
Goes to Berlin for a year. Studies there with Humperdinck	1909-1910
Returns to U.S. to marry John Ferguson Tenney. Settles in N.Y.C.	1910
Festival Prelude—for orchestra	1913
Sonata for Violin and Piano	1920
The Dancer of Fjaard—chorus and orchestra (text by G. B.)	1926
The Phantom Caravan	
Pilgrims of Destiny, solo voices, chorus and orchestra (text by G. B.)	1927
Quebec—orchestral suite	1928
Youth of the World—chorus and orchestra, (text by G. B.)	1932
Carnival Fantasy for strings, flute, harp, piano	1932
Organization of the Branscombe Choral Society	1934
Sun and the Warm Brown Earth—chorus	1934
In Paris and London *Youth of the World* performed	1935
Conducts National Chorus (1000 voices) Atlantic City, Gen. Fed. of Women's Clubs	1941
Coventry's Choir—chorus	1944
Afar on the Purple Moor—chorus	1948
Procession—solo trumpet, piano, organ	1948
Woodwinds—chorus	1949
The Lord is our Fortress—chorus	1950
Thou Shalt Not Be Afraid (91st Psalm)—chorus	1951

PHOTOGRAPH BY BRUNO, HOLLYWOOD, CAL.

GENA BRANSCOMBE

The Music of Gena Branscombe

Modern Music-Makers

SONGS

The Morning Wind [1]
Hail Ye Tyme of Holie Days [1]
At the Postern Gate [1]
Happiness [1]
Krishna; Serenade (I Send My Heart Up To Thee) [1]
Across the Blue Aegean Sea [10]
Blow Softly Maple Leaves [11]
    And many others

[1] Arthur P. Schmidt Co.
[2] Oliver Ditson Co.
[3] John Church Co.
[4] M. Witmark & Sons.
[5] C. C. Birchard & Co.
[6] J. Fischer & Bro.
[7] G. Ricordi & Co.
[8] G. Schirmer.
[9] H. FitzSimons & Co.
[10] Galaxy Music Corp.
[11] H. W. Gray Co.

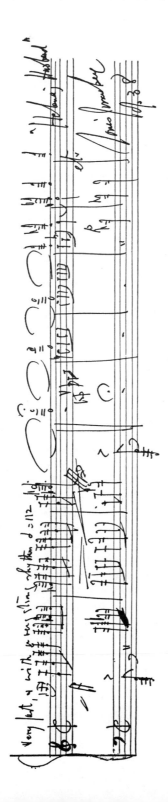

LOUIS GRUENBERG

LOUIS GRUENBERG

ALTHOUGH Louis Gruenberg has composed a large number of orchestral and chamber-music works, opera appeals to him as the type of music writing that he likes best. One of his earliest compositions was an operetta (produced when he was only twenty-one) that played successfully all over Europe. Since then he has written, up to the present time, eight serious operas—the first of these in 1912, and the last completed in 1951.

Emperor Jones, based on Eugene O'Neill's play about the Negro Pullman porter who proclaimed himself Emperor of Haiti, is the most famous of all Gruenberg's operas. He planned it as an experiment—"to get away from the old tradition of opera"—and as a study in the psychological effect of cumulative terror. By every resource of musical ingenuity—"the creepy sibilation of the strings, the spookish rattling and tintinnabulation of percussion instruments, the moaning and hollow brooding of horns, and the bloodcurdling shrieks and bellowings of the chorus," (as Paul Rosenfeld put it[1])—he tried to build up an atmosphere which he hoped would strike his audience with the same terrific emotional impact that it had produced on himself when he wrote it.

No one knew whether *Emperor Jones* would be a success or a failure. Only the day before its opening, in February, 1933, Gatti-Casazza director of the Metropolitan Opera, confessed that he wasn't sure whether Gruenberg's opera would turn out "a terrific fiasco or a tremendous success." (As he counted the curtain calls, following the first performance—there were thirty-seven in all—there was no doubt which of these alternatives was correct.)

The curtain rose, that opening night at the Metropolitan, on a jungle scene dark with creeping vines and sinister with the relentless beat of distant tom-toms. Jones, self-appointed Emperor, came stumbling through the jungle, trying to escape from the natives who had risen against him; worse still, from the 'hants of his crime-ridden past. As the ghosts of his earlier victims rose, one after the other, to confront him, the fear-crazed Negro fired his revolver at each in turn.

[1] In *The New Republic,* February 22, 1933.

92

Louis Gruenberg

Finally only one shot was left: the silver bullet which, he had boasted, was the only thing that could kill him. For an anguished moment he stopped and implored heaven's mercy in a moving spiritual: *Standing in the Need of Prayer.* Then the pursuing natives closed in with shrieks of fury; the tom-toms rose in a frenzied crescendo; with a last gesture of defiance the Negro Emperor shot the silver bullet into his own brain. . . . The curtain fell. . . . The audience burst into wild applause.

So ended the epoch-making first operatic performance of *Emperor Jones.* Eugene O'Neill's powerful drama, Lawrence Tibbett's magnificent performance, and Louis Gruenberg's striking music, all combined to make this one of the most effective productions ever to appear on the Metropolitan stage. The following day the papers were full of it. The opera rated a front-page review, and Gruenberg became the most discussed of modern composers.

Louis Gruenberg was born in Russia, in 1884, but was brought to this country when he was only a year old. His father, a violinist, came over first as an immigrant. As soon as he had put enough money aside he sent for his wife and small son to join him. Gruenberg says he can't remember anything in his childhood that was not connected with music. His father gave him his first lessons. "He would knock my head off if I didn't practice. . . ."

Louis was brought up in the downtown East Side section of New York and at an early age attended the National Conservatory of Music. Mrs. MacDowell, mother of the famous composer, was then President of the Conservatory. Gruenberg has a vivid recollection of his first meeting with Edward MacDowell. The latter was like a god to the eight-year-old boy. Louis had already written a lot of music; he went to see MacDowell at his hotel, carrying a bundle of manuscripts under his arm.

By the time young Gruenberg was ten he had made a name as a child prodigy. He gave concerts all over the country and played the entire Keith circuit, earning more money than in many a year later as a composer. But even then composition interested him more than playing. When he was nineteen—in 1903—he decided to go to Russia and study with Rimsky-Korsakoff. Just before leaving, however, he heard the celebrated pianist Busoni give a concert, and that changed the course of his career. Busoni's playing made a tremendous impression on the young musician. He decided, since he was going through Berlin on his way to Russia, that he would call on him.

"Not at home," the servant girl reported when he went to the virtuoso's house in Berlin. Young Gruenberg was not one to take no for an answer. He tried again—and again, and kept on returning. On his nineteenth visit he heard voices in the adjoining room. Still the servant refused to admit him.

"The Herr Professor has now a party," she insisted, "he cannot be disturbed."

"All right. I'll stay until the party's over," the young visitor announced firmly. Presently Busoni, curious at such persistence, came out. "Listen, Herr Busoni," said Gruenberg, "I've come thousands of miles to see you. I have been here nineteen times already, and I'll just keep on coming until you listen to me."

The final result of this remarkable perseverance—typical of much of Gruenberg's success through life—was that he "stayed with Busoni sixteen years." Busoni was so struck by the boy's ability as a pianist, and his "God-graced hands," that he insisted he must become a concert artist. In 1912 Louis Gruenberg made his debut with the Berlin Philharmonic.

He had never, however, stopped composing. The week of his debut as a pianist he won a prize offered by a German periodical (six hundred and ninety other composers had competed). For one week—"the grandest week of my life"—he was the most famous person in the musical world of Germany.

The next two years were spent in concertizing. Gruenberg toured all over Europe (he was the first pianist to play in Lapland) and he built up a considerable reputation as a concert pianist. It was at this time that he wrote his operetta; it played in more than thirty European cities. In short, Louis Gruenberg was a celebrity—that is, in Europe. In the United States he was at that time unknown.

During the summer of 1914 he went to London to see about having his operetta performed there. Just a few days after he arrived, war broke out. He had no money, no passport, a German name, and no way of proving that he was an American citizen. When he tried to get help from the American Consul the latter said, "You will have to furnish identification. There are hundreds of other Americans trying

Louis Gruenberg

to get back to the United States." So Louis Gruenberg, whose name was well known all over Europe, whose concerts had built for him a modest fortune ("the world was my oyster, and I had opened it!") now found himself a penniless tramp, with no place to go. Then a day cr so later as he walked down a London street, someone slapped him on the back.

"Hello Louis!" cried an unmistakably American voice.

At first Gruenberg didn't recognize the man. "Don't you remember me?" the latter said, smiling, "I used to be a pupil of yours. . . ."

"Quick!" cried the relieved composer. "Come with me to the American Consul and tell him who I am."

The trip back to the United States was a nightmare. He could only get passage in the steerage. All his possessions, money, over two thousand books—many of them first editions—and nineteen paintings of himself by leading foreign artists, had to be left behind. He arrived in New York penniless—unknown.

It was some time before Gruenberg's nightmare lifted. He could have continued his virtuoso career, but now he was determined to devote himself to music writing. As if to make up for the years he had spent abroad he turned wholeheartedly to the music of his own country. He began experimenting with jazz patterns, and wrote several compositions based on this idiom: *Jazettes*, for violin and piano; *Four Indiscretions* for string quartet; a *Jazz Suite* for orchestra (played by the Boston Symphony in 1930); *The Creation* and *Daniel Jazz*, both for solo voice and eight instruments. *Daniel Jazz* was chosen to represent American music at the Venice Festival of the I.C.S.M.

Finally Gruenberg's bad luck changed; he began to win prizes. An orchestral tone-poem, *Hill of Dreams* brought him the Flagler Prize; *The Enchanted Isle* won the Juilliard Foundation Award and was played by a number of leading orchestras. Next came a commission from the League of Composers, and for this he wrote *Serenade to a Beauteous Lady*. Some years later, in a contest sponsored by the Lake Placid Club, his *Quintet* for piano and strings received the $1,000 prize. He was one of the organizers of the League of Composers, President of the United States Section of the I.C.S.M. and also a member of the latter's European jury.

95

Modern Music-Makers

John Erskine, who in 1930 was head of the Juilliard School of Music, knew and admired Gruenberg's music. He had been thinking of producing an opera at Juilliard—something on a fanciful theme similar to Humperdinck's *Hansel and Gretel*. So he suggested to Gruenberg that they collaborate, he to do the libretto, Gruenberg the score. The result was "a fairy opera for the child-like": *Jack and the Beanstalk*, in which Erskine in his inimitable manner made the cow a philosopher, while the composer entered into the spirit of the occasion and produced a delightful and appropriate score—"tinged with tonal humor," as one critic put it.

This experiment in composing for the stage convinced Louis Gruenberg that opera writing was his special forte. Soon after the production of *Jack and the Beanstalk* he began work on *Emperor Jones*.

When he first came across Eugene O'Neill's play he was tremendously impressed by its dramatic possibilities. For some time he had been wanting to do an opera—preferably to an American subject (in Europe, he says, they were calling him "The American Indian" because of his devotion to New World themes). He wrote to O'Neill and asked if he could discuss the project with him. The two finally met in Paris, late one night at the Ritz-Carlton Hotel. They talked until six the next morning. O'Neill agreed to let Gruenberg set *Emperor Jones* to music and to make certain changes necessary to turn it into an opera. The actual libretto, drawn from the play, was arranged by the composer.

This period, while he was at work on *Emperor Jones*, was perhaps the happiest of Louis Gruenberg's entire life. He had just married Irma Pickora, a Czecho-Slovakian doctor of medicine. (They have one daughter, Joan Alma). After securing O'Neill's consent to the use of his drama, Gruenberg and his bride returned to the United States and took a house in the wilds of the New England woods, where he hoped he would be able to work at the new opera without interruptions. It was winter time, and their only neighbors were bears—until, a few months later, with the coming of summer they found themselves in the middle of a Salvation Army camp, and further work there proved impossible.

When Gruenberg finally completed *Emperor Jones* he showed the score to Olin Downes, who in turn recommended it to Gatti-Casazza. The famous Metropolitan manager could speak very little English,

Louis Gruenberg

and Gruenberg found it difficult to explain, half in French and half in Italian, what his opera was all about. It was especially hard to describe the psychological reactions of the demented Negro Emperor. Gatti-Casazza finally agreed, somewhat against his better judgment, to give the opera a try.

Emperor Jones proved such a success that it was carried in the Metropolitan repertory for several seasons, and was also played in Chicago, Boston, San Francisco and Los Angeles. It brought the composer the David Bispham medal, and a number of excerpts from the music have been recorded by Victor. At present there are plans afoot to produce *Emperor Jones* in Italy and other European countries—also over television in the United States.

In 1934 Gruenberg became chairman of the Chicago Music College. Three years later—"with extraordinary enthusiasm and high hopes"—he moved with his family to California.

The initial years in California proved discouraging. Then Gruenberg began writing for films, and the success of his first moving-picture music—*The Fight for Life*— established him as a film-score composer of importance. He did *The Fight for Life* in collaboration with Pare Lorentz, and his music won praise from every direction. One critic pronounced it "the most striking musical score ever heard on the screen." Underlying the whole is a rhythmic pulse, suggesting the heartbeat of the newborn child whose "fight for life" is described in the picture.

Gruenberg has written the music for a number of moving pictures. Three of his scores have received Academy nominations: *So Ends our Night, Commandos Strike at Dawn,* and *The Fight for Life.* In 1946 he did the music for *The Arch of Triumph,* and although the picture was not a box-office success, the music received special commendation.

In 1937 the Columbia Broadcasting System commissioned Gruenberg to write a radio opera. For his subject he took W. H. Hudson's delicate and fanciful story *Green Mansions,* again writing his own libretto. The music invokes the enchantment of jungle scenes and myth-like characters. He calls the work "a kind of musical pantheism, in which the world of nature becomes humanized by way of human thoughts and emotions."

97

Modern Music-Makers

In addition to his operas, six scores for films, chamber music, four symphonies (the last in 1945) and quantities of small pieces, Gruenberg has composed a number of concertos for different instruments. In 1944 Heifetz commissioned him to write a violin concerto, (he played it first in December of that year with the Philadelphia Symphony Orchestra, Eugene Ormandy conducting.) This has proved one of Gruenberg's most popular works, and has been recorded by the Victor Company. During the writing of the *Violin Concerto* Heifetz would occasionally complain that the music was getting too complicated. The composer, however, only shrugged his shoulders. "What's that to you? You're Heifetz, aren't you?"

Gruenberg's later compositions include a third *Violin Sonata*, a *Cello Concerto*, and *Pastoral Variations* for orchestra. He has been at work for the past two years on a three-act opera based on Ben Johnson's *Volpone* which he hopes will be his finest. He feels that he has learned a great deal from his film work—how, for instance, to concentrate action, to confine into the dimensions of a stage what in moving pictures is spread over acres of films.

An artist, says Gruenberg, must be able to "get out of his comfortable tradition of smugness," and imagine himself in the situation or character he wants to interpret. To reach every listener in an audience requires a powerful grasp of emotional expression, for while individually some of the group may have the mentality of a four-year-old, taken collectively an audience is a mental giant. "If I don't get the reaction of an entire audience I feel I have made a mistake."

"A great work," Gruenberg goes on to say, "must be done under compulsion. You must do it because you *have* to. Then it becomes inevitable; it gets a strength of its own—a primitive quality that annihilates criticism." The only valid basis of artistic creation, he feels, is that which is founded on emotion; for emotion is the essence of human experience, and can be understood by everyone.

Louis Gruenberg

Born August 3, in Russia	1884
Comes to United States	1885
Attends National Conservatory of Music, N.Y.	1895
Goes to Berlin to study with Busoni	1903
Graduates from State Conservatory of Music, Vienna	1912
Debut as pianist with Berlin Philharmonic	
First Violin Sonata	1913
Returns permanently to United States	1914
First String Quartet *Indiscretions*	1922
Jazz Suite for Orchestra	1925
First Symphony	1926
First Quintet for Piano and Strings	1929
Jack and the Beanstalk (opera)	1930
Marries Irma Pickora	1931
Emperor Jones	1932
Chairman Chicago Music College	1934
Green Mansions (radio opera)	1937
Moves to California	1940
The Fight for Life (film)	1940
Second Piano Concerto	1942
Concerto for Violin	1944
Concerto for Cello	1945
Second, Third and Fourth Symphonies	1941-6
Variations on a Pastoral Theme	1946
The Arch of Triumph	1947
Music to a Legend	1948
Third Violin Sonata	1948
Volpone (opera)	1951

The Music of Louis Gruenberg

LOUIS GRUENBERG

Louis Gruenberg

Chamber Music Works

Diversations [1]	1930
Second Quintet for Piano and Strings	1937
First Quartet for Strings	1937
Jazettes (violin and piano)	
Second String Quartet	1941
Third Violin Sonata	1948

Stage Works and Film Music

The Witch of Brocken (E. Malkowsky) opera [3]	1912
The Bride of the Gods (Busoni) opera	1913
Dumb Wife (Anatole France) opera	1921
Jack and the Beanstalk (John Erskine) [5]	1930
Emperor Jones (Eugene O'Neill) opera [1]	1932
Queen Helena (Philip Moeller) opera	1936
Green Mansions (radio opera)	1937
The Fight for Life (film)	1940
Commandos Strike at Dawn (film)	1942
So Ends Our Night (film)	1943
Counterattack (film)	1945
The Arch of Triumph (film)	1947
The King's Men (film)	1950
Volpone (opera)	1951

[1] Cos Cob Press.
[2] Universal Edition.
[3] C. C. Birchard & Co.
[4] Composer's Music Corp.
[5] Juilliard Sch. Pub.

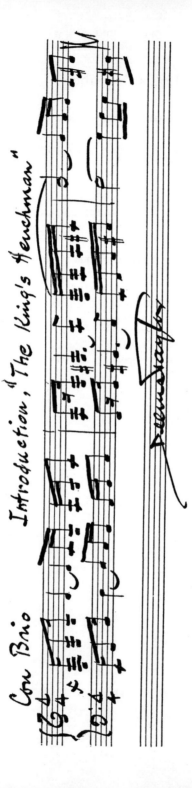

Con Brio   Introduction, "The King's Henchman"

DEEMS TAYLOR

DEEMS TAYLOR

DEEMS TAYLOR has been successful in so many different fields that it is difficult to list all of his accomplishments. Composer, writer and editor, translator, lecturer and commentator—featured on motion picture, radio and television programs—this is only a partial list of his activities.

"If the roster of my doings printed elsewhere," he writes, "seems at times to stray far afield from music, it is because I have always lived a double life. I have had to. Every composer has to. The painter, sculptor, the writer, are capable of making a living by pursuing their vocations. The composer (I mean the so-called 'serious' composer) has no such prospect. Unless he happens to write operas that are universally popular, he has no hope of making a living by writing music. So he must teach, conduct, or play an instrument as well as compose.

"I have tried teaching and found it an intolerable bore. No one would dream of hiring me as a conductor, and I am a dreadful pianist. So, long ago, I hit on a fourth choice: I would be subsidized. Therefore, for many years, I, the composer, have been supported by me, doing other things."

Deems Taylor was born in New York City on December 22, 1885, and inherited a considerable variety of racial strains, including Scottish, Irish, English, Dutch, and Swiss (a Swiss ancestor was naturalized as a British colonist in 1760).

When he was six he wrote his first musical "composition." It was in seven movements entitled *Love, Hatred, Sorroe, Gladness, Anger, Joy* and *Fetig* (Fatigue). He embellished this masterpiece with various designs, and drew the musical staves with a fine disregard for tradition—some had four, other six or more lines, all generously filled in with large fat notes placed at random. At that early age drawing and painting interested him more than music.

His father was a teacher and superintendent of public schools in New York City. He sent his son to the Ethical Culture School—forerunner of the modern progressive schools—where, among other subjects, the boy had rudimentary instruction in music reading and notation.

Modern Music-Makers

Young Taylor liked to draw and paint so well that he first considered art as a career. Music, or at any rate composing, was still closely connected in his mind with art. He enjoyed drawing notes largely because the design that they made, perched on the vertical lines of the staff, pleased his artistic sense. However, after reading a story about Mozart's glamorous career as *Wunderkind* pianist and composer, he decided that the life of a great musician might be even more interesting than that of an artist. So he composed a waltz, which he still possesses. It is written for piano and violin, (because he could not play the piano well enough to play both melody *and* accompaniment) and is described by its composer as *"no masterpiece."*

"My entry into the field of music," he writes, "was as casual as it was belated. The summer before my senior year at New York University I had amused myself by picking out a few tunes on the piano. When the time came for putting together the annual Senior Show, it was discovered that the librettist had flunked out of college and the scheduled composer had embarked on a concert career as a singer (this was Reinald Werrenrath, later a famous baritone). Another classmate (William LeBaron, now a successful motion picture producer) offered to write the book, and I, to my own intense surprise, volunteered to compose the score. I was slightly handicapped, I must confess, by the fact that my only method of writing music down was to play it on the piano and then copy the notes that my fingers indicated.

"The presence in the audience of a large delegation of friends and relatives of the cast probably had something to do with the success of our little opus. We went on to write three more for N.Y.U. The great Victor Herbert saw the second one, sent for me between the acts, and told me that I had talent. 'But,' he said, 'you know nothing of musical theory, do you?' I admitted that I did not. 'You must study,' he continued. 'Otherwise you will never get beyond this point.'

"That was enough for me. Obtaining a small subsidy from a reluctant father, I went to work with Oscar Coon, a retired bandsman and a superb musician. Time was short. Somehow I managed to get through Richter's *Harmony* and Jadassohn's *Canon and Fugue* in three months. Aside from ten months' piano lessons, at the age of ten, that was the extent of my formal musical training. Otherwise I am self-taught."

Deems Taylor

Charles Dillingham bought the fourth of Taylor's musical comedies, *The Echo* (libretto by Wm. LeBaron) and produced it on Broadway. But it lasted only ten weeks in New York, and then, as he says, "died on the road." No one would even look at his next attempt. His musical career showed signs of ending as abruptly as it had begun. Then he read in the *Musical Courier* about a prize that was being offered by the National Federation of Music Clubs for the best symphony or symphonic poem by an American composer.

"If I can't get anywhere in musical comedy," he thought to himself, "I'll go highbrow."

He had never before tried to write serious music. But he now sat down and composed a symphonic poem for orchestra called *The Siren Song*—submitted it, and to his amazement won the prize.

It was *The Siren Song* that started Deems Taylor as a serious composer. He points out that as submitted, it was so crudely orchestrated that parts of it were unplayable. So the judges gave it a *second* prize, and awarded no first. This was in 1913. In 1924 he rescored it and heard it played by the New York Philharmonic Orchestra. Taylor was at that time music critic of the *New York World,* and undertook to review the piece, pointing out that since the human body is said to renew itself every seven years, something composed eleven years before was obviously the work of a complete stranger. He found that apart from certain crudities, *The Siren Song* showed promise, and that he hoped to hear many other works by the same composer.

The year 1914 saw his first published work, a song called *Witch Woman*, published by Oliver Ditson Company. This was followed by two choral works: *The Chambered Nautilus,* for mixed chorus and orchestra, and *The Highwayman,* for women's chorus.

"In that year," he says, concerning this last, "Reinald Werrenrath was to be soloist at the annual MacDowell Festival in Peterboro, New Hampshire. One day in May he called me on the telephone. 'I've just come back from Peterborough,' he said, 'where we've been making up the program of the festival. I have promised the committee a brand-new cantata for women's chorus, baritone solo, and orchestra. For Heaven's sake, write it!' After wasting a few days hunting for a suitable text I finally chose the Alfred Noyes poem. After much blood, sweat and tears I finally managed to write the piece, orchestrate it, have the choral and orchestral parts copied, and ship the whole thing to Peterboro just in time for the rehearsals. It had its first performance on August 19th, 1914. It has had the luck to survive. In its thirty-seventh year, it is still performed."

On leaving college, Deems Taylor first went into editorial work. He was for a year on the staff of the *Nelson Encyclopedia,* then of the *Encyclopaedia Britannica.* From 1912-16 he was assistant editor of the *Western Electric News,* and following that became Sunday Editor of the *New York Herald Tribune.* He also served as war correspondent for this paper from 1916-17. Taylor was later editor of *Musical America* for two years, and he has been music critic of the *New York World,* the *New York American,* and *McCall's Magazine.*

His experience as war correspondent was largely responsible for what became his most famous work. On his return to America from Europe he had planned to compose a suite of *War Sketches* for orchestra; but when he started to write, he says, something entirely different came out. He found that he had not had time to digest his experiences sufficiently to be able to interpret them in music. He was still too close to the grim realities of war to write about them. Recalling Wordsworth's saying: "Art is emotion remembered in tranquility," he found his mind reverting to an earlier enthusiasm.

Since childhood he had been a devoted fan of Lewis Carroll's *Alice.* He never tired of rereading her *Adventures in Wonderland* and *Through the Looking Glass* (that strange land where everything is in reverse). Carroll's whimsical humor—part philosophy, part pure fantasy—appealed strongly to those same qualities in Taylor's own temperament. Now, instead of writing the proposed war sketches, he composed a suite which for the past quarter of a century has been a delight to symphonic audiences both here and abroad. It was named after Lewis Carroll's *Through the Looking Glass.*

Beginning with a lyrical *Dedication* to the "Child of the pure, unclouded brow, and dreaming eyes of wonder!" the first movement of this suite continues with *The Garden of Live Flowers.* Next comes *The Jabberwocky,* a clever burlesque describing the "brillig and burbling" of Carroll's nonsense verses. There are solo parts for clarinet and bassoon, and the movement ends with the "snickersnack" of the "vorpal blade" depicted by zylophone glissandos.

Taylor originally began the suite with what is now the third movement: *Looking Glass Insects.* This has themes describing the "Bread-

Deems Taylor

and-Butter-fly," the "Rocking-horse-fly, the Snap-dragon-fly," and the "Bee-elephant." *The Looking Glass's* last movement tells the adventures of *The White Knight,* that "toy Don Quixote, mild, chivalrous, ridiculous, and rather touching," who falls off his horse forwards whenever it stops, and backwards whenever it starts up again.

Of this work Lawrence Gilman wrote:

> He (Taylor) is wit enough to know that the peculiar distinction of Carroll's delicious masterpiece is the mood of half tender, half mocking detachment in which it is conceived; and he preserves this balance in his music with extraordinary skill and felicity. He neither burlesques nor sentimentalizes his subject. He touches it affectionately, even caressingly, as in the *Dedication;* but in his eye is a twinkle that is imperfectly suppressed.

Through the Looking Glass was written first for strings, wind and piano, and had its initial performance in 1919 by the New York Chamber Music Society. Shortly after, Taylor elaborated it into a score for full orchestra, and it made an immediate hit. Audiences always delight in music that has a humorous turn. Strauss's *Till Eulenspiegel* and *Don Quixote,* John Alden Carpenter's *Adventures in a Perambulator* and *Krazy Kat,* and Deems Taylor's *Through the Looking Glass* are perennial favorites.

During all these years Taylor had been busy with many other things besides writing music. In 1921 he was appointed music critic of the *New York World.* The ensuing four years found him not only writing music criticism but composing music for the theater. Beginning with the Theatre Guild's original production of Molnar's *Liliom,* he wrote incidental music for eight plays. These comprised *The Adding Machine* and *Rita Coventry* (1922); *Will Shakespeare* and *Humoresque* (1923); and, in 1924, *The Puppet Man.* The ballet music from his 1924 score for *Casanova* and the pantomime *A Kiss in Xanadu* have been published and are still widely performed. Another work written in that busy year of 1924 was the complete musical score for the silent picture *Janice Meredith.*

In 1925 Taylor had the unusual experience of being given three commissions in a single year. One came from Paul Whiteman, who was planning a concert tour with his band (including a trip to England

and Germany) and wanted something different from the usual jazz routine. The result was a suite called *Circus Day*, depicting a series of scenes dear to the heart of every youngster—young or old: *Street Parade, The Big Top, Bareback Riders, The Lion Cage, Tight-Rope Walker, Jugglers*, and *Clowns*. The original orchestration, made for the Whiteman ensemble, was by Ferde Grofé. In 1934 Taylor revised the piece and scored it for symphony orchestra.

Another commission came from Walter Damrosch and the New York Symphony Orchestra. For this Taylor wrote a symphonic poem *Jurgen*, based on James Branch Cabell's famous novel. The third commission, that year of 1925, was from the Metropolitan Opera Company.

One day, early that year, Edward Ziegler, then assistant general manager of the Metropolitan, invited Taylor to lunch with him. For years, he told him, they had been trying vainly to produce a successful American opera. "Now we have decided," said Ziegler, "that our best chance is to offer a commission to somebody who has had experience in the theater. Whom do you suggest that we commission?"

"Don't be silly," Taylor replied. "Why not commission me?"

"That's exactly what we planned to do. I'm glad you agree."

Ever since his college days, Taylor had been devoted to the stage, and his work in the field of incidental music had given him practical theatrical experience. When he set about fulfilling the Metropolitan's commission, he resolved to find a libretto that would be not only poetic, but "good theater." The ideal person to write such a libretto, he decided, would be Edna St. Vincent Millay—provided she would consent.

She did consent, and Taylor forthwith resigned from his *New York World* post in order to give all his time to the scheduled opera. The two spent many weeks, toying with the idea of a setting of *Snow White and the Seven Dwarfs*. Eventually Miss Millay abandoned the notion, choosing instead a story from the Anglo-Saxon chronicle which she called *The King's Henchman*. Their collaboration was an unusual one. Miss Millay's health was poor that year, so she stayed on her farm in upper New York State, mailing the libretto in installments. As soon as one arrived, Taylor would set it to music and wait for the next. "It was not too easy," he remarks, "to work on the first act without knowing what the second act would be." The opera was

Deems Taylor

completed in a little over eight months. Taylor finished the orchestration in Paris, in September 1926, and rehearsals began in October. The first performance, before a house that had been sold out weeks in advance, was February 17, 1927.

The King's Henchman was an immediate success with both the critics and the public. Lawrence Gilman pronounced it:

The best American opera we have ever heard. . . .Mr. Taylor has woven a deft and often lovely sounding score about a superb poetic text. . . .The music, as music, "sounds"; it fills the ear, is richly textured, mellifluous, has grace and movement and flexibility. It is the writing of an expert craftsman, an artist of sensibility and responsiveness.

William J. Henderson of *The Sun* wrote:

This is true opera music, dignified in melodic idiom, suited to the action and the word and throbbing with genuine emotion. There is absolute nobility in the reproach of the King, and the departure of the bearers with the body of Aethelwold is something almost elemental.

The Metropolitan promptly commissioned Taylor to write another opera. Once more came the search for an effective libretto, a search that lasted nearly three years. He finally found what he wanted in Du Maurier's novel *Peter Ibbetson*, the story of two lovers kept apart in the waking world, who meet in their dreams. From this book he fashioned his libretto.

Ibbetson made its bow before the public on February 7, 1931. This time the chorus of critical acclaim was far from unanimous. One critic announced that "a drama of exceptional sentimental appeal carried his music much farther than it would have gone of its own allure"—which is possibly why the composer chose that drama. Another was "frankly disappointed," and still another remarked, scornfully, that the music kept out of the way of the words. However, Pitts Sanborn headlined his critique:

DEEMS TAYLOR IS HAILED AS THE FIRST
AMERICAN WITH 2 OPERA SUCCESSES

Reception of *Peter Ibbetson* Indicates Great Popularity—Seen as Improvement Over His *King's Henchmen*

Modern Music-Makers

As a popular success *Peter Ibbetson* outstripped Taylor's first opera. It had eleven performances in its first season at the Metropolitan, and during the summer of 1931 there were eight performances at Ravinia Park, near Chicago. At that time Ashton Stevens wrote:

Peter Ibbetson is the most glamorous and romantic show in North America. And whatever the appraisal of the music critics, it is, I think, the most civilized thing that has happened in the American theatre since *Strange Interlude* and *Hotel Universe*. At least one million natives are standing in line. . . .waiting to hear this opera that is their very own.

The opera ran for four seasons at the Metropolitan, and there is talk of a possible revival for the season of 1951-52.

One charge hurled at *Peter Ibbetson* was that its music was "old-fashioned." The general trend in the 1930's was towards experiment and so-called ultra-modernism. Anyone who failed to follow this current style in composing was considered a reactionary. Taylor himself writes:

I sometimes wonder whether the appalling speed with which our mechanical civilization has advanced during the past thirty years hasn't lured a whole generation of composers into trying to keep up with it. . . . I sense, among a vast number and variety of composers, an uneasy impulse to keep abreast of their times, a dread of being thought old-fashioned. They must, they will tell you, reflect in their art the increased complexity and speed with which we live today; and in their effort to do so they become self-conscious and experimental. They want very much to say something, but instead of looking within themselves for their particular message, they try to translate the material world around them into terms of music. In the effort to keep up to the musical minute, they change their own style of writing from day to day. As if a man could deliberately change his style—if he has one—any more than he can change the color of his eyes. . . .

No real artist *deliberately* goes about expressing his time. In the last analysis he looks within himself for the picture he paints or the book that he writes, or the symphony that he composes. And since that self is a product of his times, it is, of course, an expression of his times, an expression over which he has no more control, and of which he is no more conscious, than your hand mirror is conscious of reflecting your face. And if the artist is a reflection of the noblest and best of his times, then his work

Deems Taylor

will be the same; and it will be understood, and loved, long after its creator is dead.[1]

Deems Taylor's radio career goes back to the fall of 1927, when he was narrator for a one-hour broadcast of *The King's Henchman* that inaugurated the opening of the Columbia Broadcasting System. In 1931, following the success of *Peter Ibbetson,* he was invited to broadcast a series of talks on the history of opera over the N.B.C. network. These led to his being appointed narrator for the first Metropolitan Opera broadcasts, during the season of 1931-32. From then on he was in fairly constant demand, with the result that except for the incidental music for Katharine Cornell's production of *Lucrece* and various choral arrangements[2], he did little composing until 1937, when he turned once more to opera and wrote *Ramuntcho,* based on the novel by Pierre Loti. It was produced by the Philadelphia Opera Company in 1942.

In 1936 Taylor became intermission commentator for the New York Philharmonic Sunday afternoon broadcasts. In these, which continued until 1943, he became widely known to radio audiences all over the United States and Canada. His well chosen talks on a variety of subjects related to music, and his happy faculty of speaking as if he were addressing each member of his vast audience personally, made him one of radio's most popular commentators.

These talks he later revised and expanded into three books: *Of Men and Music, The Well-Tempered Listener,* and *Music to my Ears,* as entertaining to read as the talks were to hear. (He has also published *A Treasury of Gilbert and Sullivan,* and *A Pictorial History of the Movies).*

In 1941 Taylor added motion pictures to his list of achievements. Walt Disney had heard him over the radio, and liked his informal approach to music. When he and Leopold Stokowski conceived the

[1] *The Well-Tempered Listener,* by Deems Taylor, Simon & Schuster, 1940.

[2] All told Taylor has produced upwards of 100 choral arrangements, some of his own composing and some of folk songs, together with an equal number of song translations from the French, Italian, German, and (with Kurt Schindler) Russian.

idea of producing an "animated" concert—Stokowski to conduct the music and Disney to interpret it in pictures—they chose Taylor to help make up the program and appear on the screen as commentator. *Fantasia* made musical history—at least it stirred up a controversy! The conservatives were horrified at the sight of Micky Mouse interpreting Dukas' classic *Apprenti Sorcier*, and were affronted by Disney's slapstick treatment of Beethoven's sacred *Pastorale* symphony. As usual, however, the general public had the last word. *Fantasia* served to make the man in the street realize that serious music was not as difficult to listen to as he might have supposed. Deems Taylor's clear and entertaining introductions added considerably to the interest of the film and made him still more popular with the public. In *Fantasia* he could be seen as well as heard by his radio audience. The picture has been revived many times, and has been seen in England and France.

Since then Taylor has appeared in two other pictures; as commentator in a film version of *The Barber of Seville*, and in *Of Men and Music*, a film featuring Arthur Rubinstein and Jascha Heifetz which opened in New York early in 1951.

Radio and pictures might well have sidetracked a lesser man from music writing. But Deems Taylor possesses the drive and determination to make a success of whatever he undertakes, and the talent for doing many things well. John Tasker Howard says that he is "so inordinately skillful that his career is a complete denial of the theory that a man may be jack of all trades and master of none."

In 1941, the year of *Fantasia*, Taylor composed a *Processional* for the annual ceremonial of the National Institute of Arts and Letters. In 1943 came *Marco Takes a Walk*. During the youngster's walk he sees a horse and a wagon; through his over-lively imagination these are successively transformed into a zebra, a reindeer, a rajah and his elephant, and a big brass band. Both the subject and his treatment of this work are typical of Taylor's love of humor and fantasy.

In that same year of 1943 he revised his *Jurgen* extensively and released it as a *Fantasy on Two Themes*. In that form it was first performed by the N.B.C. Orchestra under Frank Black, and has since been heard in Belgium and Holland. In 1944 came an *Elegy for Orchestra*, written for the Indianapolis Orchestra and Fabien Sevitzky. Also that year and again the following, Taylor invaded still another

DEEMS TAYLOR

Deems Taylor

field of music, composing the music for "Spec"—the grand parade that is a feature of the Ringling Circus performance.

An operetta based on Defoe's *Moll Flanders* occupied his spare time in 1947 and 1948, but was left unfinished. From it, in 1950, he drew a *Restoration Suite*, a series of dances evocative of the period of Charles II.

In 1947 the Schubert brothers acquired the operetta rights to the Puccini operas, and at their request Taylor made a score consisting entirely of Puccini's music. The work was completed in 1950, and was scheduled for production in the early fall of 1951.

It would be difficult to list all of the honors, prizes, and degrees that have been showered on Deems Taylor. He has been awarded a Doctor of Letters degree from Juniata College, and Doctor of Music degrees from New York University, Dartmouth, University of Rochester, Cincinnati Conservatory of Music, and Syracuse University. He is an honorary member of Phi Beta Kappa, Delta Omicron, National Federation of Music Clubs, and the Architectural League of New York. From 1942-47 Taylor was President of A.S.C.A.P. (American Society of Authors, Composers, and Publishers); he is at present Treasurer of the American Academy of Arts and Letters, as well as a member of the National Institute of Arts and Letters and of the American Philosophical Society.

In his personality and in his music Deems Taylor is distinguished for his imagination and his humor—qualities which have endeared him to all. Howard calls him "a man of unfailing good humor, a philosopher who delights in the whimsicalities of life and knows both how to fashion and enjoy a joke. . . . Through his own personal success he has both proved and disproved certain definite impressions which have clung traditionally to the composers' craft, thereby clearing a path that will make it far easier for others to proceed to worth-while achievement."[3]

[3] *Studies of Contemporary Composers* (Monograph), by John Tasker Howard, J. Fischer & Bro., New York, 1927.

Deems Taylor

The Music of Deems Taylor

[1] J. Fischer Bro.
[2] Oliver Ditson Co.

WALLINGFORD RIEGGER

WALLINGFORD RIEGGER

WALLINGFORD RIEGGER was one of the first champions of the new music in this country. Yet he did not begin to write in the modern idiom until he was past forty. Educated in a strictly conventional school, both here and abroad, he found as the years went by that the old forms could no longer satisfy him; so he broke away from that early influence and allied himself with the new movement. In his younger days, however—as a student in Berlin—Riegger disapproved heartily of modern music.

Nikisch was his idol in those days. Whenever the latter conducted at the Berlin Philharmonic young Riegger was sure to be there, sitting high in the balcony with a pocket-score in his hand so he could follow the music and study the technique of the famous conductor.

Following Nikisch's first performance of Scriabine's *Poem de l'Extase,* when catcalls and hisses of the conservatives drowned out the applause of the "modernists," Riegger remembers (to his present-day shame) that he joined vigorously with the former. He then little suspected that twenty years later his own works would be labeled "ultra"-modern, and would likewise be hissed on more than one occasion.   .

In those early days it never occurred to him that he might one day be a composer. He wrote a few pieces while he was in Berlin—one of them, an *Elegie* for cello and piano, was played by Anton Hekking—but he composed only as a pastime. His original purpose in going to Germany was to train himself as a cellist. He studied first with Robert Hausman, then with Anton Hekking; but after three years of strenuous practising he despaired of attaining an impeccable technique and decided, like a number of our most distinguished orchestra leaders who also started out as violoncellists (among them Toscanini, the late Hans Kindler, and Alfred Wallenstein) to become a conductor instead.

Wallingford Riegger was born April 29, 1885, in Albany, Georgia. His father owned and operated a lumber mill there; the mill burned down when Wallingford was three years old, and the family then moved to Indianapolis. His mother (of English, Scottish and Irish descent) was a fine pianist. She discovered, while her son was still very young, that he had unusual talent for music, and that he possessed what is known as "absolute pitch."

To amuse friends and callers she would have him demonstrate:

"Stand over there by the window with your back to the piano," she would say. And then, striking a key, "What is this note? That's right! And this? . . ." He never missed.

At an early age he picked out scales and chords on the piano and experimented with strange harmonies. "Stop that dreadful noise!" his father would exclaim, little realizing that this inventive spirit was later to lead him into a whole new world of tonality.

Wallingford and his brother both had lessons on the violin, but like average youngsters they hated to practise. When their mother went marketing and they were supposed to be practising, they would take turns standing by the window to watch for her return. When she came in she invariably found them hard at work.

Although young Wallingford didn't want to practise, he liked music, and would play passages from Beethoven's sonatas, picking them out on the piano by ear. He still remembers the first orchestral concert that he and his brother attended. "Early in the course of it there was a tremendous fortissimo, in which the kettledrums were conspicuous," he relates. "Throughout the remainder of the evening we awaited the recurrence of such an outburst, and as it did not come, went away with a decided feeling of frustration."

Another musical event that made a profound impression on him was a concert at Carnegie Hall, during his high school days, when for the first time he heard Tchaikowsky's *Symphonie Pathétique*.

Wallingford's father was an enthusiastic amateur musician. At fourteen he had been concertmaster of an orchestra in Indianapolis; he conducted a choir, sang in an oratorio society, and was an ardent chamber-music player. The Riegger family's favorite recreation was chamber music. They all took part in it: his mother at the piano, his father playing first violin, his brother second and his uncle the viola. Wallingford was elected to be cellist so he could complete the group. Those chamber-music sessions, he says, are among the pleasantest memories of his early days.

118

Wallingford Riegger

When he was fourteen the family moved to New York. After he graduated from high school his father felt that it was time for him to start earning his own living. Wallingford, however, wanted to go to college, and managed to win a scholarship to Cornell University. After finishing there he persuaded the family to let him go to the Institute of Musical Art in New York City (now the Juilliard School of Music) which Frank Damrosch then directed. The Kneisel Quartet taught there, and Wallingford studied with the cellist of the group, Alwin Schroeder. Percy Goetschius was his teacher in harmony and composition.

Except in cello and theoretical subjects, young Riegger was not by any means a star pupil at the institute. His reports stated "Attendance irregular." "I cut classes right and left," he confesses. The ear-training class frankly bored him. "I can't sing," he insisted. "May I whistle?" When it was discovered that he had absolute pitch, he was excused from the class.

About that time a fellow-whistler (he and Wallingford used to amuse themselves by whistling *Merrily We Roll Along* in parallel fifths) went abroad to attend the *Hochschule* in Berlin. This friend wrote back glowing accounts of life in the German capital, and urged Wallingford to join him there. The elder Riegger, whose own father had come from Germany, realized that such an experience would give his son many advantages: the broadening influence of a foreign environment, new languages, and the best in musical training. So he finally agreed to let him go to Berlin.

When young Riegger first went to Germany he was inclined, he says, to bore everyone at the *pension* where he stayed with eulogies of America and the American way of life. Gradually, however, he came to realize that the United States was not the only country in the world. "I got rid of a lot of nationalism," he admits. He read Goethe and the German philosophers, " 'did' the art galleries, museums and cathedrals with a vengeance, and got sidetracked on French poetry." He set himself a rigorous schedule: five hours of cello practice, two of piano, an hour or more of counterpoint, and usually each evening a concert.

"My three years' stay in Berlin was a period of intensive, extensive (and *expensive*) acquiring. I played cello in one orchestra, viola in another, belonged to smaller ensemble groups and attended one hundred and fifty orchestral concerts the first season alone, usually with small scores in my pocket which I would read on the subway."[1]

Riegger's father was not enthusiastic about the idea of music as a profession for his son, but when Wallingford decided to switch from cellist to conductor, he finally agreed, and made it possible for him to have an impressive debut. One of the best orchestras in Berlin, the Blüthner, was hired for the occasion. The young conductor rehearsed the group carefully, memorized the scores of the music he was to play, and conducted without his notes—which at that time was considered quite a feat. His concert received excellent notices.

On returning from Germany Riegger was engaged as cellist by the St. Paul Symphony Orchestra. Soon after—in 1911—he married Rose Schramm—a former high school companion. She agreed that he should become a conductor rather than a cellist, and since there were not many opportunities in his own country for an American-born orchestra leader unless he had a background of European successes, they decided to try their luck in Germany. In April, 1914, with no premonition of the war so soon to come, Riegger and his family sailed for Europe. Through a Berlin manager he obtained a position as fourth assistant conductor at the *Stadttheater* in Würzburg.

When the storm broke, the Rieggers stayed on, for at the beginning of the war it appeared unlikely that the United States would become involved. Although life in a war-engaged country was not easy, the Germans, he says, remained friendly and helped him to get food for his wife and three small daughters. They stayed in Würzburg until March, 1917, leaving just before diplomatic relations with the United States were broken off.

After Wallingford Riegger got back to his own country he went to one of the best-known concert managers and said he would like to find a position as orchestra conductor. "I have had considerable experience, and good notices," he said, handing the man a sheaf of criticisms. "And I know thirty symphonies and most of the orchestral repertoire by heart."

The concert managers, however, would do nothing for him. They insisted that foreign-born conductors with big names alone were

---

[1] The passages quoted are from Riegger's article "To the New from the Old" in the *Magazine of Art*.

Wallingford Riegger

capable of attracting audiences. Riegger finally had to fall back on his cello again. He wound up as head of the cello and music-theory department at Drake University. After remaining there four years, he moved on to the Ithaca Conservatory and later taught at the Institute of Musical Art. In 1929 the family settled permanently in New York City. Since then he has held various teaching positions there.

During his earlier years in Germany and St. Paul, Wallingford Riegger attempted little or no composing. "Of course," he says, "I realize it now—what I was doing all along was basically an act of evasion. To compose, to create, required a degree of integration which I did not then possess. A passion for perfection made me ultra-critical of every note, besides which I had not resolved the conflict between the old and the new. . . . I blushingly admit to having upheld at that time good old academic tradition."

Riegger was thirty-five when he wrote his first important composition. "After many doubts, trials and heartaches (also headaches), after rewriting whole movements and wondering why I should wish on myself the most difficult task in the world, I finally succeeded in completing a trio for piano, violin and cello."

This initial composition won for him the Paderewski prize. A later work, for four solo voices and eight instruments: *La Belle Dame Sans Merci*, was chosen from over a hundred compositions submitted for the 1924 Elizabeth Coolidge prize, and played that year at the Coolidge Chamber Music Festival in Pittsfield. Later it was performed in Paris. Riegger next tried an orchestral work. A poem by Edna St. Vincent Millay had particularly impressed him by its emotional mood of rebellion. It seemed to express something of his own feelings. For he found himself at that time, in growing conflict with the old forms of music; he wanted to develop new and freer means for interpreting his creative ideas. Now, trying to put into music what Miss Millay had said in words, he wrote an orchestral work first called by the poem's title—*Second April*—later renamed *Rhapsody for Orchestra*.

It was not, however, until *Study in Sonority*—originally named *Caprice for Ten Violins,* (written for ten violins "or any multiple thereof"—each playing a separate part) that Riegger broke entirely with the past, and "abandoned tonality."

"At Ithaca I first found myself, musically speaking—that is, when I first had the courage to break through the inhibitions of my early sur-

Modern Music-Makers

roundings and training. . . ." Speaking of atonality he goes on to say: "The abandonment of keys does not necessarily mean the complete negation of 'music,' as some excellent but conservative musicians seem to think, but rather its potential enrichment in the discovery of new tonalities, with new possibilities of texture, both harmonic and polyphonic, of melody (albeit in a new guise) and of form--all of which I felt to be not only in the line of historical development, but above all truly expressive of the age in which we live, while losing nothing of the universally human."

Riegger is a staunch champion of freedom. He once wrote in the *Magazine of Art*:

Increasingly artists in all fields are feeling the need of building a defense against those forces basically opposed to all cultural expression. . . . Little as we enjoy the prospect, it will be only at the price of continual struggle that we shall preserve those privileges which we still enjoy. As an artist, I feel impelled to continue my creative work, but I also feel, as an artist, that I must help oppose those forces which would deny humanity its heritage of culture and freedom.

In New York Wallingford Riegger met a small group of composers who had the same ideas about modern music as himself. They were explorers together in a new field. Charles Ives, although then practically unknown to the general public, had already made interesting experiments; so had Carl Ruggles, Edgar Varese and Henry Cowell. These disciples of the new music, with Riegger as one of them, formed a Pan-American Association of composers, and under its auspices gave numerous concerts both here and abroad. In their own country they met with little success; strangely enough Europe, with its long legacy of tradition and conservatism, was more open to the modern movement than we in America who have always prided ourselves on being up-to-date.

Study in Sonority was received by the apostles of the new music with enthusiasm (Henry Cowell called it "the choiring of angels"), but the general public, less accustomed to the new idiom, was outraged by its daring tone-progressions. *Dichotomy*, written three years later and one of Riegger's best-known works, fared even worse.

The name of this piece, he says, is taken from a philosophical term

Wallingford Riegger

meaning a cleavage into opposing elements, such as white and black, good and evil. As applied to music this might refer to fast and slow, loud and soft, high and low, etc. In Riegger's interpretation *Dichotomy* also refers to the ego and the non-ego, and the conflict arising from the impinging of the one upon the other.

It took some years before the critics were able to appreciate *Dichotomy*. The work was hissed on more than one occasion, but today *Dichotomy* ranks high. Following a performance of it at Yaddo, in 1946, Noel Strauss wrote:

Mr. Riegger's atonal *Dichotomy* is. . . .built up of transformation of a Schoenbergian "tone row" but without slavishly using the "twelve-tone technique" it is primarily concerned with color, being particularly remarkable for inventiveness in rich combinations of sound, intense in themselves and lent extra intensity by novel use of dissonance. Many unusual devices, some of them the composer's own, include "chord block" formations, which add to the colorfulness of the second section of the work, a fugato replete with fascinating effects. Rhythm for its own sake plays a lesser role than ordinarily in the composer's works but predominates in the closing pages, which bring the powerful and masterly opus to a brilliant termination.

Riegger has written a good deal of music for the dance—for modern ballet that is, rather than for the old-school traditional type. This latter, he explains, starts with a ready-made composition and creates a dance to interpret it. But in the modern dance, choreography comes first, and the composer must then write music to fit its rhythm, tempo and mood. Riegger found that composing music for this purpose was "a challenge to ingenuity and inventiveness." He has written scores for many of the best-known dance groups in this country, such as those of Martha Graham, Doris Humphrey, Charles Weidman, Helen Tamaris, Hanya Holm, and Anna Sokoloff. Only a few fragments of these dance scores appear on his list of serious compositions. Notably *New Dance,* arranged in seven different settings (including orchestra, two pianos, and violin and orchestra). In addition to his many dance scores, Riegger has made close to six hundred arrangements for chorus..

Wallingford Riegger's works have accumulated slowly, "interspersed with periods of unproductiveness, due partly to my own maladjustment and partly to the need of earning a livelihood. To turn an honest penny I made several hundred choral arrangements for publishers, wrote a couple of violin methods, and did editing, proof-reading and even copying. When I undertook to create, it was in spite of my environment, which I felt did not need new works so much as conditions which would enable more people to enjoy the masterpieces already created."

During the last few years Riegger has spent his life mainly on symphonic and chamber music. He composed his *First Symphony* in 1944, the *Second* a year later (written especially for school orchestras and in a comparatively simple style), and a *Third* in 1947—commissioned by Columbia University and winner of the New York Music Critics Circle Award. *A Funeral March for Band* (also arranged for orchestra) appeared in 1945, and in 1949 *Music for Brass Choir.* To his choral works he added, in 1950, a cantata for *Chorus and Orchestra.*

An interesting composition for the piano is a suite of twelve pieces titled *New and Old.* Each of the pieces demonstrates some aspect of modern music forms, such as tone-clusters, polytonality, dissonance, counterpoint, etc.

The *First String Quartet* is one of Riegger's best-known chamber music works. It has had frequent performances and has received special commendation—particularly at a concert given at the 1946 Yaddo Fall Music Festival. Since then he has written a *Second String Quartet* (1948) and a *Piano Quintet,* the latter commissioned by the University of Michigan and completed in 1950.

Few composers have had the courage to change their style of writing so completely as has Wallingford Riegger. Brought up in the classics, belonging through training and tradition to the conventional school, he found in the modern idiom his real medium of expression—and was willing to admit it. Like his comrades, Ives, Ruggles and Varese, Riegger is coming more and more to the front in the American music of today.

WALLINGFORD RIEGGER

Wallingford Riegger

Born April 29, Albany, Georgia	1885
Attends Cornell University	1904-5
Graduates from Institute of Musical Art	1907
Continues studies at *Hochschule* in Berlin	1907-9
Debut as conductor, Blüthner Orchestra, Berlin	1910
Returns to U.S., cellist with St. Paul Symph. Orch.	
Marries Rose Schramm	1911
Assistant Conductor at Stadttheater, Wurzburg	1914
Returns permanently to U.S. Heads Cello and Theory Department	
at Drake University	1917
Trio for Piano, Violin and Cello	1920
Paderewski Prize	
La Belle Dame Sans Merci	1924
Elizabeth Coolidge Prize	
Teaches at Institute of Musical Art	1925-6
Rhapsody for Orchestra (Second April)	1926
Teaches at Ithaca Conservatory of Music	1926-8
Study in Sonority	1927
Dichotomy	1931
Suite for Two Pianos	1935
First String Quartet	1938
Canon and Fugue for Strings	1941
First Symphony	1944
Second Symphony	1945
Third Symphony	1947
Second String Quartet	1948
Music for Brass Choir	1948-9
Piano Quintet	1950

The Music of Wallingford Riegger

Wallingford Riegger

Sonatina for Violin and Piano [7]	1947
Second String Quartet [10]	1948
Piano Quintet [11]	1950

PIANO WORKS

Blue Voyage [9]	1927
Four Tone Pictures [10]	1935
Evocation (Piano, four hands)	1937
New Dance (In seven different settings. Piano two hands, four hands, two pianos, orchestra, band, piano and orchestra, violin and piano)	1936
New and Old (twelve pieces for piano) [11]	1944
Piano Quintet	1950

[1] New Music.
[2] Southern.
[3] Mercury.
[4] Leeds.
[5] Associated.
[6] H. Flammer.
[7] E. B. Marks.
[8] Society for the Publication of American Music.
[9] G. Schirmer.
[10] Arrow Music Press.
[11] Boosey & Hawkes.
[12] Boletin (Bomart).

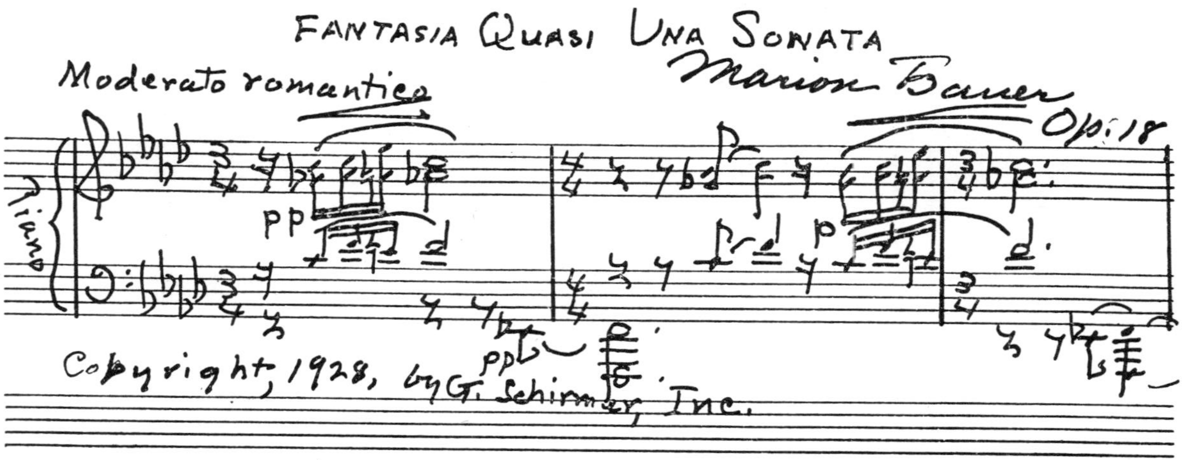

FANTASIA QUASI UNA SONATA
Marion Bauer
Op. 18
Moderato romantico
Piano
pp
p
pp
Copyright, 1928, by G. Schirmer, Inc.

MARION BAUER

PHOTOGRAPH BY BLACKSTONE STUDIO, NEW YORK

MARION BAUER

MARION BAUER

MARION BAUER'S career refutes the theory that in order to accomplish important things in life it is necessary to aim at a high goal and then labor unceasingly to reach it. She simply went along, "doing the work that was there to do," and not worrying about results. She had, as she says, "much aspiration, but few ambitions." She has always been a tireless and determined worker—but without the strain and struggle usually associated with outstanding achievement.

A young woman who was gathering material for a thesis on sociology came to interview her one day.

"Did you have a hard time convincing your parents that you wanted to be a musician?" she began.

Miss Bauer smiled. "No indeed. From the very beginning my family did everything they could to further my career."

The young woman consulted her list of questions. "Did you find it very difficult to get started? And did you have a struggle to make your way in your profession?"

"No—I just worked along naturally, with the help of my older sister—just took things as they came. . . ."

The visitor appeared disconcerted. These answers didn't fit in at all with her ideas about the difficulties of a woman's career. "But haven't you found that you met with a good deal of prejudice because you were a woman?"

"Oh no—" Miss Bauer smiled again "—I've never been disturbed by it."

Nonplussed, the young woman fired her last question. "Have you been able to reach the goal that you set yourself?"

"As a matter of fact I have gone far beyond anything I ever dreamed of," Miss Bauer replied. "I never set myself a specific goal— or definitely planned to do anything of importance."

Music started, for Marion Bauer, quite literally in the cradle. Her older sister, Emilie Frances, put her in a basket on top of the piano while she practised. From babyhood music was Marion's constant companion. Even before she could talk she knew the language of Mozart, Beethoven, and other great masters.

Her father was a natural, though untrained, musician and had a fine tenor voice. He entertained his family with an inexhaustible repertoire of operatic arias, frontier ballads, and French songs. Born in France, he came to the United States as a young man. Partly for the sake of adventure, and partly because he wanted to get out to the fabulous West Coast, he joined the army band and served in the Indian Wars. Eventually, after leaving the service, he landed in Walla Walla, Washington, (then a small frontier town) set up a general store there, and married Julie Heyman, also of French birth. They had seven children—Emilie Frances the eldest and Marion the youngest.

Julie Bauer taught languages at near-by Whitman College (fifty years later this college awarded an honorary degree to her youngest for outstanding work in music). During the absence of her mother from home, Emilie Frances looked after the younger children. She, too, had inherited her father's musical talent, and was an accomplished pianist. As soon as her little sister was old enough to sit at the piano she began teaching her.

After their father's death, the family left Walla Walla and went to live in Portland, Oregon. Emilie Frances then moved to New York, where she became well-known as a music critic. For six years she was critic of the *Evening Mail,* and she was also editor of the *Musical Leader Magazine.* When her talented younger sister finished school in the West, Emilie sent for her to come to New York so she could continue her music studies. Marion's first teacher there was Henry Holden Huss.

In the winter of 1905 the French pianist Raoul Pugno came to the United States for a series of concerts, bringing with him his wife and daughter. They met the Bauer sisters, and as they knew very little English Marion, who could speak French fluently, offered to give them lessons.

When they went back to France Pugno invited Marion to come over and visit them. "I could give her piano lessons and introduce her to the musical world of Paris," he told Emilie Frances.

This was a rare opportunity for an eager, gifted girl. So the following spring Marion went to France and spent the summer at Gargen-

Marion Bauer

ville, near Paris. Pugno was mayor of the village, and all the musicians of the countryside gathered at his home. Two strikingly handsome and talented young girls, named Nadia and Lili Boulanger, frequently joined the group. Both were accomplished musicians; it would be hard to say which was the more brilliant—Lili, then little more than a child, or Nadia, whose knowledge of harmony and counterpoint was extraordinary.

The young American girl liked the two sisters immensely. When Nadia, who wanted to learn English suggested that they exchange lessons—"If you will teach me English I will teach you harmony"—Marion was delighted. She soon had a regular English class at Gargenville, consisting of Renee Pugno, Nadia and Lili Boulanger.

After an inspiring summer Marion Bauer stayed on in Paris for the fall and winter, working harder than she ever had before. Among her teachers there were Campbell-Tipton, an American living in Paris, and Pierre Monteux, who gave her lessons in ensemble work.

On her return to the United States in 1907, Miss Bauer published her first song: *Light*, written to Bourdillon's *The Night Has a Thousand Eyes*. Mme Schumann-Heink introduced this song, and frequently sang it on her programs.

During the next four years in New York, Miss Bauer divided her time between teaching, studying and composing. She worked with Eugene Heffley, and Walter Henry Rothwell—a close personal friend almost a member of the family—gave her "musical problems" to solve and helped her to work them out.

"You have talent," Rothwell told her. "But you lack the necessary foundation. What you need is to get away from all outside distractions and concentrate on building up ground work in counterpoint and composition."

At Rothwell's suggestion, and with the ever-generous help of Emilie Frances (as well as that of other members of her family) Marion Bauer went over to Berlin and studied there with Dr. Paul Ertel. It was a valuable experience for her, though she was disturbed to find in Germany a certain amount of prejudice against American composers in general, and women composers in particular. To the Europeans of 1911, America still seemed a backwoods nation, musically speaking, with little or no individuality in its expression.

Miss Bauer resented this attitude. She knew that in her own

131

country there was a growing reaction against foreign influence, and a reaching out towards an idiom that would be representatively American—not merely a second-rate copy of the European school. Miss Bauer, then in her early twenties, wanted to be a part of the new movement; and she was also determined to prove that her sex could hold its own in music as well as in the other arts.

Before leaving Berlin she gave an informal concert of her songs, and these, like all of her music, were characterized by a breadth and vigor usually thought of as masculine in character. William Henderson, the distinguished music critic, later wrote of one of Marion Bauer's chamber music compositions:

> Those who like to descant upon the differences between the intellect of woman and that of man must have found themselves in difficulties while listening to Miss Bauer's quartet. It is anything but a ladylike composition. This does not mean that it is rude, impolite or vulgar, but merely that it has a masculine stride and the sort of confidence which is associated in one's mind with the adventurous youth in trousers.

(This, it might be added, was written in the days before adventurous youths of both sexes wore trousers . . .)

Miss Bauer's first songs were highly impressionistic in style. In spite of her year of German training, they showed the influence of the French school. This was not surprising, since her heritage was French, and her earliest allegiance had been to France's first "moderns."

In 1912 Marion Bauer came back to the United States—this time, as she thought, permanently. Soon after her return she met Arthur P. Schmidt, the music publisher who during his lifetime did much to encourage American composers. He liked her songs so well that he gave her a seven-year contract, though when he printed her *Three Impressions* (for piano) she "suspected he did it to encourage a young composer in whom he expressed faith, for they were modern and 'different.'"

Arthur P. Schmidt proved one of the most helpful personalities Miss Bauer ever had the good fortune of knowing. Another friend of this period was a gifted composer, the late Charles Griffes. His criticisms of her work and their discussions about contemporary music were invaluable to her.

Marion Bauer

At first she wrote mostly songs, then piano pieces, and after that, chamber music. For her friend Maud Powell, the well-known violinist she composed a tone poem for violin and piano. This was inspired by Miss Powell's description of a trip up the picturesque Ocklawaha River in Florida.

When Arthur Foote, celebrated Boston composer heard *Up the Ocklawaha* he said, "This is the best piece of descriptive music I ever heard!"

In 1921 Marion Bauer became a member of the American Music Guild. This gave her a chance to meet other composers, and to form a standard by which she could measure herself musically. Although she believed she had the necessary talent she was not, at that time, sure enough of her foundation to branch out into the larger forms of composition.

Emilie Frances was very proud of her youngest sister, though she agreed that Marion needed more training. She wanted her to compose in the larger forms: concertos and symphonies—big orchestral works. She felt that if she could only manage to send Marion back to France for a few more years of study, there would be no limit to what her talented sister could accomplish.

For a long time Emilie Frances worked and saved—denying herself in order to help lay aside the necessary money. Always she had been Marion's mainstay and guiding star; but this was to be the last time. Marion went over to Europe, but in 1926 was recalled by Emilie Frances' serious illness. A few weeks later, the beloved elder sister died.

During the last visit abroad, Marion Bauer studied principally with André Gédalge, professor at the Paris Conservatory and former teacher of Ravel, Milhaud and Honegger. In Paris she found Louis Gruenberg, later to become famous for his *Emperor Jones,* and he gave her valuable criticism and encouragement. While in France she wrote a *String Quartet,* and a second sonata for violin and piano which later was published as *Fantasia Quasi una Sonata.*

After Emilie Frances' death, Marion inherited the latter's position as editor and critic of the *Musical Leader.* She had often helped her sister in music criticism and had written some articles for the *Musical Quarterly.* (The first of these was based on an interesting

133

interview with Harold Bauer.) Later she collaborated with Ethel Peyser—author of *How to Enjoy Music*—in a series of six articles for the *Pictorial Review*. In 1925 she suggested to Miss Peyser that they do a book together.

"Some day I would like to write a *History of Music* for young people with you," she said.

"That's a wonderful idea," answered Miss Peyser. "Why some day? Why not right now?"

The book forthwith got under way. Miss Bauer was just then leaving for Paris, but the work continued apace, while the manuscript went back and forth across the Atlantic.

When G. P. Putnam's Sons heard about the book, they immediately offered the co-authors a contract. "I never had any problem about finding publishers after that," Miss Bauer admits. "Putnam's has published all the books I have had time to write."

This is not surprising. Marion Bauer has a special gift for expressing technical subjects in clear, easy to understand language. *How Music Grew* and *Music through the Ages* (both written with Ethel Peyser) are valuable additions to the history of music. They have recently appeared in new and enlarged editions. Since these first two collaborations, Miss Bauer has written two books on her own: *Twentieth Century Music* and *Musical Questions and Quizzes*. She is now working on a book on modern harmony.

Shortly after her last return from France, Marion Bauer was appointed to the staff of New York University. Since 1930 she has been associate professor there, teaching composition and form and analysis, and lecturing on musical aesthetics and history. She teaches at the Juilliard School of Music and at the summer school of Juilliard, and has also taught in the summer-time at Mills College in California, at the Carnegie Institute of Technology in Pittsburgh, and the Cincinnati Conservatory, and she has lectured annually at Chautauqua, New York. Miss Bauer is an active member of the Board of the League of Composers, the American Composers' Alliance, the Society for the Publication of American Music, and a number of others.

How she has been able to write music with so many time-consuming responsibilities, is difficult to understand. But Marion Bauer is not only gifted with the keen intelligence and sensitive awareness

Marion Bauer

necessary for creative work, but she also possesses extraordinary vitality, drive, and executive ability. Each year she manages to add some new work to her long list of compositions.

Roughly her music may be divided into four periods. First the songs; then music for the piano, next chamber music and, of recent years, orchestral works. These last include a *Symphonic Suite* and *A Lament* (both for string orchestra); *Sun Splendor,* a tone poem; *American Youth,* Concerto for Piano and Orchestra; and, in 1950, her *First Symphony.* She has done two works for the stage: incidental music to *Prometheus Bound,* and *Pan and Syrinx,* this last written in 1937 and performed as a choral work by the Worcester Festival Chorus and the Philadelphia Orchestra at the 1945 Worcester Festival.

Among Miss Bauer's choral compositions are a large work for mixed voices with orchestra: *China,* and three recent numbers *At the New Year* (Kenneth Patcher), *Death Spreads his Gentle Wings* (Eunice P. Crain), and *A Foreigner Comes to Earth on Boston Common* (Horace Gregory).

Chamber music has always remained one of her major interests and she has written a large number of compositions in this form. Some of the more recent of these are: *Concertino for Oboe, Clarinet and String Quartet; Pattern and Acquarelle* for double woodwind Ensemble; two *Trios for Flute, Cello, and Piano* (one in 1944 and one in 1951); *Prelude and Fugue for Flute and Strings* (1949); and *Meditation and Toccata for Organ* (1951).

Much of Miss Bauer's creative work has been done during summer months at the MacDowell Colony in Peterborough, New Hampshire. "To Mrs. Edward MacDowell," she once wrote, "I owe a debt of gratitude for having founded a haven where many other composers, writers, and painters have shared with me the extraordinary opportunity and privilege of doing creative work in peaceful, stimulating and beautiful surroundings."

At the Colony Miss Bauer has alternated between composing music and writing about it—finding inspiration for the one from the other. One year "out of sheer joy of being at the colony" she was inspired the moment of her arrival. Not waiting to unpack her trunk, she borrowed music-paper from a fellow-colonist and at once wrote down a *Prelude*—last in her group of *Six Preludes for the Piano.* An-

Modern Music-Makers

other piano suite of three pieces, called *From New Hampshire Woods,* recalls the peaceful surroundings of those quiet summers: *Indian Pipes* ("ghostly . . . mysterious . . . transcendent . . ."); *Pine Trees* ("quiet . . . listening . ."); and *White Birches,* which bears a short descriptive poem by another colonist—William Rose Benét:

> What is the meaning of their secret gleaming
> What language is in their leaves, that glitter and whisper
> Where the ghostly birches glimmer under the moon. . . .

In her early years Marion Bauer was known as one of the "ultra-moderns" among the younger composers. Today her music seems less radical. She has never believed in breaking entirely with tradition.

In May, 1951, the Phi Beta Fraternity of Music (of which Miss Bauer is a national honorary member) sponsored an entire program of her works at Town Hall, New York. This, she admits, was "one of the great events of her professional career." A month later she was awarded an honorary Doctor of Music degree from the New York College of Music. That same season, after twenty-five years of active service, she retired from the faculty of New York University.

Through her teaching and lecturing, as a member of the League of Composers, and as Chairman of the Young Composers' Contest of the National Federation of Music Clubs (1934-1947), Miss Bauer has been in intimate touch with the music of young American composers. She considers this one of the most important phases of her work—her "contribution to the future." And many are the younger music writers who bear witness to the help and inspiration which Marion Bauer has given them.

Marion Bauer

The Music of Marion Bauer

Orchestral Works

Indian Pipes	1927
Sun Splendor (orchestrated 1944)	1934
A Lament—string orchestra	1935
Symphonic Suite—string orchestra	1940
Concerto for piano and orchestra *American Youth* [1]	1943
First Symphony	1947-1950

Choral Works

Fair Daffodils, trio for women's voices [2]	1914
The Lay of the Four Winds, for men's voices [2]	1915
Three Noels [2]	1929
Here at High Morning [3]	1931
The Thinker, for mixed voices [4]	1938
A Garden is a Lovesome Thing [1]	1938
China, for mixed voices, orchestra [5]	1943-1944
At the New Year, for mixed voices (Kenneth Patcher) [6]	1950
Death Spreads his Gentle Wings—for mixed voices a cappella (Eunice P. Crain) [6]	1951
A Foreigner Comes to Earth on Boston Common (Horace Gregory)	1951

Chamber Music

Up the Ocklawaha—violin and piano [2]	1913
Allegretto Giocoso, for eleven instruments	1920
First Violin Sonata	1921
First String Quartet	1925
Fantasia Quasi una Sonata—violin and piano [1]	1928
Duo for Oboe and Clarinet	1932
Sonata for Viola and Piano (also for clarinet and piano) [7]	1935
Five Greek Lyrics for Flute alone	1938
Sonatina for oboe and piano	1939

138

Marion Bauer

Concertino for oboe, clarinet, and string quartet [8]	1940
First Trio Sonata—flute, cello, piano	1944
Pattern, for double woodwind ensemble	1948
Acquarelle, for double woodwind ensemble	
Six Little Fugues (Handel)—transcribed for woodwind quintette [9]	1948
Prelude and Fugue for Flute and Strings	1949
Second Trio Sonata—flute, cello, piano	1951
Meditation and Toccata for organ	1951

STAGE WORKS

Prometheus Bound, incidental music, two pianos and flutes	1930
Pan and Syrinx—choreographic sketch for film, flute, oboe, clarinet, string quartet, piano	1937
Three Moods for Dance	1950

PIANO WORKS

Arabesque [10]	1909
Elegy [10]	1909
In the Country—four little piano pieces [2]	1913
Three Impressions for Piano [2]	1918
Six Preludes [2]	1922
From New Hampshire Woods, three pieces for piano [1]	1923
Three Preludettes [1]	1923
Quietude	1924
Turbulence [11]	1924
A Fancy [12]	1927
Sun Splendor, also two-piano and orchestral arrangement	1929
Four Piano Pieces [8]	1930
Dance Sonata	1935
Six Little Fugues by Handel (arrangement) [12]	1940
Two Easy Pieces	1942
Patterns, five pieces	1946
Four Piano Pieces, Junior grade [13]	1949

Modern Music-Makers

SONGS

Orientale (Sir Edwin Arnold), (orchestral acc. 1934) [2]	1914
Only of Thee and Me (Louis Untermeyer) [2]	1914
The Minstrel of Romance (John S. Reed) [2]	1917
Night in the Woods (Edward Rowland Sill) [1]	1921
Four Poems (John Gould Fletcher) [1]	1924
Faun Song—contralto, orchestra	1934
Four Songs with string quartet accompaniment	1935
The Harp (Edna Castleman Bailey) [9]	1947
Swan [9]	1947

[1] G. Schirmer.
[2] A. P. Schmidt Co.
[3] H. W. Gray Co.
[4] Galaxy Music Corp.
[5] J. Fischer & Bro.
[6] Ass. Mus. Pub.
[7] Society for the Publication of American Music.
[8] Arrow Music Press.
[9] Broadcast Music Inc.
[10] John Church.
[11] E. B. Marks.
[12] Paul Axelrod.
[13] Merrymount Press.

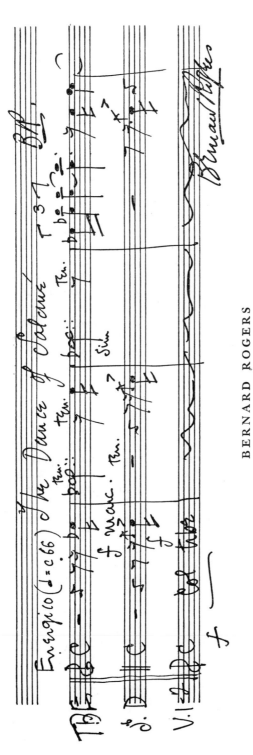

BERNARD ROGERS

BERNARD ROGERS

CREATIVE art, as Bernard Rogers explains, is both an inner and an outer process. A stimulus from without acts as a spring-board, starting the creative flow—which then sinks into the subconscious and later emerges as an individual creation. That which rouses the sleeping idea within the artist may be an object, such as a painting or a poem, or it may be an experience or even another man's work; but it is no more than the trigger that sets off the charge.

Subjects and themes from the *Bible* have often provided Rogers with the necessary stimulus for his music. One of his best-known works is an opera called *The Warrior*, built around the story of Samson and Delilah. In 1946 Columbia, through its Alice M. Ditson Fund, offered a prize for an American opera, at the same time guaranteeing $5,000 for its production. *The Warrior* was chosen, and it was produced at the Metropolitan in January, 1947.

The Warrior was a new departure in opera writing—far removed from the conventional, stock-formula type of earlier days. Its setting was severely simple: instead of elaborate scenery the stage remained bare save for two huge central pillars and a series of stairs leading to different levels. There were no intermissions or curtains during the hour-long drama—only a shifting of colored lights from one part of the stage to another, to indicate change of scenes. The music too was very different from the standard type. There were practically no arias or lyrical melodies; a parlando recitative was maintained throughout, while the orchestra remained subdued and in the background.

The Warrior was originally commissioned by the League of Composers, but when the latter decided to put it on as a radio opera, Rogers withdrew it and submitted it instead for the Diston Competition. Norman Corwin furnished the libretto. In the course of his radio career Corwin had done a good deal of experimenting with new and unusual sound effects, such as those produced by special amplifiers and echo chambers, by slowing down the frequency of recordings, or by mixing together different types of sounds. Not exactly music, but on the borderland, and with enormous possibilities for creating

142

Bernard Rogers

dramatic atmosphere through psychological suggestion. Rogers wanted to enlist some of these effects in his opera.

The music of *The Warrior*, he says, is "characteristic of our times—a kind of declaimed melody suitable to the construction of language and play.....As I feel it, poet and composer are equal partners, since the music of opera rests on two pillars: word and action, or language and situation. The composer must discipline, channel his fantasy...."[1]

Some critics felt that Bernard Rogers had disciplined his fantasy too much—that what he had written was "background music" rather than real opera. The conservatives were outraged at his venture into new techniques. Others, however, "realized that its differences from established tradition crystallize a point of departure—a practical demonstration of opera as the synchronization of several arts."[2] Ronald Eyer, while stating that *The Warrior* "came but failed to conquer," called it "a challenging and not entirely unrewarded experiment in advanced methods of wedding music to drama and speech."[3]

Rogers was prepared for criticism. He believes that opera, like the rest of music, must move with the times. "We accept changes in the other arts," he maintains, "we must accept it in opera as well.... The creative artist lives dangerously, or he merely exists—hibernates ....The opera house must open its doors to the twentieth century. It must become a laboratory for new dramatic possibilities."

Present-day development of opera, according to Roger's idea, should be away from the grandiose pageantry of old-fashioned music-drama requiring large orchestras, hosts of singers and elaborate settings, to a quasi-intimate more simplified form, of which *The Warrior* is an excellent example. Just as "little theater" groups all over the country are providing opportunities for young actors, so "chamber operas," using small orchestras and a minimum amount of expenditure for scenery and production, should furnish an outlet for our singers and musicians.

Each year sees a growing number of these younger artists. In New York there is room for only a small proportion of them; but if com-

---

[1] *Opera News*—January 6, 1947.
[2] *Christian Science Monitor*—January 25, 1947.
[3] *Musical America, January* 10, 1947.

Modern Music-Makers

munities all over the United States could establish their own orchestra and opera groups, an increased capacity for musical appreciation would soon follow. In the field of chamber opera there is a great opportunity for our younger composers.

Although Bernard Rogers has written only two other operas: *The Marriage of Aude* (produced at the 1931 Eastman Festival and winner of the David Bispham Medal) and *The Veil*—first performed at the University of Indiana in 1950; all of his music is essentially dramatic.

Some of his most powerful works have been inspired by religious themes. He himself is not conventionally religious, but he finds in the Scriptures a symbol of the force that enables man to live. This force is what he is trying to express in his works on religious subjects. The first of these a choral work, *The Raising of Lazarus* (written in 1928), typifies the transformation of darkness into light brought about by trust—the simple, child-like belief in a higher power that guides man's destiny. Next he produced *The Exodus*, (also for chorus) based on the *Old Testament* story of the crossing of the Red Sea. In 1939 another Biblical episode, entirely spectacular this time, *The Dance of Salome* —for orchestra — became the most widely played of all his compositions.

Roger's leading work on a religious subject, and the one which he considers the most important of all his compositions, is *The Passion* (first presented at the Cincinnati May Festival, 1944). He spent ten years meditating on the subject of this great choral work, which, like Bach's *Passions*, interprets the last hours of Christ. In its treatment however, Rogers' work—as might be expected—is very different. He presents the Passion as a music-drama, with neither conventional recitatives nor chorales. Tense and concentrated throughout, it would adapt itself well to dramatic action. Howard Hanson says:

Rogers approaches the gigantic problem of setting the Passion in a highly personal, subjective, deeply reverent spirit. He has poured into it the full resources of his creative ability, and it is as a consequence, far removed from the conventional. An intensely dramatic, emotional work, it embodies a strong personal reaction. It is conceived in the spirit of the East rather than that of the West, suggesting the barbaric colors of the

144

BERNARD ROGERS

Bernard Rogers

Orient. A work of startling power, it is an important milestone in contemporary writing.[4]

Many of Bernard Roger's compositions reflect his interest in art. El Greco and Rembrandt are the two painters who move him the most: the one southern and mystical, the other an austere northern type, but both virile and dramatic and especially gifted in depicting religious ideas. *The Supper at Emmaus*, an orchestral work written in 1937, is based on Rembrandt's picture by that name. In trying to reproduce the characteristics of these two men in music—violent, passionate, fantastical or mystical, as the case may be—Rogers blends his palette of tones in the same way that an artist mixes his colors. He has been called "a master of the exotic possibilities of orchestral tone."[5]

He is also strongly drawn to Oriental art. Several of his compositions were inspired by Japanese prints—notably *Three Japanese Dances* and *Fuji in the Sunset Glow*. The Japanese are great masters of understatement and economy. Rogers says that he has tried in his music to express the remoteness and simplicity of Oriental art—its flatness or two-dimensional quality.

"Every great artist gives you a hint," says Rogers. "You must go on from there. We in the West," he adds, "live under too great pressure. We work too quickly, without enough contemplation. . . ."

Bernard Roger's interest in art began at an early age. It happened, he says, through an accident of geography. He was born February 4, 1893, on the East Side of New York. His father came of English-Irish ancestry, and his mother's parents were Czecho-Slovakian. He remembers his early years as drab and uninteresting—until the memorable day when, wandering over to Fifth Avenue, he discovered the Metropolitan Museum. His parents wanted him to be an architect; but he rebelled at the dry, technical training. He preferred art, and spent all of his spare time painting pictures.

Until Rogers was sixteen, music had no part in his life. Then he

---

[4] *In Modern Music*—March-April, 1945.

[5] Bernard Rogers has recently written a book on orchestration: *The Art of Orchestration*, published by Appleton-Century-Crofts in 1951.

145

Modern Music-Makers

met a boy living in the same block who played the violin, and for the first time realized that music existed. His friend took him to one of Frank Damrosch's Symphony Concerts for Young People. This concert proved a revelation to him. At that time he was working as an office boy. He began to study music at night—soon it became his whole life.

Rogers later attended the Institute of Musical Art, where he worked with Percy Goetschius. In 1917 he was awarded a Pulitzer Traveling Fellowship, and this made it possible for him to go abroad for further study. Following that (from 1918 to 1922) he studied with Ernest Bloch. When in 1927 he won a Guggenheim Fellowship, he went back to Europe for another three years. Most of this time was spent in England, where he had lessons with Frank Bridge. He also worked with Nadia Boulanger in France.

In 1929 Rogers joined the faculty of the Eastman School of Music, where he is now head of the Composition Department. Ten years later—in 1939—he married Elizabeth Clarke, from Sacramento, California. In 1946 he was elected a member of the National Institute of Arts and Letters.

A large number of the younger generation of American composers have studied under Bernard Roger's direction at Eastman; among the best-known of these are David Diamond, Gardner Read, Burrill Phillips, Gail Kubik, and William Bergsma. As teacher of advanced composition and orchestration (largely post-graduate students) Rogers adheres to no formula, mold or cult. He respects the individuality of his pupils, and encourages them to develop in their own particular style.

According to Howard Hanson, Rogers:

believes in the creative talent of youth, and he has enthusiasm. More than this, his tolerance permits him to guide young composers who represent many different points of view. He is intolerant only of shoddy workmanship and insincerity. To the many gifted young composers from the Eastman School of Music who have had the benefit of his guidance, he has imparted his credo of artistic integrity, his belief in honest craftsmanship, and his devotion to the development of the individual.[6]

[6] Howard Hanson in *Modern Music*. Mar.-April, 1945.

146

Bernard Rogers

Rogers is inclined to be skeptical of too much facility, and feels that habitual prize-winning can be dangerous. "While awards are momentarily good for morale," he says, "like all stimulants they must be repeated." The winner is too apt to depend on them as an index of success. Someone once asked the famous conductor Karl Muck if he composed. "No," he answered. "I once sent in a work and won a prize. Then I sent a second one and again received an award. So I decided I was not a composer!"

In addition to his works based on religious subjects or on paintings, Rogers has written four symphonies and a number of other orchestral works, among them a tone poem dedicated to the fallen of the First World War (his first composition for orchestra); *The Faithful; Fuji in the Sunset Glow; Two American Frescoes; Five Fairy Tales; Invasion* (commissioned by the League of Composers and first performed by the New York Philharmonic in 1943); *Prelude to Hamlet;* a march *The Colors of War;* and *In Memory of Franklin Delano Roosevelt*—this last written shortly after the death of President Roosevelt. It is, he says, "simply a personal expression of feeling for one for whom I had great admiration and affection. I wanted to say something about it in the only way I can—in music."

Bernard Rogers's chamber-music works include a string quartet, two *Soliloquys* (one for flute and string quartet and the other for bassoon and strings); a *Pastorale* for eleven instruments; and a suite for strings, flute and oboe called *The Silver World.* He has rarely written for the piano, his main works having been orchestral and choral. His greatest works, according to Hanson, are those for chorus. Rogers also likes to experiment, and is particularly interested in unusual sound effects and the possibilities of percussion instruments.

Intensity appeals to Bernard Rogers as the most vital ingredient in an artist's nature. There should be no such thing, he believes, as the casual; every note in a composition is important and must represent a distillation of feeling. Every work must be the best a man is capable of producing.

Not many musicians can make each composition a masterpiece as could Ravel. Nor is everyone able to achieve that nice discrimination which caused Brahms to let his unworthy notes, as he expressed it, "fall under the table." On the other hand there would be fewer second-class works if all composers held to Roger's high ideals. He himself has always tried, he says, to maintain this standard—to make each of his works his *best*.

Bernard Rogers

The Music of Bernard Rogers

Bernard Rogers

[1] C. C. Birchard.
[2] Free Library of Philadelphia.
[3] E. F. Kalmus.
[4] Southern Music Publishing Co.
[5] Elkan Vogel, Inc.
[6] G. Schirmer.

Webster's Song from The Devil and Daniel Webster

I've got a ram Goliath   He was raised on Marshfield grain

Douglas Moore

DOUGLAS MOORE

DOUGLAS MOORE

DOUGLAS MOORE has a special gift for melody; he is what is called "ear-minded." Certain musicians, he explains, work by ear, others by eye. The ear-minded are usually the more inventive type, the eye-minded the performers. As a child he was always making up songs.

His music is notable for its interpretation of the American scene. Such titles as *The Devil and Daniel Webster, Pageant of P. T. Barnum, The Ballad of William Sycamore,* and *Simon Legree* are all examples of characters and incidents native to his country that have inspired him to musical interpretation.

It was not until his junior year that Moore definitely decided to follow a musical career. At that time he was asked to write the incidental music for a college production of *Quentin Durward.* He had only just begun to study harmony, for in those day (1912) the students had to wait until their third year before they could enroll in the music classes; but he was famous for his songs (one of these—*Good Night Harvard*—became Yale's favorite football rally). To compose an entire score, however, was something very different. Young Moore had not the slightest idea how to set about writing the music for the Quentin Durward play. He went to his harmony teacher, David Stanley Smith, and asked him how he should begin.

"First you must have an overture," the latter told him. "What kind of an overture do you want to write?"

Douglas looked at him in perplexity. "What kinds are there?" he inquired.

"Well—there is the sonata form. . . ."

"What's that?"

His teacher patiently explained: "A first theme, a second theme—then the development."

"What do you mean by development?"

A young man of less determination might well have decided at this point that he had better give up trying to write an overture, let alone a whole score. But Douglas Moore has always been ready to accept challenges. In spite of all he did not know about music he tackled the assignment and managed to turn out a highly satisfactory accompaniment to the *Quentin Durward* play. Even Horatio Parker, head of Yale's music department admitted that it was good.

Until that time Parker had been little more than a legend to Moore—"a great figure I'd dreamed about. . . ." One day as Douglas was playing the March from his *Quentin Durward* score, the Music Director walked in unannounced. He had overhead the playing from his office.

"Did you write this?" he asked, sitting down at the piano and playing the *March* through from memory. He nodded approvingly. "It's not bad!" Young Moore could hardly decide which impressed him the more: Parker's remarkable ear and musical memory, or the fact that he had taken the trouble to encourage an unknown student.

This was the beginning of an association that proved one of the most important influences in Douglas Moore's life. After graduating in 1915 from Yale, he stayed on for two more years of postgraduate work in order to continue his music studies with Horatio Parker.

Douglas Moore was born August 10, 1893, at Cutchogue on Long Island, New York. His parents were of earliest American stock. His father's forbears came over from England before 1640, and finally settled in Southold Town on Long Island (the oldest English-speaking settlement in New York State), while his mother was descended in direct line from Miles Standish and John Alden (as was John Alden Carpenter). The elder of Moore's two daughters has added further Americana to the family tree by marrying a descendant of Governor Bradford.

Moore's earliest memories of music go back to the days when, a child of three, he would lie in front of the fire and listen to his mother play the piano. She didn't play very well—"not at all well, in fact," he admits—but the music would throw him into a state of excitement close to ecstasy.

Mrs. Moore was president of a choral club, and there were frequent rehearsals and concerts in the big music room of their home in Brooklyn. She wanted her children to know the joy of music, and insisted that they must all have piano lessons. In order to be sure that they practised properly, she hired a "practise teacher" to come in daily and supervise their work. Unfortunately this had the opposite effect to what she had intended—at least in Douglas' case. He took such a dislike to practising (particularly scales and five-finger exercises) that he could hardly be persuaded to go on with his lessons.

His mother finally agreed to let him stop when he was thirteen. But when that time came, and he was ready to go away to school, she changed her mind and insisted that he must go on with his piano. "I felt very bitter about it at the time," he confesses. "As if I'd been betrayed...."

That year, however, music began to mean something to him. He discovered what fun it was to improvise and make up tunes. Moore spent the next few years at Hotchkiss, preparing to enter Yale. One of his classmates there was a boy named Archibald MacLeish, who was always scribbling verses. Douglas set some of Archie's poems to music. Their collaboration continued through years to come— long after both of them became celebrated.

At Hotchkiss Douglas found little opportunity for serious work in music. Moore feels rather strongly about his lack of early training and the fact that his talent was not properly channelled. Years later, when he went to Nadia Boulanger in Paris, (he was thirty-three then, and had already written his *Four Museum Pieces* and *P. T. Barnum*) she made him go back and start at the beginning with the fundamentals of music. The various clefs were like a foreign language to him, and just as it is much harder to learn a new language after maturity, so he found Solfeggio—the "a-b-c-" of music far more difficult than if he had studied it as a child.

Mlle Boulanger understood his predicament. "I know how hard it is for you to learn this now!" she said to him. Douglas Moore believes, with many another of our composers, that solfeggio (sight-reading and ear-training) should be included in the early grades of every school in this country, as it is abroad. Excellent training for any youngster, and invaluable for those who may later become musicians.

In his youth, during a vacation while still at Hotchkiss, Douglas and one of his brothers decided to put on a musical show at the club house of their father's colony. The Moore children had always been interested in dramatics. (Douglas remembers a melodrama they produced when he was seven in the "Hall Theater" of the family attic, netting the cast five pennies in admission tickets. It was entitled *The Bride's Fate;* he was manager, playwright, and leading actor of the performance. Another early diversion, forerunner of some of his later activities, was the giving of lectures illustrated with projections of colored postcards.) That summer he was fifteen—having added music to his dramatic talents, he attempted an ambitious score for the show at his father's club house, and the result was such a success that he wrote home in elation to his mother: "Now I can write any kind of music I want."

"At that time I should have been sent to a conservatory," he concludes, regretfully. Instead he completed his course at Hotchkiss and then went on to Yale. When in his junior year there he finally began to study music seriously, he worked so hard that he was largely able to make up for the years of lost time.

A memorable experience, just before his last year at Yale, was the opportunity to spend a summer at the MacDowell Colony in Peterborough, New Hampshire. His family had long been interested in that admirable place, and his cousin, Mrs. Prince, had recently contributed funds for "Colony Hall"—an old barn which was transformed into dining room and recreation quarters for the colonists. Douglas, who had been recommended to MacDowell because of his promising talent, found it "very exciting and stimulating" to be surrounded by artists, all of them working creatively. He wrote mostly songs that summer. (Since 1926 Douglas Moore has been a member of the Board of Directors of the Edward MacDowell Association.)

Horatio Parker wanted young Moore to take a teaching job following his postgraduate work at Yale. But the First World War came just at that time, upsetting many budding careers, and Douglas enlisted in the Navy. While in the service he kept on writing songs—mainly for the entertainment of his shipmates. One of these, *Destroyer Life,* became so popular and was so widely sung that John Niles, "dean of American Balladeers," believed it to be a folk song and started to include it in a collection he was about to publish. Someone however recognized the music and said, "You can't print that as a folk song—it was written by Douglas Moore."

Niles got in touch with the young composer to find out if *De-*

Douglas Moore

stroyer Life really was his song. Moore admitted his authorship and said "I should be delighted to have it appear in your collection. As a matter of fact I have a lot more songs. Why don't we do a book together?" The idea appealed to Niles, and the two of them collaborated in a racy, highly amusing volume: *Songs My Mother Never Taught Me,* (illustrated by Walgreen, cartoonist of the American Expeditionary Forces).

Douglas Moore's father, who published *The Ladies' World,* one of the early women's magazines, died shortly before the end of the war, and his eldest son took over the direction of the firm. When Douglas was released from the Navy this eldest brother said to him, "Why don't you come into the publishing business now? You've fooled around long enough with this music stuff." But young Moore was not attracted to a business career. He wanted to find out first if he could make a success as a composer. He set three of Archibald MacLeish's poems to music, then took them to his friend for advice. "How good are they?" he asked. Both MacLeish and his wife were enthusiastic. "But are they good enough to earn my living with?" Moore insisted.

That was a difficult question to answer. In those days a young composer, just out of the navy, was likely to starve before he could establish himself by writing music—no matter how talented he might be. (After the Second World War the situation became somewhat improved. At Columbia University, for instance, thirteen fellowships of $1200 each were set up by the Ditson Foundation, and these were available to promising young composers the day of their dismissal from service, thus giving them an opportunity to try out their powers free from economic worry.)

Moore, although not immediately concerned about the economical aspect, (he had inherited some money from his father) knew that if he wanted to be a first-class composer he must have further training. So he decided to go to Paris, where he entered the Schola Cantorum. There he studied composition with Vincent d'Indy, and organ with Tournemire—the last of César Franck's pupils. Through this latter teacher he became steeped in the tradition of Franck.

In Paris Douglas Moore met Stephen Vincent Benét. They soon became close friends and in the years that followed Moore set a large number of Benét's poems to music. Their collaboration culminated

Modern Music-Makers

in one of Moore's best known works: his opera *The Devil and Daniel Webster*.

In 1920, after a year abroad, Moore came home and married Emily Bailey. She returned with him for a "second marvelous year" in Paris. Then they moved back to stay permanently in the United States. Just at that time the directors of the Cleveland Museum, having recently been presented with an endowment for music, were looking for someone who could give recitals, play the organ, and supervise musical programs. Thomas Whitney Surette, at the suggestion of Archibald MacLeish, recommended Douglas Moore, and on the strength of this endorsement Moore was appointed (by correspondence) curator of music to the Cleveland Museum of Art.

He spent four years in Cleveland. The environment there was highly stimulating; in addition to artistic and musical circles he found an enthusiastic group devoted to the stage. Regular performances were given at the Cleveland Playhouse, and Moore was soon taking leading roles in these productions. It was an experience that he repeated in 1942 in Tucson, during a winter spent in Arizona with his wife.

While in Cleveland he met a number of young composers who, like himself, were interested in modern music. Among them were Roger Sessions, Quincy Porter, Bernard Rogers and Theodore Chanler. They were all pupils of Ernest Bloch, and Douglas Moore also decided to study with him. He found Bloch "the best teacher he ever had."

During the summer of 1922, again at the MacDowell Colony, Moore wrote his first serious composition, descriptive of some of the art treasures at the museum. He called it *Four Museum Pieces: Fifteenth Century Armour, A Madonna of Botticini, The Chinese Lion,* and *The Unhappy Flutist—a Statue of Rodin.* This suite was originally written for organ; later he orchestrated it and conducted the first performance of the work with the Cleveland Symphony Orchestra. In 1926 *Four Museum Pieces* brought him a Pulitzer Travelling Fellowship. He spent it in Paris, studying with Nadia Boulanger.

There have been three great literary influences in the life of Douglas Moore. First of these was Archibald MacLeish, and next Stephen

158

Douglas Moore

Vincent Benét. One day in 1923 while Moore was still at the Cleveland Museum of Art, the librarian came in.

"Who do you think is in the library?" he said. Moore stepped across to the reading room and there found one of his favorite American authors, with his nose buried in a book on Egypt—Vachel Lindsay. The two immediately struck up a friendship; it was a friendship that had far-reaching consequences. Moore claims that through his association with Lindsay he gained a new understanding of his own country. Lindsay opened the young composer's eyes to the glamour of the American scene—to the true beauty and flavor of American life. It was this new viewpoint that influenced Moore to write his first work on a typically American theme. He called it *The Pageant of P. T. Barnum* and dedicated it to Nikolai Sokoloff. The composition is in five movements: *Boyhood at Bethel; Joice Heth* (a tone poem describing the hundred and sixty-one year old Negress exhibited by Barnum); *General and Mrs. Tom Thumb; Jenny Lind;* and last a boisterous march entitled *Circus Parade.*

P. T. Barnum, according to James Rogers (in the *Cleveland Plain Dealer*) might have been written by some musical Tom Sawyer or Huckleberry Finn. He called it "clever, ingenious, with a sort of boyish exuberance in it." Willard Rhodes says:

For these alfresco pictures Moore . . . paints in brilliant colors the American scene of the 1860's. Without resorting to period stylization or naive archaism, he has recreated the charming simplicity and warm human spirit of the Currier and Ives prints.[1]

It was in 1920, on his wedding trip, that Douglas Moore first met Daniel Gregory Mason, head of the Music Department at Columbia University. Moore had written to Mason, and the latter invited the young couple to visit him at his summer home in Norfolk, Connecticut. Through the friendship thus established Moore was asked, in 1926, to join the music faculty at Columbia. The year following he became assistant professor; then associate professor and lecturer at Barnard College. Eventually, on the retirement of Mason, Moore was appointed to succeed him as head of Columbia's music department. This important position he still holds.

[1] In an article *Douglas Moore's Music,* Columbia University.

Modern Music-Makers

As teacher, lecturer, and executive, Douglas Moore has been brilliantly successful. His classes, both at Barnard and at Columbia, are the most popular in the Music Course. "The artistry with which he initiates the students into the mysteries of the musical language is a performance of sheer virtuosity."[2] Moore has gathered the essence of his lectures and music courses into two books: *Listening to Music*, published in 1932 by W. W. Norton Co., and *From Madrigal to Modern Music* (1942).

During his early years at Columbia Moore wrote a tone poem for orchestra called *Moby Dick;* then his first symphony, *A Symphony of Autumn*, dedicated to Howard Hanson. *Overture on an American Tune* (originally *Babbitt*) followed. Typical of his devotion to the American scene is a *Suite for Orchestra* written in 1950 and subtitled *Farm Journal*.

Moore's *Second Symphony* appeared in 1945. To this he has added the following explanation:

The symphony is an attempt to write in clear, objective, modified classical style, with emphasis upon rhythmic and melodic momentum rather than upon sharply contrasted themes or dramatic climax. There is no underlying program, although the mood of the second movement was suggested by a short poem of James Joyce which deals with music heard at the coming of twilight.

Moore has written a considerable number of songs, and piano and organ pieces. His chamber-music works include *The Ballad of William Sycamore* (for baritone, flute, trombone and piano) to words by Stephen Vincent Benét; a *Quartet for Strings* (1933) and two *Quintets*—one for woodwinds and horn in 1942, and one for clarinet and strings, written in 1946. He has also done a *Down East Suite* for violin and piano.

As texts for his choral music Moore has used almost entirely the poems of his three friends. Vachel Lindsay's *Simon Legree*, for men's chorus, Archibald MacLeish's *Dedication*, for mixed voices a cappella, and three by Stephen Vincent Benét: *Perhaps to Dream* (women's chorus, a cappella), *Prayer for England*, written in 1941 for men's chorus, and in 1943 *Prayer For the United Nations*. This last is for

[2] *Ibid.*

DOUGLAS MOORE

Douglas Moore

alto solo, chorus and orchestra or piano. Rhodes calls this work "one of the strongest and most deeply moving American compositions of today."

Between 1925 and 1927 Moore wrote incidental music for three theater productions: *Twelfth Night, Much Ado About Nothing,* and R. E. Sherwood's *The Road to Rome.* This led him naturally into a full-length opera based on Philip Barry's *White Wings,* and following that, an operetta to Stephen Vincent Benét's *The Headless Horseman.* Next came his famous *The Devil and Daniel Webster,* a one-act opera also to a text by Benét.

The story tells of a farmer who sells his soul to the Devil in order to gain the bride he desires. At the wedding the Devil, disguised as a lawyer, comes to claim his reward. But in the ensuing trial Daniel Webster pleads for the farmer's soul and finally wins the case by his eloquence.

Of this opera Douglas Moore wrote:

Mr. Benét and I have classified *The Devil and Daniel Webster* as a folk-opera because it is legendary in its subject matter and simple in its musical expression. As a matter of fact, this particular legend is a fiction, although related to the authentic powers of Webster as an orator, and the music makes no conscious quotation from folk tunes. The exact category into which it falls finds no convenient label. We have tried to make an opera in which the union of speech, song and instrumental music will communicate the essence of the dramatic story, enhanced but not distorted.

Some of the critics were inclined to think that the music was too subordinated to the text, but as a whole *The Devil and Daniel Webster* had excellent reviews. "Altogether it is one of the brightest and most natural of contemporary operas," wrote Otto Luening in an article for the 1931 May-June number of *Modern Music.* Alfred Frankenstein called it "as artful, eloquent, and effective a statement of the principles of American democracy as has ever been written." [3]

Moore completed a fourth opera *Giants in the Earth* in 1950. This was based on the novel by O. E. Rolvaag (libretto by Arnold Sungaard), and it was first produced at Columbia University March 28,

[3] "Plight of the American Composer" by Alfred Frankenstein in the *American Scholar,* Autumn 1943.

161

Modern Music-Makers

1951. *Giants in the Earth* was awarded the Pulitzer Prize in Music,
May 1951.

Douglas Moore's views on present day music and his own in particular were clearly set forth in an article that appeared some time
ago in the *New York Herald Tribune:*

> I feel very strongly that we are all of us overconscious today of the
> problems of idiom and esthetics. Most of us compose under the deadly
> fear of being either not modern enough or too modern. Too many of us
> worry about whether our music is properly a reflection of America, or
> suitably international, in order to please whatever faction impresses us
> the most. The particular ideal which I have been striving to attain is to
> write music which will not be self-conscious with regard to idiom, and will
> reflect the exciting quality of life, traditions, and country which I feel
> all about me . . .
>
> If we happen to feel romantically inclined, if we like a good tune now
> and then, if we still have a childish love for atmosphere, is it not well for
> us to admit the fact, and try to produce something which we like ourselves?

Moore's music abounds in "good tunes," and it is perhaps this gift
for melody that is his most outstanding characteristic. According to
Otto Luening:

> Within the variety of his output there is a unifying factor, and that is his
> melodic drive. In spite of external stylistic differences each work reveals
> a new aspect of this lyric urge. Whatever the purpose of a particular
> composition, it is achieved primarily through the melodic-rhythmic
> line. . . .A review of Moore's work leads to the conclusion that here is a
> man who has expressed his American heritage and his own ideals.[4]

---

[4] May-June 1931 *Modern Music.*

Douglas Moore

Born Aug. 10, Cutchogue, Long Island, N.Y.	1893
Receives Mus. B.A. from Yale University	1917
Enlists in the Navy	1918
Enrolls Schola Cantorum, Paris	1919
Marries Emily Bailey	1920
Curator of Music at Cleveland Museum of Art	
Four Museum Pieces	1922
The Pageant of P. T. Barnum	1924
Joins music faculty at Columbia University	1926
Moby Dick	1928
A Symphony of Autumn	1930
Overture on an American Tune	1931
Listening to Music	1932
Quartet for Strings	1933
White Wings	1935
Simon Legree	1937
The Devil and Daniel Webster	1938
Appointed head of Music Dept. at Columbia University and MacDowell Professor	1940
From Madrigal to Modern Music	1942
Prayer for the United Nations	1943
In Memoriam	1944
Second Symphony in A Major	1945
President of National Inst. of Arts & Letters	1946
Suite for Orchestra Farm Journal	1947
Giants in the Earth	1950

The Music of Douglas Moore

Douglas Moore

Adam Was My Grandfather (S. V. Benét) [10]	1937
Three Divine Sonnets of John Donne [11]	1942
The Token (Donne)	1942
The Sea That Is My Songs (Mirza Schaffy)	1942
Not This Alone (Pierson Underwood) [11]	1943

PIANO WORKS

Waltz	1920
Museum Piece [12]	1921
Careful Etta [4]	1935
Fiddlin' Joe [4]	
Grievin' Annie [4]	
Six Pieces for Piano (Prelude, Reel, Dancing School, Barn Dance, Air, Procession) [4]	

FOR ORGAN

Scherzo	1927
A March for Tamburlaine	1928
Dirge (Passacaglia) [7]	1939

MOTION PICTURES

Power and the Land (documentary)	1940
Youth Gets a Break (documentary)	1940
Bip Goes to Town (documentary)	1941

STAGE WORKS

Incidental Music, Twelfth Night	1925
Incidental Music, Much Ado About Nothing	1927
Incidental Music, The Road to Rome (R. E. Sherwood) [13]	1927
White Wings (opera), (Philip Barry)	1934
The Headless Horseman, operetta (S. V. Benét) [14]	1936
The Devil and Daniel Webster, opera (S. V. Benét) [6]	1938
Giants in the Earth	1950

[1] C. C. Birchard.
[2] Music Press.
[3] Elkan Vogel.
[4] Carl Fischer.
[5] Arrow Press.
[6] Boosey Hawkes.
[7] H. W. Gray.
[8] Society for the Publication of American Music.
[9] Harcourt Brace.
[10] Galaxy.
[11] G. Schirmer.
[12] Axelrod.
[13] Brady & Wiman.
[14] E. C. Schirmer.

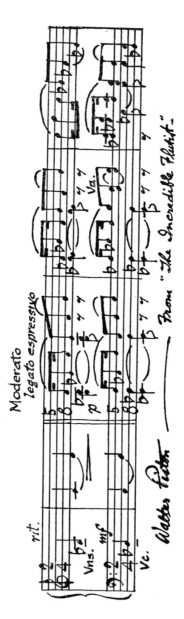

WALTER PISTON

WALTER PISTON

HARVARD'S Music School, founded in 1875 by John Knowles Paine, is located in an inconspicuous corner of the university's campus. To reach it you turn off Cambridge's busy main street, pass through high iron gates, cross a green-velvet "yard" shaded by giant elms and enclosed by dormitories of warmly mellowed brick, and finally come to a modest building with white-pillared portico labeled MUSIC DEPART-MENT.

This time-honored institution has been the musical cradle of a large number of our leading American composers, among them Edward Burlingame Hill (who became head of the department after Paine), Roger Sessions, Randall Thompson, Virgil Thomson, Leonard Bernstein, Harold Shapero, and—one of the most distinguished of them all—Walter Piston. Piston graduated from Harvard's Music School in 1924. Some years later he returned as teacher, then as assistant professor. In 1941, when Edward Burlingame Hill resigned, he succeeded him as chairman of the department.

Walter Piston would have been surprised in his early years if he had seen himself in this position. Until he was eighteen he had never thought much about music. There were no musicians in his family, and not even a piano in the home. But he may have inherited some of the traditional Italian love of music from his grandfather—a sailor named Antonio Pistone—who came over to this country from Italy, married an American girl, settled in Rockland, Maine, and finally—becoming completely American—dropped the "e" from his name.

Walter Hamor Piston was born January 20, 1894, in that same New England town. He lived there until he was ten; when the family moved to Boston. At that time art appealed to him quite as much as music, if not more. He spent four years at the Massachusetts Normal Art School, training to be a painter. While there he met a young student named Kathryn Nason, who later became a well-known painter.

Modern Music-Makers

She and her brother Tom and sister Gertrude were all exceptionally talented (a few years ago they held a "three-ring" family art exhibit in New York).

Walter Piston and Kathryn Nason were married in 1920. He claims that his wife has been largely responsible for his present career. "She painted so much better than I did that I had to give up art and become something else—a musician, or a plumber. . . ." (The latter might have proved more financially rewarding!)

It was while he was studying at the Mechanic Arts High School that Piston first became seriously interested in music. He took lessons on the violin, taught himself to play the piano, and managed to earn his way by playing in restaurants, dance halls and theaters. His early teachers were Fiumara, Winternitz, Harris Shaw and Julius Theodorowitz, assistant concertmaster of the Boston Symphony.

At the time of his graduation in 1916 from the Normal Art School Piston couldn't decide which he wanted to be; a painter or a musician. The outbreak of the First World War helped him to make up his mind. Having a natural affection for the sea—perhaps also an inheritance from his sailor-grandfather—Piston enlisted in the Navy Band. (Ironically, he never saw the ocean during his time of service. "The only battle I took part in," he explains with quiet humor, "was the 'Battle of the Charles River'!")

When he applied for enlistment he had to fill out a long page of questions: One of them was: "What is your instrument?" The only musical instruments that Piston could then play were the piano and violin—not much use in a brass band. He did some quick thinking, made a sudden choice, and put down "Saxophone."

Fortunately he was not at that moment required to prove his ability. On the way home from the recruiting office he stopped at a music store and bought a saxophone. Then he went to the Boston Public Library, asked for a book on "How to learn to play the saxophone in six short lessons" and proceeded—over night—to master the technique of his new instrument. In the Navy Band he was designated as "second-class musician," a purely technical rating—but peculiarly appropriate, he concluded, as applied to his playing of the saxophone.

Piston was assigned to the band of the Aeronautics Division then stationed at the Massachusetts Institute of Technology, across the

WALTER PISTON

Walter Piston

Charles River in Cambridge. The other members of the group apparently had had even less training than himself. Their combined efforts, he says, were little short of bedlam; for anyone with a sensitive musical ear it was a shattering experience. Piston was sure that sound of actual warfare on the battlefields couldn't be any worse than music made by out-of-tune brass instruments, badly played. He asked for a transfer to the Ensign School. But his application was refused—they considered him too valuable as a musician. "We need you in the band" they insisted.

This harrowing interlude in his career might well have put Piston off music completely; but when the war ended he decided, nonetheless, to go on (though not with the saxophone). He concentrated first on the violin, and became such a good player that he had hopes of realizing a secret ambition: to play in a symphony orchestra. With his goal near, however, he began to wonder if this was really what he wanted.

"If I become a violinist in an orchestra," he said to himself, "I'll spend the rest of my life doing what someone else tells me to do."

Having an independent and adventurous spirit, such a prospect was not enticing to him. By that time he had begun in his leisure hours to do a little music writing. Creative work is a heady drink. It has a way of so fascinating and absorbing a man that he is ready to sacrifice everything for it—even his security. Piston, now aged twenty-seven, made a sudden decision—to throw everything else overboard and train himself to be a composer.

In 1919, the year before his marriage, he enrolled at Harvard's Music Department. During the next few years he followed all the different classes in music theory, counterpoint and orchestration; conducted the University Orchestra and Pierian Sodality, and became assistant to Archibald P. Davidson. When he finished the course he graduated with highest honors—including a *"Summa Cum Laude"* in music, election to the Phi Beta Kappa Society, and the John Paine's Traveling Fellowship. Soon after, he and his wife sailed for Europe.

Piston first thought of entering the Paris Conservatory, but he found that he was beyond the age limit for admission. Several teachers had been recommended to him, one in particular named Nadia

Modern Music-Makers

Boulanger. Like many others, Piston had little faith in woman's intellect—at least when it came to technical matters. "I didn't come over to Paris just to study with a woman," he insisted.

This woman, however, was exceptional. Nadia Boulanger came of a family of musicians. Both her father and her grandfather were professors at the Paris Conservatory; her mother was also an accomplished musician, and her younger sister Lili showed great promise as a composer. In her earlier years Nadia, too, wrote music, but after her sister's death in 1918 she gave up composing and devoted herself to teaching instead.

When the American Conservatory at Fontainebleau was first established, Mlle Boulanger was put in charge of the composition classes (one of her first American pupils there was Aaron Copland). She also taught at the Ecole Normale de Musique, and later succeeded Paul Dukas as head of the composition department there. Nadia Boulanger was a fine organist and conductor as well as a remarkable teacher (she was the first woman to direct a full symphony orchestra in Paris, and has since conducted the Boston Symphony and a number of other orchestras in this country). She made her first visit to the United States in 1924, and appeared as organ soloist with the New York Philharmonic-Symphony, Walter Damrosch conducting. At that time she played a composition of her sister's and one by her talented young American pupil, Aaron Copland.

It was soon after her return from this trip that Walter Piston, having tried out several different teachers who failed to satisfy him, finally decided to go to Mlle Boulanger. She was then teaching at the Ecole Normale de Musique, (Piston later played viola in the orchestra there), and he took her some of his music "to see if she would let him in. . . ."

To his surprise, instead of the stodgy, academic, and not too brilliant professor he had expected, he found a young and attractive woman: enthusiastic, highly intelligent, with an amazing command of her subject and a rare gift for inspiring her pupils. Under Nadia Boulanger's encouraging instruction Piston gained the final mastery of his medium—a technique that has since been the admiration of all his colleagues.

"Piston's music . . . sets a level of craftsmanship that is absolutely

Walter Piston

first-rate in itself and provides a standard of reference by which every other American's work may be judged," says Aaron Copland[1] while Olin Downes called him a man "who has thoroughly mastered the ground principles of his art; who know what he wants to do and how to do it; whose basis is a thorough command of counterpoint and form, on which is superimposed brilliant treatment of the orchestra."

During his two years in Paris, Walter Piston wrote *Three Pieces for Flute, Clarinet and Bassoon* and a sketch for an orchestral work *Symphonic Piece*, first played in 1928 by the Boston Symphony with Serge Koussevitzy conducting. Since then Piston has returned several times to Europe. In 1935 he went over on a Guggenheim Fellowship, and while there wrote a *Trio* for piano, violin and cello, commissioned by the Elizabeth Sprague Coolidge Foundation.

There was nothing that Piston would have liked better than to devote his entire time to composition. But as John Alden Carpenter put it, "Even composers have to eat!" So Walter Piston, like a number of our other American musicians who have associated themselves with universities or music schools (to mention only a few: Howard Hanson at the Eastman School, William Schuman at Juilliard and Leo Sowerby at the American Conservatory in Chicago), on his return from France decided to join the faculty of Harvard's Music Department. The essence of his teaching experience there is found in three books: *Harmony* (W. W. Norton), *Principles of Harmonic Analysis* (E. C. Schirmer) and *Counterpoint.*

Piston believes that every "musicologist"—that is, everyone who is interested in the intelligent study of music—should know something of its underlying theory. In a report on the *Teaching of Theory* he said:

It has but recently become clear that the primary purpose of theoretical study in music is not the production of composers. . . .Musical theory is not a set of directions for composing music. It is rather a set of deductions arrived at by observation over a long period and attempting to describe the practise of composers. It does not teach how to compose, but it teaches how music has been composed.

It must be evident that such knowledge is indispensable to any student in any branch of music; whether his field is performing, teaching, conduct-

---

[1] In *Our New Music*. Whittlesey House, 1941.

Modern Music-Makers

ing, criticism, composition, or scholarly research. It is far more a necessity for the musicologist than for the composer.

In 1926 Piston and his wife moved to a new home in Belmont, just outside of Boston. There, during the succeeding months, he wrote his *Suite for Orchestra*, and at Koussevitzky's invitation, conducted the Boston Symphony in the première of the work. (Piston usually leads the first performances of his works, though he says that he doesn't aspire to be a conductor).

Concerto for Orchestra was composed in 1933. This, he explains, is in eighteenth century "Concerto Grosso" form, for orchestra alone and not to display the virtuosity of any single instrument. Copland called the second movement of this work "formal in design, daring in harmonic texture . . . a brilliant tour de force, making use of jazz motifs and reviving Pierrot Lunaire's device: the large *cancrizans* that reaches a central point and then proceeds, note for note, back to the starting point."

The Incredible Flutist is perhaps best known of Piston's music to the public at large, since it has been recorded and frequently played over the air. The orchestral suite is taken from a ballet composed originally in 1933 for Hans Wiener's dance group, and performed at one of the Boston Pops Concerts under the direction of Arthur Fiedler. The ballet's scene is laid in a market place where a country circus has been set up, complete with Barker, Jugglers, a Snake-Dancer, Monkey-Trainer, Crystal Gazer, and the main attraction: the Flutist—a remarkable fellow with incredible powers.

This is the only one of Piston's works that has a "programmatic," or story, basis. The suite is in eight parts, or episodes:

1. The Introduction and Dance of the Vendors
2. Entrance of Customers and Tango of the
   Merchant's Daughters
3. Arrival of the Circus and March
4. Solo of the Flutist
5. Minuet
6. Spanish Waltz
7. Siciliano Duet
8. Polka Finale

Walter Piston

Piston has written several other works featuring the flute: *Three Pieces for Flute and Piano*, a *Sonata for Flute and Piano*, and a *Quintet for Flute and String Quartet*. Other chamber music compositions include a *Suite for Oboe and Piano* (performed at a League of Composers concert), three *String Quartets*,[2] a *Quintet for Piano and Strings*, a *Trio for Violin, Cello and Piano*, a *Duo for Viola and Cello*, and a *Divertimento for Nine Instruments*. So far he has only composed one choral work: *Carnival Song*, for men's chorus and brass instruments, in 1938.

His *First Symphony* appeared in 1937, and that same year he produced a *Concertino for Piano and Chamber Orchestra*, followed in 1939 by a *Concerto for Violin*. A *Second Symphony* commissioned by the Alice M. Ditson Foundation of Columbia University won the 1943 New York Critics Circle Award and was first played by Hans Kindler and the National Symphony Orchestra in Washington, D. C.

In 1944 the League of Composers, together with the New York Philharmonic and the Columbia Broadcasting system, asked seventeen different American composers to write works commemorating some aspect of the war. Piston's contribution was a *Fugue on a Victory Theme*—based on a bugle call (the "Adjutant's Call"). That same year Elizabeth Sprague Coolidge invited him to contribute an original work for her annual Music Festival in Washington, D. C.

Some years before, he had composed two organ works for his friend—the noted organist E. Power Biggs—a *Chromatic Study on the Name of Bach* (1940) and a *Prelude and Allegro* (organ and strings—1943). Now, for his latest commission, he composed a *Partita for Violin, Viola and Organ*.

The Coolidge Chamber-Music Festivals, held in the fall in Washington, D. C., have long been highlights of the season's musical events. Attendance to these is entirely by invitation, and musicians from every part of the United States travel to Washington for the privilege of hearing the concerts. They are held in a special auditorium, built by Mrs. Coolidge in the Library of Congress Building. The festival usually lasts three or four days, with programs each evening and one or two afternoon concerts. Through her generous

---

[2] The *Third String Quartet* was written for the Music Critics Symposium held in Boston in May, 1947.

Modern Music-Makers

commissions to contemporary composers, Elizabeth Sprague Coolidge has proved an important influence in furthering the cause of modern chamber music.

The 1944 concerts were especially interesting since they marked the Foundation's Tenth Festival, and also celebrated Mrs. Coolidge's eightieth birthday. The first program was dedicated to the classics; the second included, in addition to works by Mozart and Schubert, a new sonata by Stravinsky, and *Second Avenue Waltzes* by Vittorio Rieti. The last evening was devoted to the ballet—presented by Martha Graham and her dancers—with specially commissioned music by Darius Milhaud, Paul Hindemith, and Aaron Copland.

Walter Piston's *Partita for Violin, Viola and Organ*, had its première at the third concert of the series. It was played by E. Power Biggs and two members of the Stradivarius Quartet; Wolfe Wolfinsohn and Eugene Lehner. In composing the work, Piston was directed to passages chosen by Archibald MacLeish from Carl Sandburg's humorous poem *The People, Yes*:

Wedlock is a padlock. (Take a good look at the mother before getting tied up with the daughter)

Blue eyes say love me or I die. Black eyes say love me or I kill you.

Sleep is a suspension midway and a conundrum of shadows lost in meadows of the moon.

The sea has fish for every man—every blade of grass has its share of dew. . . .

Piston had written four symphonies so far. The *Third*, commissioned by the Koussevitzky Foundation, won a Pulitzer Prize, and had its initial performance in January, 1948, by the Boston Symphony, Koussevitzky conducting. Critics commended the "lyrical tranquillity" of the first three movements, but found the finale noisy. (Piston had an explanation for this. . . . The last movement, he says, was written while an artesian well was being dug just outside his window. "I had to write music loud enough to overcome the noise outside . . . !)

His *Fourth Symphony* appeared in 1950. Other recent orchestral

174

Walter Piston

works are a *Toccata*, a *Second Suite,* and *Intermezzo for Symphonic Band: Tunbridge Fair. A Third String Quartet* was written for the Music Critic's Symposium which was held in Boston in May, 1947.

In May, 1946, Piston was awarded the degree of Doctor of Music from the Philadelphia Conservatory. He resigned from the active directorship of Harvard's Music Department when, in 1944, he became full professor. In 1951 he was appointed to the newly endowed Walter W. Naumburg chair, and became the first Naumburg Professor of Music at Harvard.

His schedule is still an exacting one, and he finds to his regret that he has far less time for composing than he would like. This is the cry of most music writers: other activities, necessary for a livelihood, fill the major part of their existence, and what is most important to them — their creative work — is forced to take second place. Nevertheless Piston has managed to produce a good deal of music, all of it distinguished for its craftsmanship and what Elliott Carter calls "love of proportion and restraint—as manifest in his compositions as in his elegantly penned manuscripts. . . . As a result of tireless concentration combined with rich native musicianship, his works have a uniform excellence that seems destined to give them an important position in the musical repertory."[3]

Piston has little time for hobbies—though now and then he enjoys a good game of chess. Painting he leaves to his wife. . . . Reserved, soft-spoken and with an engaging sense of humor, Walter Piston has been an important influence on the American music of today.

He has never been content with experiment for its own sake, or with attempts to find new harmonies or rhythms as ends in themselves. He has sought for himself a contemporary idiom based on the dissonant counterpoint of 20th Century common practise, and he has freely expressed his ideas in terms of it. His music has breadth, tenuousness, complexity and simplicity. It shows, also, a notable melodic gift which has reached considerable heights in such works as the *Concerto for Orchestra* and particularly *The Incredible Flutist.* His style has been called classical; it is on the dry side, but not excessively so; it is concise, witty, economical. . . . He believes that there is a pure, ever-flowing stream of abstract international emotion. . . . [4]

[3] Elliott Carter in *The Musical Quarterly,* July 1946.
[4] George Henry Lovett Smith in *The Magazine of Art,* February 1940.

Modern Music-Makers

Copland calls him "a representative of New England . . . [who] speaks an international language." Piston has a natural mistrust of what he calls "self-conscious striving for nationalism."

"Is the Dust Bowl more American than, say, a corner in the Boston Athenaeum?" he asks. Would not a Vermont village furnish as American a background for a composition as the Great Plains? The self-conscious striving for nationalism gets in the way of the establishment of a strong school of composition and even of significant individual expression. If the composers will increasingly strive to perfect themselves in the art of music and will follow only those paths of expression which seem to take them the true way, the matter of a national school will take care of itself. And who can predict the time of its coming? Some say it is already here. Some say it has been here since the turn of the century. Others feel it will take time to show the true significance of the enormous development of these recent years. But the composer cannot afford the wild-goose chase of trying to be more American than he is." [5]

In the whole field of contemporary music, Walter Piston occupies an important position. He has summed up the tendencies of the past twenty years both here and in Europe and given them broad and masterful expression. . . .His unique contribution is to have done this particular work with outstanding excellence in a country where few have ever made a name for themselves as thoroughly craftsmen-like artists.[6]

[5] *Ibid.*
[6] Elliott Carter in *The Musical Quarterly,* July 1946.

Walter Piston

Born January 20, Rockland, Maine	1894
Graduates from Massachusetts Normal Art School	1916
Enlists in U. S. Navy	1918
Enrolls in Harvard's Music Department	1919
Marries Kathryn Nason	1920
Graduates from Harvard with *Summa Cum Laude* and Phi Beta Kappa	1924
Awarded John Knowles Paine Travelling Fellowship Goes to Paris for two years	1924-1926
Three Pieces for Flute, Clarinet, and Bassoon	1926
Joins Harvard Music faculty	1926
Symphonic Piece	1927
Suite for Orchestra	1929
First String Quartet	1931
Concerto for Orchestra	1933
Trio for Violin, Cello and Piano	1935
Guggenheim Fellowship *First Symphony*	1937
The Incredible Flutist	1938
Concerto for Violin and Orchestra	1939
Quintet for Flute and String Quartet	1942
Second Symphony	1943
Partita for Violin, Viola and Organ	1944
Appointed full professor Harvard Music School Doctor of Music, Philadelphia Conservatory	1946
Third Symphony—Pulitzer Prize	1947
Toccata	1948
Quintet for Piano and Strings	1949
Fourth Symphony	1950
Appointed first Naumburg Professor of Music at Harvard	1951

The Music of Walter Piston

178

Walter Piston

Sonata for Violin and Piano [2]	1939
Chromatic Study on the Name of Bach [7]	1940
Quintet for Flute and String Quartet [2]	1942
Interlude for Viola and Piano [5]	1942
Prelude and Allegro for Organ and Strings [2]	1943
Partita for Violin, Viola and Organ [2]	1944
Sonatina for Violin and Harpsichord [4]	1945
Divertimento for Nine Instruments [6]	1946
String Quartet No. 3 [4]	1947
Quintet for Piano and Strings [4]	1949
Duo for Viola and Cello [4]	1949

PIANO WORKS

Piano Sonata	1926
Passacaglia [8]	1943
Improvisation [9]	1945

STAGE WORKS

The Incredible Flutist [2] (ballet)	1938

[1] Cos Cob Press.
[2] Arrow Press.
[3] G. Schirmer.
[4] Boosey & Hawkes.
[5] Boletin Latino-americano.
[6] Broadcast Music Inc.
[7] H. W. Gray Co.
[8] Mercury Music.
[9] Delkas.

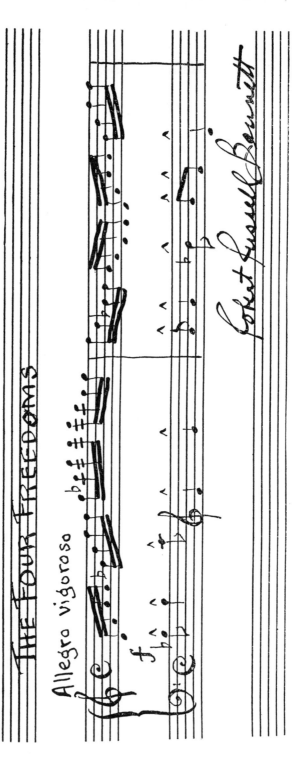

ROBERT RUSSELL BENNETT

ROBERT RUSSELL BENNETT

THE name of Robert Russell Bennett immediately calls to mind such Broadway smash-hits as *Oklahoma, Show-Boat, Annie Get Your Gun, Carousel,* and many others for which he has orchestrated the music. He has been so successful in this field that people sometimes overlook his importance as a writer of serious music. Yet he has a long list of classical compositions to his credit, including symphonies, original stage works, chamber and choral pieces—in fact nearly every type of music is represented in his work.

Bennett's success as an "arranger" began shortly after the First World War.

Early in 1919 a tall, rail-thin young man walked into the office of George Moody of the T. B. Harms and Company in New York. "Have you any music you would like to have arranged for dance, orchestra or band?" the young man asked. "I am an orchestrator," he added—with more confidence than he actually felt.

Mr. Moody looked at the applicant doubtfully. Musicians who thought they could orchestrate were always coming to him for work, but they all turned out the same banal, run-of-the-mill stuff. Would this young nobody be any different from the rest? He debated a moment, then decided to try the boy out.

"See what you can do with these," he said, handing over a pile of recently published songs.

As luck would have it, the first of the pieces Russell Bennett orchestrated became the biggest hit of the year. It was Cole Porter's *An Old-Fashioned Garden,* and not a little of its success was due to the clever arrangement of the orchestration. Bennett found himself launched on the career that was to make him famous. Even in those early years, however, "arranging" was only his means to an end. What he really wanted, then, was to conduct orchestras and to write music criticism.

Robert Russell Bennett was born in Kansas City, on June 15, 1894.

Modern Music-Makers

When he was four years old he had infantile paralysis, and the family moved to a farm some forty miles south of Kansas City, hoping that country life would restore the boy's health. He did recover almost entirely from his early affliction, and was even able to join in the sports and games of other boys (baseball was his favorite). But all during his childhood, no matter what he was doing he would "stop and run toward any music he heard."

His parents were of pure Yankee stock (Mrs. Bennett traced her descent from the second New England governor, William Bradford) and they were both musical. At the age of three, Russell startled his mother by standing in front of the piano and picking out the melody of a Beethoven sonata he had heard her play. When he was five she gave him piano lessons; then his father taught him violin and trumpet. Soon after moving from Kansas City to the country, the elder Bennett assembled the musicians of his neighborhood and organized a band-orchestra. Young Russell learned to play most of the instruments in the band; whenever one of the musicians failed to turn up he would take the absent man's place.

Before long his father let him conduct the band. At ten he appeared as soloist on a Chautauqua tour, and gave piano recitals. His parents only allowed him to play the classics—"popular music was taboo. . . ." When one day he jauntily tossed off a current popular tune, his mother "gave him a good slap on the face." This graphically taught him the difference between the two types of music, and may have been responsible for a certain sense of guilt he has felt in later years, in turning his talents to the arranging of popular music.

It was not until he was fifteen that he began to study harmony seriously. At that time he moved into Kansas City and took lessons of Karl Busch, a Danish musician. Soon after, one of his early pieces, romantically titled *June Twilight*, was printed in the *Etude* magazine.

Russell Bennett now began to search out for wider horizons. New York, he felt, was the best place for an ambitious, forward-looking young musician. But it would take money to get started in the big city. He was nearly twenty before he had saved up what seemed to him a magnificent sum, quite sufficient to launch a new career. With $200 in his pocket, "and a lot of nerve," he struck out for the East. New York was half a continent away; in order not to deplete his nest egg too much, he tramped and hitch-hiked a good part of the way.

Robert Russell Bennett

Arrived in the metropolis young Bennett took any job he could find, playing in dance halls or as a "piano-pounder" in cheap restaurants. But he liked neither the environment nor the people he had to work with. Finally he got a job at Schirmer's copying music. One of his first assignments was a piece from the musical comedy *Maytime*.

Bennett was still at Schirmer's when the United States entered the First World War. Immediately he enlisted—"lied his way into the army," as he puts it, for he was hardly fit for active duty. How he managed to get in is still a mystery. At camp Funston in Kansas the examining doctor chalked a white circle on his chest—to indicate, Bennett explains, "that his feet were no good." But in spite of a slight lameness—aftermath of his early infantile paralysis—he passed the tests and became a full-fledged doughboy in the infantry.

First he was assigned to K. P. duty. In his off hours he played the piano, and did some orchestrations and dance arrangements. These were so successful that after the war ended Bennett decided to cash in on his experience. It was then that he applied to the J. B. Harms and Company and made his first success with Cole Porter's piece.

In 1919 Russell Bennett married Louise Merrill. (They have one daughter, Jean). His wife felt that he should use his talents to more serious purpose. "You ought to compose," she told him.

Bennett was only half convinced. "Too much music has already been written," he insisted. Nevertheless, now and then he would write down a theme that occurred to him, and sometimes even a full-length piece. He began to dream of going abroad, and of studying composition seriously.

Finally in 1926, when he and his wife had laid aside a sufficient amount, they went for a year to Paris. There he worked with Nadia Boulanger, and she encouraged him to go on with his creative work. While he was in Paris that winter, Bennett wrote a number of compositions. Among them was his *First Symphony*. It received Honorable Mention in the 1926 Musical America contest.

At the end of the year the Bennetts returned to the United States, but soon after he was awarded a Guggenheim Fellowship (extended through 1928) and they were able to go back to Europe. There they divided their time between London, Paris and Berlin.

In spite of his close association with the French school, that first year when he began to work seriously, Russell Bennett's music was not affected by its influence. When he decided to write a Second Symphony, he wanted to find a subject that would be definitely American.

He was pacing the streets of Berlin one day, trying to think of something appropriate. "I had just recently been reading Lord Charnwood's biography of Lincoln," he says. "This work impressed me greatly. Suddenly the idea came to me that here was a perfect subject for my symphony."

He called it the *Abraham Lincoln Symphony*. Soon after he had finished it he heard that the Radio Corporation of America was offering a prize of $25,000 for the best composition by an American composer. At that time, in spite of the work he had already done, Bennett was still undecided as to whether he should go on writing music.

"I will make a little bargain with myself," he said. "I'll submit two works for the contest [the *Lincoln Symphony* and another orchestral piece called *Sights and Sounds*]. If either of these wins even a mention, I'll go on composing."

The judges of the contest couldn't agree on any single work submitted for the prize. It was finally divided into five parts of $5,000 each. One part went to Aaron Copland for his *Dance Symphony*, one to Ernest Bloch, and one to Louis Gruenberg. The remaining two parts were both awarded to Robert Russell Bennett. According to his bargain he had to go on writing music.

Bennett had composed six symphonies in all. The *Third* was commissioned by the New York radio station W.O.R. for publicity connected with baseball advertising. He called it *Symphony in D—for Dodgers*. The fourth movement, in chorale form, contained an announcement by Red Barber who described a fictitious baseball inning. This work was first played over the radio and later at the Stadium in New York, with Red Barber again as announcer. The *Fourth Symphony*, "On College Themes" was also a radio commission, written for football day.

Most popular of all Bennett's symphonies is his *Fifth*. In 1942 everybody in the United States was familiar with Norman Rockwell's famous *Four Freedoms*, painted for the war bond drive. The *Saturday Evening Post* commissioned Bennett, as a contribution to the war effort, to write some music describing the picture. The idea appealed to him strongly. He composed a symphony in four movements, each

ROBERT RUSSELL BENNETT

Robert Russell Bennett

interpreting one of the Four Freedoms depicted in Rockwell's painting.

Bennett's symphony won immediate success, and soon was being played all over the country. It had its first performance over the air, Frank Black conducting. Eugene Ormandy heard this broadcast and was so impressed by it that during the following season he played the *Four Freedoms Symphony* a dozen times with the Philadelphia orchestra. It was performed repeatedly during the war, both over the radio and in concert.

Bennett says he is tempted to call his *Sixth Symphony* (1948) the "First," because this last one was written exactly as he wanted it, and not at anyone else's suggestion or command. "There is nothing back of it. No commission—no special reason for writing it. . . . And no one needs to like it but me!"

Earlier in his career, Robert Russell Bennett wrote an "Operetta Ballet a l'Antique," called *Endymion*, shortly after this a one-act opera, *An Hour of Delusion*, and seven years later, *Maria Malibran*— a full length opera. This last was produced at Juilliard in February, 1935—the third American opera to be put on there. (Louis Gruenberg's *Jack and the Beanstalk* and George Antheil's *Helen Retires* were the two previous ones.)

The libretto of Bennett's opera is by Robert A. Simon—music critic at that time of *The New Yorker*. It is based on an incident in the brief life of the young singer Maria Garcia (said to have "set the world on fire" by her phenomenal voice) who was forced by her father to marry the aged libertine Malibran.

Lawrence Gilman, the late distinguished critic of the *New York Herald Tribune*, spoke highly of Russell Bennett's score:

This is not only music of rare delicacy and subtlety of facture, beautifully, knowingly, and reticently orchestrated, but it is music of a composer who has worked out for himself a very personal sort of poetic comedy—deft, sly, subtly textured.[1]

Oscar Thompson thought that *Maria Malibran* should be called a musical romance or comedy with music instead of opera, because "so

[1] *New York Herald Tribune*, April 9, 1935.

Modern Music-Makers

much of the text is spoken rather than sung and so much of the music assumes an incidental character in accompanying rather than projecting the dialogue."[2]

This style of opera writing, however, was deliberate on Bennett's part. He explains it as "a typically American approach to grand opera. . . . At all times it attempts to keep the action and story uninterrupted by arias or vocal soliloquy that are not part of the plot, thus using a formula toward which the films and musical plays of the day are gradually pointing."

From his opera Bennett drew an orchestral score—*Orchestral Fragments from the American Opera Maria Malibran*. The greater part of Russell Bennett's music has been in the orchestral field. In addition to his six symphonies he has composed *March for Two Pianos and Orchestra* (1930), *Eight Etudes for Symphony Orchestra* (1938), *Concerto for Violin and Orchestra* (1941), *Suite of Old American Dances* (1949), *Overture to the Mississippi*, and a long list of others. His chamber-music works include *Toy Symphony* and *Dance Scherzo*, both for woodwind quintet, and *Water Music* for string quartet; for violin he has written a *Sonata, Hexapoda, Five Tune Cartoons* and *Allemande*. Also a number of works featuring the flute: *Rondo Capriccioso—for Four Flutes, A Valentine—for Flute, Harp, Quartet, Five Improvisations on Exotic Scales for Flute, Piano, Cello*, and *Six Souvenirs—for Two Flutes and One Piano*. In 1946 he did an orchestral number with the flute as solo instrument: *A Dry Weather Legend*.

So far Bennett has written only a few songs. He says he would like to write more, but he hasn't been able to find the right poems to set to music. "If the poem is beautiful enough it doesn't need music—and vice versa. It's the age-old argument between words and music." (In the realm of popular music, according to Bennett, Irving Berlin is the greatest song writer of the day.)

Robert Russell Bennett's success in the 1930 RCA contest brought him inevitably to the attention of Hollywood. Before long he was in California arranging music for the films. During the years he spent in the West he found little time for his own composing. For the League of Composers, who commissioned him to do an orchestral work, he

---

[2] *Musical America*, April 25, 1935.

Robert Russell Bennett

wrote a piece which he named *Hollywood.* It was first played over NBC. *Eight Etudes for Symphonic Orchestra,* (1938) and *World's Fair for Symphonic Band,* also date from this period.

In 1940 he returned to New York to inaugurate a radio program called "Russell Bennett's Notebook." He planned the programs, personally conducted the orchestra, and wrote most of the music that went over the air. This music was partly his own, partly arrangements of familiar melodies which he wove into what he called "Music Box Operas." Among them were *Clementine, My Old Kentucky Home,* and *The Man on the Flying Trapeze.*

After Bennett returned from Hollywood he found himself more than ever in demand for orchestrating current Broadway musical shows. Popular-music writers seldom have the training necessary for intricate part-writing. Some hardly know the meaning of the word counterpoint; they can make up tunes—often good ones—but even the simplest accompaniment requires at least a little understanding of harmony, and is beyond the powers of some of the composers who have cashed in most heavily on popular favor. On the other hand professional "arrangers" can write out harmonizations but usually possess not the slightest originality.

Robert Russell Bennett's extraordinary success in this field comes from the fact that he is not only thoroughly trained in the mechanics of music, with an intimate knowledge of every instrument in the orchestra, but is at the same time a creative artist who manages to give a fresh and individual turn to whatever music he may be orchestrating.

He himself, with typical diffidence, is inclined to discount the high praise he has received for his musical arrangements. "The orchestrator's value is his sensitiveness to melody," he says. "If the melody has something to say, he can put colors into the outlines—if the melody has nothing to say, he is powerless."

The work Russell Bennett does for Broadway is to him purely a means of livelihood. "If you hold to the highest ideals in art," he says, "You have to make your living in some other way." Most of his fellow composers undoubtedly agree with him. To supplement the meager income from their creative work they hold positions as teachers and professors, as executives in universities and music schools, conductors of orchestras, or write articles and books on music.

187

Modern Music-Makers

All of these activities Bennett would call legitimate sidelines of a composer's career. But traffic with commercial music, particularly of the type found on Broadway, he feels, is a different matter. The purpose behind jazz and popular music, and most of the picture productions, is financial success rather than artistic integrity. The music, written according to a set formula, is intended solely for making money.

"Of all the 'potboiling' (as composers are pleased to call it)," says Bennett, "it seems to me that the worst is mine, which in a way prostitutes the very art I venerate. Working with music that goes from formula to formula in a desperate struggle for the utterly obvious, something must be happening to my soul, especially since I am successful at it!"

Judging from the success of Bennett's more serious music, there has been so far no damage to his creative powers. Even his gift for arrangements has been channeled into a classical mold. He has drawn "symphonic pictures" from a number of well-known popular scores, such as *Porgy and Bess, Carousel, Finian's Rainbow, Lady in the Dark, Kiss me Kate, South Pacific,* and a *Symphonic Story of Jerome Kern.* These have been widely played all over the country by leading symphony orchestras.

Today Russell Bennett, with his silver hair and tall, erect figure, looks like a distinguished and successful business man rather than the traditional long-haired musician, a type that seems to have disappeared with the romantic music of an earlier age.

Bennett now spends most of his time in New York. There, in a sunny corner of his Park Avenue apartment, he does a large part of his work. His desk is littered with knicknacks—books, ink-bottles, sheets of music paper, figurines—and "Perky."

Perky is a diminutive, much the worse-for-wear, toy cat who has been Russell Bennett's mascot for many years. He looks like a veteran, with one leg done up in splints and bandages, and a black patch over one beady eye.

"It's Perky who has written most of my music," says the composer with a small-boy grin. "When I work late at night, or get discouraged, he looks at me with that cocky one eye of his as much as to say "Keep going . . . you can do it!"

Robert Russell Bennett

Between them, Perky and his master turn out a prodigious amount of music. And so, in spite of having to give so much of his time to the orchestrating of other men's music, Russell Bennett has managed to produce a long list of his own, more serious works. These compositions place him among the eminent American composers of today.

Robert Russell Bennett

Born June 15, Kansas City, Mo.	1894
Aged ten plays on Chautauqua tours	1904
Moves to New York	1913
Enlists in army	1918
Music arranger for E. P. Harms & Co.	1919
Marries Louise Merrill	
Goes to Paris to study with Nadia Boulanger	1926
First Symphony	
Second Symphony: Abraham Lincoln	1927
Guggenheim Fellowship	
Goes to Hollywood	1931
Maria Malibran (Opera)	1932
Hollywood	1936
Dance Scherzo (Woodwind Quintet)	1937
Water Music (String Quartet)	1938
Returns to New York	1940
Inaugurates radio program "Russell Bennett's Notebook"	
Symphony in "D" for Dodgers (Third)	1941
Fourth Symphony On College Themes	
A Symphonic Picture of Gershwin's "Porgy and Bess"	1942
Fifth Symphony: The Four Freedoms	1943
A Symphonic Picture of Jerome Kern	1946
Six Souvenirs for Two Flutes and One Piano	1948
Suite of Old American Dances (for Band)	1949
Suite of Old American Dances (for Band)	1949
Overture to the Mississippi	1950

The Music of Robert Russell Bennett

Modern Music-Makers

CHORAL WORKS

Lorelei—women's chorus and piano	1927
Nietsche Variations—women's chorus and piano	1927
Aux quatre coins de Paris	1928
Crazy Cantata No. 1—based on *Three Blind Mice*	1945
Chester—based on hymn of William Billings, contralto, baritone, chorus and orchestra [3]	1945

CHAMBER MUSIC

Rondo Capriccioso—four flutes	1916
Toy Symphony—woodwind quintet	1926
Sonata for Violin and Piano	1927
Sonata for Organ [4]	1928
Dance Scherzo—woodwind quintet	1937
Water Music—string quartet	1938
Hexapoda [3]	1940
Concerto for Viola and Harp	1941
A Valentine—flute, harp, quartet	1942
Five Improvisations on Exotic Scales—flute, piano, cello	1947
Song Sonata—violin, piano	1947
Six Souvenirs—two flutes, piano	1948
Allemande, violin	1949
Sonatine for Soprano and Harp	1947

STAGE WORKS

Endymion—"operetta ballet a l'antique"	1926
An Hour of Delusion—one-act opera	1928
Maria Malibran	1932
"Music Box Operas"—for radio	1940-1941

    1 *Clementine*
    2 *Flying Trapeze*
    3 *Band Played On*
    4 *Kafoozalem*
    5 *Kentucky Home*

Robert Russell Bennett

ARRANGEMENTS

A Symphonic Picture of Gershwin's "Porgy and Bess" [5]	1942
A Symphonic Story of Jerome Kern [1]	1946
A Symphonic Picture of "Carousel" [6]	1946
A Symphonic Picture of "Finian's Rainbow" [3]	1947
A Symphonic Picture of "Lady in the Dark" [3]	1949
A Symphonic Picture of "Kiss me Kate" [3]	1949
A Symphonic Synthesis of "South Pacific" [6]	1949

PIANO WORKS

Seven Fox Trots	1927
"Vu" (Seen in Paris) [7]	1928
Sonatina	1943
Tema Sporca con Variazoni—two pianos	1946

SONGS

Three Songs (Chaucer) with string quartet	1927
Four Songs (Sara Teasdale)	1928
Seven Love Songs with Ukelele accompaniment [1]	1929

[1] Harms.
[2] Robbins.
[3] Chappell.
[4] New Music Press.
[5] Gershwin Pub. Co.
[6] Williamson.
[7] Raoul Breton, Paris '29.

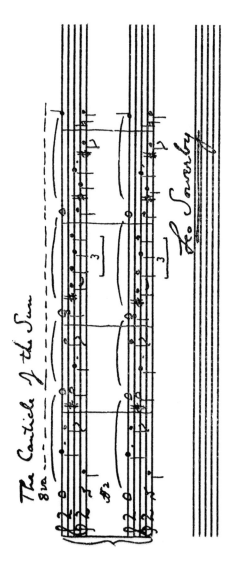

LEO SOWERBY

LEO SOWERBY

LEO SOWERBY is head of the Music Department at the American Conservatory in Chicago, and he also holds the important post of organist and choirmaster at St. James' Episcopal Church in that city. In addition to his many symphonic and chamber-music works, he has written extensively for the church, and is one of our foremost composers of ecclesiastical music.

Sowerby wrote his first publicly performed piece (a violin concerto) when he was only eighteen. At that time—1913—Glenn Dillard Gunn, music critic and champion of modern composers, decided to present a concert devoted exclusively to contemporary music. This was considered a good deal of a venture, for programs in those days were made up almost entirely of time-honored classics (as they generally are today), and the only way an audience could be made to listen to the music of native-born composers was by sandwiching an occasional work in between the older more familiar pieces. Gunn hired the Chicago Symphony Orchestra and asked a number of American composers to participate in his concert. Among them was red-headed Leo Sowerby; Gunn had heard some of his music and believed that the boy had a future.

Sowerby wrote a violin concerto especially for the occasion. It seemed to please the public, he says, though the critics insisted that "it displayed no musical ability." "They landed on my concerto with all fours," he admits, "and, as I subsequently learned, not without much justification."

He was far from satisfied with that early work; but hearing it played taught him a lot. "During the half-hour that I listened to the rehearsal I learned more about orchestration than in all the rest of my life put together." Eleven years later he "cut the concerto 50 percent and rewrote it almost entirely."

Although Leo Sowerby had gone through the regular course at the American Conservatory of Music in Chicago ("whizzed through the four years in one,") he was largely self-taught. It was his step-mother who first started him in music. Born in Grand Rapids, Michigan, on May 1, 1895, he lost his mother when he was four. Two years later his father married again, and his new stepmother became as devoted to Leo as he to her. Recognizing his talent for music, she insisted that he must have piano lessons. His teacher until he finished grammar school was Mrs. Frederick Burton.

At the age of eleven Leo decided that he would like to compose. He went to the library of his native Grand Rapids, took out a text-book on harmony, and entirely on his own proceeded to master its contents. He succeeded so well that when three years later he went to study in Chicago, his new teacher, Calvin Lampert, was amazed at the boy's knowledge. Lampert sent him to Arthur Olaf Andersen, at the American Conservatory of Music in Chicago.

The following year Leo, aged fifteen, wanted to play the organ. He couldn't afford twenty-five cents an hour for the use of an instrument to practise on. However, when Leo Sowerby wanted anything badly enough he always found some way to get it. He was "redheaded and spunky," as one writer put it,[1] "though not in an aggressive way. On the contrary . . . soft-spoken and shy. . . ."

Determined to master the organ, young Sowerby went about it in a highly original way. He stopped at a butcher shop and asked for a large sheet of brown wrapping paper. Then he took the paper to a near-by church, laid it out on the floor, and painstakingly drew a sketch of the organ's foot-pedal board. By placing the paper dummy beneath his own piano at home, he could practise exercises in foot technique—that most difficult part of organ-playing. At the same time he studied every book he could find on the subject, from the construction of the instrument to the actual technique of playing. Although he only had six actual lessons on the organ, sheer determination and hard work eventually made him one of the best performers in the country, and brought him an appointment as organist to St. James' Episcopal Church in Chicago.

When Sowerby began to compose he was so full of rules from the various textbooks he had memorized that his first efforts resembled, he says, pedantic contrapuntal exercises. Then he heard a concert by

[1] Burnet C. Tuthill in the July, 1938, *Musical Quarterly*.

Leo Sowerby

some English singers—the Fuller sisters—who specialized in folk songs. Possibly because of his own Anglo-Saxon heritage (his father was English and his mother Canadian), their music appealed strongly to young Sowerby, and he attended every concert that they gave.

About this same period he met Percy Grainger, and for a time studied with him. Grainger's music also stems from folk tunes, and his influence, together with that of the Fuller sisters, helped to bring Sowerby back to a more simple, direct way of composition. From too much concern with the technical side of his art, he now returned to the source. His first printed work, in 1916, called *The Irish Washerwoman,* was based on a folk tune—a jig attributed to an eighteenth-century Irish piper celebrated for his skill on the bagpipes. Sowerby wrote it first for piano and later orchestrated it; it is still one of his most widely played pieces. This and others in the same idiom "have a lilt and syncopation . . . a rhythmic crispness, a simplicity of tonality and a frankness and directness that belong to our native soil. His own directions for their performance characterize them accurately; 'with ginger,' 'brisk and pert,' 'at a steady trot,' 'in a free and easygoing manner' . . ." [2]

Two other important works were written in 1916, when Sowerby was still only twenty-one: *Serenade for String Quartet,* presented as a birthday gift to Elizabeth Sprague Coolidge and first performed at the 1918 Berkshire Music Festival; and *Comes Autumn Time*—originally an overture for organ, later transcribed for orchestra. This overture was inspired by Bliss Carman's poem *Autumn:*

> Now when the time of fruit and grain is come,
> When apples hang above the orchard wall
> Comes Autumn with her sunburnt caravan
> Like a long Gypsy train with trappings gay.

In January, 1917, a group of young Sowerby's friends sponsored an entire program of his works, with Eric DeLamarter directing the concert at Chicago's Orchestra Hall. Again the critics "landed on all fours." Not a single number escaped abuse. Sowerby would have been considerably discouraged if Frederick Stock, conductor of the Chicago Symphony Orchestra, had not stood up for him.

[2] Burnet C. Tuthill, *Musical Quarterly,* July, 1938.

Modern Music-Makers

"I like your music," he said. "Will you write a suite for our orchestra?"

Dr. Stock's opinion was worth more to Sowerby than that of the critics. After all, he reasoned, critics *could* be wrong. And subsequently he was justified, for later on these same men admitted that they had misjudged those early works and praised the music that at first they had condemned.

For Stock and the Chicago Symphony Leo Sowerby wrote *A Set of Four*. The ink was hardly dry on his score when, on America's entering the First World War, he immediately tried to enlist. At first the recruiting officers would not accept him because of his eyes. But he continued to "bang on the door"—as he expresses it—and was finally admitted as an ordinary private.

"You may be a musician," the Colonel of the regiment told him, "but what you need is military experience." After some preliminary training, (including the grooming of horses) Sowerby was put into the band, where he played the clarinet. A few months later he became bandleader and was elevated to the rank of Second Lieutenant.

He was still a private at Camp Grant in Rockford, Illinois, when *A Set of Four* was scheduled at one of the Chicago Symphony concerts. He asked permission to go up to Chicago to hear it. This time his music was much better received, and there were excellent reviews. On the train going back to camp, Sowerby found a group of officers reading the reviews, and they seemed highly impressed. When he reached camp his commanding officer called him in: "You have been promoted to the rank of third-class musician" he said. This, Sowerby admits, meant more to him than all the public acclaim given *A Set of Four*.

He sailed overseas with his regiment and spent six months in France. On his return he began once more to compose. Between 1919 and 1921 he wrote his *First Symphony*, a number of chamber-music works, and an organ piece *Requiescat in Pace* in memory of his fallen comrades in France.

In 1921 Leo Sowerby learned that he had been awarded the first fellowship to be offered by the recently established American Academy in Rome. "How can that be?" he asked in surprise. "I didn't compete, nor send in any compositions for approval."

The judges, he learned, had decided that none of the music that

Leo Sowerby

had been submitted was in their estimation worthy of receiving the Rome Prize; so they had awarded it to Leo Sowerby solely on the merits of his work and his reputation as a composer. The Prize entitled him to three years' residence at the picturesque villa maintained by the American Academy in Rome.

With the exception of his experience in the war, Sowerby had always led a very secluded life. His stay in Rome, with its environment of Old World culture and cosmopolitan atmosphere, together with the close association with working artists of other nationalities, helped to broaden his outlook and to give fresh impetus to his work.

King Estmere—a ballad for two pianos and orchestra—was one of his first works while in Italy. It is founded on an ancient tale of a "bright and shining princess" who is about to marry "the paynim King of Spain," but is rescued by King Estmere and his brother disguised as harper and servant.

Albert Coates conducted the first performance of this work at the Augusteo in Rome. It was a gala occasion, with many of the nobility present—and, of course, all of Sowerby's American friends. At the end of the performance, these latter broke into loud applause and shrill whistles of approval. The Italians looked at them in pained surprise. Finally there was a moment of dead silence.

"What's wrong?" one of the Americans whispered to the Roman lady who had accompanied him. "Well," the lady exclaimed indignantly, "if you don't like your friend's music, the least you could do, I should think, is to keep silent!" Then the truth of the matter dawned on him: in Italy whistling, like hissing, is a mark of extreme disapproval.

Sowerby wrote a number of compositions during his three years in Rome: chamber music; a long oratorio in five parts based on the *Book of Psalms* and scored for large chorus, organ, and full orchestra; and a suite for piano called *From the Northland*. This last has four parts: *Forest Voices, Cascades, Burnt Rock Pool*, and the final movement—in memory of his native Lake Michigan—*The Shining Big Sea Water. From the Northland* was later orchestrated.

When Leo Sowerby came back to the United States he joined the faculty of the American Conservatory of Music in Chicago as teacher of theory and music history (he now heads the department of composition there), and during every spare moment continued to write

199

Modern Music-Makers

music. In Europe he had found the foreign musicians highly interested in American jazz. Many of them were trying it out in their own music, and Gershwin's *Rhapsody in Blue*—commissioned by Paul Whiteman for his "symphonic-jazz" concerts—had just taken the United States by storm. Sowerby too had been experimenting with jazz rhythms. When Whiteman invited him to compose some classic-jazz numbers for his orchestra, he contributed two pieces which he called *Monotony* and *Sinconata*.

For the performance of *Monotony* a huge metronome was set at the front of the stage. It appeared to direct the orchestra with its swinging arm, though Paul Whiteman, concealed, did the actual conducting. The beat of the instrument never varied but maintained, through every change of rhythm, a slow monotonous ticking. The work was in four movements, each in satirical mood; one describing an argument between a married couple; another ridiculing the droning of a tiresome old preacher; and a third the shrill chattering of a group of music critics.

Sowerby next turned his attention to more serious composition. Between his "popular" pieces, such as the rollicking *Irish Washerwoman* and jazz numbers, and his serious works (especially the later ecclesiastical music) there is such a contrast that Sowerby once called himself "the Doctor Jekyll and Mr. Hyde of music."

"I have been accused by right-wingers of being too dissonant and cacophonous," he confesses, "and by the leftists of being old-fashioned and derivative." Oscar Sonneck inclined to the first opinion and once commented somewhat caustically by adding to the chestnut about the three B's (Bach, Beethoven and Brahms,) a fourth—"Sour B."

In 1925 Sowerby composed *The Vision of Sir Launfal,* a choral work with orchestra. After that came *Medieval Poem,* for organ and orchestra, dedicated to Howard Hanson and inspired by a hymn from the liturgy of St. James beginning:

> Let all mortal flesh keep silence,
> And with fear and trembling stand.

His *Second Symphony* being completed in 1927, Leo Sowerby started work on one of his best known compositions—a symphonic

LEO SOWERBY

Leo Sowerby

poem called *Prairie*. This graphically interprets the lines from Carl Sandburg's poem by the same name (from the collection called *Cornhuskers*).

Have you seen a red sunset drip over one of my cornfields, the shore of night stars, the wave lines of dawn up a wheat valley?
Have you heard my threshing crews yelling in the chaff of a strawpile and the running wheat of the wagon boards, my cornhuskers, my harvest hands hauling crops, singing dreams of women, worlds, horizons?

Sowerby constructed this symphonic poem "in such a way that sections seeking to interpret the moods of the poet's 'red sunset,' 'shore of night stars,' 'wave lines of dawn,' 'threshing crews yelling in the chaff of the straw pile' follow one another in succession without break or special line of demarcation." Lawrence Gilman in writing about *Prairie* called it "virile, poetic, imaginative. There is in it something of the sweep and largeness and mysteriousness of earth and sky and light—something timeless and elemental."

Sowerby finished a third *Symphony* in 1940, and a fourth in 1948. Serge Koussevitzky gave the first performance of this last in January, 1949.

Leo Sowerby's long list of chamber-music works includes two string quartets and two quintets for wood-winds. The second of the quintets is an amusing development of variations on the theme *Pop Goes the Weasel*. The first quintet won the award of the Society for the Publication of American Music. He had already received this honor twice before—in 1921 for the *Serenade for String Quartet,* and in 1927 for his orchestral suite *From the Northland*. Again, in 1943 a *Sonata for Clarinet and Piano* became the fourth of his compositions to be chosen by the society. Several of Sowerby's chamber-music works have been played at the Elizabeth Sprague Coolidge festivals.

He has received a long list of awards—including a Pulitzer prize in 1946 for a choral work based on St. Francis of Assisi's *Canticle of the Sun*. In addition to his other honors, the University of Rochester conferred on him in 1934 the degree of Doctor of Music. He is a member of the American Institute of Arts and Letters and an honorary member of the Bandmaster's Association; and he has received the Eastman School Publication Award and that of the Society for the Publication of American Music.

Three years after Sowerby's return from Rome, in 1927, he was appointed organist and choirmaster to St. James' Church in Chicago. Since then he has made nearly a dozen musical settings for the various services of the Episcopal Church, and has written a large number of anthems and choral and organ works. Among the best known of these latter are *Carillon; A Joyous March* ("one of the few excellent marches written for the organ"); *Pageant; Symphony for Organ* (written in 1930 and recorded by E. Power Biggs for the Columbia Recording Corporation); *Concerto for Organ and Orchestra* (played by Mr. Biggs and the Boston Symphony in April, 1938); and a *Ballade for English Horn and Organ*.

Leo Sowerby was not brought up an Episcopalian, and he says that until his appointment to St. James he had never really appreciated what the Church meant. His close contact with its services and liturgy brought him a new and deeper understanding of religion, and in the year following his appointment as organist he was confirmed in the church. Going in first as a worker, then as a member of the church through confirmation, has given him, he says, a different and more reverent approach to his creative work. "It is not possible to write satisfactory ecclesiastical music unless praise of God is the purpose."

Like Bach, who wrote at the beginning of all his works "IN NOMINE DEO," Leo Sowerby's best efforts have been dedicated to this higher source. Although he has distinguished himself in every field of music, he will be particularly remembered for his contribution to the music of the Church.

Leo Sowerby

Born May 1, Grand Rapids, Michigan	1895
Enrolls at American Conservatory of Music in Chicago	
The Irish Washerwoman	1916
Serenade for String Quartet	
Comes Autumn Time	
A Set of Four	1917
Enlists in U. S. Army. Goes to France	1917
Awarded first Rome Prize. Goes to Rome for three years	1921
First Symphony	
King Estmere	
The Vision of Sir Launfal	1925
Medieval Poem	1926
Second Symphony	1927
Appointed organist and choirmaster of St. James in Chicago	
Prairie	1929
Symphony for Organ	1930
Doctor of Music degree from University of Rochester	1934
Concerto for Organ and Orchestra	1938
Third Symphony	1940
Canticle of the Sun	1943
Awarded Pulitzer Prize	1946
Fourth Symphony	1948

The Music of Leo Sowerby

Orchestral Works

The Irish Washerwoman [1]	1916
Comes Autumn Time (overture) [1]	1916
Set of Four [2]	1917
First Concerto for Piano and Orchestra	1919
First Symphony	1921
King Estmere—two pianos and orchestra	1922
Suite from the Northland [1]	1923
Rhapsody—chamber orchestra	1923
Money Musk [2]	1924
Medieval Poem—organ [3]	1926
Second Symphony	1927
Prairie [2]	1929
Passacaglia, Interlude and Fugue	1931
Second Concerto for Piano and Orchestra	1932
Concerto for Cello and Orchestra	1933
Sinfonietta—string orchestra	1934
Concerto for Organ and Orchestra	1937
Theme in Yellow	1938
Third Symphony	1940
Concert Overture [4]	1941
Fantasy on Hymn Tunes	1943
"Classic" Concerto for organ and orchestra [5]	1944
Portrait	1946
Third Symphony	1948

Choral Works

Vision of Sir Launfal—3 solos, chorus [2]	1925
Great is the Lord—chorus, organ [5]	1934
Te Deum in D Minor—chorus, organ [6]	1936
Song for America—chorus, orchestra [5]	1942
Forsaken of Man—chorus, organ [5]	1942
Canticle of the Sun—chorus, orchestra [5]	1943

Leo Sowerby

CHAMBER MUSIC

Suite for Violin and Piano [1]	1916
Serenade for String Quartet [7]	1916
Quintet for flute, oboe, clarinet, bassoon, horn [8]	1916
Sonata for Cello and Piano	1921
Sonata for Violin and Piano [9]	1922
First String Quartet	1923
Pop Goes the Weasel—flute, oboe, clarinet, bassoon, horn [6]	1927
Second String Quartet	1935
Sonata for Clarinet and Piano [7]	1938
Second Sonata for Violin and Piano [10]	1944
Sonata for Trumpet and Piano	1945
Songs of Resignation—baritone, violin, clarinet and piano	1948

ORGAN WORKS

Symphony for Organ [11]	1930
Suite for Organ [11]	1933
Poem for Viola and Organ [5]	1942
Ballad for English Horn and Organ [5]	1948

PIANO

Suite "From the Northland" [1]	1923
Suite "Florida" [11]	1929

[1] Boston Music Co.
[2] C. C. Birchard & Co.
[3] Eastman School.
[4] Music Press.
[5] H. W. Gray & Co., Inc.
[6] H. T. Fitzsimons Co.
[7] S.P.A.M.
[8] G. Schirmer, Inc.
[9] Universal Edition.
[10] Remick Music Corp.
[11] Oxford University Press.

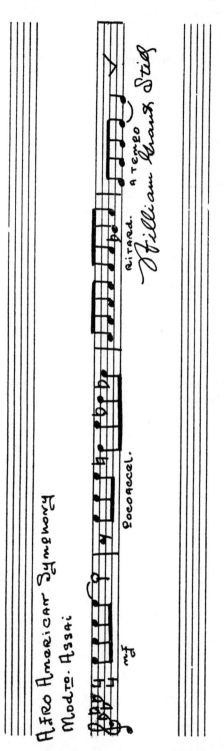

WILLIAM GRANT STILL

WILLIAM GRANT STILL

IN a book by E. R. Embree, called *Thirteen against the Odds*, William Grant Still is included as one of the thirteen greatest living Negroes. He is not only the leading composer of his own race, but he ranks among the most honored of all our contemporary composers.

Still's ancestry includes pioneer Scotch and Irish stock, Spanish, and even American Indian blood. His mother, Carrie Fambro Still, was an unusual woman—interested, as her son explains, "in everything along mental lines." She taught literature in Little Rock High School, and also lectured and had artistic leanings. She wanted her son to be a scientist, like the great George Washington Carver. Still's father was also a teacher—of mathematics, and music on the side, who had educated himself largely through his own efforts, and who had even tried to do a little composing. He would travel a distance of seventy-five miles for each cornet lesson. If he had lived he would undoubtedly have encouraged his son's talent. But he died when the latter was only a few months old.

William Grant Still was born in Woodville, Mississippi, May 11, 1895. Soon after his father's death he moved with his mother to Little Rock, Arkansas. She married again a few years later. Bill's stepfather, a postal employee, loved music—particularly opera; he invested his savings in a phonograph, and every penny that could be spared went into Red Seal records. Bill would play these records over and over. "I loved that music so much!" he says with a nostalgic sigh.

Aside from his passion for the phonograph, however, he was not at that time especially interested in music—particularly of the folk variety, though he often heard his old grandmother singing spirituals as she worked around the house. He preferred making things with his hands (Still has always been very clever with tools). Among other things he manufactured some toy violins, complete with strings and varnish. They even made music—of a kind.

Modern Music-Makers

Bill's mother gave him a real violin after he started high school, and then music suddenly became his major interest. Not that he neglected his studies. He graduated at sixteen from the Little Rock High School, a First Honor Bearer and Valedictorian of his class.

He begged his mother to let him go to Oberlin Conservatory. But she "couldn't see a musical career for him," so to please her he went instead to Wilberforce University. There he met other students who, like himself, were music fans. They would go together to neighboring Dayton to attend the opera. Bill took lessons on the clarinet and joined the college band. Before long he was made leader and gradually learned to play many different instruments.

Most of his allowance while at Wilberforce was spent on music books and opera scores. He arranged music for the band and for the college string quartet, and even wrote some original pieces that were played at a concert during his last year at Wilberforce. His other studies, however, did not interest him particularly. During French class he usually had his nose in a music book.

Bill was always, according to his admission, "up to some devilment or other." Four months before graduation he left Wilberforce, struck out on his own, and was briefly married. His mother was sadly disappointed when he failed to receive a diploma with the rest of his class. She little suspected that Wilberforce would not only eventually grant him the degree he missed, but would also confer on him an honorary Doctor of Music.

Still now went to Columbus, Ohio, where he had to make his living as best he could. One of his first jobs netted him $6.00 a week. Gradually he got into musical work—joined a band and played with a small orchestra at the Athletic Club.

At twenty-one he received a small legacy from his father's estate, and decided to go to Oberlin Conservatory. His mother did not help him—she insisted that he must do it on his own. He understood her attitude. "She was wise . . . I wouldn't criticize her," he says. "I don't believe either in coddling anyone."

His legacy didn't stretch as far as he had hoped. To supplement it while at Oberlin he played in picture shows, waited on table and helped the janitor. When he was supposed to be sweeping out the library, he studied Wagner's scores. ("It mean everything to me to be able to get at them!")

William Grant Still

Theory was young Still's favorite subject. He would spend hours and hours at it. The theory teacher, Professor Lehman, was so impressed by the clever musical setting of a poem he turned in one day that he said "Why don't you study composition?"

The young man looked away for a moment before answering. Then he faced the issue squarely. "Because I haven't the money!"

That evening Professor Lehman called a meeting of the Theory Committee. "This student has exceptional talent," he told them. "He could become a first-rate composer if he had a chance to go on with his studies. Couldn't we create a scholarship in composition?"

The committee voted on the matter, and finally decided to establish a special scholarship, which they awarded to William Grant Still. He was tremendously encouraged by their faith in his ability. Now, he felt, his mother might be willing to admit that he had been justified in choosing a musical career.

In 1918, when the United States entered the First World War, Still enlisted in the Navy. He went to New York—his first visit—and walked the streets until he was ready to drop with fatigue. Then he got on a streetcar. "Suddenly there in front of me was the Metropolitan Opera House!" A performance of *Rigoletto* was just about to begin; he climbed up to the Family Circle, and that evening, he says, turned out to be one of the high-lights of his life. Opera has ever since remained his greatest love.

Still was assigned to a transport going overseas, and had to wait on table at the officers' mess. When they heard that he could play the violin they decided (much to his relief) to let him entertain them with music at meal-time instead of waiting table.

When the war ended, Still got a job in New York with W. C. Handy—"father of the Blues." He arranged music for him and played in his band, and when Handy's *Shuffle Along* went on tour, Still accompanied the show. By this time his original twenty-five dollars a week had been increased to sixty, and he had been able to lay aside a little money. So he decided to go back to his music studies and learn serious composing.

While *Shuffle Along* was playing in Boston, Still called on George W. Chadwick at the New England Conservatory. The latter was so

Modern Music-Makers

impressed by the young man's talent that he not only accepted him as a pupil, but offered to teach him free of charge.

After a few months with Chadwick, Still returned to New York and became recording manager at the Black Swan Recording Company. Just about that time Edgar Varèse was looking for a talented young Negro to whom he could give a scholarship in composition. Still won the scholarship and for the next two years studied with Varèse. "He taught me to express myself," he says. "Before that I had just been groping."

How thoroughly he had absorbed his teacher's ultra-modern idiom, Still did not realize until he heard the first public performance of one of the pieces he wrote while under Varèse's tutelage: *From the Land of Dreams*. This was played in February, 1925, at Varèse's recommendation, at a concert given by the International Composer's Guild.

Still intended the piece "as an expression of the evanescence of dreams," but its "pure cacophony" raised a storm of protest. People didn't know what to make of the peculiar noises. "They *were* peculiar, all right," he admits.

Olin Downes felt that Varèse had driven the young composer's "original and entertaining music out of him. . . . Is Mr. Still unaware that the cheapest melody in the revues he has orchestrated has more reality and inspiration in it than the curious noises he has manufactured?"

Still now realized that he had been trying to imitate his teacher rather than to express what he wanted to say in his own language. Today he calls that early effort, "the musical picture of an owl with a headache." The score of *From the Land of Dreams* has been lost. He hopes it will never turn up.

For the next few years William Grant Still earned his living in theater orchestras, vaudeville and night clubs. He played the banjo at the Plantation Club, then was promoted to orchestra leader there. Next he did orchestrating for a number of popular entertainers (among them Sophie Tucker, Earl Carroll, and Paul Whiteman) and for Willard Robinson's "Deep River" radio hour. Later, at the request of the men in the orchestra, he was made conductor of the group, and

William Grant Still

when in 1936 he conducted at the Hollywood Bowl, he was the first of his race to lead a major symphony orchestra.

During these years of close connection with the popular field of entertainment, Still became intimately acquainted with jazz. What nowadays passes for jazz Still feels is cheaper and less musical than the original product. In his estimation Tin-Pan Alley usually lacks sincere emotional content, intellect, and spiritual depth. But that does not disprove the value of the idiom. He believes that from the elements of jazz—i.e., rhythm, tone-color, fluency—a great musical form can be built.

Real Jazz isn't cheap, and it isn't haphazard. Most important of all is the fact that Jazz and its exponents have made friends for the Negro. In doing so, they have helped race relations in this country and in other parts of the world. [1]

Still's experience with orchestras had one important result. He learned, largely through trial and error, how to get the effect he wanted by various combinations of instruments, and gradually evolved his own style of orchestration. "You learn much more when you have to do a thing yourself," he explains. "Then you develop your own individuality."

I never try to find out the best way to orchestrate an idea or theme. The orchestration is already worked out as soon as the sketch is completed. I think 'orchestrally,' that is, in terms of orchestra. It may or may not be a fortuitous circumstance, but I never learned to play the piano. Almost from the beginning I worked with orchestras, consequently I think in terms of the orchestra. Some composers first write out their ideas as piano compositions and orchestrate them later. To me, they sound consciously orchestrated.[2]

In trying to find his own, personal idiom, Still eventually turned to the folk music of his people. There he found such a rich storehouse of

[1] William Grant Still as quoted by Douglas Cook in *Opera, Concert and Symphony*, November, 1946.
[2] *Ibid.*

material that since then he has used it as the inspiration of much of his music.

His earliest published compositions were songs, and he wrote his first orchestral work in 1924. Its theme was "the triumph of a people over their sorrows through fervent prayer"; he called it *Darker America.*

The first performance of the work was by the Barrere Little Symphony in New York; later Howard Hanson played it in Rochester. From the beginning Hanson has generously sponsored and encouraged the works of William Grant Still. "Dr. Hanson has done more, perhaps, than anyone in the United States for the music of this country," says Still, with grateful appreciation. "Although he himself is a composer, he goes out and works hard for other composers. . . ."

Still's next work, written two years later, was in lighter vein. *From the Black Belt,* in seven parts, is full of vigorous humor—particularly the first movement: *Lil' Scamp,* which is only eight measures long. Two other movements are called *Mah Bones is Creakin',* and the last—contagiously rhythmical—*Clap Yo' Han's.*

In 1929 Still produced the first of his important orchestral works. *Africa* is in three movements: *Land of Peace, Land of Romance,* and *Land of Superstition.* The Barrere Ensemble again was the first to perform the work, and Howard Hanson also played it. *Africa* has been heard abroad, in New York and, in 1936 under the composer's own direction at the Hollywood Bowl.

Still made six different revisions of *Africa* before he was finally satisfied with it.

William Grant Still's best-known work is his second, or *Afro-American Symphony.* This he describes as "a composite musical portrait of those Afro-Americans who have not responded completely to the cultural influences of today. . . ." Nevertheless one who hears it is quite sure to discover other meanings which are probably broader in their scope.

When Still first began to outline the *Afro-American Symphony,* it occurred to him, "That it would be a splendid idea to use an original theme in Blues idiom as a basis for the work." This Blues motif forms the principal theme of the first movement—called *Longing.* Each of the four movements represents a different emotion, and is headed by an excerpt from the poems of Paul Laurence Dunbar.

William Grant Still

Second is *Sorrow,* third *Humor.* The fourth—*Sincerity*—is prefaced by a verse beginning:

"Be Proud, my Race, in mind and soul."

The *Afro-American Symphony* won praise from every direction. "There is not a cheap or banal passage in the entire composition," said one critic. Another found it "full of melody, straightforward in expression of mood, cumulative in effect."

"This work is remarkably scored," wrote Lawrence Gilman. "Mr. Still's orchestra laments, rejoices, longs and aspires, with a prismatic beauty and exquisiteness of hue."[3]

Howard Hanson gave the first performance of the *Afro-American Symphony* in Rochester, and later played it in Germany. Stokowski included it on his nation-wide tour with the Philadelphia Orchestra, and it was heard in New York under Hans Lange with the New York Philharmonic. During the war the OWI had the symphony microfilmed and sent to various foreign countries as representative American music.

Third in Still's trilogy is the *Symphony in G. Minor* (dedicated to Isabel Morse Jones). Subtitled *Song of a New Race,* at Leopold Stokowski's suggestion, it was first played by him in December, 1937. This symphony, according to the composer, forms "a sort of extension, or evolution" of the preceding one. Its principal theme, in the opening movement, is closely related to the main theme in the last movement of the *Afro-American Symphony.* While this latter represents the freed-man of the days after the Civil War, the *Symphony in G. Minor* interprets "the American colored man of today, in so many instances a totally new individual produced through the fusion of White, Indian, and Negro bloods."

Music connected with the stage has always been close to the heart of William Grant Still. His first work in that field was for the ballet. *La Guiablesse* (written in 1933) was suggested to him by Adolf Bolm, who wanted to do a ballet based on Lafcadio Hearn's tales of Martinique, and felt that Still was the composer who could best in-

[3] In the *New York Herald Tribune,* January 22, 1935.

Modern Music-Makers

terpret the West Indian atmosphere. The story concerns a beautiful sorceress — *La Guiablesse* — who lures her young lover to his destruction.

The ballet, performed several times by Bolm and the Chicago Grand Opera Company, also in New York, was acclaimed "far above the average ballet music . . . both in quality of invention and in the value of its themes and imagination. It is a highly-colored, vivid, evocative, gorgeous score."[4]

The scene of Still's next ballet, *Sahdji*, is laid in Africa. Before starting it, he spent more than a year studying African music and legend, so that he could create an authentic atmosphere. The work is scored for ballet and chorus, and makes effective use of native drums. *Sahdji* received high praise. "*La Guiablesse* is a work of talent," said one critic—"*Sahdji* is a work of genius!"

Still's ballets were only a prelude to what he considers the most important of all his work. Since his earliest days, when he listened to his step-father's records, he has "always lived and dreamed opera." He has written a dozen or more, but has discarded most of them.

The first of Still's operas—*Blue Steel*—concerns a young Birmingham Negro named Blue Steel, voodooism, and black magic. (A theme from this opera was later used in his *Lenox Avenue Suite*). Next came *Troubled Island,* based on Langston Hughes' play *Drums of Haiti,* which describes the struggle of the Haitian Negroes to liberate themselves from the French. *Troubled Island* was presented by the New York City Center Opera Company in April, 1949, and was recorded and broadcast over a Voice of America program.

Still has also written *A Bayou Legend* (1940); *A Southern Legend* (1942) and another more recent opera *Costaso.*

Many prizes and honors have come to William Grant Still. At the beginning of his career, in 1928, he received the Harmon award, given annually for the year's most significant contribution to Negro culture. He has been twice granted a Rosenwald Fellowship, and twice a Guggenheim Fellowship. Both Wilberforce and Howard Universities, and more recently Oberlin, have conferred on him honorary Doctor of Music degrees. In 1949 the National Association of Amer-

[4] Herman Devries in the *Chicago American.*

214

William Grant Still

ican Composers and Conductors awarded him a citation "for untiring efforts and distinguished contribution to the cause of American music."

In 1938 Still was chosen from a group of American composers to provide a musical theme to be used at the New York World's Fair. His score was played several times daily throughout the duration of the Fair. In 1945 he received a $1,000 War Bond for a *Festive Overture* written for the Cincinnati Orchestra's Fiftieth Anniversary. Thirty-eight composers submitted scores; Still's won by unanimous vote.

In the fall of 1945 he was accorded a signal honor when an entire program of his works was played in Paris, under the direction of the English Negro conductor from British Guiana, Rudolph Dunbar. The latter had already performed Still's music several times in England, where it was enthusiastically received, and in Paris it met with equal success. He was dubbed "the American Tschaikowsky."

During the war (in 1943) Still, on learning that the first American soldier to be killed in action was a Negro, wrote a moving tribute called: *In Memoriam: To the Colored Soldiers Who Died for Democracy.*

William Grant Still is not a crusader, but in his gentle, large-minded way he has done much to encourage race tolerance. His choral work *And They Lynched Him on a Tree*, to a poem by Katherine Garrison Chapin, is a strong plea for greater understanding between men. The poem—"created purely as a human document and not intended for propaganda"—appealed to him because of its lack of bitterness, and because it stressed tolerance. In the words of the final chorus:

> Oh trust your brother, and reach out your hand
> And clear the shadow, the long dark shadow
> And clear the shadow that falls across the land.

And They Lynched Him on a Tree was first performed in June, 1940, at the Lewisohn Stadium in New York City. The critics joined in praising the "deeply moving and tellingly dramatic music. . . ."

The following year Still set another of Miss Chapin's poems to

Modern Music-Makers

music: *Plain Chant for America*—a protest against Fascism. He dedicated the composition to President and Mrs. Roosevelt.

In 1934 William Grant Still moved permanently to Southern California and there met Verna Arvey, a noted writer and concert pianist, who helped him with his correspondence and secretarial work. As a result of this partnership Miss Arvey became deeply interested in Still's career, and wrote a number of articles about him and his work.[5] The close association and mutual interests of William Grant Still and Verna Arvey culminated, in 1939, in their marriage. They now have two children, Duncan and blond-haired Judith, and make their home in Los Angeles.

Under his wife's encouragement William Grant Still has produced the greater number of his most important compositions. Before meeting Verna Arvey he had written practically no music for the piano. Now he turned to this medium, and produced a number of scores, among them *Three Visions;* a short piece called *Quit dat Fool'nish; The Black Man Dances* (with orchestral accompaniment); and *Kaintuck*—a piano concerto. This last he dedicated to Verna Arvey and she has played it in public a number of times, including a performance with the Los Angeles Philharmonic under Otto Klemperer.

Verna Arvey has written program notes for most of Still's works, and texts for several (among them the two operas *A Bayou Legend* and *A Southern Interlude*). Two of his orchestral works: *Dismal Swamp* and *Poem for Orchestra* are prefaced by original poems by Miss Arvey.

Still spends twelve to fourteen hours a day composing. Most of his work is painstakingly transcribed on a music typewriter. While he produces slowly, he labors so continuously and systematically that he turns out a prodigious amount of material. Only once has he given himself a real vacation. In 1945, after a particularly arduous period of work, he stopped composing entirely for nine months. During that period he spent his days building furniture and toys for the children. But finally he "had to go back to composing. . . ." He then concentrated on a large orchestral work which he believes, may be his most important composition: *Archaic Ritual.* Since then he

---

[5] Miss Arvey is also the author of *Choreographic Music*, published in 1941 by E. P. Dutton and Company.

WILLIAM GRANT STILL

William Grant Still

has written a *Fourth Symphony*, (1949), *Wood Notes* (a suite for orchestra), *From a Lost Continent*, a large choral work, and the opera *Costaso*.

William Grant Still is completely dedicated to his music. When he works he is oblivious of time and the outer world. One day a friend came to visit him and remarked on the heat. Still looked up in surprise "Is it hot?" he asked. "Then I'd better take off my coat!"

Although essentially serious-minded, he possesses a saving sense of humor. Once at a meeting when he was called on to contribute a few words following a succession of lengthy speeches, he rose—said quietly, "I wonder if everyone is as hungry as I am?"—and sat down amid loud applause.

William Grant Still possesses the humility of greatness. He is by nature a philosopher, and in the truest sense, a philanthropist. He once stated his ideal as, "The study of life with a view to learning that which will enable me to make my life more serviceable to mankind."

William Grant Still

The Music of William Grant Still

ORCHESTRAL WORKS

Darker America [1]	1924
From the Black Belt [2]	1926
La Guiablesse (suite from ballet) [2]	1927
Africa	1930
Sahdji (suite from ballet) [3]	1930
First Symphony Afro-American [3]	1931
Kaintuck (piano and orchestra) [3]	1935
Dismal Swamp [4]	1936
Lenox Avenue (suite from ballet) [3]	1937
Second Symphony in G. Minor [3]	1937
Song of a City (orchestra and chorus) [3]	1939
Victory Tide (also for band and for voice) [3]	1939
Can'tcha Line 'Em	1940
Old California (also for band) [3]	1941
In Memoriam: The Colored Soldiers Who Died for Democracy [5]	1943
Festive Overture [2]	1944
Bells (also for piano) [5]	1944
Poem For Orchestra [5]	1944
Fanfare for the 99th Fighter Squadron	1945
Third Symphony	1945
From the Delta (for band) [6]	1945
Archaic Ritual	1946
Woodnotes	1947
Fourth Symphony	1947

CHORAL WORKS

Three Negro Spirituals [7]	1937
Rising Tide [3]	1939
Victory Tide [3]	1939

219

Modern Music-Makers

And They Lynched Him on a Tree (orchestra score on rental) [3]   1940
Plain Chant for America [3]   1941
Those Who Wait   1943
The Voice of the Lord [9]   1946
Wailing Woman   1946
Carry Him Along [8]   1947
From a Lost Continent   1949

CHAMBER MUSIC

Incantation and Dance (for oboe and piano) [2]   1942
Suite (violin and piano) [5]   1943
Pastorela [9]   1946

PIANO WORKS

A Deserted Plantation [10]   1933
Three Visions [3]   1935
Quit Dat Fool'nish [3]   1935
Seven Traceries [3]   1940
Marionette [5]   1945

STAGE WORKS

La Guiablesse (ballet) [2]   1927
Sahdji (ballet) [2]   1930
Blue Steel (opera)   1935
Troubled Island (opera) [6]   1938
A Bayou Legend (opera)   1940
Miss Sally's Party (ballet) [3]   1940
A Southern Interlude (opera)   1942
Costaso (opera)   1949

William Grant Still

Winter's Approach [11]	1927
Breath of a Rose [11]	1927
Twelve Negro Spirituals [7]	1937
Caribbean Melodies [8]	1941
Here's One [12]	1941
Bayou Home [10]	1944
Songs of Separation [5]	1945

[1] C. C. Birchard.
[2] Carl Fischer.
[3] J. Fischer.
[4] New Music Edition.
[5] Delkas.
[6] Leeds.
[7] Handy Bros.
[8] Oliver Ditson.
[9] Witmark.
[10] Robbins Music.
[11] G. Schirmer.
[12] John Church Co.

221

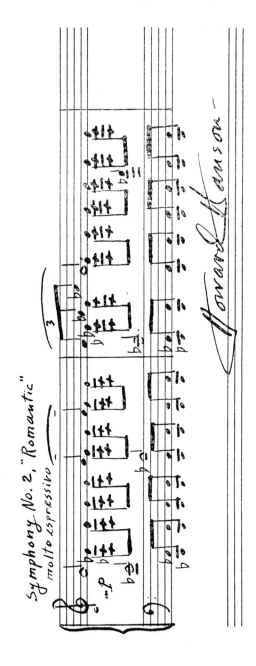

HOWARD HANSON

HOWARD HANSON

HOWARD HANSON, distinguished head of the Eastman School of Music, began his career as an educator before he was twenty.

In the spring of 1916 President Seaton of California's College of the Pacific went East to find a teacher of theory and composition for his music department. He was particularly impressed by the brilliant record of a senior in Northwestern University's Music School. But when he met the lanky, tow-headed youth, he looked at him a little doubtfully. "How old are you?" he asked.

Howard Hanson flushed. He knew that his fair coloring—a heritage from Scandinavian ancestors—made him appear even younger than he actually was. (Later he tried to remedy this by raising a mustache and Van Dyke beard). "I'll be twenty next fall," he replied.

"Rather young for a college professor!" the president exclaimed, smiling. "However—I'm willing to take a chance if you think you can handle the position."

Hanson was quite sure that he could. Since childhood he had been a leader. When only nine years old and already an able pianist, he organized a string quartet; since there were no cellists in his small home town, he learned to play the cello so that he could complete the quartet. Howard enjoyed sports and outdoor games; but his favorite recreation was making music with the quartet; and also with the school orchestra, of which he soon became conductor. In all things musical, young Hanson was years ahead of other youngsters of his age in the town.

His mother had a good deal to do with this. Howard's grand-parents, Hans and Hannah Hanson, came to the United States from the province of Skane, in Sweden. They settled in the little town of Wahoo—not far from Lincoln, Nebraska—and their son married the daughter of Per and Hannah Eckstrom who had migrated to Omaha from the same part of the old country. Wahoo (whose Indian name seemed made to order for college yells) was a Swedish community. The life of the people there centered around the Lutheran Church and its large chorus. Each year they held music festivals and joined in singing the old Lutheran hymns and oratorio classics.

223

Modern Music-Makers

Howard, born October 28, 1896, heard music from his earliest days. His mother, Hilma Hanson, was a fair pianist, and as soon as he reached the age of six she taught him to play the piano. Almost at once he started to compose, and his mother carefully cherished these early efforts. Opus I, Hanson recalls, was "a trio of doleful melodies, very much under the influence of Greig." It was natural, because of Hanson's Swedish heritage, that this great Scandinavian composer should have been the boy's first musical hero.

Young Howard showed such marked musical talent that before long, in spite of his youth, he was admitted to classes in harmony and counterpoint at the neighboring Lutheran College. He graduated from this college when only sixteen, with highest scholastic honors. The superintendent of his high school advised him strongly against taking up music as a career.

"Music is not a *man's* job," he insisted. "With your ability you could make a success in some really important field!"

But Howard, although at one time he had thought of joining the Lutheran ministry, had made up his mind that music should be his life's work. He had had lessons at the University School of Music in Lincoln, in addition to his college course; now he wanted to continue these studies in New York. To earn the necessary money, he spent the summer of 1913 on a Chautauqua tour, playing one-night stands all over the country.

In New York young Hanson entered the Institute of Musical Art and completed the course there in a year. At that time he was urged to become a concert pianist. James Friskin was his teacher. But Dr. Goetschius, head of the composition department, thought his talent for composing more important.

After another summer's Chautauqua touring Hanson won a teaching fellowship to Northwestern University's Music School, and worked there with Arne Oldberg and Peter Christian Lutkin. It was during the latter part of his stay at Northwestern that he met President Seaton of San José's Pacific College. In September, 1916, Howard Hanson moved out to California.

Most of the pupils at Pacific College were older than their new harmony professor. But even in those early days Hanson proved himself a born teacher. His keen intelligence, enthusiasm and vitality, and especially his disarming sense of humor, made him then,

PORTRAIT BY BYRON MORGAN

HOWARD HANSON

Howard Hanson

as now, a highly efficient instructor and personally popular with the students as well. Three years later, at twenty-two, he was elected Dean of the College's Conservatory of Fine Arts—the youngest on record to hold such a responsible position.

Hanson did not neglect his composing during the years in California. He wrote his first three orchestral works there: *Symphonic Poem* (1916), *Legend* (1917) and, in 1919, a *Symphonic Rhapsody*. These compositions brought him to the attention of Walter Henry Rothwell, then director of the Los Angeles Philharmonic. Rothwell became interested in the young composer and invited him to come to Los Angeles and conduct the orchestra in a performance of his *Symphonic Rhapsody*. This was the greatest event, so far, in Hanson's life. "I have conducted many excellent orchestras since that time," he says, "but I never hope to get in this world the thrill which I had in hearing the first chord of my own music from a great orchestra."

While in California Hanson also conducted the San Francisco orchestra, and in 1920 he was commissioned to write and to direct the music for the California Forest Play, given out-of-doors under giant redwood trees.

In 1921 the newly established Music Department of the American Academy in Rome held its first open competition. Hanson submitted his fourth orchestral work, *Poem Before the Dawn,* and this won for him the coveted Rome Prize. He had never been abroad; the opportunity for a three year's stay in Rome appealed to him strongly.

When he arrived in Europe, early in 1922, he found a hot-bed of musical rebels. The younger composers of the day had turned against the traditional style of music writing, especially if it savored of the romantic period, and "neoclassicism" was the rage. They were all striving for ultra-modern effects; originality at any price was the keynote. Groups of young musicians sat about in the cafés, arguing over the relative merits of atonality and polytonality, and as to whether they should compose in three or four keys at once.

Alfred Hertz, for many years conductor of the San Francisco Orchestra helped to steer Hanson away from this sophisticated trend.

Modern Music-Makers

"Come up to my hotel and show me what you have been writing," he said, when the two met in Paris.

Hanson, like the rest of the younger set, had been experimenting with the new idiom, so he sat down and played his latest atonal effort.

"Interesting," commented Hertz briefly. "But haven't you something else?"

Hanson thought a moment. Then he played the slow movement of his *First Symphony*—the *Nordic*—which he was then working on.

When he had finished "Papa" Hertz came over and put his arm around him.

"Young man, you don't have to write that other kind of music. You have *talent!*"

These words made a profound impression on Hanson. Already he was growing convinced that his real interest lay in a different direction from the current modern trend. The style of the moment seemed to him of less importance than being true to his own inner urge, and faithful to the principles which he believed to be right. Most of the so-called modern works appeared to him mainly a mental product —a sort of abstract experiment in tonal relationship. Music, Hanson feels, is fundamentally an expression of the emotions. More than this: it is an exact language, capable of interpreting every gradation of emotion—from the mildest state to actual hysteria—something which is not possible in words.

As a reaction against the music he encountered abroad, Howard Hanson deliberately went to the other extreme. He even called his *Second Symphony*—commissioned by Koussevitzky in 1930 for the Boston Philharmonic's Fiftieth Anniversary — the *Romantic*. In writing of this work he says:

I recognize, of course, that romanticism is, at the present time, the poor stepchild, without the social standing of her elder sister, neoclassicism. Nevertheless, I embrace her all the more fervently, believing, as I do, that romanticism will find in this country rich soil for a new, young and vigorous growth.

The real battle, Hanson reasons, is between two completely different conceptions of art, and the terms "neoclassicism" and "neo-

226

Howard Hanson

romanticism" are used to describe, rather inaccurately, fundamental differences in philosophy. It is not a question of consonance versus dissonance, but rather of the introvert versus the extrovert. Music reveals a composer's personal aesthetic and moral philosophy.

Hanson's outlook is reflected in all of his music. The sagas of the North, and the open spaces of the West, have furnished the outer inspiration for much of his work. But the real source lies in his own personal philosophy which sees life as a Force striving towards the light—that *"Lux Aeterna"* which he symbolizes in several of his compositions. The symphonic poem called by this name (written in 1923 while he was in Rome) is meant, he says, to express the "struggle between light and darkness and the groping of the spirit of man toward the realization of light."

Pan and the Priest, written three years later, also symbolizes man's inner strife, dramatizing, as Hanson explains in the program notes, the result of inner forces and emotional conflicts.

"Pan" might be said to represent the pagan spirit which lives in every artist, the spirit of freedom, of exuberant life, of unfettered emotions. The "Priest" represents the religious influence, the artist's tendency to seek relief from the too insistent rhythm of life in meditation and philosophic contemplation, the spirit of emotional restraint and asceticism.

While in Rome, Hanson wrote his *First Symphony,* and he called it *The Nordic,* because it was inspired by the sagas of his Scandinavian forbears. The first movement, "sings of the solemnity, austerity, and grandeur of the North, of its restless surging and strifes, of its somberness and melancholy." The second movement, in contrasting mood—gentle and serene—is inscribed "To My Mother," while the third movement, rugged, energetic and built on Swedish folk songs, bears the title "To My Father." Hanson has always been deeply devoted to his parents. When his father died he wrote a moving memorial—his fourth, or *Requiem* symphony:

One of the noblest works ever written in America, this symphony does not merely play with structural problems—a technical, intellectual practice that may be highly ingenious and interesting and yet degrade the psychic, emotional factor to relative unimportance.[1]

[1] *Serge Koussevitsky—The Boston Symphony Orchestra and the New American Music* by Hugh Leichtentrit, page 42.

Modern Music-Makers

During his years abroad, Hanson composed a number of symphonic works. These were first played by the Augusteo Orchestra in Rome and conducted by the young composer himself. In addition to the *Nordic* Symphony and *Lux Aeterna,* he wrote a tone poem called *North and West* and a *String Quartet,* the latter commissioned by Elizabeth Sprague Coolidge. He also began a large choral work entitled *The Lament of Beowulf.* This was completed a year later, after his return to the United States.

The Lament of Beowulf is one of Hanson's finest works. The epic poem, which he read while on a visit to England, inspired the work. The first sketches were written in Scotland, he says, "in an environment rugged, swept with mist, and wholly appropriate to the scene. . . ."

My intention has been to realize in the music the austerity and stoicism and the heroic atmosphere of the poem. This is true Anglo-Saxon poetry and may well serve as a basis for music composed by an American. The music follows closely the text and the text presents with epic vigor and terse eloquence the scene of Beowulf's burial.

The tone poem describes the great burial ground by the sea where Beowulf's funeral pyre has been built, piled high with the trophies of his battles. The chorus sings of the King's heroic deeds, and laments his passing in the moving phrases:

> In such wise they grieved, the folk of the Geats
> For the fall of their lord, e'en they his hearth fellows;
> Quoth they that he was a world king forsooth,
> The mildest of all men, unto men kindest
> To his folk the most gentlest, most yearning of fame.

In *The Lament of Beowulf* Hanson's talent for choral writing—one of the most distinctive features of his music—is particularly evident.

While Hanson was on a visit home, in 1924, Walter Damrosch invited him to conduct the New York Philharmonic in his tone poem *North and West.* On that same visit he played the *Nordic Symphony* with the Rochester Orchestra. This visit to Rochester changed Hanson's whole career. While there he met George Eastman, the Kodak magnate who had recently endowed a Music School at the University of Rochester. Eastman and Dr. Rush Rhees, President of the University, were looking for a director to take over the management of what was to become the great Eastman School of Music. They were both impressed by young Hanson's forceful personality and executive ability and decided that he was just the man they were looking for. Shortly after Howard Hanson returned to Rome he received a letter from President Rhees asking him to become director of the new music school.

It was difficult for the young musician to give up his work abroad. He had already made a name for himself as a composer. To be the head of a great organization, he knew, would mean a life so full of responsibility and activity that he would have little leisure for his own work. But at the same time he realized that in this new school there would be tremendous opportunities to further the cause of music. He did not hesitate long. In 1925 Howard Hanson returned to the United States and was installed as head of the school.

A man with less vision, vigor, and determination might have found himself swamped by the endless duties of such a position. But Hanson's extraordinary capacity for work has made it possible for him to carry on his executive work and still to find time for writing music. Through the years he has continued to compose—though he has been obliged to do most of his work at night, and also to sacrifice much of his personal life. "In the creative field," he states with a certain wry humor, "It is necessary to fight for every bit of leisure."

Hanson "never had time for a wife" until recently. In the summer of 1946 he married Margaret Elizabeth Nelson. Now, somewhat to his surprise, he finds that he is doing more composing than before.

The long list of Hanson's compositions includes the four symphonies: *Nordic* (1922); *Romantic* (1930)—his most popular work; the *Third*, commissioned by the Columbia Broadcasting Company in 1937; and the *Fourth*, awarded a 1944 Pulitzer Prize. Among his choral works, in addition to *The Lament of Beowulf* and *Heroic Elegy* are *Drum Taps* (the latter to a poem by Walt Whitman is one of Hanson's most eloquent scores); *Hymn for Pioneers;* a transcription of Palestrina's *Pope Marcellus Mass;* and *The Cherubic Hymn* (1950). His more recent chamber-music works are a *Serenade* for

Modern Music-Makers

Flute, Harp, and Strings, and *Pastorale* for Oboe and Strings, written in 1949.

One of Howard Hanson's most famous works is his opera *Merry Mount*, produced at the Metropolitan in 1934. The libretto of this opera, by Richard L. Stokes, is based on an episode of Puritan times (taken from Hawthorne's tale *The Maypole of Merry Mount*). The story tells of an austere Puritan pastor named Bradford whose religious convictions are at war with his natural impulses. He falls in love with Marigold, one of Merry Mount's gay but unregenerate cavalier company. In a series of dramatic episodes, "Wrestling Bradford" struggles to save the girl's soul—only to lose his own. The opera ends with a dramatic burning of the village by the Indians, while Bradford seizes Marigold and marches with her into the flames as the Puritans chant the Lord's Prayer.

The original cast of *Merry Mount* included Lawrence Tibbett, Gladys Swarthout, and Edward Johnson—later manager of the Metropolitan. At the end of the opera, performers, composer, and librettist had to return for fifty curtain calls—an all time record for the Metropolitan.

Olin Downes wrote that Hanson's opera received "the most enthusiastic reception given any native music drama that has been produced in ten years or more." He thought the music at times "conventional and noisily effective," but he joined Lawrence Gilman in praising the choral writing. They felt that this was the most successful part of the opera. "The choruses of *Merry Mount* will prove, in all likelihood, to be its most memorable artistic achievement."

Shortly after taking up his new position at the Eastman School of Music, Howard Hanson inaugurated a series of American Composers' Concerts which has had a far-reaching effect on the music of this country. Realizing from his own experience how useful it is to a young composer to hear his works played, he resolved to "create in Rochester a center of musical composition which would serve the needs of the young composer."

What seemed to be necessary. . . .was the creation of a laboratory for composers, a place where the young composer might come and hear his

Howard Hanson

works performed by a competent orchestra under conditions sufficiently sympathetic to give his compositions a fair test. . . .

On May 1, 1925, the first American Composers' Concert was given in the Eastman Theatre. . . .The public reaction was favorable. Listeners began to discover for themselves the fascinating adventure of hearing new music. Sometimes they suffered, but they came again and again, and in increasing numbers. . . .

The reactions, however, were by no means favorable. Some felt that this "coddling" of the young composer was a waste of money. After all, was it not a tradition of good composers to starve in the garret and be "discovered" after they were dead? One ultra-conservative critic remarked to Mr. Eastman that the concerts had been going on for five years and he had not observed that we had discovered any Beethovens. George Eastman's answer was characteristic of the man, "If we discover one Beethoven in fifty years I shall consider this venture an enormous success.[2]

Each year now, in addition to the Composers' Concerts, a spring Festival of American Music is held in Rochester and new scores are always in demand. More native music has been played at these concerts than in all the rest of the United States put together. Hanson and the Eastman Orchestra have recorded a large number of the new works played at their concerts. These recordings are filed and catalogued in the Eastman School's extensive music library. They form one of the most valuable existing records of modern music writing in America.

In 1933, under the auspices of the Oberlaender Trust of the Carl Schurz Memorial Foundation, Hanson carried his crusade abroad. He gave concerts of American works in Berlin, Leipzig, and Stuttgart, and was largely influential in making the composers of our country known abroad. He has probably done more to further the cause of contemporary American music than anyone in this country today.

The list of Hanson's musical activities is endless. Besides his work at Eastman (which includes an advanced class in composition) he serves on numerous committees and juries throughout the country, and lectures extensively. He has received countless honors both here

[2] Howard Hanson in the *Eastman School Festival of the American Music Bulletin,* 1945.

Modern Music-Makers

and abroad; among others he was elected in 1935 to the National Institute of Arts and Letters, and in 1938 became a Fellow of the Royal Academy of Music in Sweden. He has been President of the National Music Council, the Music Teachers National Association, and the National Association of Schools and Music. He holds the honorary degrees of Doctor of Letters, Doctor of Laws, and Doctor of Music from twelve different universities, colleges and music conservatories, among them Columbia, Northwestern, Syracuse, and the University of Nebraska.

Every person's achievement mirrors his special qualities; Hanson's reveals a genial spirit and a sensitive awareness to beauty. His name will stand high in the annals of American musical history both because of his own creative work, and because of the generous support he has given to younger composers. He believes that we are today in the midst of the greatest creative period in American music. No one has worked more wholeheartedly to bring this about than Howard Hanson.

Howard Hanson

Honorary Degrees—Mus. Doc., L.L.D. D.H.L.; Litt.D.;—Fellow Royal Academy Sweden—member National Institute of Arts and Letters.

The Music of Howard Hanson

Howard Hanson

235

Modern Music-Makers

Songs

[1] C. C. Birchard & Co.
[2] G. Schirmer, Inc.
[3] Carl Fischer, Inc.
[4] Harms, Inc.
[5] J. Fischer.
[6] Composers' Music Corp.
[7] Theodore Presser.
[8] White-Smith Pub. Co.

Four Saints in Three Acts

music by Virgil Thomson

text by Gertrude Stein

VIRGIL THOMSON

VIRGIL THOMSON

VIRGIL THOMSON, widely known as composer, and distinguished music-critic of the New York Herald Tribune, is one of the most eclectic and thoroughly trained musicians in the United States today. He has been called "America's musical satirist"—a reputation that goes back to his *Four Saints in Three Acts*. Until the production of this opera, with text by Gertrude Stein, he was relatively unknown in this country. But with the first performance of *Four Saints*, which created one of the greatest sensations ever known on Broadway, he became among the most discussed of contemporary composers.

The audience hardly knew whether to be outraged or amused, that first night. The curtain rose on a stage decorated in white tarletan palm trees and sky-blue cellophane clouds. ("Witty, delicious and iridescent, based on. . . .modern painting; a sort of whimsical coquetry with the baroque that is a fresh step in stage decor," said one critic.[1]) An all-Negro cast in fantastic ecclesiastical costumes solemnly began to chant:

To know to know to love her so
Four saints prepare for saints.
It makes it well fish
Four saints prepare for saints it makes it well fish it makes it well fish
    prepare for saints. . . .

On and on went the purposely meaningless words to an accompaniment of singularly effective music

Pigeons on the grass, alas
Pigeons on the grass alas
Short longer grass short longer longer shorter yellow grass. Pigeons large
pigeons on the shorter yellow grass alas pigeons on the grass. . . .

Four Saints in Three Acts was a combination of opera, music-

[1] Stark Young in *The New Republic*, March 7, 1934.

Virgil Thomson

drama, and what one critic called "delectable imbecility." Those in the audience who were able to "check their limitations" (as Olin Downes put it in an excellent recipe for broad-mindedness[2]) enjoyed themselves hugely. "Everyone had a good time—the audience, the cast, and the conductor....A gorgeous piece of kidding."[3]

There were sixty performances of *Four Saints* that first season. It became not only the talk of Broadway, but of all musical America. So did Gertrude Stein and its composer, Virgil Thomson who had long been an admirer of Gertrude Stein's. Her rambling poetry-prose ("like the speech of a little child who loves to run words together") appealed to what Copland calls Thomson's "uncommonly acute sensitivity to the inner rhythm of English." While still at college Thomson set a number of Miss Stein's poems to music—mainly because it was fun. "Since you didn't know what the meanings were," he says, "there was no temptation to be descriptive; the sound and cadence were all that mattered."

Later Thomson met Gertrude Stein in Paris ("the marriage of true minds was performed by Antheil", say Howard Barlow) and they collaborated in a number of vocal works—including the famous *Capital Capitals* which he made into a twenty-minute long cantata. Everyone liked these songs; so Thomson said to Miss Stein: "Why don't you write an opera libretto for me?"

The two debated long over the subject matter. Should it be legendary? Mythological—with a tragical ending, recitative and arias? Historical? ("but *not* the Colonial period—we didn't think the costumes would look well.")

"What about the lives of the Saints?" Miss Stein finally suggested.

"Fine," answered Thomson. "But the Italian saints have been overdone, and the Renaissance racket isn't very fresh...."

They finally decided on Spanish saints—two of them. ("Everything in life goes by twos." Thomson explains. "The Democratic party and the Republicans—Columbia and the N. B. C.—Macy's and

---

[2] "Granted that no one of us can possibly escape from the limitations of his temperament and prejudices—which amount to about the same thing—we should try to check our limitations with our hats when we enter a new place, and see if there is not something to be found there that is entertaining." *New York Times*, February 25, 1934.

[3] Harry Hansen in the *World Telegram*, February 23, 1934.

Modern Music-Makers

Bloomingdale's.") St. Ignatius was chosen—the "theological-military type"—and St. Theresa, the "club type." The cast actually included two St. Theresas, since Thomson believed that one person would find it too strenuous to manage the entire part. In fact there were some thirty saints and four acts—not four saints and three acts. The title was just part of the general nonsense and the stage directions were as mixed-up as the rest.

Thomson's idea of having negro actors was an inspired one. He had heard them sing in night clubs and chose them, he says, for the simple reason that they speak more clearly. "The negro sings with greater ease, putting himself into the various moods demanded by the opera, fanciful and devotional, a thousand times better than a white artist could." The superiority of the negroes' choral singing, combined with their clarity of diction and the fact that they are satisfied with the pure beauty of sound rather than its meaning—in other words have no intellectual barriers to break down or make them self-conscious—all these things influenced Thomson to use negro performers.

Although the critics—like the rest of the audience at that first performance of *Four Saints in Three Acts*—were bewildered, their reaction was for the most part favorable. Carl Van Vechten thought *Four Saints* "as original in its conception as *Pelleas and Melisande*." He wrote that the performance was "a good deal like a dream in which you lie back indolently and let things happen to you, and through you—pleasant things to see, pleasant things to hear, pleasant things to feel. Possessed by a dozen contradictory moods in as many moments, you fall a prey to conflicting emotions and are at the mercy of author and composer."

Olin Downes was not quite as enthusiastic about *Four Saints*. It was performed, he said, "with great éclat for the precious. . . . The trail of foppishness and pose and pseudo-intellectuality is over it all." Downes admitted, however, that Thomson's "great skill in combining music and text" impressed him. "When he wanted to make a phrase tell he found for it a rhythm, accent, and shape of the melodic line that fitted the words like a glove."

Lawrence Gilman liked the music better than the libretto:

Of Mr. Thomson's music it may be said that it is deceptively simple. . . .a little self-consciously candid and naive, actually very wily and deft and

VIRGIL THOMSON

Virgil Thomson

slick, often subtly and wittily illusive, distinguished in its artful banality. This is a suave and charming score. Using Miss Stein's syllabic patterns as a framework, Mr. Thomson has derived from them a rhythmic and melodic structure of disarming simplicity and undeniable attractiveness.[4]

Because of his revolt against what he considers the too-involved pretentiousness of most modern music, and because he deliberately tries to write in a simple, straightforward way, some people have hesitated to take Virgil Thomson seriously. Critics have accused him—perhaps not always without justice—of occasionally reverting to the banal and commonplace. Yet even then, as Gilman said, his music is "deceptively simple. . . ."

Virgil Thomson was born of pioneer stock in Kansas City, Missouri, November 25, 1896. He had his first music lessons at the age of five from a cousin. Two cousins played violin and piano; Thomson's most vivid early remembrance is hearing them perform the *Intermezzo* from *Cavalleria Rusticana*. He was so enthralled that he "rolled on the floor in ecstasy." He remembers too the wonder of the early gramophone, and "the excitement of pumping a pianola. . . ."

His father was definitely not musical. "My father and his mother before him," writes Thomson in his book *The State of Music*[5] "were what used to be called 'tone deaf.' They never sang or whistled or paid any attention to musical noises. The four to six hours a day piano practise that I did for some years in my father's house never fazed either of them. They would read or sleep while it was going on as easily as I read or sleep in a railway train."

At twelve, Virgil played accompaniments for singers, had a job in a church as organist, studied harmony, and began composing songs. He particularly enjoys writing for voice. "You always like to do what you do well," he explains, and certainly Thomson has, as Copland states in his book *Our New Music*,[6] "an extraordinary felicity in the handling of the vocal text. . . . His gift for allowing

4 *New York Herald Tribune*, February 25, 1934.
5 Wm. Morrow & Co., 1939.
6 Whittlesey House, 1941.

Modern Music-Makers

English to be natural when sung is almost unique among American composers."

Thompson went from Kansas City to Cambridge and entered Harvard, where he received his major training. He worked there with Archibald T. Davison and Edward Burlingame Hill, and took piano lessons from Heinrich Gebhard and organ from Wallace Goodrich. Later he studied composition in New York with Rosario Scalero.

Young Thomson's college work was interrupted, during the war, by a year and a half in the aviation service. But after that he returned to complete his music course and won a scholarship that made it possible for him to go abroad in 1921 for a year's study with Nadia Boulanger. Then he went back to Harvard, this time as assistant music instructor and conductor of the Harvard Glee Club. He remained there mostly until 1925. During these years he also served as organist and choir master at King's Chapel in Boston.

Virgil Thomson composed his first important works for the organ: a *Passacaglia* and *Two Preludes and a Christmas Pastorale*, both in 1922 in Paris. Two choral works: *Three Antiphonal Psalms*, and *Missa Brevis* for men's choir, were written at Harvard in 1924. Ten years later he produced a second Missa Brevis, for women's voices a cappella.

In 1925 Thomson again went to Paris and remained, with only occasional visits home, until 1940 when the war drove him back to the United States. In Paris he soon became a leading member of artistic and musical circles. He and George Antheil organized a series of concerts that made them both notorious. Antheil's cacophonous *Ballet Méchanique* had its first performance at one of these concerts. The programs, held at the homes of the Parisian "*haut monde*" were devoted mainly to contemporary works. They helped considerably to make modern American music fashionable in Paris.

Thomson, like all the rest of the younger composers, was at that time experimenting with new harmonies and combinations of tones designed chiefly to startle by their originality. To this period of his career belong his *Sonata da Chiesa* (1926) for five instruments, which he himself admits "makes a funny noise"; *Five Phrases from the Song of Solomon* for soprano and percussion (1926); and a *Symphony on a Hymn Tune* (1928). This latter contains, according to

242

Virgil Thomson

Thomson, a "half-in and half-out-of-focus harmonization of two Southern hymns, one a Sunday School melody."

It wasn't long, however, before Thomson began to draw away from the ultra-moderns—or "Neoclassicists" as they liked to call themselves—and to return to simpler forms of expression. He became one of the first to embrace the "Neoromantic" movement. He was, in fact, one of its founders. Among the first fruits of his conversion were a group of chamber-music works — *Synthetic Waltzes and a Sonata for Violin, Serenade in Five Movements* for flute and violin, and two *String Quartets*. Samuel Barlow calls the first string quartet "pure Louis Philippe . . . ."

There is the carved elegance founded on classic lines (most of the figuration is Mozartian), the black walnut and tassels, the humor, and then the abrupt endings, just to show that the Victorian can be streamlined. . . . The *Second Quartet* is more diffuse and less immediately charming, but the waltz chases its tail in the best Haydn-seek manner; and in both quartets there is continuous good writing for the instruments, an almost constricting use of classical form, and a pleasing and personal melodic line. . . .They are well made, vastly entertaining, and often lovely—like a seashell door stop. . . .[7]

Thomson's first orchestral work was written in 1923, while he was still in Boston. He called it *Two Sentimental Tangos*. His next two after the *Hymn-time Symphony*, were *Oraison Funèbre*, for tenor solo to a text by Bossuet, with orchestral accompaniment; and a *Second Symphony*. (1931) This symphony, he explains, contains "no formal exposition, nothing but continuous variation and transformation of the musical material with which it starts. . . .(it belongs to) the Neoromantic school of thought. . . . Its guiding motive is the wish to express sincere personal sentiments with a maximum of directness and of spontaneity."

In 1947 Thomson added *The Seine at Night* to his orchestral works, then *Wheat Field at Noon* and, in 1950, *Concerto for Cello and Orchestra*.

After *Four Saints in Three Acts* appeared in 1934, Thomson found himself very much in demand for writing incidental music for plays.

[7] S. L. M. Barlow in *Modern Music,* May-June, 1941.

Modern Music-Makers

He composed the scores for *A Bride for the Unicorn* (1934), *Injunction Granted* (1936), Leslie Howard's production of *Hamlet* (also in 1936), and *Anthony and Cleopatra* (1937). Better known are his symphonic accompaniments for two documentary films, from which he has drawn orchestral suites that have been widely played. *The Plough that Broke the Plains* (text by Pare Lorentz) was commissioned in 1936 by the Farm Security Administration of the United States' Department of Agriculture. It tells the story of the vast Southwestern farming territory, and its destruction by wrong farming methods. It describes the ploughing of the plains, the devastating droughts and consequent disintegration of the soil and, finally, the westward migration of the "Okies" and other farmers to the Pacific Coast.

> This is a record of land. . . .
> of soil, rather than people —
> a story of the Great Plains.
> The 400,000,000 acres of
> wind-swept grass land that
> spread up from the Texas
> Panhandle to Canada. . . .
> A high, treeless continent,
> without a river, without streams. . . .
> A country of high winds,
> and sun. . . .
> and of little rain. . . .

Virgil Thomson handled this score with singular deftness and understanding, using tom-tom, wood-block, cowbell, guitar and banjo to add local color. The second film, *The River* written the following year, was based on the history of the mighty Mississippi's career, and is more elaborate in its scoring.

In 1937 Thomson wrote, in collaboration with Marc Blitzstein, the music for another documentary film—*The Spanish Earth*. That same year he produced his first and so far only, ballet: *Filling Station*. The music is "in the American vernacular," filled with themes that resemble old American tunes, but no quoted songs except *I Won't Go Home Until Morning*. *Filling Station* has been on tour all over the United States and South America. Music for still another film—

244

Virgil Thomson

Louisiana Story—was written in 1948. From this were drawn two orchestral suites, the second entitled *Acadian Songs and Dances.*

Thomson wrote a second opera in 1947: *The Mother of Us All* also to a text by Gertrude Stein. (She completed it only a short time before her death). The leading character is Susan B. Anthony, famous woman-suffragist; but with fine disregard for time and fact, Miss Stein included in the cast such time-separated characters as John Adams, Daniel Webster, Ulysses S. Grant, Lillian Russell and —for good measure—a "Gertrude S." and a "Virgil T." The opera was first performed in May 1947.

In *The Mother of Us All* Thomson again demonstrates his particular genius for setting words to music. To quote from a review in *Time*:

Since the business on stage. . . .was pretty complicated, Thomson kept his music harmonically simple, rarely dissonant and sometimes hymn-like, and his adroit handling of the voices added some new inflections to Steinese.

Although Thomson himself does not paint, he has a lively appreciation for art, and some of his best friends in Paris were artists— among them Picasso, Hans Arp, Tchélitcheff, Bérard, Léonide and Eugene Berman, Maurice Grosser, and Florine Stettheimer, who designed the sets and costumes for his opera *Four Saints.*

Famous among Thomson's compositions are his "musical portraits." He has done over a hundred of these, ranging from short piano, organ and violin pieces, to elaborate chamber-music works. He does these just as a painter would do a portrait, only using notes instead of a brush. Posing his subjects he sits before the model "looks at him a bit—then starts 'painting.'" It doesn't matter so much what the person looks like, he says, it is what he feels—the general state of his mind—the qualities of his character that are implied; these Thomson translates, or "paints" in terms of music. He has been surprisingly successful in his portraits. Twelve or more of them he has orchestrated, and a number of these latter have been played by leading symphony orchestras. Among them are pictures in music of such varying notables as Aaron Copland, Fiorella LaGuardia, Picasso, and Dorothy Thompson.

245

Modern Music-Makers

Some of the portraits are serious, some amusing, and some even tragical. Thomson has a keen sense of the ironical. He admits that he "is not averse to a musical joke." This ability for seeing the humorous side of situations has made him particularly successful as critic and author.

Thomson started his writing career with articles for a number of magazines, including such widely different periodicals as *Vanity Fair* and *Modern Music*. Then in 1939 he published a book *The State of Music* [8] ("full of things which only Thomson has the keenness and the wit to say, presented in the most provocative manner possible"). In 1940 he succeeded the late Lawrence Gilman as critic of the *New York Herald Tribune*. In this capacity he has established a reputation for his "fresh and frank judgments"—with a "keen insight and a sharp and witty tongue." His reviews are always entertaining, usually stimulating, and "never ambiguous, verbose or fence-straddling." A collection of these reviews, entitled *Music Right and Left* was published in 1951. [8]

Since his return from Europe Virgil Thomson has been living in a sunny top-floor apartment of the old Chelsea hotel, overlooking the southern part of New York. Here—a genial host—he indulges his hobbies for cooking (he has quite a reputation as a chef) and provocative conversation. Mornings he works in bathrobe and pajamas—usually at his music. Composing, he says, is a necessity for him. "If I don't write music, I get sick!"

In his book, *The State of Music*, Thomson tells "what it feels like to be a musician."

Mostly it is a feeling of being different from everybody, but other musicians and of inhabiting with these a closed world. This world functions interiorly like a republic of letters. Exteriorly it is a secret society and its members practice a mystery: the mystery is no mystery to us, of course; and any outsider is free to participate if he can. Only he never can. Because music-listening, and music using are oriented toward different goals from music-making, and hence nobody really knows anything about music-making except music-makers. Everybody else is just neighbors or customers, and the musical world is a tight little island entirely surrounded by them all.

[8] Henry Holt & Company.

Virgil Thomson

"There is no more sharply-drawn musical personality in America today than Virgil Thomson's," says Samuel Barlow. "He is one of the very few American-born composers with an international reputation, he is a most lively writer, he was a *Chef d'Ecole* in his thirties, and he possesses the snappiest brain in the confraternity." [9]

[9] S. L. M. Barlow in *Modern Music*, May-June, 1941.

Virgil Thomson

CHRONOLOGICAL CHART OF MAIN EVENTS AND WORKS

Born November 25, Kansas City, Mo.	1896
Enlists Field Artillery, later transferred to Air Service	1917
Discharged as Second Lieutenant	1918
Goes to Paris studies organ & composition with Nadia Boulanger	1921
Assistant music instructor and conductor of Glee Club at Harvard, organist King's Chapel, Boston	1922
Passacaglia (for organ)	
Graduates from Harvard	
Three Antiphonal Psalms (for chorus)	1924
Returns to Paris, to remain until 1932	1925
Sonata da Chiesa	1926
Symphony on a Hymn Tune	1928
Four Saints in Three Acts (first performed in 1934)	1928
Violin Sonata	1930
First String Quartet	1931
Second String Quartet	1932
Stabat Mater	1932
The Plough that broke the Plains	1936
Filling Station (ballet)	1937
The River	
Returns permanently to U.S.	1940
Seventy-five *Portraits for Piano*	1928-1940
Twelve Portraits for Orchestra	1944
The Mother of Us All	1947
Two Suites for Orchestra from Louisiana Story	1948
Concerto for Cello and Orchestra	1950

The Music of Virgil Thomson

ORCHESTRAL WORKS

Two Sentimental Tangos	1923
Symphony on a Hymn Tune [1]	1928
Second Symphony [2]	1931
Suite from The Plough that Broke the Plains [3]	1941
Suite from The River [3]	1942
Twelve Portraits [3]	1944
The Seine at Night [2]	1947
Suite #1 from Louisiana Story [2]	1948
Suite #2 from Louisiana Story—Acadian Songs and Dances [2]	1948
Wheat Field at Noon [2]	1948
Suite from The Mother of Us All [3]	1949
Concerto for Cello and Orchestra [4]	1950
A Solemn Music—for band [2]	1949
At the Beach—concert waltz for cornet solo and band [2]	1949

CHORAL WORKS

Three Antiphonal Psalms, a cappella, women's voices	1924
Missa Brevis, a cappella, men's voices	1924
Capital, Capitals (Gertrude Stein) 4 men's voices and piano [6]	1927
Missa Brevis #2, women's voices, percussion	1934
Medea Choruses (Countee Cullen), women's voices, percussion [3]	1934
Scenes from the Holy Infancy: Joseph and the Angels, The Wise Men, The Flight into Egypt, a cappella, mixed voices [3]	1937
Hymns from the Old South: My Shepherd Will Supply My Need (1937), *The Morning Star, Green Fields, Death 'tis a Melancholy Day* [5]	1949

CHAMBER MUSIC

Sonata da Chiesa—chorale, tango & fugue, for five instruments [6]	1926
Seven Portraits, for violin	1928
Five Portraits, for quartet of clarinets	1929

Modern Music-Makers

Violin Sonata	1930
First String Quartet [7]	1931
Second String Quartet [7]	1932
Serenade in Five Movements, flute and violin [1]	1932
Sonata for flute alone [8]	1943

STAGE WORKS

Four Saints in Three Acts (Gertrude Stein) opera [3]	1928
A Bride for the Unicorn (Dennis Johnson) incidental music	1934
Injunction Granted (Living Newspaper) incidental music	1936
Hamlet—incidental music	1936
The Plough that Broke the Plains (Pare Lorenz) film score	1936
Filling Station—ballet [7]	1937
Antony and Cleopatra—incidental music	1937
The Spanish Earth (Hemingway & Ivans) film in collaboration with Marc Blitzstein	1937
The River (Pare Lorentz)—film score	1937
The Trojan Women (Euripides)—radio	1940
Oedipos Tyrannos (Sophocles)—men's voices, wind, percussion	1941
Tuesday in November (John Houseman)—film	1945
The Mother of Us All—opera (Gertrude Stein) [3]	1947
Louisiana Story (Robert Flaherty)—film	1948

SONGS

Susie Asado (Gertrude Stein) [7]	1926
Five Phrases from the Song of Solomon soprano and percussion	1926
Preciosilla—recitative and aria (Gertrude Stein) [2]	1927
La Valse Grégorienne—4 poems (Georges Hugnet) [9]	1927
Les Soirées Bagnolaises, Le Berceau de Gertrude Stein— (Georges Hugnet)	1928
Le Singe et le Léopard (La Fontaine)	1928
Oraison Funèbre (Bossuet)—tenor	1930
Stabat Mater (Max Jacob)—soprano, string quartet [7]	1931
Beauty Asleep (Georges Hugnet)—soprano [2]	1931
Air de Phèdre (Racine)—soprano	1932
Old English Poems: The Sunflower, The Tiger (Blake) *Dirge* (Webster)	1920-39

Virgil Thomson

ORGAN

Postlude and a Christmas Pastorale [5]	1922
Passacaglia	1922
Variations and Fugues on Gospel Hymns—4 sets	1927
Come Ye Disconsolate	
There's Not a Friend Like the Lowly Jesus	
Will There Be Any Stars in My Crown?	
Shall We Gather at the River?	
Wedding Music	1940

PIANO

Synthetic Waltzes (for 2 pianos) [8]	1925
Ten Easy Pieces and a Coda	1926
Five Inventions	1926
Four Sonatas [3]	1930-1940
Piano Portraits (40 in 5 Volumes) [8]	1928-1940
Ten Etudes [10]	1943

[1] Southern Music.
[2] G. Schirmer.
[3] Mercury.
[4] Ricordi.
[5] H. W. Gray.
[6] New Music.
[7] Arrow Music Press.
[8] Elkan-Vogel.
[9] L'Usage de La Parole.
[10] C. Fischer.

From "The Trial of Lucullus" (1947)

ROGER SESSIONS

ROGER SESSIONS

Roger Sessions has been called "a composer's composer." Mark Schubart, however, believes that his music is too free to fit such a limited description.

In the validity of his actions and the breadth of his knowledge and experience, he is most certainly a musician's musician. . . .Of composers practising their art in the United States today, few have had a more profound influence on the course of music here than Roger Huntington Sessions. It has not been a spectacular influence. . . .But it is a substantial and important influence none the less. For it springs directly from the integrity of Sessions as a composer and as a teacher.[1]

Music, for Sessions, began while he was still an infant. One day a hurdy-gurdy stopped beneath the window of his nursery, and began to play. It woke him up, but instead of showing distress "his eyes opened wide, his face grew pink, his hands moved excitedly. It was evident that he was listening. 'That child's going to be musical!' cried the nurse. 'Look at him, he's all stirred up!' "

Before young Roger could talk he was able to sing, and "he kept it up from morning till night, in his bath, his baby-carriage, and his bed." He could reproduce any song that he heard—without the words, to be sure, "but perfectly correct and recognizable in time and tune. People used to stop and demand the name of the 'singing baby.' "

These and other tales about her precocious son were recorded by Roger Sessions' remarkable mother in a book of memoirs called *Sixty-Odd*.[2] Ruth Huntington Sessions came of a long line of New England ministers and free thinkers. Her father had been ordained

[1] Mark Schubart in *The Musical Quarterly*, April, 1946.
[2] *Sixty-Odd*, by Ruth Huntington Sessions, Stephen Daye Press, Brattleboro, Vermont, 1936.

in the Episcopal Church, having turned against his own father's Unitarian beliefs. He later became Bishop. Mrs. Sessions was musically talented, before her marriage she had spent some years studying in Germany, and from her father she inherited a keen mind and analytical nature. These endowments she passed on to her son.

He was born a few days after Christmas—December 28, 1896—and they christened him Roger Huntington. The family was then temporarily living in Brooklyn, New York, on the same street where Aaron Copland began life four years later. Roger spent a good part of his early life at Northhampton, Massachusetts, on a country estate that had belonged to the Huntington family for generations.

It was natural that he should be musical, for he came by it from his father's side, (the latter's sister was a professional singer) as well as his mother's. When Roger was three years old his mother took him to his first symphony concert. Walter Damrosch conducted the program, and began with the Overture to *Tannhäuser*. Suddenly Mrs. Sessions became aware that people in the audience below were looking up at her proscenium box, smiling. She turned to find Roger "standing there with one hand in the air, following Damrosch's baton with absolute fidelity, beat by beat, a broad grin on his countenance."

This first introduction to Wagner made a deep impression on young Roger Sessions. His mother started giving him piano lessons when he was four. Although he had no regular harmony or composition instruction, at twelve ("still under the spell of Wagner") he began—and what's more remarkable, completed—an opera: *Lancelot and Elaine*. He had taught himself to read when he was only three; likewise on his own he discovered how to set notes down on paper. "If one really wants to do a thing," he insists, "one usually does it!"

Roger attended Kent School, in Kent, Connecticut, and at fourteen entered Harvard University. During his junior year there he was made editor of the *Harvard Musical Review* and wrote a number of articles for it, including several about Strauss, whose *Elektra* he particularly admired. At this period he first encountered the moderns—Stravinsky, Scriabin and Schoenberg, and was so captivated by their music that he bought all the scores of their music that he could find.

After graduating from Harvard in 1915 Sessions planned to go to

Roger Sessions

France, to study with Ravel. But it was not possible then, because of the war, so he went instead to Horatio Parker at Yale. (Later when he tried to enlist in the army he was rejected because of his eyes). During his two years at Yale he composed his first orchestral piece, an *Overture*.

On completing his studies with Parker, Sessions was appointed in 1917 to the music faculty of Smith College, where he remained for four years. While there he continued to write music, and even began a symphony. He was not, however, satisfied with his work. "I wasn't getting the results I wanted," he says. Finally he decided to write to Ernest Bloch, whose music he had always greatly admired, and ask his advice.

"I knew that he would probably say 'Give it up. . . .!' " As it turned out, Bloch did say exactly that. When Sessions instead of appearing discouraged admitted that this was just what he had expected, "Bloch was the most surprised man in the world, for he wasn't accustomed to young American composers who were willing to admit that they didn't know much."

Sessions took an occasional lesson from Ernest Bloch (whenever he could afford the price) and found him an inspiring teacher. "A good teacher," says Roger Sessions, "is one who doesn't discourage his pupil, but corrects him by telling him all the facts."

After Bloch became head of the Cleveland Institute of Music he recommended Sessions as his assistant there. Four years later, in 1925, when Bloch left the institute, Roger Sessions also resigned.

While teaching at Smith, Sessions had thought of writing an opera. A friend in the Dramatics Department suggested as text a picturesque and colorful drama by the Russian Andreyev, called *The Black Maskers*. Sessions was struck by its possibilities, though at the time he did nothing about it. Then shortly after going to Cleveland he received a telegram saying that the Drama Section at Smith was planning to put on this very same play, and wanted him to write a musical score to accompany *The Black Maskers*. For this production he composed a score in seven parts which formed an almost continuous accompaniment to the play.

The Black Maskers is an allegorical story dealing with the conflict within the soul of man. "The castle is the soul; the lord of the castle is man, the master of the soul; the strange black maskers are the

255

powers whose field of action is the soul of man, and whose mysterious nature he can never fathom."

Every man (says Sessions), as I afterwards came to see and understand, was like that rich and distinguished gentleman who arranged a gorgeous masquerade in his castle and illuminated his castle with lights; and thither came from far and wide strange masks, whom he welcomed with courteous greetings, though ever with the vain inquiry: "Who are you?" and new masks arrived ever stranger and more horrible!

Sessions dedicated *The Black Maskers* to Ernest Bloch. Later he rearranged the original score into an orchestral suite in four parts:

I. *Dance* . . . a wild melody in which are heard malicious laughter and despair, and someone's low, sad plaining.

II. *Scena* . . . in which the festive gathering is gradually overwhelmed by the increasing horde of Black Maskers—Lorenzo's song.

III. *Dirge* . . . interspersed with reminiscences of the wild trumpetings of the Black Maskers and later by trumpet calls announcing from the turrets of the castle the death of Lorenzo.

IV. *Finale* . . . music of final scene; as his castle is overwhelmed by the conflagration, Lorenzo finds redemption in the symbolic purity of the flames.

When Roger Sessions left Cleveland in 1925, he went to Europe. Several awards—notably a Guggenheim Fellowship in 1926 (renewed the following year) and, in 1928, the Rome Prize, made it possible for him to remain in Europe altogether eight years—with occasional visits home. He spent three years in Florence, three more in Rome, and two in Berlin. This long association with the music and culture of foreign countries, together with the intellectual inheritance of his family background, have given Roger Sessions a breadth and an "innate cosmopolitanism" that is evident in all his work.

ROGER SESSIONS

Roger Sessions

In Paris, at the home of Nadia Boulanger, Sessions met another young American composer: Aaron Copland. The two had many discussions about the sad plight of native composers in the United States. In Europe modern music was accepted with open-minded interest—if not always with enthusiasm—(a number of the younger Americans achieved reputations abroad long before they were accepted in their own country). But in the United States the situation was very different.

Sessions and Copland felt that this was largely due to the fact that contemporary works were frequently played abroad, but seldom in the United States, and they believed (somewhat optimistically, as it turned out) that if American audiences had a chance to hear more modern music, it would become more popular. The two young composers decided to sponsor a group of concerts devoted exclusively to the works of contemporary American composers.

The resulting series, called the Copland-Sessions Concerts, proved one of the earliest, and most important, means of bringing the music of the younger composers before the public. Sessions, however, did not long maintain an active part in these concerts, for just at that time he was awarded the Rome Prize and went to stay three years at the American Academy in Rome.

While in Florence he wrote three *Chorale Preludes* ("remarkably austere—without a trace of the emotional spirit of the *Black Maskers*"[3]) and his *First Symphony*. The latter had its initial performance in April 1927 by Koussevitzky and the Boston Symphony.

Randall Thompson called Sessions' *First Piano Sonata* (written in 1930) "a work of elegance, nobility and passion....No superfluous detail....Polished without being precious—strong without display of strength."[4] Copland pronounced it "a cornerstone upon which to base an American music." Sessions completed a *Second Piano Sonata* in 1946. He has also produced a *Duo for Violin and Piano* (1942), and two *String Quartets*, the last of these in 1951.

Roger Sessions returned permanently from Europe in 1933. He taught for a time at the Delacroze Institute in New York, and in 1935 was appointed to Princeton's Music Department. That same

[3] Nicolas Slonimsky in *American Composers on American Music*, edited by Henry Colwell.
[4] Randall Thompson in *Modern Music*, April, 1935.

summer the University of California invited him to come to Berkeley to conduct a summer class in composition. This visit to California proved an important prelude to his later career and to his personal life. In Berkeley he met Elisabeth Franck, and they were married soon after (he for the second time). They now have two children—John and Elisabeth.

In 1936 Sessions went back to the University of California for a second summer course; again three years later and finally, in 1945 (after ten years at Princeton), he became full-time head of California's Music Department. He enjoys teaching, and his natural friendliness and simplicity have made him popular with students and faculty alike.

In his teaching, Sessions draws constantly on his creative faculties, and it is this generosity that gives him a remarkable understanding of his pupil's problems, and sympathy with their purposes. He is both informal and tolerant with them, and never seeks to influence them in matters of style and esthetic. He believes that the role of the teacher of advanced pupils is, first, to see that they themselves understand what they are trying to do and, secondly, to help them do it. Unlike some other teachers, whose pupils sit at the feet of the master and write in his manner, Sessions prefers that his pupils retain their independance, and that each write according to the dictates of his own ear, sharing with his colleagues only those principles of musicality common to all composers.[5]

Sessions' *First String Quartet* was composed during his second visit to California. Then for ten years, with the exception of a *Chorale* for organ, a few short piano pieces *(Pages from a Diary)* and a choral work *Turn O Libertad,* he produced no new work of importance. He had several up his sleeve, however, and in preparation.

In 1946 he completed a *Second Piano Sonata,* written for Andor Foldes, and played by him in New York; also a *Second Symphony* (under the auspices of Columbia's Ditson Fund, though for some years in preparation). This symphony—dedicated to Franklin D. Roosevelt—was first played in San Francisco, with Pierre Monteux conducting. It received a Naumburg Award, and after its performance in 1951 by Mitropoulos and the New York Philharmonic-

[5] Mark A. Schubart in the *Musical Quarterly,* April, 1946.

Roger Sessions

Symphony, was given the Music Critics' award for "the best orchestral composition of the year."

The music took the shape which it had to take, (Sessions explains[6]) and I strove, as I always do, to be simply the obedient and willing servant of my musical ideas. But it must be remembered always, I think, that for a composer musical ideas have infinitely more substance, more reality, more specific meaning, and a more vital connection with experience than any words that could be found to describe them. . . .

Composing is a spiritual thing. Kurt Sachs. . . .concludes that in composition there is two percent inspiration and ninety-eight percent technique. My own idea is that music is not abstract and that technique is actually the power of articulate speech. Technique is not something one learns in school (except the basis or necessary foundation of technique), it is something personal: imagination. But one can't have imagination until one has a medium by which it can be expressed. . . .

What may seem emotion to some will be to others rich in feeling, depending on experiences shared or known. One's own relationship to a thing also changes or develops with time. . . .If you hear my *Second Symphony* next year, or the next, it is possible that it will have a different meaning to you than when first you heard it.

This is true of all modern works. Music which at a first performance may seem to have no meaning whatsoever becomes reasonably clear and intelligible after repeated hearing. Arthur Rodzinski once remarked: "You should never criticize a new work until you have heard it at least ten times. . . ."

According to this criterion it is too soon to pass judgment on Session's *Second Symphony*. *Time* called it "hard work for musicians and audience alike, and added that Sessions "is probably the most difficult of United States composers." But Alfred Frankenstein, critic of the San Francisco *Chronicle* pronounced it "big . . . challenging . . . important . . . austere." He also said that it was "fiendishly difficult . . . a complex of forceful and fruitful ideas which can be studied for a long time before they yield all their secrets."

Sessions himself claims that all that is required in order to perform his works is good musicianship—plus good will on the part of

[6] In an interview with J. Douglas Cook, *In Opera, Concert and Symphony*, May 1947.

the players. For instance, he explains, in *The Black Maskers* there is a difficult entrance for the bassoons. When played by large orchestras the conductors are apt to give this part to another instrument. But if by a less pretentious group then the bassoonist "takes it home and learns it."

Sessions' *Violin Concerto*, written in 1935, has the reputation of being "impossible to play." Yet, he explains, fairly unknown violinists have been able to learn it. Although his works may demand a little practise, the results are worth the effort.

His primary aim, he says, is not so much to reach the public, as simply "to write good music. If a thing is good enough it will get to the public eventually." Music that is functional, but which does not depend on immediate popular success is, to him, the best of all. Bach wrote functional music, but in the last analysis it didn't matter whether anyone liked it or not. "He didn't write to flatter the public. There was no one demanding larger gate receipts...."

Sessions does not entirely approve of subsidies. "Great talents are not fostered—they foster themselves," he says. Subsidies, fellowships, etc., are too often given "not because of art but because composers must be kept alive. Classics grow with acquaintance. Most modern works do not...."

The best conditions existed, he believes, in the time of Bach, Haydn and Mozart. Theirs was *employment*, not subsidy. Their music was functional in the highest sense; it was written for a purpose: to be performed. They were asked to produce music, but allowed to work it out their own way.

Lazare Saminsky called Roger Sessions "a neoclassicist of the Hindemith-Prokofiev kind." Sessions himself says that he rejects any kind of dogma or platform.

I am not trying to write "modern," "American," or "neo-classic" music; I am seeking always and only the coherent, and living expression of my musical ideas. I dislike rhetoric, over-emphasis, vulgarity, but at the same time believe that perfection in art consists in a sort of equilibrium which can be neither defined nor counterfeited.

He has no sympathy with consciously sought originality.

"My interest is in form; and by this I mean that I accept my musical ideas, try to give them living shape, without theorizing as to their source or their other than musical meaning. Musical ideas are impulses, emotional impulses, if you will, which come from subconscious sources. . . . Any kind of creative activity is a mystery, and works of art are, in my opinion, to be judged largely with the imagination and not with reference to any set of opinions.[7]

Until recently, *The Black Maskers* was Sessions' only "programmatic" work. But he had always wanted, since his earliest venture *Lancelot and Elaine,* produced at the age of twelve, to write an opera. In 1935 C. A. Borghese (son-in-law of Thomas Mann) suggested to Sessions that he collaborate with him in making an opera of a book Borghese had written about the ancient Emperor Montezuma. Sessions was fired by the dramatical possibilities of the book's setting, and agreed. For several years now, off and on, he has been working at this opera.

When he first began it he felt, he confesses "a certain uneasiness" since he knew comparatively little then about operatic technique. So by way of practice he decided to try his hand at a shorter work. For this he chose a play by the German writer Berthold Brecht: *The Trial of Lucullus.*

This powerful denunciation of tyranny and oppression was originally written for radio, and had its first broadcast from Zürich at the time of Poland's invasion. It tells of a Roman general who stands trial after his death to see whether he shall be assigned to Hades or to the Elysian fields. The jury questions his witnesses and they tell what his wars did to their lives. "Their homely talk, so powerful because so simple and true, swells to an indictment that speaks for all the suffering masses in the world today."

The Trial of Lucullus as a one-act opera was first performed April 18, 1947, by the students of the Music Department at the University of California. (Stravinsky's *Histoire du Soldat* was on the same program.)

Roger Sessions feels strongly about the condition of opera in this country. He believes that it is too largely dominated by commercial considerations. In Europe every large city has its opera house and company, with ample opportunities for the development of young

[7] Roger Sessions as quoted in the *Boston Symphony Program Notes,* April 22, 1927.

Modern Music-Makers

artists; the state considers opera a necessary part of cultural education, and subsidizes the performances. As a result new works are encouraged. In the United States, however, new operas tend to be actually discouraged, since they involve too much of a financial risk.

"This situation must be changed," says Sessions, "if American opera is to become an accomplished and historic fact comparable to what it is in Europe."

During the past few years Sessions' time has been largely taken up in writing two books on music: *The Musical Experience,* published in 1950 by the Princeton University Press, and *Harmonic Practice* (Harcourt Brace and Co., 1951). He has also been at work on two symphonies, his *Third* and *Fourth,* which he expects to complete in 1951, and a group of pieces for orchestra entitled *Burlesque, Elegy,* and *Pastorale.*

Roger Sessions, according to Lazere Saminsky, is "not a stylizer, not a clever manipulator of tired pasticcio, but a man aroused by a vision of the orderly frames of the classical world, intoxicated by their lucid reason."[8]

Aaron Copland writes of him:

The music that he has composed is more often than not of a surpassing technical difficulty. This makes it hard to perform and hard to listen to, particularly for the ordinary concert-goer. But you must be willing to accept these conditions of his art, so to speak, or you will never get closer to an appreciation of the music itself.

Sessions is by nature a perfectionist. Every work signed with his name is sure to be the result of extraordinary care, perhaps exaggerated meticulousness. . . . But that does not mean that his music is precious; on the contrary, it is solid, full-blooded, robust . . . of real quality . . . of an almost tactile sensibility. . . . And all his music, slow or fast, is written with the same consummate technical finish.[9]

[8] Lazare Saminsky in *Modern Music,* Jan.-Feb., 1936.
[9] Aaron Copland in *Our New Music,* Whittlesey House, 1941.

Roger Sessions

CHRONOLOGICAL CHART OF MAIN EVENTS AND WORKS

Born December 28, Brooklyn, N. Y.	1896
Graduates from Harvard	1915
Studies with Horatio Parker at Yale	1915-1917
Appointed to Music Faculty of Smith College—Steinert Prize	1917
Appointed assistant to Ernest Bloch at Cleveland Institute of Music	1921
Incidental Music to The Black Maskers	1923
Goes to Europe for eight years	1925
Three Chorale Preludes for Organ	1924-1926
Guggenheim Fellowship (renewed in 1927)	1926
First Symphony	1927
Rome Prize	1928
Pastorale for Flute	1929
With Aaron Copland established the Copland-Sessions Concerts	1931
Returns permanently to U. S.	1933
Concerto for Violin	1931-1935
Appointed to Princeton's Music Department	1935
Summer Session at University of California	
Marries Elizabeth Franck	
First String Quartet	1936
Elected to National Institute of Arts and Letters	1938
President of U. S. section of International Society for	
Contemporary Music	1936-1941
Appointed Professor at University of California	1945
Second Symphony	1946
The Trial of Lucullus	1947
Naumburg Award (for *Second Symphony*)	1949
Music Critics' Prize for *Second Symphony*	1950

The Music of Roger Sessions

ORCHESTRAL WORKS

First Symphony [1]	1926-1927
Suite from The Black Maskers [1]	1928
Concerto for Violin [2]	1931-1935
Symphony No. 2 [3]	1946
Burlesque, Elegy, Pastorale (to be completed in 1951)	
Third Symphony (to be completed in 1951)	
Fourth Symphony (in preparation)	

CHORAL WORKS

Turn O Libertad—mixed chorus, piano four hands	1944

CHAMBER MUSIC

Pastorale for Flute Solo	1929
Sonata for Piano—First [4]	1930
String Quartet No. 1 [5]	1936
Duo for Violin and Piano [6]	1942
Second Piano Sonata [7]	1946
Second Quartet	1951

ORGAN WORKS

Chorale Prelude [1]	1924
Two Chorale Preludes [1]	1926
Chorale [8]	1938

PIANO WORKS

Four Pieces for Children [9]	1935
Pages from a Diary [7]	1937-1940

SONGS

On the Beach at Fontan [10]	1930

Roger Sessions

Music for the Stage

Incidental Music for The Black Maskers	1923
Incidental Music for Turandot (Vollmüller)	1925
Two pianos and percussion	
The Trial of Lucullus (opera)	1947
Montezuma (opera—in preparation)	

[1] Cos Cob Press.
[2] Edgar Stillman Kelley Soc.
[3] G. Schirmer.
[4] Schott.
[5] Arrow Music Press.
[6] New Music Edition.
[7] Ed. B. Marks Corp.
[8] H. W. Gray Co.
[9] C. Fischer.
[10] Cos Cob and Sylvan Press, London.

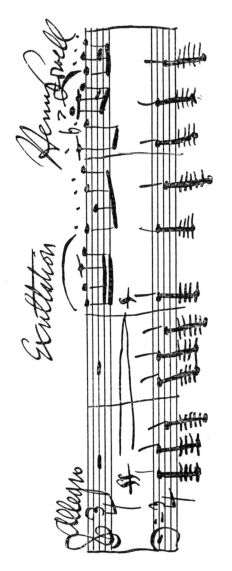

HENRY COWELL

HENRY COWELL

HENRY COWELL at the beginning of his career was one of the most radical of contemporary composers. His first public concert, in 1921, made something of a stir. After his second appearance before a larger audience in New York, at which he gave an entire program of his own works, his reputation as a startling innovator spread across the country. From 1924 to 1935 he toured the United States yearly, and people flocked to listen to his strange new music.

Those who heard him in those early days will not have forgotten the impression which his curious way of playing made. Leaning with his whole arm on the keyboard, to produce the "tone-clusters" for which his music is famous—standing up to pluck the strings inside the piano or tapping various rhythms on the sound-box itself—Cowell's performance was fascinating to watch, if a little difficult for the average person to understand. The music sounded a good deal like bedlam to unaccustomed ears ("congealed nightmares of sound" some called it), though certain of the lighter, descriptive pieces, using the full resources of the "String and Percussion Piano" that is, an ordinary piano played Cowell-fashion—captivated the public with their charming and unusual effects. Today, however, as we have grown more accustomed to the modern idiom, those early pieces of Cowell's no longer seem radical.

While still a young child Henry Cowell began to experiment with sound effects. He trained himself to recognize and to set down, in his own method of notation, the various sounds that intrigued him. He did everything he could to develop his musical perceptions, deliberately "practising sounds" and experimenting in many fields.

Henry Cowell was born in Menlo Park, California, March 11, 1897. When only four he learned to play on a curious instrument called the "mandolin-harp." His father, who had come to this country from Ireland (son of an Episcopal Dean in Kildare) and his mother—sensitive, poetic, and a writer by profession—both encouraged their son's interest in music. They bought him a small violin, and before long he was playing in recitals. However, this proved too much for his health; when he was eight he had to give up the violin.

Henry then decided to be a composer, for he felt that a composer's life would be less strenuous than that of a virtuoso. And also more interesting! He was always making up songs. Whenever his mother read poetry to him, the words inevitably wove themselves in his mind into a pattern of music.

There was no piano in the modest home where the Cowells then lived, near Palo Alto, California. Young Henry saved up for years to buy one. He herded the neighbor's cows, helped with the gardening and did all the odd jobs that a delicate boy could handle. Finally in 1911, when he was fourteen, he bought a second-hand upright piano and felt that his musical career was launched.

The piano as an instrument fascinated him. He explored it inside and out. By plucking the strings he found that he could reproduce the pizzicato of a violin, and by running his fingers lightly over the strings he was able to create an eerie, wind-like effect quite different from the instrument's usual tone. Again, when he struck the sounding board with his knuckles, strange resonances of various pitches were revealed. Before long Henry began to put these sound-effects into weird pieces full of glissandos like the wailing of Irish banshees.

About a year later, young Cowell made another discovery. He wrote some incidental music for a play to be given at Carmel's picturesque Forest Theater. At the rehearsal, finding that his music sounded disappointingly thin on the lone piano under the trees, and that his ten fingers couldn't make enough sound to satisfy him, the enterprising young composer supplemented his fingers by using his fist—then his whole forearm.

The result was so gratifying that a few months later he used the new technique in an opera based on an Indian myth. This was performed in a field near the beach, seventeen miles south of San Luis Obispo, the stage lit by auto headlights covered with colored cellophane. The piano accompaniment, with its massive "forearm chords" made quite an impression.

Henry was so pleased with his new sound effect, and so sure that it must have a scientific basis, that he decided to make a serious study of acoustics. He used the word "tone-clusters" to describe his multiple-note chords, and wrote a set of short pieces—*Adventures in Harmony*—to demonstrate his arm-playing technique. During the first years after he began experimenting with the possibilities of what he christened the "string and percussion piano," young Cowell turned out over a hundred pieces, all of them short, and none of them according to rule. Because, as he says, he "didn't know any rules."

In 1912 Arthur Lewis, of the San Francisco Symphony, was walking in the country not far from Stanford University when he heard strange and unfamiliar music coming from a small cottage in the hills. He listened a moment. Then he knocked at the door.

A slight, delicate-looking boy with a sensitive face and a large head, came to the door.

"Who was playing the piano just now?" Lewis asked.

The boy admitted shyly that it was he. "But the music," the other insisted, "where did you find it?"

"I wrote it myself," admitted the young musician, and showed Lewis some of his extraordinary pieces. When the latter learned that the fifteen-year-old composer was entirely self-taught he was so impressed that he took the boy to Charles Seeger, head of the Music Department of the University of California.

Dr. Seeger saw at once that here was a brilliant and unusual talent, and offered to train young Cowell. He was wise enough, however, not to try to force him into a conventional mold. While giving him a solid base of harmony and counterpoint, he allowed him to work out his own ideas in composing. For the next three and a half years, Cowell studied "legitimate" ways of writing music. But it had little or no effect on his own originality, and he continued to turn out unorthodox compositions.

In 1917 he enlisted in the army, where he served with one of the bands. After his discharge he enrolled at the Institute of Musical Art in New York City. This was Cowell's first experience with cut and dried rules and regulations. He didn't like it. One day, when an exercise in composition came back to him covered with even more blue-pencil marks than usual he decided, in exasperation, to try a little experiment of his own. He copied out a Bach *Chorale* and turned it in. When this too came back with blue marks Cowell presented the sheet, together with the original, and asked for the return of his tuition money.

Following this short flight into orthodoxy, Cowell studied for a time with Huntington Woodman at the Institute of Applied Music in New York. He also had a few lessons with Carl Ruggles. But the young composer was impatient with conservative methods. He was the despair of both teachers and friends, who could see no excuse for the unconventionality of his ideas.

Cowell continued to write music in his own individual style. Soon he began to give concerts of his works, and his music roused so much controversy that he became one of the most discussed of the new music composers.

Everyone who has heard his weird glissandos, interpretative of the ghost of his Irish ancestors, the "Banshee" rendered directly on the piano strings, will admit that as a new orchestral color it is an undeniable acquisition. Pizzicato on the piano strings, as well as the entire gamut of percussion, conjured up from the pianistic entrails, make the piano a richer instrument without impinging on its historical dignity.[1]

In the middle 1920's, a player-piano manufacturing company invited Cowell to make some recordings for their instrument.

Several months later he happened to be in a music store where the automatic pianos were sold. Without mentioning his name, he asked to hear one of his recordings. The clerk put in the selected roll, turned on the mechanism—then looked down at the pianola in consternation. First all the notes on one side of the keyboard went down, then all those on the other side.

"There must be something wrong with this player," he said apologetically. "I'll try another one." But again the same thing happened. The distraught salesman was about to call in a repair man when Cowell finally explained the phenomenon of tone-clusters.

Henry Cowell's discovery of these tone-clusters came quite naturally, he says, while searching for a means of reinforcing sound. The massed chords add greatly to the deep, resonant tones in the bass (whether used orchestrally or on the piano alone), while in the

[1] In *American Composers on American Music,* edited by Henry Cowell, Stanford University Press, 1933.

Henry Cowell

treble they create an effect of scintillating brilliance. The composition of these clusters, Cowell explains, is based scientifically on the law of overtones.

As any music-student knows, when a note is struck, a corresponding series of overtones is automatically set into motion, stretching upwards in mathematical progression. Debussy employed this principle, holding down the pedal to bring out the overtone vibrations, and thus giving to his music a rich, sonorous texture. Cowell, instead of using the pedal alone, plays the actual tones in multiple chords of from twelve to fifty-six notes each. In a single instrument he is able to create sweeps of sound similar to orchestral effects.

The tone-clusters, he points out, are in reality a simple use of acoustical laws—*i.e.*, chords based on seconds instead of, as is usual, on thirds or fourths. Although at times the tone-clusters give an impression of extreme dissonance—as in the piano pieces *Tiger, Antinomy, Advertisement,*—where they are used softly as an accompaniment to a leading melody, the effect is enriching rather than dissonant.

Cowell denies that he is deliberately dissonant, or seeks only to innovate:

To write extreme dissonance is not necessarily to innovate: it is possible to innovate only by unique handling.

There is a tendency on the part of the concert going public to regard all dissonant music as original, and all music on concordant basis as old-fashioned. . . . Not because of striving for originality, but on account of the compelling urge of the musical idea, I find necessary in certain compositions the use of new materials, which, upon analysis afterwards, prove to be new tone qualities, new cross meters and rhythms, new extensions of melodic line, new types of harmony and counterpoint, and materials which are themselves combinations of new and old styles.

Cowell was not actually the first to invent "tone-clusters." Some years before, Charles Ives had used chords which were supposed to be played with a ruler, or board. A Russian named Rebikov also experimented with the same idea of massed-notes, and so did Ornstein. But none of these composers carried their experiments beyond the initial stages.

Cowell, on the other hand, developed the tone-cluster technique to the limit of its possibilities in extended works for orchestra as well as

271

Modern Music-Makers

for single instruments, using the multiple chords both as moving harmonic masses and as the result of the crossing of several polyphonic lines.

Later he made a thorough study of the science of tone combinations, of rhythm and chord formation, and also worked out a special notation or way of writing down his new sound effects. His book, *New Musical Resources,* published in 1930 by Alfred Knopf, explains his theories and discoveries. The object of the book, he writes in the introduction, is "to point out the influence the overtone series has exerted on music throughout its history . . . how, by various means of applying its principles in many different manners, a large palette of musical materials can be assembled."

While studying the laws of rhythm and vibration, Cowell conceived the idea of an instrument which would be capable of reproducing rhythmical patterns of varying complexity. With Professor Theremin, inventor of the famous ether-wave instrument, he constructed what they called a "rhythmicon"—using a new principle (now a basic part of television) in which broken light rays play on a photoelectric cell. This invention, which makes it possible to play any kind of rhythm by holding down certain keys on an organlike keyboard, relates rhythm to sound in a scientific manner "so that a sonal harmony corresponding to the rhythm in vibration ratio is always heard."

For this instrument Cowell composed an orchestral suite of four movements which he called *Rhythmicana.* Another composition for rhythmicon and violin was played in San Francisco in May, 1932.

Mr. Cowell used his rhythmicon to accompany a set of violin movements which he had written for the occasion. The accompaniment was a strange complexity of rhythmical inter-weavings and cross currents of a cunning and precision as never before fell on the ear of man, and the sound pattern was as uncanny as the motion.[2]

Between the years of 1921 and 1935, Cowell made five successful concert tours through the leading cities of Europe. Wherever he appeared, his music aroused interest and amazement. It had every kind of reception—from "gnashing of teeth to sober praise from competent critics."

[2] Homer Henley in *The Argonaut.* May 20, 1932.

272

HENRY COWELL

Henry Cowell

At his first European concert, in Leipzig, pandemonium broke loose. The police were finally called in, and arrested twenty people whose arguments had turned into a free-for-all on the stage. Cowell sat calmly through the fracas and continued playing. . . .

In Russia he was more favorably received. Although some accused him of "bourgeois psychology" and "false futurism," most of the people there recognized in the young American composer a fellow revolutionary, one who was seeking new ways to express old truths— new bottles for old wine, and some new wine to boot. Cowell's music represented to the Russians the clamorous machine age of America. One listener, after hearing him play at the Leningrad Institute of Arts and Sciences, wrote that the music brought before his eyes the towering sky line of New York and the floodlights of Broadway.

In 1932 Cowell returned to Berlin on a Guggenheim Fellowship and made a study of comparative musicology. Insatiably curious about everything concerning music, he was intensely interested in the way other nations expressed themselves in rhythm and melody. The music of the East fascinated him particularly. He made a collection of the recordings of Far-East countries, and learned to play some of their instruments—notably the Javanese *Gamelang* and the *Shakuhachi*, the flute of Japan. In Berlin Cowell made an extensive study of Oriental music with Erich von Hornbostel.

As a result of this study, Cowell has become recognized as a leading authority on the music of the East. Because of his knowledge of the subject, in 1943 he was appointed Music Editor to the Office of War Information, and was put in charge of the selecting of music used on the propaganda broadcasts to foreign countries.

Cowell's music divides rather sharply into two different styles, one scientific, technical, and not easy for the layman to listen to, (*Polyphonica*, for twelve instruments, is a typical example) the other written with such simplicity that it appears, at first hand, naive. Actually it is very subtle, says Charles Seeger in an article written for the July, 1940, *Magazine of Art*.

The music is almost without 'content.' It seems calculatedly shallow. One often suspects the tongue-in-cheek, but I doubt if it is there. . . . This music is not easily relatable to other contemporary music. It seems to exist

Modern Music-Makers

in a universe of its own. It is more than 'unconventional'. . . I can think of no composer whose work is more difficult to evaluate.

The influence of Cowell's Irish ancestry is apparent in much of his work. Many of the titles reflect his love for the old Celtic legends and folklore. For instance *The Tides of Mannanen,* using rolling tone-clusters to depict the swelling waves; the *Gaelic Symphony;* a *Suite for String and Percussion Piano and Chamber Orchestra,* whose numbers are entitled *The Banshee, Leprechaun,* and *Fairy Bells.*

He has written a large number of piano pieces, most of them with descriptive titles such as *The Whirling Dervish* and the *Aeolian Harp* (this last played entirely on the open string of the piano). Typical of Cowell's inventive spirit are *Synchrony,* for dancers and orchestra, *Toccanta*—a cantata-toccata for piano, flute, cello and soprano voice, and a chamber-music work called *Mosaic Quartet.*

The *Mosaic Quartet* is perhaps the most original of Cowell's chamber-music works. It is made up of four very short movements, (each about a minute and a half long), and these can be combined in any sequence that may be desired, the players thus building their own "mosaic." Of the initial performance Olin Downes wrote: "The first (movement) harmonizes perfectly a conventional and chorale-like strain in queer ways . . . like the exercise of an inept harmony pupil who finally got it right by the time the last measure arrived." The third he called "a thing of faint buzzings and whines against a cello monologue of unctuous brevity," while the last, he said, was "really funny. The audience had a good laugh. This is music written with a pleasing insolence."

Tales of Our Countryside, for piano and orchestra, has four movements based on earlier piano works, each written in a different part of the United States: *Deep Tides* (California), *Exultation* (New York), *The Harp of Life* (Iowa), and *Country Reel* (Kansas). Cowell played two of these in their original piano version at a recital in Boston, in the late 1920's. One of the critics at that time took him severely to task for writing such cacophonous music. But when the pieces were played there again in 1940 by Stokowski and his Youth Orchestra, the same critic remarked that "he had expected radical modern music, but could see nothing in *Tales of Our Countryside* to justify his considering Cowell as a particularly *modern* composer."

Henry Cowell

Which goes to show that dissonance has become so much a part of today's music that Cowell's tunes, based on broad melodies in folk-ballad style, now seem natural rather than startling.

Leopold Stokowski performed Cowell's *Tales of Our Countryside* at the opening concert of the New York Philharmonic-Symphony's centennial season, with the composer as soloist. Following the concert Virgil Thomson wrote:

Henry Cowell is a charming composer. His approach to the folk-style is muscular and sentimental, and he writes folksy tunes that are as bouncing and as buoyant as real ones but which are nevertheless personal expressions, not quotations from the books. All this gives to his music a character of directness and of sincerity that is utterly pleasing.

In 1943 Cowell set to music, for orchestra and chorus, Robert Frost's poem *Fire and Ice*, and in the same year (for women's chorus with piano accompaniment) he wrote *American Muse*, from Stephen Vincent Benèt's *John Brown's Body*. This latter, together with his series of *Hymns and Fuguing Tunes* (five in all, of which the *Second* has been most widely played), represents Cowell's idea of what the old New England church music would have grown into if it had been allowed to develop from its early beginnings to the present time. He feels that this might well have become an individual and definitely American classical style.[3] His *Violin Sonata* (1947) uses an extension of this style in its materials, though it is written in sonata form. The five movements are titled: *Hymn, Fuguing Tune, Ballad, Dance,* and *Finale.*

The list of Henry Cowell's compositions is endless. He has written close to nine hundred in all, among them five symphonies (the last of these played in 1949 by Hans Kindler and the National Symphony Orchestra, and in 1950 by Izler Solomon at the Columbia University Festival); a large number of pieces for band; chamber music in endless combinations of instruments and, of course, the piano compositions which were the basis of his early reputation. He has also written many choral works. One of the most recent of these: *Day, Evening,*

[3] Cowell's interpretation of the old "fuguing tune" is in interesting contrast to William Schuman's treatment of the same subject in his *William Billings Overture.*

275

Modern Music-Makers

Night, Morning has been sung on tour for two seasons by Leonard de Pauer's Infantry Chorus.

In 1941 Henry Cowell married Sidney Robertson, well-known authority on folk songs. Mrs. Cowell spent several years collecting folk music from different parts of the United States (records of which are on file in the Library of Congress). She has published a book on the native songs of California.

Henry Cowell too has written several books: *New Musical Resources;* a symposium called *American Composers on American Music;* and *The Nature of Melody* — a textbook on melody writing. In addition he founded, and for several years was editor of the quarterly, *New Music.* He has contributed numerous articles, and has lectured extensively both in this country and abroad. At various times he has been on the faculties of the University of California, Stanford, Bennington, Mills College, Columbia, The New School, and Adelphi College. As director of musical activities at the New School for Social Research he organized concerts of modern music and established the first composer's forum. Cowell has been an active member of the New Music Society of California, the Pan-American Association of Composers, and the International Exchange Concerts—whose purpose is to make the works of contemporary composers known in other countries besides their own. As John Tasker Howard says: "Cowell is the friend of all modern tendencies and the tireless proponent of American musical life."[4]

Henry Cowell's music, and his experiments in tone-production and acoustics, have added greatly to our present day musical palette, and equally important has been his contribution to the cause of modern music. For this cause he has worked wholeheartedly, lending his time and energy, advice and support. Charles Seeger considers him "a kind of catalytic agent among the disparate elements of American musical life."

[4] John Tasker Howard, *Our Contemporary Composers,* Thomas Y. Crowell Co., New York, 1943.

Henry Cowell

The Music of Henry Cowell

Henry Cowell

To America—chorus, two orchestras [8]	1946
Saturday Night at the Firehouse [5]	1947
Fifth Symphony [5]	1948

Symphonic Band

Animal Magic [9]	
Fanfare [10]	1928
Grandma's Rumba [8]	1929
Hymn and Fuguing Tune #1 [9]	1930
Shipshape Overture [6]	1941
Schoonthree [7]	1940
A Curse and a Blessing [11]	1951

Chamber Music

Ensemble—2 violins, viola, 2 cellos [3]	1925
Seven Paragraphs—trios, violin, viola, cello	1926
Quartet	1927
Suite—violin, piano [3]	1927
Ensemble for Wind Quintet [15]	1930
Six Casual Developments—clarinet, piano	1934
Movement [12]	1934
Mosaic Quartet—string quartet [12]	1935
Seven Associated Movements—violin, piano	1935
United Quartet—string quartet	1936
Vocalise—soprano, flute, cello, piano	1937
Processional (organ) [18]	1938
Toccanta—soprano, flute, cello, piano	1939
Three Ostinati with Chorales—oboe, piano [21]	1940
Two Bits (flute & piano) [13]	1940
How Old Is Song—violin, piano, strings	1942-1944
Action in Brass [14]	1943
Sonata—violin, piano (revised 1947) [3]	1945
Tall Tale (2 trumpets, horn, 2 trombones, tuba) [7]	1947
Tom Binkley's Tune (baritone horn & piano) [9]	1947
Saxophone Quartet (2 altos, tenor, baritone) [16]	1948
Tune Takes a Trip (5 B flat clarinets) [17]	1948

279

Modern Music-Makers

Choral Music

The Thistle Flower (women's voices a cappella)	1928
The Coming of Light (soprano, alto, tenor, bass) [19]	1939
Fire and Ice (2 tenors, bar, bass, orch. or band) [20]	1942
American Muse (soprano, alto, piano) [21]	1943
United Nations Songbook [8]	1943
Canon: Air Held Her Breath (SATB a cappella) [21]	1944
To America (SATB a cappella) [8]	1944
The Irish Girl (SATB with piano) [8]	1945
The Irishman Lilts (SSA or SATB with piano) [8]	1945
The Road into Tomorrow (SATB with piano) [5]	1947
Sweet Christmas Song (SATB a cappella) [17]	1948
Day, Evening, Night, Morning (TTBB a cappella) [15]	1948
Ballad of the Two Mothers (SATB a cappella) [15]	1948
The Lily's Lament (SSA with piano) [17]	1948
Brookside at Eventide (TTBBB a cappella) [15]	1949
Luther's Carol (TTBB a cappella) [9]	1949

Stage Works

The Building of Banba—ballet	1915-1916
Atlantis—ballet	1926
Mr. Flagmaker—film	1942
O'Higgins Chile—opera	1950

Piano Works
(Using Tone Clusters)

The Tides of Manaunaun [5]	1915
Antinomy [5]	1915
Dynamic Motion [5]	1915
The Voice of Lir [5]	1916
Advertisement [5]	1916
The Hero Sun [5]	1916
Amiable Conversation [5]	1916
Exultation [5]	1918
The Snows of Fuji-Yama [5]	1921
It Isn't It [22]	1921
The Harp of Life [5]	1925
Lilt of the Reel [5]	1926
Tiger [23]	1927

Henry Cowell

The Irishman Dances [24]	1931
The Irish Minstrel Sings [24]	1931

(Using the piano strings)

Piece for Piano with Strings [26]	1924
Aeolian Harp [25]	1925
The Banshee [25]	1925
The Fairy Answer [25]	1927
Sinister Resonance [5]	1927

(Using customary keyboard technique)

Six Ings: Floating-Fleeting-Wafting-Seething-Frisking-Scooting [5]	1916
Fabric (three interweaving rhythms) [5]	1917
Maestoso [12]	1930
Heroic Dance [27]	1931
Woof Nos. 1 and 2 [12]	1935
Hilarious Curtain Opener [12]	1938

SONGS

St. Agnes Morning [21]	1918
Where She Lies [29]	1924
Manaunaun's Birthing [29]	1924
Rest [12]	1928
Sunset [12]	1928
How Old Is Song [28]	1944
The Donkey [21]	1946

[1] M. Senart.
[2] Edition Adler.
[3] Associated Music.
[4] Arrow Music Press.
[5] Ass. Music Pub.
[6] G. Schirmer, Inc.
[7] Mercury Music Corp.
[8] Broadcast Music Inc.
[9] Leeds.
[10] Boosey Hawks.
[11] Peer International.
[12] New Music.
[13] Gundy-Bettoney.
[14] Edition Musicus.
[15] Merrymount.
[16] Peer International.
[17] Marks.
[18] Grey.
[19] Harold Flammer.
[20] Boston Music Co.
[21] Music Press.
[22] Transition.
[23] State Edition.
[24] C. Fischer.
[25] Shilkret.
[26] Courier Musicale.
[27] Instituto Interameri.
[28] Williams.
[29] Curwen.

Opening part of Passacaglia Theme for String Orchestra.
in ms. preparation.

ROY HARRIS

ROY HARRIS

IT has been said of Roy Harris that he is "the most American of all our composers." Since he belongs both by heritage and upbringing to the pioneers, and since an artist's creative expression inevitably springs from his own personal experience and background, it is natural that Harris' music should reflect the sturdy individualism of the early settlers.

He was born in a log cabin on Lincoln's birthday, February 12, 1898, in Lincoln County, Oklahoma. "Ever since," he confesses, "the shadow of Abe Lincoln has remained with me." His parents of Scotch, Welsh, and Irish descent, migrated westward in the wake of the Cimarron rush. Like other pioneers they carried with them only the barest necessities: a gun, an axe, and a few provisions. When their covered wagon reached Oklahoma, Elmer Harris staked out a claim near Chanler, cut down trees to build a log cabin, and established a farm.

Two of Roy's brothers died there of malaria. When his mother, too, showed signs of failing, the family decided to move further West— this time to Southern California. Roy was five at the time. The elder Harris bought a small piece of grazing pasture from Lucky Baldwin (who owned vast stretches of land just east of Pasadena), and again started farming. In the years following, the Harrises were to see startling changes in that section of the country. The orange groves gradually disappeared; speculators bought up the land and subdivided it into a network of small towns and country estates. During his youth, Harris says, he witnessed "the end of the pioneer days and the beginning of commercial, standardized America."

As Roy grew older he helped his father with the farm chores and the ploughing. Although the elder Harris had never been musically trained, he had a natural ear for music, and sang or whistled as he worked. One of his favorite tunes was the old Civil War ballad *When Johnny Comes Marching Home*. "He used to whistle it with jaunty bravado when we went to work on the farm in the morning, and with

283

sad pensiveness as we returned at dusk behind the slow, weary plodding of the horses."

Elmer Harris knew scores of folk songs and ballads. In later years, although he was vastly proud of his son's accomplishments, he found Roy's music a little baffling to his understanding; so he suggested that it might be an advantage if the two "made a team"—he to provide the tunes, his son to set them to music. One of Harris' most popular works is an overture based on that old favorite of his father's: *When Johnny Comes Marching Home*. The *Folk Song Symphony* utilizes other American ballads.

One day when Roy was still a child—it was soon after Edison had invented the phonograph—Elmer Harris brought home a curious instrument consisting of a square box surmounted by a large horn, and a set of round wax cylinders. When he wound the machine up, music issued from the gaudy horn. Roy was entranced. Evenings, after the day's work was done, the family would gather round the phonograph and listen to those primitive records.

Another early acquisition was a piano—the only one, at that time, for miles around. Mrs. Harris, an ardent if untrained musician, could play anything by ear, and soon Roy followed suit. His mother taught him as best she could, then a local teacher was found, and before long the boy played at recitals and school functions. He went to the Covina Public School and later played clarinet in the high-school band.

His fellow pupils, however, were inclined to look down on his musical accomplishments. In those days people were apt to consider the "long-haired arts," as they called them, effeminate. Roy, anxious to prove his virility, decided it would be better to give up music and go in for athletics. In the process (as a football player) he broke his nose and arm and ended all possibility of a pianist's career by badly injuring one of his fingers.

Music might have been permanently side-tracked, during his high-school years, if he hadn't at that time met a group of young liberals. Guiding spirit of the band was an older man who had come to America from Scotland. On Sundays he played the organ at a local church, and on week-days was accountant for the Fruit Grower's Association. His studio-home at Sierra Madre, with its fine collection of books, pictures, phonograph and Steinway grand piano, became

Roy Harris

their meeting place. Here they gathered to discuss world problems, and to listen to music. They played chess, took long hikes, and went in to Los Angeles to hear symphony concerts and opera. Through this association young Harris found "faith in beauty, peace of mind, ideas, spiritual aspirations, and individuality."

Roy was sixteen when the First World War broke out. He enlisted two years later in the heavy artillery and spent a difficult year trying to get used to army life. When the war ended he found himself, with thousands of other sensitive and thoughtful young men, unable to adjust to ordinary living. He was, by nature, insatiably curious. Everything in life interested him. This led him, some years later, on a voyage across the country; he slept under the stars, in haystacks and on park benches, and did odd jobs to keep going—once even acting as gate-keeper for a rodeo.

At twenty-two Roy Harris had "neither money nor connections." He got a job as truck-driver with a dairy company and for the next four years earned his living delivering milk, eggs and butter. He couldn't afford to buy tickets so in order to hear concerts he acted as usher at the Los Angeles Philharmonic auditorium. For a time he was also music-critic on the *Los Angeles Illustrated Daily Newspaper*. In spite of this unexciting routine those years, he says, were filled with enthusiasms. "Each new harmony, each new melody, each new composer discovered was a milestone for me."[1]

For two years Harris attended the University of California at Los Angeles. There he studied everything he could find, from sociology to Eastern philosophy, that would help him to understand life. But he was unable, he says, to discover any stable or dependable values—either in actual living, in relationships, in his studies, or even in philosophy—that "endless web of words modified by more words."

He came at last to believe that it was not what he saw or heard that was important, but what he felt about things. It was in music that he finally found stability. "I gradually realized that any given harmony or melody or reiterated rhythm always imparted its peculiar feeling. Here was something to depend on . . . values which I could count on and learn to use as the tools with which to discover and create new worlds."[2]

[1] Roy Harris, "Perspective at Forty," *Magazine of Art*, November, 1939.
[2] *Ibid.* ("Perspective at Forty.")

Modern Music-Makers

Every hour that he could spare from his work, young Harris studied music and tried to compose—though with little success at first. He had a few lessons in harmony and composition with Fannie Dillon, later with Modest Altschuler and Arthur Bliss, but his main teacher was the California composer Arthur Farwell. Farwell, from the start, recognized his pupil's unusual talent. Some years later he wrote a long article on Harris and his music, and began it with a paraphrase of Schuman's famous introduction of the young Chopin. "Gentlemen, a genius—but keep your hats on!" Farwell was convinced that Roy Harris would make his mark. "I predict for him . . ." he said "a wide, dynamic and enduring influence upon the art of music."[3]

At the time he first began studying with Farwell, however, Harris was not only unknown—he couldn't even set down the music he wanted to write. Within a year or so he had managed a string quartet, entitled *Songs of a Rainy Day* (played by the Zoellner Quartet in Los Angeles) and a *Fantasy for Trio and Chorus* performed by the Pasadena Community Chorus. But these were nothing to the big works he had in mind. Finally in desperation he decided to try a piece for orchestra—*Andante* he called it.

Farwell was so enthusiastic about the *Andante* that with the help of Altschuler and Artie Mason Carter (Founder of the Hollywood Bowl) he persuaded Hoogstraten to play it, that summer of 1926, at a Hollywood Bowl concert. The latter "had to be browbeaten to go on with it," after he saw the manuscript, but later changed his opinion and played it a second time, that summer, at the Lewisohn Stadium in New York City.

Meanwhile Harris's music had been brought to the attention of Howard Hanson, who agreed to give it a performance in Rochester. The young composer was invited to go East for the event. He left California for a two week's trip—and stayed away five years.

The success of the early *Andante* had far-reaching results. Harris was given an opportunity to work at the MacDowell Colony that summer—and after that to go to Paris for study with Nadia Boulanger. In order to test his ability, Mlle Boulanger asked him to write twenty melodies in different styles. Instead of twenty he brought her over a hundred. . . .

---

[3] *The Musical Quarterly,* June, 1932.

Roy Harris

When he first went abroad he felt very much of an alien, and was a little afraid of being submerged by the cultural life of Europe. He had decided ideas about music and composing, and was unwilling to submit to the discipline required in the formal study of counterpoint and harmony. At that time he believed it more important to develop technique firsthand, through his own experience. Nadia Boulanger called him her "autodidact," and wisely let him go his own way, that first year. As he says, "she had the patience of an angel. . . ."

It was through a concentrated study of Beethoven's *String Quartets*, according to Harris, that he eventually changed his point of view entirely. He bought the scores of the quartets, went to concerts, and studied the music in minutest detail.

> Beethoven became a wise, confiding, copiously illustrative teacher. . . . I learned about the passion and discipline of uninterrupted eloquence. . . . In short I became a profound believer in discipline and form. . . . Technique is the manner of formulating a long accumulation of choices and disciplines . . . the mastery with which continuity of impulse must be achieved with materials chosen for their unity and relationships.[4]

At the end of six months in Paris, Roy Harris wrote a *Concerto for Piano, Clarinet and String Quartet* that established him as one of the most important of the younger American composers. The work was performed in Paris, that spring of 1927, and later broadcast over C.B.S. It also won for him a Guggenheim Fellowship, this latter extended a second year, which made it possible for him to stay on in France. He was there altogether four years.

His work, however, was interrupted by an accident which he calls "a blessing in disguise," since it taught him how to read and write music without depending on a piano. Harris was living at the time just outside of Paris, in the little village of Juziers; he slipped on the stairs, fell on his back, and broke three vertebrae. He was taken back to the United States on a stretcher, and in New York had to undergo a serious operation in which a segment of his shin bone was transplanted to the spine. For six months he remained flat on his back in a plaster cast. Nevertheless he continued to compose. "In one short, concentrated period I gained freedom from the room-with-a-piano-

[4] "Perspective at Forty," *Magazine of Art*, November, 1939.

Modern Music-Makers

in-it which might have cramped my whole life," he says. During those months he wrote his first *String Quartet.*

Harris' eventual return to active life in his own country was not easy. He missed France—the country "where art was a part of the process of being civilized." In America he found the historical perspective missing, and the attitude towards music and composers was very different from that abroad. He wrote with some bitterness:

Society believed and acted on the assumption that all great music had been written; that new mechanical devices were more important than new music; that the performances were more important than the music performed; that only *poseurs* and maladjusted eccentrics really stood for new music, which was a sort of fad, that a musician's business is to teach and perform music, not create it. . . . In short, that the more serious a composer is, the more he is to be regarded as a liability to the social structure.[5]

He was advised to go to the Library of Congress in Washington. There, in the Music Division, he discovered a rare collection of the complete works of the great masters, and books dealing with every aspect of music. While in Washington, and on later visits, he made an intensive study of the historical development of music through the ages. More composers, he feels, should take advantage of this gold mine of information.

At the Library of Congress Harris also saw the special auditorium that had recently been built and endowed by Mrs. Elizabeth Sprague Coolidge for chamber music. Little did Harris then suspect what this auditorium held in store for him—the many performances of his works by great chamber music artists before distinguished and enthusiastic audiences, and the much coveted Elizabeth Sprague Coolidge medal "for eminent services to chamber music."

In California, where he now went to join his family, Harris was met everywhere with the question, "Well what are you going to do now?" It was expected that he would teach, lecture, or get a job at something connected with music (possibly as a piano salesman). Composing was considered "only an indulgence. Of course if I could

[5] Roy Harris in *The Musical Courier,* May 19, 1934.

288

PHOTOGRAPH BY DON CRAVENS

OY HARRIS

Roy Harris

have the energy left to write a few little piano pieces and songs or even some choruses not too difficult to perform, that would boost my teaching value."[6]

No one was particularly interested in whether he wrote music or not. To be sure, a *Piano Sonata* (with a scherzo reminiscent of *Turkey in the Straw*), had created quite a stir among the musical intelligentsia. But that didn't pay the doctor's bills, or the grocer's either. At this low ebb in his career, a group of liberal-minded Pasadena citizens helped tide him over. Believing that talent deserves support—at least until it can be self-supporting (as in earlier days wealthy patrons subsidized artists so they could work without worry over material considerations)—they presented him with a Creative Fellowship of $2,000 from their Music and Arts Association.[7] Ernest Batchelder was chairman of the association. His wife, the late Alice Coleman Batchelder, well-known pianist and founder of the Coleman Chamber Music Concerts in Pasadena, played the piano part at the first performance of Roy Harris' *Fantasie* for piano, French horn and wind instruments.

Harris now settled down to a steady pace of music writing—a pace which has never since slackened. Orchestral works, chamber music, choral compositions, all followed in quick succession. He first completed, at Mills College, what was originally called *Choral for Six Groups of Stringed Instruments*. This "is conceived as a modern expression of the choral form which is a variation development of a given traditional theme, generally of a religious nature." Harris feels strongly that the early Protestant hymn tunes have had an important influence on American music. They possess "a simple direct beauty which is near to the spirit of America."

Serge Koussevitzky, with his usual flair for recognizing new talent, next commissioned Harris to write a symphony. This *First Symphony,* composed in 1933, nearly met with disaster. A suitcase, containing the newly completed work together with all the orchestral parts, was stolen from a parked car while he was in New York. Anyone who knows the infinite labor involved in writing a symphony can imagine

---

[6] *Ibid.*

[7] Today various endowments or foundations have taken on the role of the old-time individual patron of the arts; among them the Guggenheim, Pulitzer, Alice M. Ditson, Koussevitzky, MacDowell, Trask (Yaddo), and a number of others.

Modern Music-Makers

Harris' state of mind. Fortunately the thief, disgusted at finding only musical notes instead of bank notes, decided the loot wasn't worth destroying, and dropped the suitcase at a subway entrance. There it was eventually recovered by the police, and returned to the frantic composer.

Koussevitzky was enthusiastic about the *First Symphony* and said it was "unmistakably American." He gave the first performances of all of Harris' symphonies after that—with the exception of the *Fourth*, which is really a choral work and has recorded three of them: the *First* with Columbia, the *Third* and *Fifth* with Victor.

When Harris heard his *First Symphony* played by Koussevitzky and the Boston Symphony it sounded even better than he had expected. "I mean to become a really great composer," he wrote in a letter to Nicolas Slonimsky. According to the latter, "At the completion of each new work, Harris experiences a state of musical euphoria so spontaneous and so utterly devoid of falsity that it cannot be offensive except to critical prudes."[8] Walter Piston once made a similar remark: "His personality is contagiously enthusiastic, and his honest appreciation of the beauties of his own work is refreshing."[9]

Before long all the leading orchestras were playing Harris' music. In 1935 an entire program of his works was given at the New School for Social Research. He had composed, by that time, a great deal of music, including two symphonies, two string quartets and a string sextet, a piano trio (played at the Coolidge Musical Festival in the Berkshires, September, 1934), and a piece for piano, flute and string quartet curiously titled *Four Minutes and Twenty Seconds*—written to fill in an extra side on the recording of his *First Symphony*. Also, in 1933, the famous overture *When Johnny Comes Marching Home*[10] commissioned by R.C.A. Victor.

Johnny's tune turned up again in the last movement of the *Fourth*, or *Folk Song Symphony*. This "vocal symphony" with five movements based on American songs was written, he says, "to bring about a cultural co-operation between the high school, college and com-

[8] In the *Musical Quarterly*, January, 1947.
[9] *Modern Music*, January-February, 1934.
[10] A younger composer, Morton Gould, has also used *When Johnny Comes Marching Home* in his *American Salute*. This has been widely played, particularly by Army, Navy and high school bands.

Roy Harris

munity choruses of our cities and their symphony orchestras which are frequently too remote socially from their communities."

The *Folk Song Symphony* in its completed form was first performed by Harris' good friend Artur Rodzinski in Cleveland, January, 1941. (Previously a part of it had been played at an Eastman Music Festival.) One critic was so carried away by the music that he wrote: "Forty-five minutes swept by like a second and left one listener with the excited consciousness of having heard something like the American continent rising up and saying hello. This music is nothing if not one-hundred percent United States of America."[11]

Harris' *Third Symphony* has been acclaimed his greatest (though Slonimsky thinks the *Fifth* is still better). Koussevitzky called it "The first truly great orchestral work produced in America." Since the latter's initial performance of the work in Boston, February 2, 1939, it has been played repeatedly all over the United States as well as abroad. In one season alone (1941-2) there were thirty-three performances of the *Third Symphony*. The final seal of popular approval came to Harris in a letter from the manager of a baseball team: "If I had pitchers who could pitch as strongly as you do in your Symphony, my worries would be over."

Some people, it is true, were less enthusiastic. Alec Templeton said that in his opinion the *Third Symphony* sounded "like a lot of people moving furniture around. . . ."

Walt Whitman has always been to Roy Harris a kindred spirit—as he has to many of our other American composers. Harris has tried to do in music, he says, what Whitman has done in poetry. A number of his choral works are based on the American bard's poems, among them *Whitman Triptych* (1927), *Symphony for Voices* (1936) *American Creed* (1940) *Walt Whitman Suite* (1944) and *A Song for Occupations*. This latter, an early work, was commissioned by the League of Composers, and dedicated to The Workers of the World. "It is an expression of my belief," wrote Harris, "that the workers are the most important part of any civilization."

Among Roy Harris' chamber-music works, to many people the *Piano Quintet*—composed in 1939—stands highest. Lazare Saminsky

[11] Herbert Elwell in the *Cleveland Plain Dealer*.

called it his greatest work. "The *Passacaglia* is, in my opinion, the best piece of American music that has been written during the three hundred years of its history." Harris has composed a large amount of chamber music, though recently he has turned more to the larger forms.

He was in the midst of writing his *Fifth Symphony* when he received a telegram from the Soviet Embassy in Washington. At that time Russia was heroically battling the German invaders and Stalingrad appeared about to fall. Yet in spite of the chaotic conditions the people were making plans to celebrate the twenty-fifth Anniversary of the International Arts Congress in Moscow. They asked Harris as a representative American composer to send a message of greeting. The American sympathies, at this time, were all with the Russian allies.

Harris felt so touched, he says, that he wondered what he could say to a people who, under such circumstances, were still able to remember the arts. He couldn't find the right phrase for his greeting— everything seemed trite and worn-out. He walked and walked, vainly seeking inspiration. Finally he came home and saw, spread out, the sheets of the new symphony he was working on. So he dedicated the *Fifth Symphony* to Russia "as a gesture of respect to the courage, faith and vitality of a great people."

After he had done this, he remembered that the Boston Symphony was to give the first performance of the work—and that Koussevitzky was a White Russian. He called the maestro long distance and explained what he had done. There was a long silence. . . . Finally Koussevitzky said, "Roy, you are a courageous man. I will send a telegram too!"

The Russian Government's reply to Harris' dedication was the following cablegram:

U.S.S.R. SOCIETY FOR CULTURAL RELATIONS WITH FOREIGN COUNTRIES WARMLY GREETS GREAT ARTISTS OF GREAT FRIENDLY NATION. MUSIC IS MIGHTY MEANS FOR COMMUNION OF PEOPLE. IT HELPS STRENGTHEN RANKS OF DEFENDERS OF LIBERTY AND DEMOCRACY. WE WOULD LIKE TO HEAR YOUR SYMPHONY HERE.

Roy Harris

When the *Fifth Symphony* was broadcast to Russia, nine of their leading composers joined together in sending a message of congratulation:

GREETINGS TO ROY HARRIS FROM THE COMPOSERS OF USSR! WE GREET IN YOUR PERSON YOUNG MUSIC OF AMERICAN PEOPLE. ACROSS SEAS AND OCEANS WE EXTEND YOU OUR HAND IN SINCERE FRATERNAL HANDSHAKE. LONG LIVE OUR VICTORY.

> (*Signed*) GLIERE, SHOSTAKOVICH, PROKOFIEFF, MYASKOVSKY, KHACHATURYAN, KABALEVSKY, MURADELI, KHRENNIKOV, BIELY.

The *Fifth Symphony* was performed a number of times in Russia, and one of the Soviet musicologists wrote:

Harris occupies today the most important position among composers of the United States. His works are performed by the leading orchestras and are recorded by gramophone companies; extensive essays are published on his musical style. It should be noted that on his road to fame Harris never made any concession to the prevalent fashion and the tastes of the large public. His music is closely bound in thematic essence with the spiritual strivings of the nation, its musical folklore and its literature, but it remains austere and somewhat uncouth, making it sometimes difficult to understand.[12]

"For tender or untutored ears," says Nicolas Slonimsky, "it is still a disquieting art. But listeners who hear Harris' symphonies without environmental prejudices, warm up to it."

According to Copland:

The late start in his musical education was at first held to be responsible for a certain awkwardness, both in manipulating materials and in writing for instruments. But gradually, as if in spite of himself, this awkwardness became part and parcel of his style, taking on a charm of its own.[13]

---

[12] *Contemporary American Music*, by Gregory Schneerson.
[13] *Our New Music*, by Aaron Copland. Whittlesey House.

Modern Music-Makers

The late Lawrence Gilman, in a special Sunday edition article on Roy Harris wrote:

Certainly Mr. Harris would qualify as the hero of an American Success-Story. Yet Harris' success-story differs from many others because it has been achieved without any sacrifice of the ideals and standards of a singularly high-minded, sincere, and uncompromising artist. The melodies, the harmonies, the rhythms, the counterpoint, have lived their own way with an independence and a power that bespoke the presence of that rarest thing in art, a genuinely individual voice.

During the war Harris wrote a number of pieces inspired by the world conflict—notably *Ode to Friendship* (1941) and *March in Time of War* (1943).

Harris' *Fifth Symphony*, composed in 1942, was radioed to troops at home and overseas, and elicited a spectacular response. His *Sixth Symphony*, also completed during the war, brought over ninety letters of appreciation from soldiers in the armed forces. These letters, Harris says, more than repaid him for the time and effort that went into his symphony. He was glad to learn that during three years of broadcasting musical programs to the troops, the request for serious music increased more than three-hundred percent.

Harris has written only a few scores for stage and films. Three for ballet: *From This Earth, What So Proudly We Hail,* and another on the subject of war (all for Hanya Holm); and one film score for a documentary picture about negro life in the South: *One Tenth of a Nation.*

Copland feels that in his incidental music Harris lacks adaptability, or "extra-musical imagination." It may be that he is too much of an individualist to subordinate himself to stage requirements. He functions best in "independent music," (which, as he puts it, is "a complete emotional aural experience in itself"), as against the "incidental music" required for theater or films.

In 1945 Roy Harris composed a charming orchestral piece, *Memories of a Child's Sunday,*[14] dedicated "to little Richard Rodzinski, aged one and a bit," (the small son of his good friends Artur and

[14] Harris conducted this work five times with the New York Philharmonic during the spring of 1946.

Roy Harris

Halina Rodzinski); and in 1946 wrote *Celebration*, dedicated to another close friend: Howard Hanson, containing variations on a theme from the latter's *Third Symphony*; and a *Two-Piano Concerto* (labeled "wild and daring" by the *Denver Post*). This last was played in Denver in January, 1947, by the composer's wife, Johana Harris, and Max Lanner.

Other recent works include an *Overture: The Quest*; a *Concerto for Accordion and Orchestra* (played by Andy Rizzo in Chicago); a *Mass* for men's voices and organ, performed in 1948 at Columbia University; an *Elegy and Paean* for viola and orchestra played by William Primrose and the Houston Orchestra; a *Scherzo: Kentucky Spring* first performed in 1949 in Louisville, Ky.; a piece for symphonic band, *Fruit of Gold*, played at the University of California in Los Angeles; and in 1951 a concerto for orchestra—*Cumberland Concerto*, commissioned by the Cincinnati Symphony. He is also at work on another symphony—his *Seventh*—commissioned by the Koussevitzky Foundation.

Johana Harris, Roy's second wife, is an accomplished musician in her own right, and has been an able interpreter of her husband's piano works. The two were married in 1936 and have remained in close comradeship, sharing the same interests and working together. At present they live with their three small children, Paddy, Sharen and Daniel, in Nashville, Tennessee, where Harris is "composer-in-residence" at the Peabody College for Teachers. He was connected for several years with the Music Department of Colorado University, and before that was at Cornell.

For the last ten years Harris has been extremely active in music education, particularly in the teaching of composers. He has adopted the practise of inviting the most gifted of his students as resident artists in his own home, teaching them much in the manner of the old Italian tradition of apprentices. A number of his students now hold responsible positions in universities and colleges, and some are in radio as composers, arrangers, and producers.

During the last ten years Roy and Johana Harris have also been active in radio education. They have given over a hundred educational programs over the air. Their series "Let's Make Music" was voted the highest citation award by the National Radio Education Convention held in 1944 in Chicago.

Modern Music-Makers

Because of his interest in young composers Roy Harris has been elected President of the Fellowship of American Composers—a group which is doing important pioneer work for the performance of young, unknown American composers. He has received many prizes, honors, and degrees— among them two honorary doctor's degrees, one from Rutgers University and one from the University of Rochester—and he has lectured widely and written for a large number of papers and periodicals. In 1951 he was invited, under the Mellon Grant, to become composer in residence at the Pennsylvania College for Women, and his wife as artist in residence and teacher of advanced piano students. While there Harris plans to complete a book on music theory for the United States Government, and also gather data for a five volume history of musical materials. He has recently signed a ten year contract with Ricordi, a music publishing company which is planning to concentrate on an extensive American music catalogue.

Harris is singularly expressive in discussing both his own work and music in general. His articles form a valuable addition to the literature on what—to the layman at least—is one of today's most baffling subjects: modern music.

He feels that in America the time is ripe for the development of the arts, and particularly of music. When a civilization has reached its full vigor, yet is young enough to have retained the qualities of naïveté, curiosity, and the faith of youth, then conditions for cultural expression are at their best. An indispensable factor, says Harris, is a new faith or enthusiasm. In past centuries religion was the main impetus (Bach, for instance, was largely a product of the Lutheran Reformation). The French Revolution, socialism, democracy—whatever the enthusiasm may be, acts as a kind of wine in the blood and inspires new art. In America today, and especially among the younger generation, belief in justice for all is the motivating factor. It is fast growing to the point of fervor necessary to stimulate creation.

Our own country and times are uniquely adapted to a blossoming of the arts. We have here economic security and freedom from want and fear; great universities and libraries; art exhibits and concerts— all available to everyone. Until recently there were many musical illiterates; but now through radio and the phonograph (which are to music what the printing press is to literature) music has been brought to the multitudes. Also there are unlimited new technical resources

Roy Harris

for the composer's use, such as modern developments in harmony and asymmetrical rhythms, a new school of brasses and orchestral effects.

All these factors have enormously stimulated the output of music in the United States, and a wide interest in the subject as well. Today we no longer depend as we did so largely in the past on foreign composers and performers; nor is our own music patterned, as it mostly was in the past century on their models. We are gradually evolving an idiom that belongs to our own country and way of life.

Roy Harris has done much to develop this idiom. As Koussevitzky summed it up:

> I think that nobody has expressed with such genius the American life, the vitality, the greatness, the strength of this country. . . . Roy Harris seems to be the answer to our desire for the Essential American. He is among those who have come to stand for the beliefs the people cherish and to be the means of interpreting those beliefs abroad. He is the man who is probably the most widely performed of our composers, whose fame came to him because he has striven in the American way toward ideals Americans as a people hold.[15]

15 *The International Musician.*

Roy Harris

The Music of Roy Harris

ORCHESTRAL WORKS

Andante	1926
Andantino	1931
First Symphony	1933
When Johnny Comes Marching Home (also for chorus)[1]	1934
Second Symphony	1934
Farewell to Pioneers [1]	1935
Prelude and Fugue for String Orchestra [1]	1935
Time Suite [1]	1936
Third Symphony[2]	1937
Fourth, or Folk Song Symphony [1]	1939
American Creed [2]	1940
Ode to Truth [2]	1941
Evening Piece [2]	1941
Acceleration [2]	1941
Ode to Friendship [2]	1941
Fifth Symphony [2]	1942
Fanfare [2]	1942
Folk Rhythms of Today (also for band)[2]	1942
March in Time of War [2]	1943
Chorale for Orchestra [2]	1944
Sixth Symphony [2]	1944
Memories of a Child's Sunday [3]	1945
Children at Play (also for piano)[3]	1946
Melody [3]	1946
"Celebration," Variations on a Theme from Howard Hanson's Third Symphony [3]	1946
Concerto for Two Pianos and Orchestra [3]	1946
Radio Piece (orchestra and piano) [3]	1946
Mood [2]	
Work [2]	
Concerto for Accordion and Orchestra [4]	1947
Overture The Quest [4]	1947
Elegy and Paean for Viola solo and orchestra [4]	1948
Concerto for Violin and Orchestra [2]	1948-1949

Kentucky Spring, scherzo for orchestra [4]	1949
Fruit of Gold for symphonic band [4]	1949
Cumberland Symphony	1951

CHORAL WORKS

Fantasy for Trio and Chorus	1925
Whitman Triptych (women's voices and piano)[1]	1927
A Song for Occupations [1]	1934
Sanctus [1]	1935
Symphony for Voices [1]	1936
Railroad Man's Ballad (chorus and orchestra)[2]	1938
Rock of Ages (chorus and orchestra)[2]	1940
Challenge (chorus and orchestra) [1]	1940
A Red Bird in a Green Tree [2]	1940
Songs of Democracy [2]	1941
Sons of Uncle Sam [2]	1942
Walt Whitman Suite (chorus, string orchestra, 2 pianos) [2]	1944
Alleluia (chorus, brasses and organ)[2]	1945
Blow the Man Down (chorus, band and strings) [1]	1945
Israel—motet for tenor, chorus and organ	1946
Sammy's Fighting Sons (chorus and band)[2]	1946
Mass for men's voices and organ	1948

CHAMBER MUSIC

Songs of a Rainy Day	1925
Concerto for Piano, Clarinet and String Quartet [5]	1927
Piano Sonata [5]	1928
First String Quartet	1930
String Sextet [6]	1932
Three Variations on a Theme (Second String Quartet) [1]	1933
Piano Trio [7]	1934
Four Minutes, Twenty Seconds (String Quartet and Flute) [2]	1934
Poem for Violin and Piano	1935
Piano Quintet [1]	1936
Third String Quartet [2]	1937
Soliloquy and Dance (viola and piano) [1]	1938

Roy Harris

Viola Quintet	1939
Violin Sonata [2]	1942
Four Easy Pieces for Violin [2]	1942
Toccata for Organ and Brasses [2]	1944

PIANO WORKS

Little Suite [1]	1938
Variations on an Irish Theme [2]	1938
Children at Play [3]	1942
Ten American Ballads for Piano [2]	1946

MUSIC FOR BAND

Cimarron [2]	1941
First Concerto for Piano and Band [2]	1942
Folk Rhythms of Today [2]	1942
Fantasy for Piano and Band [2]	1943

SONGS

Waitin' (voice and piano) [2]	1940
Lullaby (voice and piano) [2]	1940
Freedom's Land (voice and piano) [2]	1942
Sons of the U. S. A. (voice and piano) [2]	1942
Take the Sun and Keep the Stars (voice and piano) [2]	1946

STAGE WORKS

One-Tenth of a Nation (music for a film)[2]	1940
From this Earth (ballet) [2]	1941
What So Proudly We Hail [2]	1942
Ballet on Subject of War [2]	1945

[1] G. Schirmer.
[2] Mills Music Co.
[3] G. Fischer.
[4] Carl Fischer Co.
[5] Cos Cob Press.
[6] H. Flammer.
[7] New Music.

HARL MCDONALD

HARL McDONALD

HARL McDONALD, whose Scotch name proclaims his ancestry, was born on a ranch in the Rocky Mountains near Boulder, Colorado. Soon after, the family moved to El Solano, then to San Jacinto in the cattle-ranch country of Southern California. Later they settled in Redlands, and there Harl spent most of his early years. His life was divided between a typically Western out-of-doors existence, with daily horseback riding and bronco busting (he carries a silver patch in his skull as a memento of one of these episodes), and music.

Both his parents were musical. His father played the piano and horn, and his mother was not only an accomplished Lieder singer, but knew a good deal about music theory. She started young Harl at the piano when he was four, and a year later with elementary harmony. He took to it like a duck to water. He still recalls his initial enthusiasm for Bach's *Inventions* and *Well-Tempered Clavichord*— and, for that matter, for all things musical. This enthusiasm has never left him. "Music is like poison in your veins," he says, a little ruefully. "You can't get rid of it!"

During those years on the ranch he was exposed to more than one kind of music. Mexican bands and circuses often came to the little California town near which he lived, and for fifteen cents young Harl could take in the whole show—trapeze artists, jugglers, ballet dancers, and best of all—the dance music. "I got an ear-full of Mexican music," he says, with a grin. And even at that early date he was trying to put the rhythms he heard into his own original tunes. When he was seven he wrote a set of dances—another group when he was ten. These were published, much to his delight at the time; but today he "shudders to think of their being in print!"

All through these early years his classical training went on, with hours of daily practise and occasionally, as a great treat, a trip to Los Angeles to a symphony or opera (there were no movies or radio in

303

Modern Music-Makers

those days). In addition he heard the songs and music of the cow hands—they all played mandolin, or banjo, or guitar—and the visiting Mexican bands.

Young Harl learned to play many different instruments, including piano and organ, violin, cello, clarinet and horn. When he announced that he wanted to be a musician, however, his father objected strenuously. Whereat Harl, then in his early teens, left home in protest—determined that he would carry out his plan alone. He got a job as horn player with the Los Angeles Symphony Orchestra, and earned enough in that way (and later as choir director) to pay for his musical education.

Father McDonald eventually resigned himself to his son's choice of a profession. "All right," he agreed. "But if you *must* be a musician at least don't be a velvet-coated one. Get out and earn a degree!"

Harl heeded the advice. He took the music course at Redlands (where he lived for several years), then went to the University of Southern California and got his B.A. degree there in 1918. His early teachers were Vernon Spencer, Ernest Douglas (organist at St. Paul's Pro-Cathedral in Los Angeles) and Jaroslaw de Zielinzki—a Russian who had been Rimsky-Korsakoff's assistant at the Moscow Conservatory.

After graduating from U.S.C., McDonald spent a few months in the army, at Fort MacArthur, but he didn't get overseas as the war ended that same November. The next couple of years he "batted around—just a cub," playing accompaniments, teaching a little, and composing. Two of his pieces were played by the Los Angeles Symphony under Adolf Tandler, and later another by Walter Henry Rothwell with the Los Angeles Philharmonic.

At twenty-one McDonald appeared as soloist with the San Francisco Orchestra under Alfred Hertz in an early piano concerto he had recently completed. It was very hot the day of the rehearsal and the perspiring musicians had difficulty with the tricky Hispanic-Indian rhythm of his concerto. He recalls how Hertz mopped his shiny bald head with a handkerchief as large as a table-cloth. "Shentlemen—mind the rhyt'm," he cried. Finally soloist and orchestra got together, and the concert turned out to be the greatest triumph of McDonald's early career.

For relaxation, at this period, he took up boxing—with results some-

304

HARL McDONALD

Harl McDonald

what disfiguring to his physiognomy. At one time he held an amateur championship in the Southwest.

While still more or less at loose ends, young McDonald was fortunate enough to win two prizes—one offered by the American Federation of Music Clubs, and the other jointly by the Los Angeles Philharmonic and Ballet Association. This enabled him to go abroad for further study. In Germany, at that time, the inflation made it possible for an American "to live like a king on next to nothing." McDonald went to the Conservatory of Music in Leipzig, from which he received a diploma in 1922, and studied with Augustus Steiner and Teichmuller.

Before leaving the United States, McDonald had outlined a *Symphonic Fantasy* based on the Indian legends of California with the Mojave Desert as a background. In Germany he rewrote *Mojave,* as he named the piece, and Steiner played it at the Berlin *Staadtsoper.* The success of this performance caused the young American's name to become known in other foreign countries. He was invited to lecture at the *Académie Tournefort,* in Paris, and his *Mojave* was played again by Albert Coates in London.

McDonald returned to the United States for a two-year period of free-lancing. Then he went back for one more year of study in Europe and finally, in 1925, settled down—more or less—in Philadelphia. He married Eleanor Gosling (a widow with two young sons), and they now have two daughters. The younger has inherited her father's musical talent; one of her compositions has been played by the Philadelphia Orchestra.

Harl McDonald has always been a dynamo of energy. After moving to Philadelphia he divided his time between many activities—gave piano recitals, did editorial work, and lectured. In 1927 he was appointed head of the University of Pennsylvania's Music Department. At the same time he directed a number of choral groups—including the University Men's Glee Club, the *A Cappella* Choir, Women's Glee Club, Chamber-Music Society, Choral Society, and the Mendelssohn Club—and also served as organist and Music Director at the Church of the Holy Apostles. As if such a schedule were not sufficiently formidable he undertook, on a Rockefeller Foundation Grant, (in collaboration with two engineers and a physicist), to do special research work in acoustics and the analysis and measurement of sound. The

Modern Music-Makers

results of these experiments proved so valuable that McDonald was elected to the honorary society of Sigma Xi.

There was not much time left, during those busy days, for composing. Leopold Stokowski, then conductor of the Philadelphia Orchestra, felt that McDonald was making a serious mistake in sidetracking his creative work. "You should cut down your outside activities," he told him. "Drop all the unimportant stuff and get back to your composition."

McDonald agreed, and finally decided to make a drastic change in his schedule. Although he continued as Professor of Music at the University, he let most of the other things go and devoted the major part of his time to music writing. During the next years he turned out a large number of works (there are over 150 on his list)—including single pieces for various instruments, three trios, three string quartets, a piano concerto and one for two-pianos, (this last beginning "in traditional European style" and ending "with a finale that is decidedly American—Hispanic in feeling"), a violin concerto, two tone-poems, four orchestral suites and four symphonies.

His First Symphony, called *The Santa Fe Trail*, is perhaps the best known of the four. Its colorful locale has to do with the coming of the Anglo-Saxons to the Southwest. McDonald, in his boyhood, heard many tales about the early days of the Santa Fe Trail, among them those related by some old prospectors who had known the Santa Fe Colony in the days of the gold rush—at a time when they still had to have the protection of the United States Cavalry against the Indians.

The *Santa Fe Symphony* commemorates those pioneer days. The first movement has to do with the early explorers; the second describes the life of the Spanish settlers; and the third, and last, reflects the many influences that have helped to shape the great Southwest: Anglo-Saxon, Spanish, and Indian.

McDonald's *Second*, or *Rhumba Symphony* as he calls it, is fittingly subtitled *Reflections on an Era of Turmoil*. In this work, according to John Tasker Howard:

He succeeds admirably in presenting graphically the modern restlessness, the hectic, brooding emotionalism, and the avid lust for wild and fiery pleasure that outwardly characterize much in the present era.[1]

[1] John Tasker Howard, *Our Contemporary Composers*, Thomas Y. Crowell, 1943.

Harl McDonald

The *Scherzo* from the *Rhumba Symphony,* which has been widely played as a separate piece, is one of McDonald's most popular orchestral works. It has been recorded by Victor, as have a number of his other compositions.

Of all his symphonies McDonald himself prefers the *Third,* or *Choral Symphony,* subtitled *Lamentations of Fu Hsuan.* This moving paean to despair is based on a Chinese poem which was translated for him by a Chinese student at the University of Pennsylvania. It is in three main parts: *Apprehension, Realization of Loss,* and, finally, *Resignation.*

The *Fourth Symphony* has no special name. When asked to supply program notes, McDonald stated that while the work was probably in a sense autobiographical, "he would refrain from boring his listeners with details of experiences that were important to him as a composer, but would be most improper as part of the program notes." He has drawn the thematic material of the *Fourth Symphony* from a wide range of subject (such as a cakewalk in the *Scherzo*), typical of different parts of the United States.

Harl McDonald's compositions represent a wide variety of interests and enthusiasms. Whatever moves him is apt to be translated into music.

He considers that music greatest which has the greatest universality of appeal, emotionally. His own works, he says, spring from compulsion to express in music his inner impressions of things from which he gets emotional reactions. Music is essentially an emotional language, he believes, and his principal criticism of contemporary composition is that there is too much cerebration, too much experiment with sterile, intellectual forms and idioms. Music should not be written objectively, but "from the inside out," in his opinion. Only then does it have appeal and import for the listener.[2]

Typical of a work representing emotional reaction is one written at the time of the Lindbergh kidnapping called *Lament for the Stolen.* During the war McDonald was moved to write a symphonic poem to the heroes of Bataan; also an *Overture 1941,* and a *Symphonic Suite My Country at War.*

[2] Ronald F. Eyer in *Musical America,* March 10, 1944.

Modern Music-Makers

One of his recent works is a cycle of songs composed for the great American soprano, Helen Traubel. These songs are uniform in style but differ widely in mood, and offer sufficient variety for an entire program. "Too frequently the groups of American songs on a program are 'confetti'—that is, written in too many different styles," he says. "The Italian classics have a uniform quality—so do the German lieder. But our composers vary so greatly in character that it is difficult to make a representative group of American songs."

Harl McDonald's other recent works include a *Fifth Symphony, Children's Symphony on Familiar Tunes,* a Cantata for Mixed Voices and Orchestra, *God Give Us Men,* and an *Overture for Children.*

In 1934 Harl McDonald was appointed to the Board of Directors of the Philadelphia Orchestra. Five years later he became manager, and still continues in that capacity.

His fine work in that organization speaks for itself. He has brought to it a sympathetic understanding of the musicians, rare tact in dealing with conductors and soloists, keen insight into the manifold business problems that come to the fore in running a major orchestra, and what is most important, a grand sense of humor which helps everyone concerned over the rough places.

McDonald's sense of humor crops out occasionally in amusing ways. On a December, 1939, concert, the Philadelphia Orchestra featured a *Miniature Suite* by one John C. Smith. Judging from the style of the music, the critics decided that "Smith" must be the Anglicized version of Johann Christian Schmidt—one of Handel's contemporaries. McDonald smiled up his sleeve. It was his own creation—a hoax to prove that present-day composers could write in eighteenth century style if they so desired.

In latter years, with the direction of a great orchestra on his shoulders—endless details, tours to plan, constant traveling from one city to another—Harl McDonald would long since have had to stop composing if he had not learned to make use of every moment of leisure. Week-ends, late into the night, he is usually to be found with a sheet of music paper. A lot of his work has been done while traveling, on the train and in hotels.

"Necessity generally dictates working conditions," he insists. "The

Harl McDonald

hours spent in train coaches mount up to an enormous amount of time. Not being addicted to gin rummy, the only alternatives are looking out the car windows at the landscapes, reading, or just plain daydreaming. I'd rather work!"

Always good-natured and able to adapt to any condition, there is nevertheless one thing that never ceases to irk him. "I have been in a great many hotel bedrooms," he says, "but never yet have I found one with a desk large enough to accommodate a manuscript sheet of music . . . If any other composer is forced to spend much of his time in hotels, my advice to him is to take out the bottom drawer and mount it upside down either on the knees or the arms of the chair. The drawer makes an excellent work bench and is ample enough for a full manuscript sheet."

At least during the summer months McDonald can work uninterruptedly. He has a country place in Maine—"with no phone—and I don't intend ever to have one!" While there he doesn't read mail, he says, not even telegrams. "I throw them into the ocean. But if they're washed up on shore," he adds with a twinkle of his Scotch-blue eyes, "then I know Fate decrees I must read them. . . ."

American music is at the present time "in a state of ferment," says Harl McDonald. But this he regards as a normal and healthy sign.

It would be illogical for music to have found a settled, cut-and-dried course in this country at this stage of its evolution. While McDonald himself is affected most by Hispanic influences, he considers it logical and proper that American composers should make use of the so-called folk music of various types, including jazz, cowboy, negro and hill-billy idioms, etc., and that each should employ them as his individuality dictates.[3]

In an article: "Problems of the American Composer," written for the December, 1937, *Magazine of Art*, McDonald puts it in this way:

I do not believe that nationalism in music has any purpose as an aim in itself. The use of native source material is valuable to the composer in that it tends to discourage artificiality, and helps him to maintain emotional poise in harmony with humanity. . . .

[3] Ronald F. Eyer in *Musical America*, March 10, 1944.

Modern Music-Makers

Many of us have had the good fortune to have spent our formative years in close association with some of the highly individual forms of native music. . . . It is true that these many types never have been fused into a true national form or style. Neither have the people of this country become one people, except in certain matters of temper, spirit, and habits.

As an expression of this temper and spirit, Jazz is our nearest approach to a completely native art. But our people are drawn from many races and the music of our country must be drawn from many sources.

I would suggest that the composer who would benefit from native source material had best give his attention to the music of his locale or racial group. He need not necessarily be confined to it but he should remember that there are a surprising number of undiscovered gold mines in people's back yards.

Harl McDonald has drawn considerable riches from his own back yard. What he calls the "Hispanic-Indian Anglo-Saxon combination of the Mexican border region" has furnished material for many of his compositions.

In an analysis made by *Musical America* of the 1942-3 symphony orchestra programs, Harl McDonald ranked as one of the ten most often heard contemporary composers of that year. The late critic, William J. Henderson, considered him typically representative of his own country. He called him "As American as Pike's Peak."

Harl McDonald

The Music of Harl McDonald

NOTE: All works published by Elkan-Vogel. Others, not
listed, published by Theodore Presser, G. Schirmer, and
Breitkopf & Härtel.

ORCHESTRAL WORKS

Mojave—Symphonic Fantasy	1922
First Symphony—The Santa Fe Trail	1934
Second Symphony—Rhumba	1935
Three Poems on Traditional Aramaic Themes	1935
Third Symphony—Tragic Cycle (Soprano, chorus, orch.)	1936
Concerto for Two Pianos and Orchestra	1936
Fourth Symphony (*Scherzo Movement: Cake Walk*)	1937
San Juan Capistrano—two Nocturnes for Orchestra	1938
Miniature Suite (After John Christopher Smith, 1784)	1939
The Legend of the Arkansas Traveller	1939
Chameleon Variations	1940
From Childhood—Suite for harp and orchestra	1940
Overture 1941	1941
My Country at War—Symphonic Suite	1943
Bataan—Symphonic Poem	
Concerto for Violin and Orchestra	1943
Mississippi—Suite for Orchestra	
Fifth Symphony—Children's Symphony on Familiar Themes	1948
Overture for Children	1950

CHORAL WORKS

Missa Patriem (double chorus a cappella)	1937
The Breadth and Extent of Man's Empire (mixed chorus)	1938
Songs of Conquest (mixed chorus)	1938
Lament for the Stolen (women's chorus, orchestra)	1939
Come Quickly, Lord, and Take my Soul to Rest (mixed chorus)	1939
The Sea (mixed chorus and string orchestra)	1939
Dirge for Two Veterans (women's chorus, orchestra)	1940
Evening (women's voices)	1940
Wind in the Palm Trees (women's voices, string orchestra)	1940
Day Break (high voice and orchestra)	1941

Harl McDonald

The Lover's Lament (English Drinking Song) (men's chorus) 1941
Pioneers, O Pioneers (mixed chorus) 1941
God Give Us Men (Cantata for mixed voices & Orchestra) 1950

CHAMBER MUSIC

Trio in G Minor—Piano, Violin, Cello 1931
Two Miniatures 1931
Fantasy for String Quartet 1932
Second Trio 1932
Quartet on Negro Themes 1933
Prelude in G Minor 1933
Monkeyshines 1939
Serenade 1940

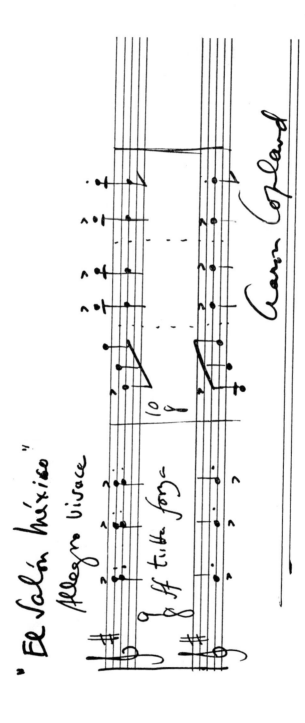

AARON COPLAND

AARON COPLAND

AARON COPLAND and Roy Harris have both been called "typically American"—but they differ as widely in style and temperament as they do in background and heritage. This is not, however, as paradoxical as it might appear, for our country is made up of many different regions, states, and cities, each with its own characteristics yet each representatively American. Those of our composers whose music reflects the special attributes of their particular environment might all be said to be typically American.

Copland's music belongs unmistakably to the United States—which shows how quickly a single generation living in a new country can absorb the idiom of that country. For both of his parents were Russian-born.

The name was originally transliterated as "Kaplan." When Copland's father passed through England on his way to America, the immigration officer asked him how he spelled his name. Kaplan knew only the Russian alphabet; finally the officer wrote it down as it sounded to him: "Copland." Kaplan let it stand. To him it was symbolical—a new country, a new life, and a new name.

He settled in Brooklyn, just outside of New York. The elder Copland was thrifty and hard-working; he established a thriving general-store that became the "Macy's" of Brooklyn, and brought up his five sons and daughters as American children. The four older ones all had music lessons—not because the Coplands were themselves musically inclined, rather because it seemed a usual part of education in this, their adopted land of boundless opportunities—but by the time the fifth child was born, November 14, 1900, they had come to the conclusion that music lessons were a waste of time and money. So young Aaron—the only really musically gifted one in the family—had no early musical instruction.

Possibly because he felt slightly cheated, music assumed an intensely desirable aspect in Aaron's eyes. When he was eleven he persuaded his older sister to give him lessons on the piano. This only whetted his appetite for more, so at thirteen—quite on his own —he went to a neighboring teacher, Leopold Wolfsohn, and asked if he could study with him. Later he had piano lessons with Victor Wittgenstein and Clarence Adler. It was not long before young Copland wanted to write music as well as play it. He subscribed to a correspondence course in harmony; but the results, he confesses, were not highly successful. Then he heard about Goldmark.

A few months before the United States entered the First World War, Rubin Goldmark—teacher of composition and nephew of the famous Goldmark of *Queen of Sheba* fame—answered a knock at his door. He opened it to admit a tall, gangling youth of seventeen, with eager eyes behind thick-lensed spectacles.

"I want to be a composer," the boy announced.

Goldmark looked at him severely. "What for?" he asked.

Aaron Copland could hardly explain his reasons. He only knew that he wanted, above everything else in the world, to be able to write music. And since he was a young man of resolution, industry and also of great talent, he not only reached the goal he set himself in those early days, but went far beyond it.

Rubin Goldmark had been trained in a strictly conservative school. In his day only a few had dared to break away from tradition, and those bold ones were frowned upon as radicals and heretics. Goldmark had no use for "modern" music, and because he disapproved, young Copland was all the more inclined to experiment.

When he brought his teacher a piano piece entitled *The Cat and the Mouse*, Goldmark gave it one glance and then scornfully threw the piece to one side. Aaron, he felt, took a perverse delight in breaking all the rules he had so painstakingly tried to teach him. "How do you expect me to criticize such music?" he asked sarcastically.

During all these early years, Copland had been living the unexciting life of the average Brooklyn schoolboy. There was nothing in his environment to stimulate him artistically, and it was only some deep urge within himself that kept him on his chosen path. There were times when he felt very lonely. None of his friends were interested in music; he longed to meet others who were working in the same field. His personal world was far removed from that of his everyday life. He had, as he puts it, a sense of isolation and of working too much by himself.

What he wanted more than anything else was a chance to go abroad to study. After the war, the music center of Europe shifted from Vienna and Berlin to Paris. In the spring of 1921 Copland saw a notice in a magazine about a summer school that was to be opened for American students of music and art in Fontainebleau, just outside of Paris. He sat down at once and sent in his application. As it turned out, Aaron Copland was the first pupil to be enrolled at the Fontainebleau School of Music.

In Paris he at last found himself in his element. There he became aware of a congenial group of composers who, like himself, were interested in the new idiom. Among them were Stravinsky and the French *Groupe des Six,* and two Americans: George Antheil and later Virgil Thomson. All of these men were experimenting with new forms of composition. Now at last, thought Aaron, he would be able to learn more about modern music writing. To his disappointment, however, the teacher at the Fontainebleau School—Paul Vidal of the Paris Conservatory—turned out to be "a French version of Rubin Goldmark, except that he was harder to understand."

Copland had just about made up his mind that he would have to struggle on by himself if he wanted to write in the style that appealed to him, when a fellow student told him about the remarkable new teacher of harmony, Nadia Boulanger. "You should visit one of her classes," he said.

Copland, like many another, was at first skeptical. "I finished with harmony years ago," he replied. "And besides, how could a *woman* be a good teacher of composition? Name me one outstanding woman composer. . . ."

"Just come to Mlle Boulanger's class and see for yourself," the friend insisted.

Largely to satisfy his curiosity, Copland finally agreed. When he reached the classroom he was surprised to find, instead of the elderly, dried-up spinster he had expected, a bright-eyed, eager-faced young woman who, with contagious enthusiasm was explaining to her enthralled students the harmonic structure of Moussorgsky's *Boris Godounoff.*

By the time the class ended, Aaron Copland was completely won

over. Never before had he heard such a clear exposition of fundamental principles, nor met anyone with such a rare gift for inspiring
the creative powers of her pupils. He decided to study with Mlle
Boulanger, and this was, he says, the most important decision of
his life—the one to which he owes the most.

That fall, after the summer school at Fontainebleau closed, Copland stayed on in Paris and became Nadia Boulanger's first full-time
American composition pupil. Since then, a large number of our
younger American composers have at one time or another worked
with her. It would be difficult to estimate the influence that this
inspiring teacher has had on contemporary music.

Copland remained for three years in Paris. He came to know
personally the leading composers of various countries, and heard
much of their music played. Each spring a Russian conductor named
Serge Koussevitzky gave a series of concerts in the French capital
which were devoted to modern compositions. Koussevitzky was
even then a staunch champion of "new" music. As he once humor-
ously put it: "A balanced symphonic diet must include Vitamin C:
C-ontemporary music."

Shortly before Copland left Fontainebleau for his first winter in
Paris he played, at a student's concert there, one of the compositions
that had so startled his early teacher Goldmark: *The Cat and the
Mouse.* Jacques Durand, the music publisher (printer of Debussy's
works) heard this piece and was so struck by its originality that he
offered to buy it for $25. Young Copland felt that now, at last, he
had really "arrived." *The Cat and the Mouse* was his first published
composition.

Most important of his works composed in Europe was a one-act
ballet, *Grogh*—a set of dances full of strange syncopation—founded
on a German film about a magician who had the magic power to
make the dead dance. He wrote it after a summer spent in Berlin.

Koussevitzky had just then been appointed conductor of the
Boston Symphony. When he came to Paris for his closing season of
"Concerts Symphoniques" Mlle Boulanger took young Aaron Cop-
land to call on him.

"Here is a young composer from the country you are about to visit
for the first time," she told him. Koussevitzky was interested in all
young composers. "The creative force in music is a continuous one,"

Aaron Copland

he once said. "Each generation adds to the sum total." He saw that Copland had brought a score with him. "Won't you play it for me?" he asked kindly.

The young musician, "with all the assurance of youth," as he tells it, played the *Cortege Macabre* from his ballet *Grogh*. Koussevitzky immediately said that he would perform the piece at one of his concerts in the United States. Copland "left his presence walking on thin air."

Some years later, after returning to the United States, Aaron Copland took three of the numbers from *Grogh* and made them into what he called a *Dance Symphony*. This was early in 1929, when prosperity had reached its peak and few dreamed of the disastrous depression so soon to follow. The R. C. A. Victor Company offered a prize of $25,000 for the best symphonic work by an American composer. Copland set to work on an ambitious *Symphonic Ode*, but a short time before the competition's closing date he realized that he would never be able to finish the work in time. So he resurrected his ballet Grogh, cut it down in size, and submitted this shorter *Dance Symphony* instead. The judges were unable to decide on any one entry, so finally the prize money was split up into five parts, and Copland's *Dance Symphony* received a $5,000 award.[1] Its first performance was by the Philadelphia Orchestra, Stokowski conducting in April, 1931.

Later he completed the *Symphonic Ode*, begun for the R. C. A. competition, and it was played at the Fiftieth Anniversary of the Boston Symphony. In speaking of this work, Copland quotes a passage from André Gide that might apply to all creative work:

What interests me especially is what I have put into my book without my own knowledge—that part of the unconscious that I should like to name *"La part de Dieu."*

Shortly before he left Paris, Mlle Boulanger asked her "first American pupil" if he would write a composition for her to play the following fall at her American debut. She was an accomplished organist as well as a teacher of harmony, so Copland started work

---

[1] The other winners were Robert Russell Bennett, Louis Gruenberg, and Ernest Bloch.

Modern Music-Makers

on what he called an *Organ Symphony*—a concerto for organ with orchestral accompaniment (he later rearranged it for orchestra alone).

When he got back to the United States, the only job he could find was as pianist with a summer resort hotel trio in Milford, Pennsylvania. After he had finished playing for the hotel guests he would work late into the night trying to get his *Organ Symphony* done. But he found he couldn't do both things at once. He finally had to hire a substitute to take his place in the hotel trio, so that he could finish the symphony in time for Nadia Boulanger's first concert. It took place in New York with Walter Damrosch conducting the New York Symphony Society.

When Dr. Damrosch saw the score of Copland's work he lifted his eyebrows. He knew what the reaction of his conservative audience would be. But since Mlle Boulanger insisted that this was what she wanted to play.....

At the end of Copland's *Organ Symphony* there was polite but unenthusiastic applause. Damrosch turned to the audience.

"If a young man at the age of twenty-three can write a symphony like that," he commented, "in five more years he will be ready to commit murder!"

Copland in telling of the incident concludes: "His prophecy luckily came to nothing."

Aaron Copland returned from Paris in 1923. That fall, after his hotel trio interlude, he opened a studio and hopefully sent out cards announcing himself as a teacher of harmony, piano and composition. But, he confesses, "the effect of this move was nil. It produced not one pupil."

What was to be done? Here he was—a thoroughly trained musician, whose works had already received public recognition (if not acclaim)—and no income. How was he to live?

Fortunately, at that crucial period in his life, the Guggenheim Memorial Foundation having recently been established, Copland applied for and received the first fellowship ever given to a composer. The grant, on its completion, was extended, so during the following two years he was able to devote himself to composition free of financial worries.

But his troubles were not entirely ended. Early in his career he

AARON COPLAND

Aaron Copland

had discovered that his best hours for composing were at night, between 8 P.M. and 2 A.M., when the noises of the outside world had quieted down and there was less danger of interruption. "Music is largely a product of the emotions," he insists, with shrewd humor, "And I can't get emotional early in the day."

However, he found that neighbors seldom approve of music—emotional or otherwise—in the small hours of the night. Copland moved from one place to another, and wherever he went there were sure to be indignant protests from the people above and below. Once, when he was working on his *Piano Variations* (an experiment, as he himself confesses, "spare in sonority—lean in texture—difficult to perform and difficult for an audience to comprehend") there came a violent knock at his door. He tried, at first, to ignore it. When finally he opened the door a large, fierce-looking man pushed his way in and strode over to the piano. Copland had visions of ivory keys and broken strings flying around the room. Instead, the man only peered with frowning intensity at the manuscript.

"What I want to know," he said belligerently, "is how you make the left hand go. I can get the right, but the left, now...."

It didn't occur to Copland to move out of New York to some quiet spot in the country where he would be far from troublesome neighbors. He was essentially a child of the city, and life to him was inseparable from the bustle and stimulation of a busy metropolis. So he kept on moving, and eventually—it was a good many years later—he located what for his needs proved an ideal spot—a large studio at the top of a loft building. There at last he was able to work in complete privacy. The business firms below closed their doors by 6 P.M., and he could make music at any hour that struck his fancy.

Like most of our modern composers Copland, at the beginning of his career, was fascinated by jazz rhythms. When he came back from Paris—possibly to prove that he was not under French influence, he wanted to write something with a truly American flavor. The *Organ Symphony*, he felt, was slightly Boulangesque in character; jazz appealed to him as the most representative medium for his new work. He sketched out a suite for small orchestra (later called *Music for the Theater*) and tried to settle down to work. But it didn't seem to jell. There were too many interruptions.

"Why don't you go to the MacDowell Colony?" a friend suggested.

Modern Music-Makers

Copland had heard of the colony. He applied for admittance, was accepted, and moved up to New Hampshire, where he completed *Music for the Theater*. He has returned many times to the colony, and a number of his important works have been written there (including part of the *Third Symphony*, in 1946). It was at the Mac-Dowell Colony that he first met another young American composer who, like himself, was then comparatively unknown—Roy Harris.

Copland's next composition, *Concerto for Piano and Orchestra*, (written in 1926) was also an elaboration of jazz.[2] Oscar Thompson called this "the most impressive symphonic work in jazz idiom of any composer." "In truly alchemic manner the concerto transmutes the dross of jazz into a fantastic and scintillant symphonic style," wrote another critic. Of this work Copland himself says:

This proved to be the last of my "experiments" with symphonic jazz. With the *Concerto* I felt I had done all I could with the idiom, considering its limited emotional scope. True, it was an easy way to be American in musical terms, but all American music could not possibly be confined to two dominant jazz moods: the "blues" and the snappy number. The characteristic rhythmic element of jazz (or swing, to give it its new name), being independent of mood, yet purely indigenous, will undoubtedly continue to be used in serious native music.[3]

The *Piano Concerto* won more hisses than applause—at least, in its early days. In Mexico City—where Copland himself later played the solo part with the Mexican Symphony Orchestra—the audience reacted violently. Some of the listeners began almost at the first notes to hiss their disapproval. Others, more sympathetic, cried "*Silencio.*" The music could hardly be heard above the general hubbub. Copland wondered if he should go on, but Carlos Chavez—who was conducting—stuck grimly to his post. At the conclusion of the performance, Copland likes to remember, the applause won out over the hisses.

On his first trip to Mexico, Copland fell in love with the country. He liked the easy-going, picturesque natives, the beautiful mountain-encircled country with its warm sunshine and mild climate, and he

[2] Gershwin's *Piano Concerto* appeared in 1925—*The Rhapsody in Blue* a year before that.
[3] In *Our New Music*, Whittlesey House publishers, 1941.

Aaron Copland

especially liked the colorful, rhythm-filled music. Even the banal melodies of the night clubs fascinated him. These popular Mexican songs furnished the themes for one of his most widely played works: *El Salon Mexico.*

From the very beginning, the idea of writing a work based on popular Mexican melodies was connected in his mind with a popular dance hall in Mexico City called "Salon Mexico." He felt, in a very natural and unaffected way, a close contact with the Mexican people. It wasn't the music, but the spirit of the people which inspired him.

El Salon Mexico, first heard in 1938 over N.B.C. under Sir Adrian Boult, was chosen that same year as one of the only two American compositions played at the festival of the International Society for Contemporary Music in London.

Copland has returned several times to Mexico. In the little village of Tepotzlan, about sixty miles from Mexico City (it might have been six hundred, he says), where there was no electricity, nor movies, newspapers or prying neighbors—and above all, no radio—he found an ideal place to work.

Copland has written only a few chamber-music works. *Vitebsk,* a trio for violin, cello and piano, (founded on the Jewish melodies of his racial heritage) and two pieces for string quartet, were comparatively early compositions. His main interest has been centered in music for orchestra, films, radio and ballet. Since the early *Grogh,* Copland has written several ballet scores. These include, *Hear Ye, Hear Ye!, Rodeo,* and *Billy the Kid.* In the latter, cowboy tunes form the basic material. "Whatever cliché he seizes upon—a cowboy ditty, a Spanish tune, a New England hymn—is transformed into an unmistakably Coplandesque configuration." wrote Arthur Berger in the March-April *Partisan Review* of 1943.

Appalachian Spring, a ballet commissioned by Elizabeth Sprague Coolidge, is one of Copland's most delightful scores. He wrote it for a special performance in honor of Mrs. Coolidge's eightieth birthday, and Martha Graham and her dancers first performed it on October 30, 1944, at the Library of Congress in Washington.[4] Miss

---

[4] Walter Piston's *Partita for Violin, Viola, and Organ* was also composed to honor this occasion.

Modern Music-Makers

Graham suggested both subject and title. The following short description of *Appalachian Spring* appeared on the program:

Spring was celebrated by a man and a woman building a house with joy and love and prayer; by a revivalist and his followers in their shouts of exultation; by a pioneering woman with her dreams of the Promised Land.

The ballet contains eight sections, played without interruption. One of its later themes—a quiet, tender melody—is taken from an old Shaker song entitled *Simple Gifts:*

'Tis the gift to be simple,
'Tis the gift to be free
'Tis the gift to come down
Where we ought to be.
And when we find ourselves
In the place just right
'T'will be in the valley
Of love and delight.

Copland has transcribed orchestral suites from *Rodeo, Billy the Kid* and *Appalachian Spring;* these are widely played at symphony concerts, and are among his most popular compositions.

In addition to the *Dance Symphony,* taken from the ballet *Grogh,* and the *Symphonic Ode,* there are three major works for orchestra: the *First Symphony* (adapted from the organ concerto written in 1924 for Nadia Boulanger) a *Short Symphony* (No. II) (1933) and the *Third Symphony,* commissioned by the Koussevitzky Music Foundation and one of the most important of Copland's compositions. It was first performed in October, 1946, by Koussevitzky and the Boston Symphony and again the following month in New York.

Lincoln Portrait found its inspiration at the beginning of the last war. André Kostelanetz, well-known conductor, believing that "the magnificent spirit of our country could be expressed through a musical interpretation of great American characters," suggested to Virgil Thomson, Jerome Kern and Aaron Copland that they write orchestral portraits of three outstanding patriots. Kern took Mark Twain as his subject; Thomson chose Fiorella La Guardia; and Aaron Copland planned to interpret "the patron saint of all American

324

Aaron Copland

composers: Walt Whitman," but was asked to do Abraham Lincoln instead. At first Copland hesitated, feeling that it would be impossible to "match in musical terms the stature of so eminent a figure." But he finally solved the problem by letting Lincoln speak for himself. The score of *Lincoln Portrait* includes the texts of several of the great emancipator's speeches and letters, delivered by a narrator to the music's accompaniment.

Recent works of Copland's are *Preamble for Orchestra* (also with speaking voice); a choral work *In the Beginning* (for mezzo-soprano and mixed chorus) using as text excerpts from the first two chapters of Genesis; and, in 1950, a song-cycle *Twelve Poems of Emily Dickinson;* a *Quartet for Piano and Strings,* and *Old American Songs Newly Arranged.*

The music of any period, Copland points out, is shaped by the needs of that period. Just as Palestrina, and later Bach, composed music of a religious character for the Church, and Haydn and Mozart wrote light, entertaining scores to amuse their royal patrons, so today an entirely new type of music and of audience is coming into being through radio, phonograph, and moving pictures. In schools and in educational projects, too, music is playing a greater role than ever before.

Aaron Copland has composed for all these different fields. For the schools he wrote an *Outdoor Overture* and *The Second Hurricane.* The latter, a "play-opera" with a thoroughly modern plot is "for young people from eight to eighteen." *The Second Hurricane* was planned originally for the Music School of the Henry Street Settlement in New York City; the children themselves managed every detail of the production: they designed and built the sets, acted, sang and played in the accompanying orchestra.

Copland has always aimed to make his music as straightforward as possible—to "say what he had to say in the simplest possible terms." For this reason it has been eminently suitable for radio and films. As W. H. Mellers [5] says: "its hollowness, sparseness, the sharp clarity of its harmonic scheme poised between diatonic consonance and an acute dissonance. . . .is by nature suitable to the microphone and to mechanistic treatment generally."

[5] "An American Perspective," *Kenyon Review,* summer of 1943.

Modern Music-Makers

The "spaciousness and open-airiness" of Aaron Copland's music probably had something to do with the title selected for a radio work commissioned in 1937 by the Columbia Broadcasting Company. Copland couldn't decide on a name for the piece, so they asked the radio audience, after hearing it played, to suggest a name that would describe the music. Over a thousand titles were sent in, proving the truism that music can be interpreted in many different ways—according to the temperament of the individual. *Saga of the Prairies* was finally chosen as the most appropriate.

Copland had no "program" in mind when he wrote the work. He believes that to give music a title at once limits it. He himself calls the piece simply *Music for Radio*.

After looking at long reels of silent films, Copland decided that without music they were cold and lacking in reality. "Music," he says, "is like a small flame put under the screen to help warm it."

While realizing that the music written for films must play a subordinate part ("after all, film music makes sense only if it helps the film") he maintains that a successful score must so perfectly interpret the atmosphere and emotion of the particular story it accompanies that the music becomes an integral part of the film, helping to tie together the many different scenes; and should not be—as it too often is—a casual appendage tailored to fit specific time requirements.

The score that he wrote for the screen production of *Our Town* illustrates how perfectly music can interpret and produce mood. Thornton Wilder wrote *Our Town* while at the MacDowell Colony in Peterborough. The scene is laid in a New England village that could have been Peterborough itself, with its winding roads and quaint old houses set among ancient elms and maples; with its old Town Hall and picturesque graveyard on a sunny slope overlooking the river. Copland, equally familiar with the New Hampshire countryside, has caught its atmosphere in his musical score. The underlying theme of *Our Town* suggests a quiet New England village where life moves at a serene, unhurried pace.

Copland has done a number of other moving-picture scores: *Of Mice and Men, The North Star* and two documentary films: *The City* and *The Cummington Story*. (The latter for the O.W.I.) More recently he wrote the music for *The Red Pony*, from which he drew a

326

Aaron Copland

Children's Suite for orchestra, and *The Heiress*. For this last he was awarded an Oscar by the Academy of Motion Picture Arts and Sciences for the best film-score of 1950.

Writing for the new medium of films, radio and educational fields is one of the modern composer's greatest opportunities Copland believes. The concert hall can reach only a selected few, but radio and the films are for the millions. To bring music to the youth of the country is to broaden and develop understanding and appreciation in a coming generation of listeners. "For the first time democracy has entered the realm of serious music," says Copland. He considers the new means for reproducing music through radio, phonograph and films as important as the invention of the printing press.

Aaron Copland has been one of the most active among our native composers in advancing the cause of modern music. In the late twenties he and Roger Sessions inaugurated the "Copland-Sessions Concerts." These were devoted exclusively to the works of American contemporary, and in many cases unknown, composers, and played a leading part in bringing new music before the public.

Copland has also written two important books: *What to Listen for in Music,* (Whittlesey House, 1939), and *Our New Music,* (Whittlesey House, 1941). As a writer he expresses himself with unusual lucidity, and has the rare faculty of making an abstruse subject intelligible even to the layman. Anyone who wants to understand modern music will find much in Aaron Copland's books to enlighten him. He speaks not only for the music of today, but for the composer as well. In the preface to *Our New Music* he says:

The art of music during the past fifty years has undergone a violent upheaval. Audiences everywhere have shown signs of bewilderment at the variety of styles and tendencies that all pass muster under the name of modern music. . . .

Although this break with the past began more than forty years ago, there are still some people who have not yet recovered from the shock. Music has been changing, but they have remained the same. Nevertheless, inwardly, they know that change in music, like change in all the arts, is inevitable. After all, why should I or any other composer living in a time like ours write music that reflects some other period? Isn't it natural for us to try to develop our own kind of music? In doing so, we are merely following the example of revolutionaries like Beethoven and Wagner. They too sought new expressive possibilities in music—and found them.

The fact is that the whole history of music is a history of continuous change. There never was a great composer who left music exactly as he found it.

It will be interesting to see, some twenty or thirty years hence, just which of our present-day composers are most responsible for changing—or at any rate of modifying—the world's musical idiom. Aaron Copland's name will undoubtedly be close to the head of the list.

Aaron Copland

The Music of Aaron Copland

ORCHESTRAL WORKS

Symphony for Organ and Orchestra [1]	1924
Dance Symphony [1]	1925
Music for the Theatre (suite for small orchestra)[1]	1925
Concerto for Piano and Orchestra [1]	1926
First Symphony [1]	1928
Symphonic Ode [1]	1929
Short Symphony (No. 2) [1]	1933
Statements [2]	1934
El Salon Mexico [2]	1936
Music for Radio (*Saga of The Prairie*) [2]	1937
Outdoor Overture [2]	1938
Billy the Kid (suite from ballet) [2]	1938
Quiet City, trumpet, English horn, string orchestra [2]	1940
Our Town (music from film score) [2]	1940
John Henry (small orchestra)	1940
Lincoln Portrait [2]	1942
Danzon Cubano [2]	1942
Fanfare for the Common Man [2]	1942
Music for Movies [2]	1942
Four dances from Rodeo [2]	1942
Jubilee Variation (on a theme by Goossens)	1944
Letter from Home [2]	1944
Appalachian Spring (suite from ballet) [2]	1944
Third Symphony [2]	1946
Children's Suite from *The Red Pony* [2]	1948
Clarinet Concerto [2]	1948
Preamble for Orchestra with speaking voice [2]	1949

PIANO WORKS

Scherzo Humoristique: The Cat and The Mouse [2]	1920
Passacaglia [3]	1922
Sentimental Melody [4]	1926
Piano Variations [1]	1930

Aaron Copland

Two Children's Pieces [5]	1936
Piano Sonata [2]	1941
Four Piano Blues [2]	1948

CHORAL WORKS

Four Motets—mixed chorus, a cappella	1921
Two Choruses for women's voices, a cappella [6]	1925
What Do We Plant—Junior High Chorus, piano [2]	1935
Lark—mixed chorus, baritone solo, a cappella [6]	1938
Las Agachadas (The Shake-Down Song) mixed chorus, a cappella [2]	1942
The Younger Generation [2]	1943
Song of the Guerrillas men's voices with baritone solo and piano [2]	1943
In the Beginning, mezzo-soprano solo, mixed chorus, a cappella [2]	1947

CHAMBER MUSIC

As It Fell Upon a Day, soprano, flute and clarinet [7]	1923
Two Pieces for Violin and Piano [4]	1926
Two Pieces for String Quartet [1]	1928
Vitebsk, violin, cello and piano [1]	1929
Elegies, violin and viola [1]	1932
Sextet, string quartet, piano, clarinet [2]	1937
Quiet City, trumpet, English horn, string orchestra [2]	1940
Episode, organ [8]	1941
Danzon Cubano, two pianos [2]	1942
Fanfare for the Common Man, brass and percussion [2]	1942
Sonata for Violin and Piano [2]	1943
Quartet for Piano and Strings [2]	1950

SONGS

Old Poem [3]	1920
Pastorale	1921
Song (E. E. Cummings) [9]	1927
Vocalise [10]	1928
Twelve Poems of Emily Dickinson, song-cycle for voice and piano [2]	1950
Old American Songs, newly arranged, voice and piano [2]	1950

Modern Music-Makers

[1] Arrow Music Press.
[2] Boosey-Hawkes.
[3] Salabart, Paris.
[4] Schott, Mainz.
[5] C. Fischer.
[6] E. C. Schirmer.
[7] New Music Pub.
[8] H. W. Gray.
[9] Cos Cob Press.
[10] Alphonse Leduc.
[11] C. C. Birchard.

GEORGE ANTHEIL

GEORGE ANTHEIL

"MANY composers develop a certain style and never change," says George Antheil. "They are more concerned with maintaining their style than with the music itself. Others write as if music were like a fashion in dressmaking—this year a certain color or fabric, next year another. I used to be like that. I've gone through many things, but now I know that there is only one thing that counts: to continue the great art of music. It must follow along the grand line."

It took a good many years before Antheil came to the above conclusion. In his early days he was known as "the Bad Boy of Music" —a reputation which began when he was only three. At that time he demanded a piano. "A real, *big* piano. . . ."

His father, owner of "Antheil's, A Friendly Family Shoe Store" was amused; but his mother, who was more sympathetic (she had played the piano in her youth) bought him a toy piano. Georgie was furious. Even at that early age, for him it had to be "everything or nothing." He took the piano down to the cellar and broke it into bits. When he was punished for his vandalism he felt overwhelmed by the injustice of the world. The breaking up of the toy piano was symbolical; it started him on an iconoclastic career.

He was born July 8, 1900, in Trenton, New Jersey. The family lived next door to a machine shop—though Antheil insists that this had nothing to do with the theme of his early, most notorious work, the *Ballet Mécanique.*

He began writing music when he was ten. Two years later, to immortalize the tragic disaster of the *Titanic,* he composed what he considered his first important work; *The Sinking of the Titanic.* He called it a "sonata"; it was full of rolling chords, representing the surging waves, and ended with a touching transcription of *Nearer*

George Antheil

My God to Thee. George thought so highly of this masterpiece that he invited the members of his E. G. Club ("E.G." stood for "Easy Going") to hear him play it. They were "really impressed," and the twelve-year old composer, always pleased with applause, decided then and there on a public career.

For a number of years he studied piano with Constantine von Sternberg, at one time a pupil of Liszt; then composition with Ernest Bloch, who encouraged him to write his *First Symphony.* This was completed in 1920 and shortly after, young Antheil went over to Germany on a concert tour, eventually appearing—with startling effect—in most of the larger European cities.

He usually played some of his own pieces on the programs. The music was new, and to say the least, disturbing. His *Airplane Sonata,* written soon after he went abroad, and several later compositions caused riots on more than one occasion.

George did not object to the demonstrations (he has never been adverse to publicity) but he *did* want to be heard. He bought a small pistol and had a special holster made so he could carry it beneath his left armpit. At a return engagement in Budapest, where he had previously been unable to finish his concert because of rioting, he ordered the ushers to lock the doors. Then he drew out his pistol—laid it on the piano beside him, and went on with his program. This time the audience listened to the end—in respectful silence.

Soon after Antheil went to Germany, the Berlin Philharmonic played his *First Symphony.* Although this work was mild, compared to his later ones, the critics didn't like it, and said so in no uncertain terms. This was less of a disappointment to him, however, than might have been expected. For he had just then met and immediately fallen in love with a young Hungarian girl named Boski Markus (pronounced "Beshka"). Later, in Paris, she became his wife.

Life in Paris was a delirious round of social events and concerts, with occasional side trips to Switzerland and Morocco. The Antheils became part of a group of artists, writers and musicians from every country who, like themselves, had found their Mecca in the gay French capital. One of their best friends there was the American composer Virgil Thomson.

Antheil was only twenty-three when he first arrived in Paris, and with his round, guileless face and short stature he looked like an

335

unsophisticated schoolboy. But his music was far from unsophisticated. It both startled and entertained the Parisians, and made him one of the most conspicuous figures in the musical world. His *Sonata Sauvage,* an "impressionistic portrait" dedicated to Boski, (which caused a major disturbance when first played at the *Théâtre des Champs Elysées), Death of the Machines, Mechanisms,* and finally the climax of them all, the *Ballet Méchanique* gave him the reputation of being a radical of the first degree. At that time new effects were all the rage, and Antheil's *Ballet Méchanique* (which he describes as "a mechanistic dance of life") outdid the wildest of them. It was scored for eight electric pianos, xylophones, buzzers and other hardware, and an instrument reproducing the noise of an airplane propeller.

In 1926 George Antheil and Virgil Thomson organized a series of recitals at the home of a wealthy American woman who lived not far from the Eiffel Tower. It was there, at the opening concert, that the *Ballet Méchanique* had its first performance. The salon of the apartment was unusually spacious, but by the time eight grand pianos, xylophones and other instruments were crowded in (some even overflowed into the hall and stairs) there was scarcely any room left for the audience. All the important social and musical people of Paris had been invited. They managed to squeeze in somehow, but many were practically sitting on top of the pianos—others "hanging by the chandeliers. . . ."

The first blaring chord ("not exactly a quiet one," Antheil admits) nearly blew the walls out. People's hair stood on end and they clutched their ears. How they managed to sit through the noise at such close quarters is still a mystery. However, they not only stayed to the end (to be sure, there was no possibility of escape) but they actually seemed to like the *Ballet Méchanique.* At least they were amused. . . .

The first public performance caused a riot second only to the epic reception of Stravinsky's *Sacre du Printemps.* Subsequent French performances always drew packed houses—though many people came principally out of curiosity. For by this time Antheil had become notorious.

In the United States the *Ballet Méchanique* met with less enthusiasm. In fact it was a complete fiasco. Elaborately produced at Car-

GEORGE ANTHEIL

SAMUEL BARBER

The Music of Samuel Barber

ORCHESTRAL WORKS

(Published by G. Schirmer, Inc.)

Overture to "The School for Scandal"	1932
Music for a Scene from Shelley	1933
First Symphony (in one movement)	1936
Adagio for Strings	1936
Essay for Orchestra	1937
Concerto for Violin and Orchestra	1939
Second Essay for Orchestra	1942
Second Symphony	1944
Capricorn Concerto	1944
Concerto for Cello and Orchestra	1945
Medea (suite from the ballet *Cave of the Heart*)	1946

CHORAL WORKS

(Published by G. Schirmer, Inc.)

The Virgin Martyrs (Helen Waddell after the Latin of Sigebert of Gembloux)—women's voices a cappella	1935
Let Down the Bars, O Death (Emily Dickinson) mixed voices a cappella	1936
Reincarnations (James Stephens)—mixed voices a cappella	1936-1940
1. *Mary Hynes*	1936
2. *Anthony O'Day*	1940
3. *The Coolin'*	1940
A Stopwatch and an Ordnance Map (Stephen Spender) men's voices a cappella and kettledrums	1940
Knoxville: Summer of 1915 (soprano solo) (text by James Agee)	1948

CHAMBER MUSIC

Serenade for String Quartet (or *String Orchestra*)	1929
Dover Beach—baritone and string quartet	1931
Sonata for Cello and Piano	1932
String Quartet in B Minor	1936

Modern Music-Makers

SONGS
(Published by G. Schirmer, Inc.)

The Daisies (James Stephens)	1927
With Rue My Heart Is Laden (A. E. Housman)	1928
Dover Beach (with string quartet)	1932
Bessie Bobtail (James Stephens)	1934
Three Songs from Chamber Music (James Joyce)	1936

1. *Rain Has Fallen*
2. *Sleep Now*
3. *I Hear an Army* (with orchestra)

Heaven-haven (*A Nun takes the Veil*) (Gerard M. Hopkins)	1937
The Secrets of the Old (W. B. Yeats)	1938
Sure on This Shining Night (James Agee)—with orchestra	1938
Nocturne (Frederic Prokosch)—with orchestra	1940
The Queen's Face on the Summery Coin (Robert Horan)	1942
Monks and Raisins (José Garcia Villa)—with orchestra	1943

PIANO WORKS
(Published by G. Schirmer, Inc.)

Excursions	1942
Sonata	1949

STAGE WORKS
(Published by G. Schirmer, Inc.)

Cave of the Heart—(ballet)	1945

Marc Blitzstein

Flight; then the *Ballad of History and Mythology,* tracing the development of man's earliest efforts to be "Airborne."

> Phaëthon had wings on the brain
> Mad for to fly, and walk the sky. . . .
> Icarus had wings on the brain. . . .
> Archytas of Tarentum tried a wooden pigeon
> But it wooden pigeon. . . .
> Leonardo designed a fine propeller model
> Never sweller model. . . .[4]

Next comes *Kitty Hawk* and the Wright Brothers. Part II deals with the war; it includes a moving section dedicated to "Wounded Cities," and the saga of young aviators "walking on the wind-still sky." Part III contains *"Ballad of Hurry Up"* and a slow section—*Night Music*—with a hauntingly tender *Ballad of the Bombardier.* The closing part is entitled *The Open Sky,* beginning "Glory, Glory, Victory. . . ." while the monitor intones:

> Whose Victory—Whose Glory?
> Shall men, once again ready to resume the conquest of the skies,
> Once again be stopped? Once again create—
> The enemy? [5]

The Symphony ends in a shrieking chorus of jubilation:

> Open sky. Open sky.
> Free the air for the Airborne . . . [6]

Scarcely to be heard above the din (in spite of the considerable assistance of loud-speakers) the Monitor continues to admonish:

> Not without grief! Not without warning!
> Warning!
> Warning! [7]

[4] *Ibid.*
[5] *Ibid.*
[6] New York City Symphony Program Notes, April 1-2, 1946.
[7] *Ibid.*

Modern Music-Makers

Leonard Bernstein and the New York City Symphony gave the *Airborne Symphony* its first performance in April, 1946, with Orson Welles as Monitor. They played it again in October of the same year with Robert Shaw in the speaker's part.

"Not often has a new symphony had such an approving reception in this city," wrote Olin Downes. "The work gripped the audience by its subject and its musico-dramatic treatment. . . . It is a significant score, in its quality, expressive purpose, and relation to urgencies of today." Another critic called the *Airborne Symphony* "a monumental masterpiece."[8]

All of Blitzstein's orchestral works, with the exception of a *Piano Concerto* (1931) include chorus or solo voice. His first composition —*Gods*— written in 1926, is for mezzo-soprano, string orchestra and cello solo. He has written only a few chamber-music pieces: a *String Quartet* (1930) and *Serenade for String Quartet* (1932)—both of them performed at Copland-Sessions and The League of Composers concerts, and at Yaddo Festivals.

In addition to his own musical dramas Blitzstein has produced incidental music for a number of plays, among them an American Repertory Theater's production of *Androcles and the Lion* and Lillian Hellman's *Another Part of the Forest*—both in 1947; and *King Lear*, in 1951. He has done two ballets—*Cain* (an early work) and *The Guests*, with Jerome Robbins, produced by the New York City Ballet in 1949. His latest opera, *Regina*, was commissioned by Koussevitsky for production at Tanglewood. It is adapted from Miss Hellman's *The Little Foxes.*

All of Blitzstein's dramatic works contain an underlying theme. Music, he feels, must teach as well as entertain—must have a social as well as an artistic base; it should broaden its scope and reach not only the select few but also the masses. This is his personal creed, and he has the talent, the intelligence, and the enterprise to express it. Marc Blitzstein is a force in the musical world to be reckoned with.

---

[8] Grena Bennett in the *New York Journal American.*

Marc Blitzstein

The Music of Marc Blitzstein

Marc Blitzstein

Incidental Music for Another Part of the Forest (Lilian Hellman)　　1947
The Guests–ballet (with Jerome Robbins)　　1949
Regina–opera　　1949
Incidental Music for King Lear　　1951

[1] G. Schirmer Inc.
[2] B. Schott's Sönne.
[3] Chappell.

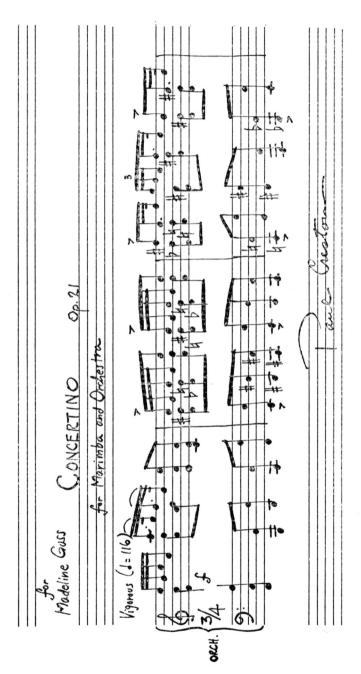

PAUL CRESTON

PAUL CRESTON

PAUL CRESTON has been commended for his "clear and straight-forward musical thinking" and for "the general skilfulness and sound-worthiness of his instrumentation."[1] Yet he is almost entirely a self-taught composer.

He was born in New York City on October 10, 1906. His father, a house-painter by profession who had come to the United States from Sicily, was delighted when the younger of his two sons showed musical promise. At an early age the boy learned the old Italian folk songs, and would listen enthralled while his father sang and played the guitar, or told him stories of sunny Italy. He dreamed of visiting that enchanted land where winter never comes, where—so his father told him—oranges hang on trees waiting to be picked (not wrapped in tissue paper at a price small boys could seldom afford) and where, best of all, there was always music in the air.

This dream of a trip to Italy came true when he was six. At that time his mother took her two sons on a visit to Sicily. Every detail of that journey remained, sharply etched on the boy's awakening mind. The gay singing of the peasants and the rhythm of their dances made a special impression on him. His most vivid memory was a circus in Palermo where his uncle played the clarinet in the band. Soon after, he returned to America. He was glad to get back to the East Side flat on Twenty-Ninth Street; after all, he had been born in New York, and the United States was his country.

He first wanted to be a pianist, and begged his father to let him have a piano. There was little money to spare, but his father could never say no where music was concerned, and finally bought him a second-hand piano for ten dollars.

The older brother was given a violin, but it was the younger one who first learned to play on it and soon could reproduce anything that

[1] Olin Downes, New York Music Critics' Circle.

371

he heard by ear. If the hurdy-gurdy ground out a waltz beneath the window he would amuse himself by improving on the tune—or by making up a better one. But composing in those days was "only a pleasant pastime"—something with which to while away an idle hour or to entertain his friends. He was more interested at that time in literature. When he was thirteen he started an ambitious novel, but after working on it for some time finally gave it up. In later years he was to write a number of essays, poems and articles; fiction, however, has never been his medium.

He was a typically active, fun-loving boy—more aggressively American, perhaps, than many of those with generations-long claim to the title. Grafted onto the artistic sensitivity of his Italian forbears was the energy and enterprise typical of the new country in which he had been born.

Learning was his passion. After school hours he would haunt the libraries, devouring books on every conceivable subject, from graphology, and astrology to hypnotism (which latter he practised on his playmates with awe-inspiring success). When he wanted to learn shorthand he sent for a course he'd seen advertised. He didn't have the money to pay for it, but in the five days that he was allowed to keep the books "on trial," he laboriously copied out the lessons, word for word—sent the course back, and proceeded to master stenography. Since that time he has invented three systems of shorthand. This painstaking determination has always been a leading characteristic of Paul Creston. No effort is too great for him if it serves his purpose.

Creston's family name was Gultoveggio, and he was christened "Giuseppe" (shortened to "Joe"). But he found the name unwieldy; people had trouble remembering it—let alone spelling it correctly. Also he felt that it sounded too foreign for an American-born citizen.

While he was in high school it occurred to him that it might be a good idea to change his name. His companions dubbed him "Cress" after a character which he had impersonated in a school play called *The Fan.* After leaving high school he lengthened the "Cress" to Creston, added Paul, "because he liked it," and adopted Paul Creston as his permanent name.

During the three years following high school, young Creston set

Paul Creston

himself a strenuous, almost fanatical schedule. Before going to work in the morning he practised for two hours. Then he worked all day, practised again in the evening, and studied until two or three in the morning. When sleep threatened to overpower him he smoked coffee beans to keep awake.

"Edison got along on four hours of sleep," he reasoned. "So I should be able to do the same!"

He held a number of different jobs. First with the MacFadden Publications; then in the Foreign Exchange Department of the Irving Bank; and finally with the Metropolitan Life Insurance Company. Meanwhile he continued studying and reaching out in every direction (his interests at that time included natural therapeautics, cryptography and Eastern philosophy), and worked hard at his piano. Randegger and Dethier were his teachers, and he had organ lessons with Pietro Yon.

In July, 1927, shortly before his twenty-first birthday, he married Louise Gotto—like himself of Italian ancestry, born in America. She was at that time a dancer in Martha Graham's company and continued with that group for some years longer. The Creston's first child was born ten years after their marriage, but only lived a few weeks. In 1938 and 1942 two other sons, Joel and Timothy, joined the family.

It was not until five years after his marriage that Paul Creston thought seriously of becoming a composer. He had always kept up his music, and had even written a few songs and piano pieces. But he had never had any formal instruction in harmony or composition.

He realized, now, that if he wanted to be a serious composer he would have to start at the very beginning. Since he couldn't afford a first-class teacher, he made up his mind that he would learn by himself. He studied every book he could find on harmony, theory and counterpoint; with the power of intense application gained through years of self-discipline, he managed in a relatively short time to acquire a thorough knowledge of his subject.

The New York libraries, lectures and concerts, were his universities. In a radio interview he once stated:

I am entirely a product of Manhattan. All my work has been done here and my education was in this city. I never felt it necessary to study in foreign lands because, first of all, I didn't have the money to get there—and

373

Modern Music-Makers

more importantly, because Europe has come to us. We have the best that the world can offer, right here in the shadow of the Empire State Building!

It was really his friends, Creston claims, who were responsible for turning him into a professional musician. "Why don't you have some of your pieces published, Cress?" they asked him.

"Who would want to publish stuff like this?" he answered (though to himself he probably confessed, as MacDowell once did about his early compositions: "In my heart I had the greatest love for them, and would not willingly have changed a single note.").

One day Creston screwed up his courage and took a group of pieces—*Seven Theses for the Piano*—to the New Music Publishing Company. Henry Cowell was then editor, and recognized at once that the young composer had outstanding talent. He agreed to publish the pieces, and it was largely due to this encouragement that Creston decided to go on writing music.

After he had mastered the fundamentals of composition, he branched out into every subject he could find that was related to music, such as the evolution of harmony, Gregorian chant, seventeenth and eighteenth century music, acoustics, and the philosophy and psychology of music. One thing that interested him greatly was musical therapy. He feels that this science—music as a curative power, both physical and mental—has enormous possibilities, and should be put on a more practical basis. Considerable research has been done on the subject, but the results need more co-ordination. Trained scientists, he believes, or some endowed society such as the Rockefeller Foundation, should make an exhaustive study of musical therapy.

The next few years, while Creston was training himself, were not easy. Having definitely decided on a composer's career, he now gave up all non-musical activities. For a time, to keep the family fires burning, he played the organ in a moving picture theater. Then, in 1934 he was appointed organist to St. Malachy's Church—a post he still holds. Later he was engaged to direct some radio programs over the Blue Network. He conducted the A.B.C. Orchestra and composed and conducted for "Storyland Theatre" and the "Hour of Faith" programs.

It takes years for most composers to win public recognition, and

374

Paul Creston

Paul Creston was no exception to this rule. But finally the tide began to turn. In 1938 he received a Guggenheim Fellowship—renewed the following year—and his first composition for full orchestra, called *Threnody,* was played by Fritz Reiner and the Pittsburgh Symphony. This work, written at the death of his first child, bears a moving introduction in Gregorian chant style, followed by a "human" theme of intense emotion. The latter leads to a violent climax which gradually returns to the choral-like first theme. The work ends with a quiet passage for flute and muted strings.

Creston's *First Symphony,* completed in 1940, made his name widely known to the public. It received a citation from the National Association of American Composers and Conductors, a $1,000 grant from the American Academy of Arts and Letters, and the 1943 New York Music Critics Circle award. Creston's work was selected from a group of compositions by Aaron Copland *(A Lincoln Portrait),* Roy Harris *(Fifth Symphony),* Morton Gould *(Spirituals for String Choir and Orchestra),* and William Schuman *(Prayer in Time of War).*

In choosing Creston's *First Symphony* Olin Downes, then president of the New York Music Critics Circle voiced the opinion of the judges:

Mr. Creston's composition gave us much satisfaction by . . . its balance of lyrical, rhythmic and contrapuntal elements . . . the contrast and balance within the unity of the framework of the different movements, and the style which did not ride to death some technical theory, form or formula. Here is a score which reflects, though in no greatly individual or epochal manner, the composer's intention to provide, without pretense, apology or braggadocio, a soundly wrought and interesting symphony.

Following the first performance of the work, in February, 1941, Virgil Thompson spoke of its "gusto and buoyancy," and said that Creston's "musical facility and technical command are more like what we import from Europe than what we currently grow here." Olin Downes called it "one of the most workmanlike symphonies by an American that we know."

Creston's *First Symphony* is in four movements, titled *With Majesty, With Humor, With Serenity,* and *With Gaiety.* The second movement, based essentially on rhythm, has been frequently heard alone under the name *Scherzo*. Stokowski and his first Youth Orchestra played it a number of times on their South American tour.

Paul Creston is particularly interested in the rhythmical side of music. He feels that the other elements—melody, harmonic development, color, form, etc., have so far received the greater attention. There are many books on harmony and counterpoint, but few on rhythm. The four parts of rhythm: meter, pace, duration, and accent, can be used in practically endless combinations. Creston tries to find the rhythmic possibilities of a theme before working out its harmonic relations. When beginning a new composition he first decides on the mood, then the rhythm that best interprets that mood. Only after this comes the melodic and harmonic development.

When Creston received the Guggenheim Fellowship in 1938, his first work was based on dance rhythms. He had always been interested in the dance, partly because of his intuitive feeling for rhythm and also because of his wife's connection with the stage. A number of his works are in this medium.

Two Choric Dances was originally scored for chamber orchestra— later for full orchestra. *Prelude and Dance* and *Pastorale and Tarantella,* for full orchestra, were both composed in 1941. *Dance Variations* is for soprano solo and orchestra. Creston has also written a ballet: A *Tale about the Land* (1940).

Paul Creston may or may not agree with the old gag "there must be music in the saxophone since it never comes out." At any rate he has written several works for this instrument—a *Suite* and a *Sonata* (with piano accompaniments) and a *Concerto for Saxophone and Orchestra.* He has also composed the only work in serious form for the marimba. This *Concerto for Marimba and Orchestra,* written as a commission for Frederique Petrides, was commended by the critics. They called him, "a composer with ideas and invention . . . [who] writes with rhythmic bite and variety and, occasionally with a delightfully lyric strain." [1]

In 1947 he produced a *Fantasy for Trombone and Orchestra;* in 1949 a *Concerto for Piano and Orchestra* (commissioned as a memorial to the late Joseph D. Malkin); and in 1951 a *Concerto for Two*

[1] *New York Times,* April 30, 1940.

PAUL CRESTON

Paul Creston

*Pianos and Orchestra,*this last as a commission from the duo-pianists Luboschutz and Nemenoff.

Creston's chamber-music works include a *String Quartet* (1936); a *Suite for Viola and Piano* (1937) and one for violin and piano (1939); a *Partita* for flute, violin and strings; and, in 1947, a *Homage* arranged for viola, harp and piano, (also for viola and piano, cello and piano, or for string orchestra.) In choral music Creston has composed for a cappella choir *Three Chorals* based on Tagore's *Gitanjali,* and two Masses: a *Missa Pro Defunctis* (1938) and a *Missa Solemnis* (1949).

Most of his later works have been for orchestra. Among them are a *Fantasy* (piano and orchestra); *Chant of 1942; Frontiers; Dawn Mood;* and a *Second Symphony* (1944). This last well illustrates the two dominant characteristics of Paul Creston's music: rhythm and melody. He calls his *Second Symphony* "an apotheosis of the two foundations of all music: Song and Dance." The work is in two main parts (each of these in two sections) *Introduction and Song* and *Interlude and Dance*—the first tender and simple in character, the last a complex fabric of rhythmic patterns.

A *Third Symphony* was commissioned in 1950 by the Worcester County Musical Association, and first played at the Worcester Festival in October of that year. Since then it has had performances in New York and other leading cities. The music of the *Third Symphony* is based on Gregorian plain chant, and is subtitled *The Three Mysteries: The Nativity, The Crucifixion,* and *The Resurrection.*

Paul Creston does not write what is known as "program music." He says he is not interested in telling stories or painting tone pictures. His mind works from the abstract side rather than from the personal. The form of composition is not born of the title, but the title invented to fit the form.

When someone once asked Creston if he was an "innovator" he replied: "There is no such thing as an innovator in music—in any of the arts, for that matter. The things that we create today are built upon the beginnings of many yesterdays. The works of Bach himself evolved from patterns that men before him had set down. In short, I believe in evolution—not revolution."

Creston divides his days between composing, directing radio programs, playing the organ at St. Malachy's, teaching composition,

Modern Music-Makers

piano and organ, and his family. He finds time for all these only because of his exceptionally methodical nature. He daily sets himself definite tasks—so many hours for creative work, so many for outside activities, so many for copying music (usually at night). He often spends six months to two years thinking over a composition before he actually sets it down. Then he works out the details on the piano.

Like Chopin, who rambled over the piano until he struck what he called his *"note bleue,"* most artists have some touchstone that releases their creative energy. Some find it through quiet introspection, an indrawing. Others again (like Gershwin, for instance) are stimulated by noise and confusion; the outer clamor actually helps them to collect their ideas. Great masters such as Beethoven and Brahms have found their "blue note" in Nature—a quiet walk into the country puts them in touch with the source of creative power. Ravel, on the other hand, shut himself in a tiny room with black walls and somber hangings when he wanted to write music. . . .

Paul Creston often finds his inspiration at a concert. "A performer will start to play," he says, "and in the middle of the concert, or whatever he may be playing, an idea will hit me; it may be a theme or a rhythmic figure—any number of things. Well, from that point on, I don't hear what's going on around me. It's just a blur, and all of a sudden I realize that the people around me are going home—the concert has ended."

Paul Creston had none of the advantages available to most young music students, such as conservatories, music schools, training abroad—all, in a sense, shortcuts to achievement. He was obliged to work everything out for himself. But the old saying: "What you learn by your own efforts you know best," has proved true in his case. Enterprise and industry, added to his natural musical endowments, have won for him an assured place among the American composers of today.

Paul Creston

The Music of Paul Creston

Paul Creston

Psalm XXIII, voice and piano [1]	1945
Homage—(for viola, harp & organ or viola & piano	
or cello & piano or string orchestra)	1947

PIANO WORKS

Five Dances [5]	1932
Seven Theses [3]	1933
The Bird of the Wilderness [1]	1933
Four Songs to Death	1935
Three Sonnets	1936
Sonata	1936
Five Two Part Inventions [1]	1937
Five Little Dances [1]	1940
Prelude and Dance No. 1 [6]	1942
Prelude and Dance No. 2 [5]	1942
Dance Variations, soprano & orchestra	1942
Six Preludes [2]	1945-1946
Three Songs for High Voice & Piano	1950
Thirteen French-Canadian Folk Songs (arranged for voice & piano)	1950

BALLET

A Tale About the Land	1940

[1] G. Schirmer, Inc.
[2] Leeds Music Corp.
[3] New Music.
[4] Pro-Art.
[5] Axelrod.
[6] Mercury Music.

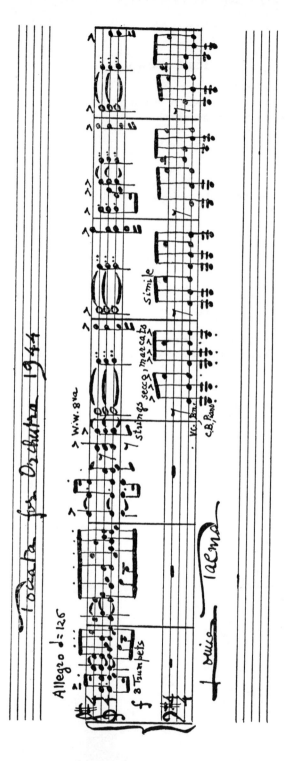

LOUISE TALMA

LOUISE TALMA

LOUISE TALMA began her career as a composer by writing songs. Choral music still remains her favorite medium, though she has produced a number of interesting piano and chamber-music works as well. Her first orchestral composition was an elaborate *Toccata*, completed in 1944.

When Reginald Stewart, conductor of the Baltimore Symphony Orchestra, decided to play the *Toccata* at one of his concerts the following winter, this was the greatest event, so far, in Miss Talma's career. She went down to Baltimore to hear the rehearsal and performance of her piece. A heavy blizzard delayed the train. By the time she reached Baltimore the orchestra was just beginning the rehearsal. It was the first full orchestral performance of her work, and she was so overcome, she says, that for at least ten minutes she could scarcely hear the music.

When the musicians finished playing they laid down their instruments and applauded warmly. The concertmaster leaned over and said to her, "A fine piece of work!" After the public performance of the *Toccata* the critics, too, agreed. "Unquestionably an important contribution of which we shall hear more," they wrote, and stated that the composer "showed great skill . . . in the handling of modern medium."

No later success could mean as much to Louise Talma. Her only regret was that her mother could not have lived to witness this triumph. It would have meant to her "the culmination of a lifetime of devotion and effort and self-denial and hope." Whatever success Miss Talma may have in life, she feels, will be owing to her mother's influence. Mrs. Talma was a singer, but she gave up her own career in order to direct her daughter's training. Louise's father died when she was very young, and life was a hard struggle for the widow. In spite of severely straitened circumstances, however, she managed to provide Louise with every advantage. She gave her lessons in piano and solfeggio, directed her reading, and taught her languages

Modern Music-Makers

(they had regular set times for speaking French, German and Italian together).

Louise's first piano lesson was given to her as a birthday present when she was five, and from that moment she wanted to be a musician—probably a concert pianist, her mother thought. At the age of nine she tried to write an opera to Victor Hugo's *Notre Dame de Paris,* but finally concluded that she was not meant to be a composer.

The Talmas lived abroad for some time. Louise's main education, however, was in this country. She graduated from Wadleigh High School in New York, after winning a Greek Prize and the John G. Wight Scholarship for the best academic record, and also attended the Institute of Musical Art. At that time she still had no thought of becoming a composer (though three times, while at the Institute, she won the Isaac Seligman prize for composition). She took the courses in harmony, counterpoint, etc., mainly in order to understand music better.

At the music school, Louise was considered the "bad girl" of the class—always upsetting the others by asking questions. She had a disconcerting way of wanting to know the "why" of all the rules. Then she would bring in examples from the masters to refute them. None of her teachers then thought her especially gifted—though she played the piano well.

While Louise was at the Institute of Musical Art a fellow pupil, who went over to attend the summer school at Fontainebleau, returned—"starry-eyed"—to tell of her experiences in France. Louise and her mother decided that some way, somehow, she too must go to France. With great effort and self-denial they raised the necessary money.

At Fontainebleau Miss Talma worked mainly with the celebrated piano teacher Isidore Philipp. When fellow students advised her to join Nadia Boulanger's harmony class she gave the idea little attention, since she thought that "she had already completed this branch of study at the Institute of Musical Art." But during her second year at Fontainebleau the students gave a performance of Fauré's *Requiem* and some choral works by Mlle Boulanger's sister Lili. Nadia came to the final rehearsal and spoke to the students. Louise Talma was deeply impressed by the Frenchwoman's magnetic personality, and finally decided that she must attend her classes.

384

PHOTOGRAPH BY BERNICE B. PERRY, WILTON, N. H.

LOUISE TALMA

Louise Talma

Like most young musicians, Miss Talma went through various stages of musical enthusiasms. During her first year at Fontainebleau, Brahms and the German romantics headed the list. She wrote a piece that pleased her mightily—only to discover that it was "a carbon copy of Brahms." Next she switched to Scriabin and the Russians, and unconsciously followed their pattern in a second chefd'oeuvre.

When she went to her first lesson with Nadia Boulanger, she took these two pieces with her.

"Let me see what you have there," said the Frenchwoman, looking briefly through the scores. Then she turned with the charming smile that so endeared her to her pupils. "You love Scriabin very much, don't you?"

Nadia Boulanger had the extraordinary gift of being able, in a cursory glance, to "hear" and also to remember the notes on a page of music. Now, to Louise's amazement she sat down at the piano and without looking at the notes played the beginning of the girl's composition. Then she went through the whole piece pointing out the weak spots.

The young composer would have been discouraged if Mlle Boulanger had not assured her that there was promise in her work. One memorable day towards the end of the summer, her teacher said, with flattering earnestness, "Louise, you have got something—you really have talent! You ought to work to prepare yourself so that some day you can apply for a Guggenheim Fellowship." Louise Talma could hardly believe that Mlle Boulanger was in earnest. She had been struggling along, not daring to hope that she had any special talent. This was the first time anyone had suggested that she might one day qualify as a real composer. Nadia Boulanger's words gave her immense self-confidence, and that same day she received further encouragement from Gerald Reynolds, director of the Women's University Glee Club and liaison officer at Fontainebleau, who asked her if she would write some songs for his chorus.

The result of Reynold's commission was a set of *Three Madrigals*—her first serious compositions. He liked them so much that the following year he asked for more. This time she wrote a choral number called *La Belle Dame Sans Merci* and it was even more successful than the *Madrigals*.

Modern Music-Makers

Louise Talma returned from France full of ideas for her future work. Then fate stepped in and for a time halted her newly begun career. Her beloved mother was stricken with paralysis. In order to care for the invalid and meet the heavy expenses of her illness, Miss Talma was obliged to give up her own work and devote herself to teaching. The diploma she had received from the Institute of Musical Art was not enough, she found, to qualify her for an accredited school—a college degree was necessary. With the help of Marion Bauer, always so generous in aiding younger musicians, she managed in record time to complete the music course at New York University, and later took an M.A. degree at Columbia. While at Columbia she won the Joseph H. Bearns Prize, and in 1946 was awarded a Guggenheim Fellowship. This was renewed in 1947—the first time a woman has twice received this award in music.

Miss Talma has taught at the Institute of Musical Art and the Manhattan School of Music, and for a number of summers held a solfeggio class at the Fontainebleau School—the only American on the staff. At present she is Assistant Professor in the Music Department of Hunter College.

When, at her mother's death, she was able to return to her creative work she found, as many do who are obliged for one reason or another to interrupt their careers, that it was very difficult to get started again. Try as she would, nothing seemed to come. At that moment she was, as she puts it, "empty of ideas. It was the lowest point in my existence." Then an opportunity came to spend the summer at the Mac-Dowell Colony in Peterborough, New Hampshire.

Shy and reserved by temperament, she was at first almost afraid to go. The idea of meeting new people and other artists working in the same field, terrified her. Then too, she felt a great sense of responsibility to produce something worthwhile while there. During her first weeks, beyond one song—the opening one in the *Terre de France* cycle—and a theme for a piano piece (which by the end of the summer developed into the *Piano Sonata)* nothing would come. She was in despair. Mrs. MacDowell, however, wise with many years' handling of temperamental artists, reassured her. "Don't worry," she said, "it takes a few weeks to get started. Give yourself time. . . ."

A fellow composer at the colony, that summer, was young Lukas Foss. Louise had recently heard him play his *Prairie* (in his own

386

individual piano version) and it had made a deep impression on her. When she was asked to perform one of her compositions at a concert given for Mrs. MacDowell at the colony's library, she sent home for some manuscript music, picked out a half-forgotten piano piece called *Four-Handed Fun,* and asked Lukas to play it with her. Their performance, which really *was* "four-handed fun" marked the beginning of a close friendship between the two.

Young Foss was enthusiastic about Louise's piece. This encouragement, together with the inspiration of colony surroundings and of her secluded studio in the woods, proved just the stimulus that she needed. Now her creative powers began to flow. Before the summer's end she had completed her *Piano Sonata.*

In addition to her early *Madrigals* Miss Talma has written a number of of choral works—among them *Fourteen Variations on Thirteen Ways of Looking at a Blackbird* (words by Wallace Stevens) for three women's voices and piano; a motet *In Principio Erat Verbum,* for mixed chorus and organ—which won the Stovall prize—and *Carmina Mariana,* three duets for two sopranos and piano. Her many songs include three cycles: *Five Sonnets from the Portuguese,* A *Child's Fancy,* and—one of her finest works—*Terre de France.* This last was composed "as a tribute to much-loved France"; it has for text poems by Péguy, Du Bellay, Ronsard, and Charles d'Orleans. The *Terre de France* songs were first heard at the W.N.Y.C. Festival of American music in February, 1946, and again that same fall at the Yaddo Festival.

Miss Talma's *Piano Sonata,* which she herself played at a League of Composers concert, received excellent reviews. It contained, according to one of these, "passages hinting at the existence of a genuinely vigorous talent." In 1947 the *Piano Sonata* won the $1,000 North American Prize offered by the E. Robert Schmitz School in a competition open to composers from Mexico, Canada, and the United States.

It was, however, the *Toccata* that made Louise Talma's name known to the public. Following its Baltimore performance this work was played in May, 1946, at the orchestral concert of the Columbia Music Festival, and that same year received the Juilliard Publication Award. The *Toccata* was well received at the Columbia concert; its

Modern Music-Makers

"gay, buoyant and youthful spirit," and its "rich orchestration and design" were especially commended. Olin Downes wrote:[1]

Miss Talma's treatment of the Toccata form reminds me more of one of the baroque Eighteenth Century Toccatas in the variety and style presented before it is finished, than of one of these machine pieces which most present-day composers succeed in writing on the basis of a single short figure repeated and variegated sufficiently to fill a few pages. . . .

Louise Talma's mind is filled with more ideas than she can set down, she says—ideas accumulated during the enforced years of her creative inactivity. Her most ambitious work, so far, is an oratorio *The Divine Flame,* for mixed chorus and orchestra, mezzo-soprano and baritone. She worked on it for three years, finally completing it in 1948. In 1950 she composed another choral work: *The Leaden Echo and the Golden Echo,* to a poem by Hopkins. (His poetry appeals to her especially, and most of her later songs have used his words as texts.) Her most recent work is for violin and piano—*Song and Dance*—first played in February, 1951 at the W.N.Y.C. American Festival by Paul Makovsky.

Louise Talma has always kept in mind the ideals instilled in her during her early childhood. Strong religious faith and creative work are, she feels, the most important things in life. The latter, to her, is only a practical application of the former. "Creative work means to live well whatever life the Lord gives you to live," she says. "Whether it be scrubbing floors or writing symphonies, the dignity of the work is exactly the same and its worth in direct proportion to the quality of the execution. A well-scrubbed floor is better praise of the Lord than an ill-made symphony."

Louise Talma is in all things a perfectionist, and in this sense her faith and work are one. To them she brings intensity and devotion, and her music, in consequence, is true "praise of the Lord."

---

[1] *The New York Times,* May 5, 1946.

Louise Talma

CHRONOLOGICAL CHART OF MAIN EVENTS AND WORKS

Born October 31	1906
Graduates from Wadleigh High School, New York	1922
John Wright Scholarship	
Attends Institute of Musical Art	1922-1930
Isaac Seligman Composition Prize 1927, 28, 29	
Attends summer school at Fontainebleau	1926-1939
Studies with Nadia Boulanger	1928-1943
Three Madrigals	1929
La Belle Dame Sans Merci	1930
M. A. degree from Columbia Music Department	1933
J. H. Bearns Prize	
In Principio Erat Verbum	1939
Four-Handed Fun	
Appointed Assistant Professor Music Department Hunter College	1942
First visit to MacDowell Colony	1943
Piano Sonata	1943
Toccata for Orchestra	1944
Alleluia	
Terre de France song cycle	1945
Juilliard Publication Award (*Toccata*)	1946
North American Prize (*Piano Sonata*)	1947
The Divine Flame	1948
Appointed Associate Professor Music Department Hunter College	1949
The Leaden Echo and the Golden Echo	1950

The Music of Louise Talma

Toccata [1]   1944

Choral Music

Three Choruses for Women's Voices and String Quartet (Wyatt) [2]   1929
La Belle Dame Sans Merci (women's voices, baritone solo, organ)
  (Keats)   1930
Thirteen Ways of Looking at a Blackbird (women's voices and piano)
  (Stevens)   1938
In Principio Erat Verbum (mixed chorus and organ) (St. John)   1939
Carmina Mariana (women's voices and piano) (The Missal)   1943
The Divine Flame: oratorio. (mixed chorus and orchestra; mezzo-
  soprano and baritone) (The Bible and Missal)   1945-1948
The Leaden Echo and the Golden Echo (mixed chorus and piano)
  (Hopkins)   1950

Piano Music

Two Dances   1934
Four-Handed Fun (piano four hands) [3]   1939
Piano Sonata [3]   1943
Alleluia in the Form of Toccata [3]   1945
Italian Suite   1946
Pastoral Prelude [3]   1949
Bagatelle   1950

Organ

Wedding Piece   1946

Violin and Piano

Song and Dance   1951

Louise Talma

[1] American Music Center, Juilliard Edition.
[2] J. Fischer.
[3] Carl Fischer.

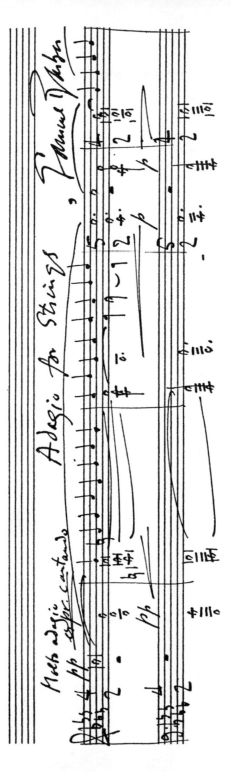

SAMUEL BARBER

SAMUEL BARBER

SAMUEL BARBER

WHEN Toscanini took over the direction of the NBC Orchestra, the first work by an American to be played on his program was Samuel Barber's *Adagio for Strings.*

At the time there was some criticism of Toscanini's choice. Certain modern music devotees felt that Barber was too much of a "romantic" to be validly representative of his country's music. Americans, practical and matter-of-fact, are inclined to be suspicious of anything resembling sentimentality, though most have a deep-lying, if unacknowledged, urge to translate the commonplace into terms of beauty. This is what "romanticism" really is, and what Barber's music does for us—particularly in its slow movements, which show his lyrical qualities at their best.

From the day of his birth, March 9, 1910, in West Chester, Pennsylvania, Samuel Barber lived in close contact with music. His father, a physician, had no special talent, though he loved music; but his mother, the former Marguerite Beatty (sister of the famous Louise Homer), came from a family where music was the main concern of life. There were five brothers and three sisters, all of them musically gifted. They made up their own miniature symphony, and were always playing or singing together. Louise had the best voice—a rich, full contralto. When she went to Boston to study, her teacher there was Sidney Homer. She married him later, and as Mme Homer became the world-famous Metropolitan opera singer.

Sam often visited at his aunt's home in New York or, during the summer months, at Cape Cod and Lake George. Wherever the Homers lived they invariably had two studios—one for the opera singer and the other for her composer-husband. Their six children, Sam's cousins, were all musical too, and he often joined them in making music. Years later he and his aunt and several of her children appeared together in a "family" concert at West Chester, at which Louise Jr., the eldest, sang duets with her mother, and Kay, one of the twins, made her debut as accompanist. Sidney Homer and Sam contributed songs for the occasion.

Modern Music-Makers

It was no doubt inevitable that Sam should have followed the family pattern. Exceptions to the contrary, early environment does play a large part in predisposing a child's interests. Where music is the daily fare in a home, if talent exists it will find early recognition and encouragement, and every chance for development. Mozart is the outstanding example of this.

Sam was six when he began piano lessons in West Chester with a teacher named William Hatton Green. Some months later his mother heard him playing a doleful melody. "What's that?" she asked. "I made it up," he answered. "It's called *Sadness. . . .*" She wrote it down for him, and he still has the faded manuscript tucked away among his papers.

By the time he was twelve, Sam had become a first-class organist as well as pianist, and had a regular position in one of West Chester's churches. But even then his ideas about music were unorthodox. After a year or so he resigned.

In 1924 the Curtis Institute of Music in Philadelphia opened its doors for the first time. Generously endowed by Mary Curtis Bok this institute was to become, with Eastman and Juilliard, one of the three great music schools in the United States. Fourteen-year-old Samuel Barber was a charter pupil. He had now definitely decided to make music his career, and since Curtis offered opportunities for training in every department, he wanted to sample as many as possible.

Only the finest available teachers were engaged for the new school; at that time there were few outstanding American-trained music instructors, so the faculty was chiefly made up of foreigners. The list of Sam's teachers sounds like an international roll call. He had piano lessons with George Boyle, an Australian—later with Mme Vengerova, a Russian; conducting with Fritz Reiner, a German; and composition with Rosario Scalero, an Italian.

It was in Scalero's class that Barber first met a fellow student a year younger than himself, who was to become his closest friend. Gian-Carlo Menotti, born in Milan, July 7, 1911, had just come over from Italy. He had attended the conservatory there, but he was more interested in the operas at the famous La Scala Theater than in his academic studies. Even in those early days young Menotti wrote music with amazing facility, and could not understand why he should

394

Samuel Barber

have to bother with rules and regulations. When he was seventeen his mother decided to bring him to the United States to study with his countryman, Rosario Scalero. At Curtis Institute he was at last convinced that he could never become a serious composer unless he first mastered theory and counterpoint. Menotti spent five years at Curtis and proved one of the most brilliant pupils ever to graduate from this institute which has been the training school for so many of our fine young American composers.

Menotti and Barber had much in common, not least of which was their love of melody. In the former's case this was based on his Italian heritage and early association with opera, and in Barber's on his experience as a singer. While at Curtis Barber studied singing with Emilio di Gogorza—husband of the opera singer Emma Eames. Sam had a fine baritone voice, and for a while it looked as if he might follow in his aunt's footsteps, and take up a singer's career. But his creative gift was even greater than his interpretative talent, and as he continued with his music studies, composition attracted him more and more.

In Philadelphia he had a unique opportunity to hear the most recent contemporary works. Leopold Stokowski, then conductor of the Philadelphia Orchestra, and one of modern music's earliest and most important champions, usually included some contemporary work on his programs—in spite of determined and often indignant opposition from the audiences, (who even objected to Debussy in the early days). With his ability for recognizing genuine talent, Stokowski has helped to launch many an unknown composer who later made a name for himself.

The concerts of the Philadelphia Orchestra gave young Barber a chance to hear what other composers in the same field were doing, and also stimulated his desire to write music of his own. He composed a number of songs while at Curtis, a *Serenade for String Quartet*, a *Sonata for Violincello and Piano* and, during the last of his eight years there an *Overture to the School for Scandal*. This orchestral work, based on Sheridan's immortal comedy is a gay, humorous piece set in a classical pattern. The Philadelphia Orchestra played it at Robin Hood Dell.

After graduating from Curtis, Gian-Carlo Menotti and Sam Barber, together with another of their fellow students—John Bitter—decided to go to Vienna for the winter. Barber wanted to continue his vocal studies. He worked in Vienna with an American teacher, John Braun, and made his debut there singing German lieder and a number of his own songs. Years later Victor made a recording of Samuel Barber's *Dover Beach,* with the composer singing the solo part to a string quartet accompaniment. The combination is so delightful that it makes one regret Barber could not have maintained both careers: singer and composer. But he was wise enough to realize that the demands of public appearances leave little time or energy for creative work. It is difficult, and in most cases impossible, to combine the two successfully.[1]

While in Vienna Sam, Menotti, and John Bitter (who later became leader of the Miami Symphony Orchestra and assistant conductor on Stokowski's Youth Orchestra tour to South America), pooled their resources and hired a "practise orchestra" of some thirty pieces, so they could practise conducting.

Sam's German was not always equal to the occasion. "I had *'umlaut'* trouble," he explains ruefully. "When some of the orchestra failed to enter correctly I told them, in my best German, that they must *count—'sie mussen zahlen'* and they looked at me in blank astonishment. You see, I should have said *'sie müssen zählen.'* Without the *umlauts* I was telling them they had to *pay.* . . ."

After several months of rehearsing, the aspiring conductors decided to give a concert. Barber and Menotti each wrote a piece especially for the occasion, hired a hall (used during the week for socialist gatherings) and set the date for a Sunday. There was considerable unrest in Vienna at the time. The socialists resented the Dollfuss regime and frequent clashes between government and workers flared up.

Regardless of the turmoil, Barber, Menotti and Bitter went on with their plans for the concert, and finally the event came off without untoward incident. But the day after this debut, the socialist hall where the concert had been held went up in a mighty explosion. Barber later learned that the bombs and ammunition for this demonstration had been stored directly under the platform on which he conducted.

[1] Leonard Bernstein is one of the few exceptions to this rule.

Samuel Barber

It was after his return to the United States that Samuel Barber wrote his next orchestral work—*Music for a Scene from Shelley* ("in tender mood . . . with shimmering color," as one critic described it). He explains how he came to write it:

In the summer of 1933 I was reading Shelley's *Prometheus Unbound*. The lines in Act II, Scene 5, where Shelley indicates "Music," suggested the composition. It is really incidental music for the particular scene, and has nothing to do with the figure of Prometheus.

> "Hearest thou not sounds i' the air
> which speak the love
> Of all articulate beings?
> Feelest thou not
> The inanimate winds enamoured of Thee
> List!" (Music)

Werner Janssen and the New York Philharmonic gave the first performance of this work in March, 1935.

Music for a Scene from Shelley brought Barber honors from every direction. First he was awarded the Bearns Prize (he had already received this once before in 1928 for his *Sonata for Violoncello and Piano*); then the 1935 Pulitzer Prize; and finally a Fellowship to the American Academy in Rome. He again received the Pulitzer award the following year for his *Symphony in One Movement*, thus becoming the first composer to be so honored two years in succession.

Barber wrote the *Symphony in One Movement* while he was "in residence" at the American Academy in Rome. It was played there in May, 1936, by the Augusteo Orchestra under the direction of Molinari. The performance was not an unalloyed success. One elderly princess remarked loudly, as she left the hall, "That young man should have been strangled at birth!"

Others, however, had a very different reaction. Those who liked modern music hailed Barber's symphony with enthusiasm. Artur Rodzinski was so impressed that he performed it in Cleveland the following January, in New York in March, and again that same summer at the Salzburg Music Festival. It was the first time an American's music had ever been played at one of these festivals.

Barber was staying, that summer, in the mountains of the Salz-

Modern Music-Makers

kammergut, not far from Salzburg in a small hunting chalet near Lake St. Wolfgang. The chalet belonged to a forest warden, whose wife served Barber as cook and general housekeeper. Although the two peasants had never been to a concert they both loved music ("they were always singing Schubert songs by ear"). It was a great event in their lives to have a real musician and composer in their home—even though his music did sound a little strange after Schubert. When Sam returned from the first Salzburg performance of his *Symphony in One Movement,* he was touched to find that by way of celebrating the event, the two good people had decorated the chalet with pine boughs and had set up the main theme from his symphony in large cardboard notes.

While he was abroad, Samuel Barber often visited the Menottis in Italy. His friend Gian-Carlo had been raised in a picture-book environment near the village of Cadegliano, on beautiful Lake Lugano. There were eight children in his family; one of the six brothers played the cello, others the violin, while Gian-Carlo—most gifted of them all—officiated at the piano. Evenings they always played chamber music. The Menotti children built their own marionette theatre, painted the scenery for it, made the costumes, and wrote their own plays. Gian-Carlo began composing little pieces when he was five, and at the age of eleven turned out an entire opera for the marionette theater. This was the first of a long line of operas that have since made him famous. *Amelia Goes to the Ball* was his first public success; next *The Old Maid and the Thief* (written originally for radio). *The Medium* and *The Telephone* both played for several seasons to sold-out houses on Broadway, as did *The Consul,* a tragic story of intrigue during war time, and so far his most ambitious work. For all these operas Menotti has written the words as well as the music. Contrary to the general belief that Italian is the ideal language for setting to music Menotti, equally at home in both tongues, claims that English has a greater variety of inflexions and accents, and lends itself better to opera.

It was on one of his visits to the Menottis that Samuel Barber first met Toscanini. The Maestro was spending the summer at his villa on a small island on Laggo Maggiore. Sam took his courage in hand and decided to call on him. He hired a boatman to row him across.

Samuel Barber

But as he rang the bell he was suddenly overcome with shyness. "Is—is *Signora* Toscanini at home?" he faltered.

Samuel Barber was a handsome youth, with an engaging smile and pleasing manner. The servant considered him a moment. "I will inquire, Signor. . . ."

In a moment the man returned. "The Signora is not at home," he announced. "But—" he added with a smile, noting the visitor's crestfallen expression, "*Il Maestro* will see you if you wish."

The visit that followed was like one of Samuel's dreams come true. Toscanini received him with the greatest friendliness, wanted to hear all about his music, invited him to stay for dinner and—to cap the climax—got out a score of Monteverdi's *Orfeo* which the two of them spent the evening performing together, the silver-haired Maestro singing Eurydice while young Barber took the part of Orpheus.

Since that early visit, Toscanini has followed Samuel Barber's career with the greatest interest. He thinks highly of the young man's music; in fact he considers him perhaps the most talented of all the younger American composers. Samuel Barber's *Adagio for Strings* was given its world première by Toscanini on November 5, 1938.

The *Adagio for Strings*, dedicated "To my aunt and uncle, Louise and Sidney Homer," was taken from a *String Quartet* Barber wrote while in Rome. It is a short but moving piece, sincere and full of a noble feeling that is almost religious in character. Lawrence Gilman called it:

full-throated and noble music. Mr. Barber is not ashamed to write simply, gravely and with emotion. He is not afraid to let the instruments sing. He is not only willing, but able to spin a long and expressive cantilena, one that unfolds itself with naturalness and seeming spontaneity; so that one does not think of an anxious and self-conscious experimentalist striving to make the hearer sit up, but of a tone-poet allowing music to speak through him as it will.

Barber's next symphonic work, another short piece called *Essay for Orchestra* was also first played by Toscanini.

Barber had for some time felt the necessity for a short orchestral form, abstract rather than descriptive in character—corresponding in length and organization to the literary essay. He fashioned a subtle two-part form—completely contrasting in mood and color yet with reciprocal interplay of thematic material. Definite restraint . . . little emphasis on orchestral sensuousness, or sound for the sake of sound . . . terse and epigrammatic . . . music of disenchantment.[2]

A *Second Essay* was written in 1942 for the Centennial of the New York Philharmonic. In between Barber did a *Concerto for Violin and Orchestra,* first played by Albert Spalding and the New York Philharmonic.

Samuel Barber was in France when the war broke out. He heard the London première of his *First Essay* from the cellar of the Paris hotel where he was staying, during a blackout. Fortunately he was able, soon after, to get back to his own country. In 1942, he was inducted into the United States Army. Even then, as corporal in the Air Force, he went on composing, and at the request of the Government wrote his *Second Symphony.*

While in the service Barber often accompanied the pilots on their trips. The night flights impressed him particularly; the heroism of the young aviators, the tragic implications of an existence almost mystic in its detachment from ordinary life, the sense of aloofness, of being alone in the universe, together with the complete stillness, except for the droning motors and eerie sound of the beam. All these things Barber tried to put into his *Second Symphony,* not seeking to describe them literally, but trying rather to interpret their underlying emotional content.

Koussevitzky and the Boston Symphony Orchestra first played the *Second Symphony* on March 3, 1944, in Boston and, shortly after, in New York. A few days before that, the New York Philharmonic had given a revised edition of Barber's *First Symphony.* During May in one week alone there were five performances of his works at Carnegie Hall. According to one analysis, made by ASCAP in 1942, Samuel Barber's music had at that time been played more often than that of any other American symphonic composer.

The *Second Symphony* was recorded by the Office of War Information and broadcast all over the world, and scores of the work were

[2] Robert Horan in *Modern Music,* March-April, 1943.

Samuel Barber

flown to England and to Russia. On his recent visits abroad, Barber has found an increasing interest in American music. Throughout Europe the people are familiar with the names of our leading composers, and are anxious to get scores of their works. These scores, however, are seldom available, says Barber, since American publishers have not yet become sufficiently convinced of the commercial value of our own "moderns" to make their compositions available to foreign markets— or even to print them, in many cases.

Since he first began composing, Barber had been particularly successful in writing songs and choral works. Of the songs perhaps the most outstanding is *Monks and Raisins* (1943) to a poem by José Garcia Villa, while among the choral compositions *Anthony O'Daly* (from James Stephens' *Reincarnations,* for mixed voices a cappella) and A *Stopwatch and an Ordnance Map* (words by Stephen Spender) both written in 1940, head the list. The latter is an effective work for men's voices a cappella with an accompaniment of kettledrums. Horan says that it has "a strangely ominous and haunting quality achieved by the curious indefinite pitch of the tympani . . . unique in cumulative and elegiac desperation. These two choruses together with the *Second Essay* and *Adagio for Strings* contain Barber's finest writing."

In 1945 Samuel Barber wrote his first ballet, *Cave of the Heart,*[3] for Martha Graham and her dance group. This was performed several times in May, 1946, before enthusiastic audiences at Columbia's Festival of Modern American Music. Another brilliant success at this same festival was Gian-Carlo Menotti's opera, *The Medium.*

The most important musical event in Europe after the war took place in Prague in May, 1946. At that time the Czecho-Slovakian Government invited leading composers and conductors from all over the world to represent the music of their respective countries at the hundredth anniversary celebration of the founding of the Prague Symphony Orchestra. Leonard Bernstein was chosen as United States conductor, and Samuel Barber as composer.

Immediately after the final United States performance of his *Cave of the Heart,* Barber flew to Prague. There he conducted a program

---

[3] This, and incidental music for Mary Kennedy's *One Day of Spring* (produced in Florida in 1935) are the only scores Barber has so far composed for the theater.

of his own works including, among others, the *Capricorn Concerto*, a *Suite* drawn from the new ballet, and *Adagio for Strings*.

From Prague Barber flew to England, and conducted several concerts of his own works with the London Symphony, the B.B.C. Orchestra, and other groups. He found everywhere a tremendous interest in music—particularly among the young people of England. Their main recreation during the war years had been concerts and listening to music over the radio. Barber led the "Three Choir's Festival"—most famous in England—during their 250th celebration in Hereford Cathedral. At Birmingham the average age of the audience, he says, was between fifteen and seventeen years. After Barber's concerts the young people brought back the scores of his music and asked him to autograph them. *Adagio for Strings* was especially popular. He learned that in England this is the most performed of all American compositions.

When Barber returned to the United States after the outbreak of the war, he and Gian-Carlo Menotti decided to pool their resources and buy a place in the country. They finally found just what they wanted near Mt. Kisco, New York—an attractive, rambling house designed by Lescaze, on a knoll overlooking Lake Croton and the surrounding woods. The house is large enough so they can have widely separated wings where each works undisturbed by the other's music.

They called the place "Capricorn," and Barber used that name for a *Concerto for Chamber Orchestra*, written in 1944, which he conducted that same November at Chicago University's Mandel Hall. At Capricorn Barber and Menotti have recreated the charm and the leisurely atmosphere of the life that they shared abroad. Their home has become a meeting place for many of the younger artists, musicians, poets and writers of the day. One of the latter, Robert Horan, who shares the house with them, has been quoted before in this chapter. He concludes his article in the March-April, 1943, issue of *Modern Music* by saying:

Barber's music . . . is of particular importance because of its concentration on the beauty and possibility of design; because of its alive and moving personality and its entirely musical integrity. . . .

[It] is absurdly romantic in an age when romanticism is the catchword

402

Samuel Barber

of fools and prophets. It is written intensely for strings in a period when music is written intensely for brass. Its intention is wholly musical. Its convention is rare, in that it establishes a personality before an idea, but a meaning before an effect. It is economical, not of necessity but of choice. It is cerebral only in the perspective of its craft, it logic and its form. It cannot properly be called "the answer" to anything, or the direction that music must take, for its distinction is entirely individual. It lacks casualness and often spontaneity, and sometimes fails in the incident of irony or humor. But it is composed. On the paper and in the ear, its design and its articulateness reveal a profound elegance of style, and a personal, anti-mechanical melancholy.

All through Samuel Barber's music runs the "sensitive and penetrating design of melancholy." This melancholy is often felt by the true artist, who experiences a sense of frustration because of his inability to transcribe, as he would like, the vision that has inspired him. Barber's music reveals more than a glimpse of that initial inspiration. It expresses, as Olin Downes once put it, "beauty and sincerity . . . genuine and noble feeling."

Samuel Barber

The Music of Samuel Barber

Orchestral Works
(Published by G. Schirmer, Inc.)

Overture to "The School for Scandal"	1932
Music for a Scene from Shelley	1933
First Symphony (in one movement)	1936
Adagio for Strings	1936
Essay for Orchestra	1937
Concerto for Violin and Orchestra	1939
Second Essay for Orchestra	1942
Second Symphony	1944
Capricorn Concerto	1944
Concerto for Cello and Orchestra	1945
Medea (suite from the ballet *Cave of the Heart*)	1946

Choral Works

(Published by G. Schirmer, Inc.)

The Virgin Martyrs (Helen Waddell after the Latin of Sigebert of Gembloux)—women's voices a cappella	1935
Let Down the Bars, O Death (Emily Dickinson) mixed voices a cappella	1936
Reincarnations (James Stephens)—mixed voices a cappella	1936-1940
1. *Mary Hynes*	1936
2. *Anthony O'Day*	1940
3. *The Coolin'*	1940
A Stopwatch and an Ordnance Map (Stephen Spender) men's voices a cappella and kettledrums	1940
Knoxville: Summer of 1915 (soprano solo) (text by James Agee)	1948

Chamber Music

Serenade for String Quartet (or *String Orchestra*)	1929
Dover Beach—baritone and string quartet	1931
Sonata for Cello and Piano	1932
String Quartet in B Minor	1936

Modern Music-Makers

WILLIAM SCHUMAN

WILLIAM SCHUMAN

WILLIAM SCHUMAN believes that the most important thing in a musician's life is to be true to his own convictions. "A composer must create on his own terms," he says. "Not simply write what the public thinks it wants at the moment. If his music has worth, the world will subsequently come to understand it. Publicity, salesmanship and the like may confuse the issue in a temporary sense, but in the long run values will emerge as they truly are."

Bill Schuman was nineteen when his values first began to emerge. Before then he had been an ardent Tin Pan Alley fan, had written melodies for popular songs, and had even organized a jazz band of his own. Classical music he had always imagined to be dull and uninteresting.

His mother tried for years to get him to a symphony concert. Finally she put it up to him as a kind of challenge: "I can't imagine anyone so lacking in curiosity as not to be willing to listen at least once to some serious music!"

Just to satisfy his mother, Bill finally bought a ticket for Carnegie Hall and prepared to endure a dull evening. When the orchestra began to play, his first reaction had nothing to do with music. "How can all those fiddles manage to bow with exactly the same beat?" he marveled, remembering the jaunty independence of his own jazz players. But as he listened to the music he suddenly discovered that he wasn't bored at all. In fact he was actually enjoying this "highbrow stuff." With a growing feeling of excitement he realized that he had never in his life been so thrilled. He came away from that first concert feeling as if a door into another world had opened up.

William Schuman's early life was in no way exceptional. He was born August 4, 1910, on the upper West Side of New York, and was brought up in a comfortable, though not wealthy home. His grandparents came from Germany and Alsace. His father, vice-president of a lithographing company, gave the two Schuman children—Bill and his sister—the advantages common to average American young-

WILLIAM SCHUMAN

William Schuman

sters. As to music—"Well," states Bill with the engaging grin that has made him so popular, "my parents were undoubtedly very musical. My father was an expert on the pianola (his favorite piece was the *William Tell Overture*), and my mother could play Rubinstein's *Melody in F* by ear. We used to gather around the piano and sing together. Our home environment was happy and idealistic."

When Bill was about twelve he wanted to join the school band. He had never had music lessons, but his father now bought him a cheap violin and he soon learned to play well enough to qualify.

From the start, young Schuman showed an enterprising spirit (a trait later evident in an exceptional gift for organization and executive ability). At fifteen he and a friend planned an Outing Club for younger boys. Each afternoon when school was over they called for the eight or nine members of the group and entertained them until five with baseball, football, or—if it was raining—with games in a gymnasium. Saturdays they took the youngsters for an all-day outing, with trips into the country. This experience led naturally, a few years later, into summer camp counselor work. While at Camp Cobbossee, Maine, Bill wrote his first music. He and another boy produced a musical comedy that was a camp hit. Two of the songs were later published.

Encouraged by this success, Bill—on his return to New York—organized and directed his own jazz band. He sang with it, played violin in it, and made musical arrangements for it. With Frank Loesser (now a topnotch lyric-writer in Hollywood) he turned out a popular song sentimentally titled, *In Love with the Memory of You*. Scores of similar numbers followed, all more or less variations of the first. Bill soon found that the formula for a successful popular song was practically stereotyped: the more sentimental it was, the more it followed—even imitated—existing songs, the more of a hit it was bound to be.

At first Schuman wrote only the melodies of the songs, and let the "arrangers" add the accompaniments. But these didn't satisfy him, so he tried to do his own piano parts. Melody writing had always been easy for him, but now, to his considerable surprise, he discovered that harmonizing accompaniments was a slightly more complicated process.

He began by trying to orchestrate some jazz dance music. After laboriously writing out the parts for the different instruments, he took the music to a low-class dance hall, and by bribing the musicians with some cigarettes got them to play it through for him. The result, to put it mildly, was startling. "It sounded," he says, "like chaos!" But the experience was valuable; it taught him a lot about how *not* to write music. He took note of the criticisms (freely offered) and kept on trying. When he felt that he had made some progress, he went a step higher in the entertainment world and enlisted the help of the Biltmore Hotel orchestra. They played his music for him in the kitchen during intermissions.

In this experimental way young Schuman learned a good deal. But it was hardly more than a beginning. He soon discovered that what he needed was regular instruction. On a sudden impulse he gave up the business course he was attending (on the side he had been doing advertising for a candy store) and enrolled in the Malkin Music Conservatory. Just so he could write better jazz!—that is, until the fateful evening at Carnegie Hall.

Schuman's introduction to classical music started him on a new life. From that moment and for the next five years he "ate, slept and lived" at Carnegie Hall (with occasional nights off to attend a concert at Town Hall instead), soaking up music as a sponge soaks up water. Such a program, even with the cheapest general admission tickets, would have been prohibitive to his limited means. But Bill was always resourceful . . . Armed with books and a sandwich he would retire, between the afternoon and evening concerts, to a retreat ("gentlemen only") where he was sure of being undisturbed, and in this way made his afternoon ticket cover both performances.

By following the music, score in hand, and by listening intently and comparing what he heard with the original, Schuman gained a great deal of practical knowledge about composition and orchestration. It was a rare experience to be thus introduced at maturity to these new horizons. Having no precedent in knowledge or training, he came to music with a completely fresh viewpoint. One after the other of the great masters claimed his enthusiasm. There was the early period when César Franck "could do no wrong"; then Strauss held the stage with *Till Eulenspiegel*. Tschaikowsky's *Pathétique* filled the picture until Wagner appeared. Next came Beethoven, Mozart, and finally Debussy, Ravel and last the moderns. It was not

William Schuman

until some years later that Schuman discovered Bach and still earlier composers. For a time then, he says, he was very condescending to all the others. Now he enjoys them all and has learned to judge each composer in terms of his intentions, in fact considers this the only true aesthetic.

After five years of this intensive listening, young William Schuman was thoroughly familiar with the repertory of symphonic music; he had learned the resources of each orchestral instrument—its tone-color, range of pitch and possibilities of expressions; and he was well acquainted with the individual language of each of the great musicians. "The student-composer should know the music of the masters so perfectly that he could write in the special style of any one of them," he insists. "The writer doesn't have to worry about originality. He either is or isn't. If he isn't, nothing in the world will make him so and if he is, nothing in the world could stop him from being so."

Carnegie Hall did not at first entirely take the place of Tin Pan Alley in Bill Schuman's life. Although "popular" music ceased to interest him, his songs and arrangements — while not particularly lucrative — did bring in some money, and this could not be ignored. But as he delved deeper into the classics he made an interesting discovery. The more good music he absorbed, the less he was able to write the banal songs that had formerly flowed from his pen with such ease. As soon as his music began to develop along serious lines, it had less chance of being popular and its commercial value was questionable.

William Schuman, having "graduated" from Tin Pan Alley, feels rather strongly about its limitations, especially from an artistic standpoint. Jazz, in his opinion, is another matter; he considers it a creative expression, and entirely appropriate to its own field. "Art," he says, "cannot be considered in terms of values divorced from appropriateness. There can only be genuine comparison where the intentions of the writers were similar. There is no point in comparing a Sousa march with a symphony by Brahms. Who can say that one is more successful than the other?—and it is certainly obvious that they are not interchangeable in functional terms. Surely from a listener's point of view Beethoven, for example, is not the equal of Jerome Kern when it comes to dinner music or musical-comedy stage music, even though he is infinitely to be preferred in the concert hall."

411

Modern Music-Makers

Soon after he discovered Carnegie Hall Schuman began the study of harmony with Max Persin, and counterpoint with Charles Haubiel. Always interested in the educational angle of music, he decided when he was twenty-three that he would like to teach. He enrolled at Columbia as a student in the music course and from that university eventually received both Bachelor of Arts and Master's degrees.

He began, too, to try his hand at serious music writing. In 1935 Schuman won a Mozarteum scholarship, and with the privilege of studying in Salzburg. He went there ostensibly to learn conducting, but felt that the honor of a Mozarteum scholarship also called for serious creative effort. At Salzburg he composed his first long work— a symphony for eighteen instruments.

That same fall of 1935, a new professor was introduced in the Music Department of the fashionable and progressive Sarah Lawrence College in Bronxville, New York. He was young, tall, good-looking, with a pleasing and enthusiastic personality and a talent for the informal that ranged from sweaters and no ties to a casual but highly effective classroom manner. The girls flocked to his classes and all wanted to sing in his chorus. This choral group—eventually it had to be limited to eighty-five members—became the most popular extracurricular activity of the school. The college paper called it "The football team of Sarah Lawrence," headlining the article "They Had Knute, But We Have Bill."

In spite of the casual manner that endeared him to his pupils, Schuman took his position at Sarah Lawrence very seriously. He has a special gift for inspiring the enthusiasm and co-operation of any group he conducts—largely because of his own interest in whatever he may be doing. The chorus at Sarah Lawrence made musical history. A number of concerts were given and, highlight of their public career, the girls were invited by Koussevitzky to sing with the Boston Symphony.

During his years at Sarah Lawrence Schuman produced a large number of choral works for women's voices and for mixed chorus. In 1946, he wrote one for men's voices: *Truth Shall Deliver*, which was first performed by the Yale Glee Club, Marshall Bartholomew conducting, in December of that year.

The year of 1936 marked two important events in Schuman's life— his marriage to Frances Prince, and the beginning of a friendship

William Schuman

that was to prove an outstanding influence on his musical career.

For some time already, he had been a great admirer of Roy Harris' music—it excited and stimulated him more than any other contemporary composer's work. That summer while teaching at Columbia, he learned that Harris was to give a class in composition at Juilliard, just across the street. Schuman walked over and registered in the class.

Soon the two became close friends. Harris went through the younger composer's *First Symphony* and other works with him, and was impressed by the talent and vitality of these compositions. He saw that Schuman, like himself, was working towards the same goal—a music truly individual and truly American in character.

"Harris helped me to formulate my point of view," says Schuman. "Basically our aesthetic springs from the same direction."

When William Schuman wrote his *Second Symphony* Aaron Copland was so impressed by its originality that he personally recommended it to Koussevitzky. Schuman recalls with emotion a letter that came from the famous maestro, asking if he might see the new symphony. The score was sent on at once, and Koussevitzky, recognizing that here was a talent worth encouraging, decided to give the work a hearing.

The *Second Symphony* had already been tried out by a W.P.A. orchestra in a performance that had considerably discouraged young Schuman. Koussevitzky understood this reaction. "It is important that a composer should hear his music *well* played," he said. "To be sure, your symphony will probably have no *succès* with my public. But," he added with a smile, "with *me* it has a *succès!*"

That was quite enough to satisfy Bill Schuman. He was prepared for the audience's icy reception of his *Second Symphony*. As a matter of fact, "Ice would be an understatement!" he confesses ruefully. "At the afternoon concert the ladies were too polite to hiss. But in the evening there were plenty of hisses from those brave enough to express their feelings." A few cheers, however, came from a group of Harvard men. As to the critics: they said the work was a disgrace. Koussevitzky admitted that it was "an experiment."

When the Boston Orchestra played Schuman's *Third Symphony* six years later, both audience and critics gave this one a very different reception. "He has changed!" they insisted. "But," Schuman explains, "it was *they* who had changed. I would be perfectly satisfied if people would only admit: 'I don't understand what you are trying to say, and I don't like it.' But they pretend to know and criticize without basic knowledge."

Schuman later withdrew his first two symphonies from circulation. "They will be released again," he stated, "if ever I find time to revise them. I am counting on running out of ideas at some point in the next fifty odd years, and then I'll have a chance to take another look at these first major works."

So far William Schuman shows no sign of running out of ideas. Each year sees the addition of important works to his long list of compositions.

In 1939 a week's festival of American music, under the sponsorship of ASCAP, was held in Boston and New York. Koussevitzky asked Schuman to compose a piece with which to open the festival. He responded with *American Festival Overture*—one of his most popular works. "The first three notes of this piece," he wrote in the program notes, "will be recognized by some listeners as the 'call to play' of boyhood days. In New York City it is yelled on the syllables 'Wee-Awk-Eee' to get the gang together for a game or a festive occasion of some sort. This call very naturally suggested itself for a piece of music being composed for a very festive occasion."

A choral work, *Prologue for Chorus and Orchestra,* had its première that same summer of 1939 at the Lewisohn Stadium in New York, Alexander Smallens conducting. Shortly after this, Schuman heard a broadcast from the Chicago World's Fair by the People's Philharmonic Society—a large group made up of amateur singers from different trades, including needle-makers, furriers, shoe manufacturers, carpenters, painters, laundrymen and many others. This great chorus so fired his imagination that he wrote a work especially for them, and called it *This Is Our Time.*

As usually happens when a new work in an unfamiliar idiom is first presented, the critics had different reactions. Some liked *This Is Our Time* (Frances Perkins spoke of its "noteworthy largeness of utterance and vividness of expression"), others felt that he "was not yet ready to tackle a work of the proportions of this cantata."

With the *Third Symphony,* completed in 1941, William Schuman reached his full stride. He dedicated this work to Serge Koussevitzky,

William Schuman

who first performed it on October 18th. A week later the Boston Symphony played it again in New York.

Once more the critics were divided. Olin Downes wrote:

This symphony is full of talent and vitality, from first to last, and done with an exuberance and conviction on the part of the composer that carry straight over the footlights. . . . Although couched in 18th Century contrapuntal forms or moulds. . . .in its pages the old bottle was filled with a new exhilarating wine. The chosen formula did not prevent the young composer from writing lusty, audacious surefooted music.

Others were less complimentary. Some insisted that Schuman's *Third Symphony* held nothing beyond technique, and called it "a gallery of counterpoint exercises on a gigantic scale. . . . It breathes emotional sterility." Schuman, however, considers the work "a song from beginning to end. My music," he adds, "is completely melodic. I write by singing, not by sitting at the piano."

The Music Critics Circle of New York City chose the *Third Symphony* as the best new orchestral work played locally during the season of 1941-2. Schuman has been granted many awards. Among them: a Guggenheim Fellowship in 1940 and 1941; a Pulitzer Prize in 1943; a joint fellowship from the American Academy of Arts and the National Institute of Arts and Letters (1943); a citation from the National Association of American Composers and Conductors, and a mention by the *Encyclopaedia Britannica* as "Composer of the Year" (both in 1942).

Schuman also received an appointment as "Composer in Residence" for a year at the Metropolitan Opera House. This "Grant-in-Aid" was established by the Carnegie Foundation to give promising young composers and librettists an opportunity to learn about opera at first hand. During their year in residence they are allowed the run of the Metropolitan, and in this way gain an understanding of practical technique from backstage as well as audience reaction. Unfortunately in Schuman's case the proposed libretto failed to stimulate his desire to write an opera, and nothing came of the experience—except a further enlarging of his musical horizon.

During World War II Schuman turned his attention to music connected with the war effort, since the army refused to accept him for active service. He wrote incidental music for a propaganda film to

Modern Music-Makers

be presented abroad, called *Steel Town* (showing the steel mills of Youngstown, Ohio, which at that time were alone producing as much steel as the entire Japanese nation). *A Free Song,* a cantata adapted from Walt Whitman's *Drum Taps,*[1] also was inspired by the war; it contains a dirge for the mistakes of the past and the horrors of battle and, in the second part, a *Song of the Banner at Daybreak."*

Prayer in Time of War (originally called *Prayer* 1943) was composed at a time when things were going badly overseas. It is a moving expression of hope as well as of despair. "The work is not program music in the usual sense of that overworked term," says Schuman. "There is no story, nor is any realistic event being depicted. The title is merely some indication of the new kind of feeling that went into the composition. . . . Prayer is not only introspective, it can also be demanding—shrieking for help. . . ." ("Ear-splitting in its dynamic intensity," said one critic, who felt that the *Prayer* "revealed more cool intelligence than emotional conviction.")

In 1941 Schuman composed a *Fourth Symphony,* and following that, a *Symphony for Strings* (commissioned by the Koussevitzky Foundation and first played in November, 1943, by Koussevitzky and the Boston Symphony Orchestra.) A *Sixth Symphony* was commissioned by the Dallas Symphony Association, and presented there in February, 1949, with Antal Dorati conducting.

In the chamber-music field Schuman has written a *Canon and Fugue for Violin, Cello and Piano;* a *Choreographic Poem for Seven Instruments;* a *Quartettino for Four Bassoons;* and four *String Quartets.* The last of these was commissioned by the Elizabeth Sprague Coolidge Foundation and played in October, 1950, by the Hungarian String Quartet at a Library of Congress concert.

Schuman says that of all types of composing he most enjoys writing music for the theater. His first work in this field was *Side Show,* for Billy Rose's *Seven Lively Arts.* Next came incidental music for a production of Shakespeare's *King Henry the VIII.* Then Anthony Tudor, choreographer of the Ballet Theater, suggested to Schuman that they do a ballet together. They discussed it for some time; Tudor explained the idea in general terms and the final result was *Undertow*—a ballet which made a sensation at its first performance, April

---

[1] Howard Hanson has likewise made a choral setting of this poem.

William Schuman

10, 1945, at the Metropolitan. From this ballet Schuman made a symphonic version (first heard with Wallenstein conducting the Los Angeles Philharmonic).

Night Journey, Schuman's next ballet, was commissioned by the Elizabeth Sprague Coolidge Foundation for Martha Graham. The musical score of this work is "as dark and inexorable as the drama itself, and its very static quality and slow, cumulative power intensify the effect of the movement."[2]

In 1949 the Louisville Philharmonic Society asked Schuman to do another ballet for Martha Graham. This time Miss Graham chose the story of *Judith,* with a theme freely adapted from the Apocryphal story. She presented the ballet with the Louisville Symphony at Carnegie Hall in late December, 1950.

William Schuman brings a keen intelligence to the mechanics of his art. He approaches a new work as if it were a problem in geometry. Starting with certain premises—the given "known"—the problem, he says, is to work out the solution without changing this known. A good example is found in his *William Billings Overture.* Here the "given" is a simple, old-fashioned psalm-tune. Schuman's aim has been to work out a solution that maintains the basic material while clothing it in original form, *i.e.* without altering the given.

Leonard Bernstein takes strong exception to some people who claim that Schuman's music is a mixture of Harris, Hindemith, Copland, and even Sibelius. In an article in *Modern Music* (Jan., 1942) Bernstein says:

If there be resemblance, well and good. A composer's output is the sum of all his experience, musical or otherwise; yet a composer with more original creative spirit than Schuman's is rare indeed....

Almost as exciting as hearing the music itself is to observe how Schuman's progress is manifested in the *Third Symphony*—a progress alive, radiant, optimistic. It is, in fact, all one piece—his development and his music—a pattern of health and youth, and work, and hope.

Schuman is particularly interested in the educational side of music. He has written a number of works for school orchestras, bands and glee clubs, including *News Reel*—a group of short pieces bearing

[2] *Musical America.*

417

Modern Music-Makers

titles sure to appeal to youngsters: *Horse Race, Fashion Show, Tribal Dance, Monkeys at the Zoo* and *Parade; Holiday Song*—commissioned by a group of schools for a Field Day celebration; and several others widely played and sung by children of grammar and high school ages. *George Washington Bridge*, an *Impression for Band*, was first played at the National Music Camp in Interlochen, Michigan, July, 1950.

Schuman considers it his privilege and duty, as a composer in the American democracy, to contribute works for the layman to perform. This, he insists, is essential in order that a wider audience than that of concert hall and stage may be reached. In an article written for the *New York Times* of June 30th, 1940, he expresses his views on the subject:

Only in this manner can we communicate to our countrymen in intimate fashion the unique feelings of the contemporary composer. For, regardless of one's opinion concerning the merits of modern American works, the fact remains that these compositions and these alone are the result of direct contact with the present American scene.

An important consideration for the American composer is that he can have abundant performances and a vitally interested audience if he is willing to create music that is serviceable to other than strictly professional groups. Unfortunately the original music used by the large majority of our amateur groups (including, alas, the schools) has been written by hacks or by casual composers with questionable, if any, artistic convictions. If this situation is to be appreciably altered the composers whose music is performed by our leading symphonic organizations must devote a portion of their energies to music for amateurs. This music must be in addition to, not at the expense of, other works. Furthermore the composer writing for the amateur must make his compromise in technical matters and never in the emotional or intellectual validity of his offering.

In the spring of 1945 Schuman resigned from the music department of Sarah Lawrence in order to become director of publications at the G. Schirmer Company in New York. The following year he was elected president of the Juilliard School of Music. To this important position he has brought fresh ideas and vitality, keen enthusiasm and a wide capacity for executive work. Under his direction the school's activities have been expanded to include public concerts, radio

William Schuman

broadcasts, recording of new music, and highly specialized individual training.

This educational work appeals strongly to William Schuman. As he once stated, he is "at heart a teacher." With his broadminded grasp of present-day music and his understanding of the individual student's problems, he can do much to encourage new talent and to bring it before the public. As in his younger days he was helped by Harris and Copland, so now he wants in his turn to be of service to other beginners. "I can think of nothing more inspiring," he once remarked, "than to have younger composers come to me and ask for advice."

William Schuman has many such opportunities at Juilliard. It is to be hoped that the exacting responsibilities of a large institution will not crowd out his own creative work. As one of the most brilliant of today's composers, he should continue to add important contributions to the music of America.

William Schuman

The Music of William Schuman

421

Modern Music-Makers

Requiescat—for chorus of women's voices and piano
    (also arranged for mixed voices) [1]   1942
Holiday Song—for chorus of mixed voices and piano (also arranged
    for women's voices) (Genevieve Taggard) [1]   1942
A Free Song—secular cantata No. 2 for chorus of mixed voices and
    orchestra (Walt Whitman) [1]   1942
Te Deum—for chorus of mixed voices [1]
    (from incidental music for Henry VIII)   1944
Truth Shall Deliver—for chorus of men's voices [1]   1946

CHAMBER MUSIC

Canon and Fugue for Violin, Cello, and Piano	1934
Choreographic Poem, for seven instruments	1934
String Quartet No. 1	1936
String Quartet No. 2 [5]	1937
Quartettino for Four Bassoons [6]	1939
String Quartet No. 3 [4]	1950
String Quartet No. 4 [1]	1950

STAGE WORKS AND FILM MUSIC

Steeltown (Music for a film)	1944
Henry VIII (Music for a play) [1]	1944
Undertow (ballet) [1]	1945
Night Journey (ballet) [1]	1947
Judith (ballet)	1949

SONGS

Orpheus with His Lute—soprano with piano accompaniment [1]   1944

PIANO

Three-Score Set [1]   1943

[1] G. Schirmer, Inc.
[2] J. & W. Chester.
[3] C. Fischer.
[4] Boosey & Hawkes.
[5] Arrow Music Press.
[6] Boletin Latino-Americano de Musica.

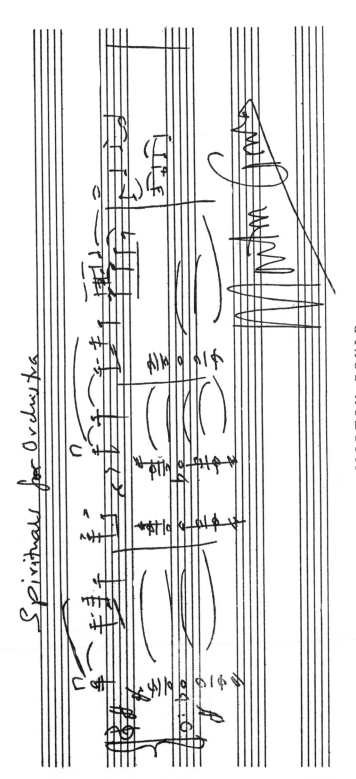

Spirituals for Orchestra

MORTON GOULD

MORTON GOULD

MORTON GOULD'S career has been unique in that from the very start he had to use a good part of his music for practical purposes. The influences that molded his style were not only personal but also the result of his daily contacts. He first made his name in commercial fields, and for that reason he has always had to "fight tags," as he puts it. "People think it's another Gershwin case," he says. "But actually the opposite is true."

Gould came to jazz through the classics; his early training was academic. But instead of solving his economical problem by teaching or lecturing, as have so many of our composers, he turned some of his talents to the entertainment world, and became widely known as director and arranger of a number of radio programs. For these programs he has composed a great deal of music. Yet in spite of full-time work and the rush of meeting dead-lines, he has managed to produce a surprising number of original works.

Writing music is not only Morton Gould's profession, but his recreation as well. "Hobbies?—well," he says "I would rather compose than do anything else." While he confesses to an interest in miniature trains and railroad magazines, for relaxation and sheer enjoyment give him a few sheets of music paper and a quiet place free from interruption. Because of this intense preoccupation and his consistent use of that margin of time usually given over to idle recreation, Morton Gould has become one of the most prolific and, through his radio work, one of the best known of our younger composers.

He was born December 10, 1913, at Richmond Hill on Long Island, New York. Neither his father, who came to this country from Austria, nor his mother (of Russian descent) were professional musicians, but they did everything they could to encourage their son's talent.

When still a very small child, Morton was fascinated by the family player-piano. Like young Gershwin before him he would

MORTON GOULD

Morton Gould

watch the keys go down and try to follow them with his own small fingers. Soon he could reproduce some of the simpler phrases. Then he began to experiment with the tunes he heard. On Armistice Day in 1918 Morton, not yet five, heard a brass band blaring Sousa's *Stars and Stripes Forever.* He came home and surprised the family by picking out the tune on the piano, note for note, without a mistake. Before long he could play by ear anything that he heard, and made up tunes of his own as well. On his sixth birthday he blossomed into a full-fledged composer with a waltz appropriately named *Just Six.*

When Morton was eight his parents took him to Walter Damrosch, at that time head of the New York Institute of Musical Art (later the Juilliard Institute of Music). Damrosch was so struck by the boy's talent in improvising that he gave him a scholarship at the institute.

At thirteen, with Abby Whiteside as piano teacher, young Gould began giving concerts and playing over the radio, and he acquired a certain reputation in forearm and elbow technique. Dr. Vincent Jones taught him harmony and counterpoint, and encouraged him to continue composing.

At sixteen he gave a concert of his compositions at New York University. Critics were impressed by the unusual span of his right hand (he could reach several notes over an octave), by his "innovational piano-technique," and most of all by his music which showed, so they reported, "the flash of unmistakable originality."

All this strictly classical musical training, in addition to his regular schooling, kept young Gould very much occupied until he was seventeen. Then for the next few years, because of economic necessity he worked wherever he could, playing the piano in moving-picture theatres and with bands and dance orchestras, and occasionally over the radio.

It was only at this period that he discovered jazz. Instead of graduating into the classics by way of popular music, as in the case of a number of the younger composers, Gould came to jazz by way of serious music—but, he insists, without prejudice or "high-hat" convictions. In fact he acquired both admiration and respect for jazz, and considers it "a wonderful idiom—completely legitimate for use in serious composition."

Gould has composed a number of works which have their roots in this idiom. *Boogie Woogie Etude* was written for and played by

425

Modern Music-Makers

José Iturbi—also recorded by him. *Concerto for Orchestra* (commissioned by Eric Leinsdorf and first played in 1945 by the Cleveland Orchestra) shows an effective use of jazz rhythms with a second movement in classical "blues" style. *Chorale and Fugue for Jazz* is another well-known example.

During those early years of knocking about, young Morton often had to "arrange" music—popular and otherwise—for the groups that he worked with. Here was a new application of the academic exercises in harmony which he had expected would be used in more classical ways. But the work gave him, as he says, a certain routine and technique of the actual mechanics of putting music and orchestrations down on paper, and brought him in close touch with the popular music of the country. Then too, he was constantly faced with practical problems—for instance, how to make an orchestra of twenty sound like one of forty instruments. All this provided a valuable basis for his later work in original composition. Eventually young Gould's skill in arranging music brought him a position on the staff of Roxy's Music Hall and, later, on that of the National Broadcasting Company.

The first highlight of Morton Gould's career came, he states, at the age of fifteen, when Schirmer published a piano suite of his called *Three Conservative Sketches.* The second came six years later, when he was twenty-one.

At that time Leopold Stokowski and the Philadelphia Symphony represented the ultimate in American orchestral performance. When Stokowski decided to play Gould's *Chorale and Fugue for Jazz,* Morton could hardly believe his good fortune. To hear for the first time his own work played by a symphony orchestra—and this the world's greatest was a thrilling and stimulating event.

In later years, however, Gould has developed an actual phobia about sitting in the audience when his own works are played. Someone with no use for modern music is bound to sit near him, he explains, and will invariably say: "Now why do they have to put things like that on the program?" "It makes me feel like a criminal!" he confesses with an apologetic grin.

Another important event in Morton Gould's life occurred when he was twenty-one. The director of one of New York's radio stations (WOR), recognizing the young man's ability both as musician and

Morton Gould

organizer, offered him a radio program of his own. Gould managed this so successfully that a few years later he was chosen to direct the "Cresta Blanca Hour"—an elaborate broadcast with a large orchestra, and Alec Templeton as soloist. Since then Morton Gould has conducted other important radio programs—including the "Chrysler Hour"—and has appeared as guest conductor with most of the major symphony orchestras in programs of his own compositions and other American composers.

Few people realize the work involved in preparing a program for broadcasting. For instance, the "Cresta Blanca Hour" required the combined efforts of six people working the entire week, in addition to Morton Gould's own concentrated planning. Although he had no thought in these programs of writing classical music he discovered—to his own surprise—that many of the things he wrote for radio later found their way into the symphonic repertoire. Among these are what he calls "Symphonettes," his Americanized version of the old term *Sinfonietta*—an abridged form of symphony appropriate for short radio programs. Of four works written in this form, the *Latin-American Symphonette*, containing four movements in *Rhumba, Tango, Guaracha,* and *Conga* style, has proved the most popular (it was recorded by Iturbi and the Rochester Symphony Orchestra for Victor), while *Pavanne,* from the *Second Symphonette* (1938) has been more widely played than any of Gould's compositions. *Pavanne* has been arranged for almost every conceivable combination of instruments, and half a dozen or more orchestras—both classical and jazz—have made recordings of the work.

Besides the "Symphonettes" Gould has written two miniature "Concertettes," for piano and orchestra and for viola and orchestra; also two full-length concertos for the same combination of instruments. The ballet hit *Interplay* is based on the *Piano Concertette.*

A great many of Morton Gould's works use themes stemming from native folk music. The *Homespun Overture*—a "gay and buoyant work"—calls for a banjo in addition to the usual symphony instruments. This overture was first played in 1938 by Alfred Wallenstein and the N.B.C. Orchestra. About that same time Gould became interested in Stephen Foster's music. He made an extensive study of original manuscripts, and at the request of Fritz Reiner transcribed a number of Foster's more important songs into a symphonic syn-

Modern Music-Makers

thesis which he called *Foster Gallery*. This has been recorded by Victor with Arthur Fiedler and the Boston Pops Orchestra.

To the concert-going public, Morton Gould is chiefly known by his *Spirituals for Orchestra*. This work, as he explains, is "an expression in modern terms" of our rich heritage of spirituals—both Negro and White. There are five movements: *Proclamation, Sermon, A Little Bit of Sin, Protest,* and *Jubilee*.

In program notes on his *Spirituals* Gould wrote:

I have tried to write music the way one speaks. I tried to make it as direct and simple as possible. Part of the *Jubilee* section is in boogie-woogie pattern. Of course many contemporary jazz effects coincide with certain rhythmic patterns in our Spirituals. . . .

My starting premise was that our Spirituals develop a wide gamut of emotions, musically. These emotions are specifically American. The songs range from strictly spiritual ones that are escapist in feeling, or light and gay, to those having tremendous depth and tragic impact.

My idea was to get five moods, widely contrasted in feeling. The titles are self-explanatory. Although most of the work is original as far as thematic material goes, I have used fragments of folk tunes here and there. [1]

Spirituals for Orchestra was first performed in 1941 under Gould's own direction at New York City's Festival of American music. Arthur Rodzinski and the Cleveland Symphony gave it the first major orchestral presentation, and since then it has been played by most of the leading symphonies. Gould confesses that he is tired of hearing it. On his guest conductor appearances, he says, he has never yet conducted his own *Spirituals*, since they have usually "just been done" before his arrival. Rodzinski has recorded the work with the New York Philharmonic for Columbia.

Morton Gould's first full-length symphony was written in 1942, soon after the United States entered the Second World War. The work is dedicated "to my three brothers in the Armed Forces of the United States and their fellow-fighters." The first movement—called

---

[1] In the program notes of the April 7, 1946, New York Philharmonic Concert.

428

Morton Gould

Epitaph—is a memorial to all the soldiers who lost their lives in the war. The second—*Dances*—is based on rollicking folk tunes and popular airs. Then comes *Pastoral and Battle Music,* and lastly *Resolution* with an anthem-like finale. The first performance was by Fritz Reiner and the Pittsburgh Symphony.

Gould's *Second Symphony* was commissioned for the Centennial Celebration of the Y.M.C.A. and first performed in June, 1944, Vladimir Golschman conducting the New York Philharmonic Symphony. It is based on Civil War melodies, including the *Battle Hymn of the Republic* and *When Johnny Comes Marching Home.*[2] This last, which he considers one of our country's finest marching tunes, Gould has also used in *American Salute,* and in a series of marching songs written during the war called *Salutes to the Allies* (including *New China March*—the main theme taken from a modern Chinese song— and *Red Cavalry March).*

When the Soviet Government suggested to the United States an exchange of contemporary composers' music, Gould's *Spirituals* and *Lincoln Legend* were among the American scores that were microfilmed and flown across the sea to Russia. *Lincoln Legend,* inspired by Carl Sandburg's book on the great American patriot, was written in 1942 and first played by Toscanini and the NBC Orchestra that same November.

Morton Gould, in his music, has finally availed himself of the many different idioms existing in our wide land. In addition to *Spirituals* he has written a *Cowboy Rhapsody,* based on the vigorous songs of the West; *Folk Suite,* in "musical slang" composed especially for high school orchestras; a musical comedy called *Billion Dollar Baby;* incidental music for the United Artist's film *Delightfully Dangerous* (in which he also appeared); and numerous shorter works— many of them for college and high school symphonic bands.

Gould is particularly interested in music for young people.

The destiny of American music is in the hands of its young people.... To my way of thinking, the most progressive and stimulating contributions to today's music are being made by our high school and college music

[2] Roy Harris has also used this tune in his Overture *Johnny Comes Marching Home.*

groups. The school field is assuming more importance to the performer and the composer. . . .

If more good American composers will do their best work in composing for school bands and other school music groups they will do much to assist in the building of an American music culture and to foster sound relations between composers, performers and audiences. [3]

Morton Gould's *Third Symphony* was first performed (in revised form) by Dimitri Mitropoulos and the New York Philharmonic-Symphony in October, 1948. He has written incidental music for three films, and the scores for two ballets: *Interplay* (1943) and *Fall River Legend* (1948). So far he has produced only one choral work—based on Thomas Wolfe's *Of Time and the River* (a cappella). His chamber music includes three piano sonatas, a *Prelude and Toccata* and *Boogie Woogie Etude* (also for piano), and a *Suite for Violin and Piano*. Gould's most recent works are: *Philharmonic Waltzes, Serenade of Carols, Guajjira* (a popular dance), *Big City Blues*, and *Family Album*. This last, for band, was directed by Morton Gould leading the U. S. Marine Band at the March, 1951, Bandmaster's Convention. Three earlier works for band are *Cowboy Rhapsody, Jericho, and Ballad*.

Unlike many composers who have had contact with foreign sources, and whose work more or less reflects that contact, Morton Gould's music is entirely a "home product." His daily work has kept him in close touch with American life. Jazz and folk idioms, according to his estimate, are among the important origins of material for our music. "Foreign composers have used popular melodies," he says. "Why is it that so often when we in America do the same thing we run up against a snobbish attitude?"

A composer, to Gould, is largely a craftsman. "Not that I deny inspiration or talent, but music should be written to be heard, and with a consistency of output and application. A composer should be able to turn out a variety of things—short entertainment pieces as well as symphonies. The great musicians of the past wrote mostly on commission—light things as well as serious. We are now once

[3] Morton Gould, *The New York Times*, August 17, 1941.

Morton Gould

again in an age that can commission works, or sponsor composers, through radio, records, moving pictures, fellowships, and foundations." Morton Gould, with most of his fellow composers, feels that today—and particularly in our country—we are living in a period that is highly significant for the development of music.

Morton Gould

Born December 10 at Richmond Hill, Long Island, New York	1913
Scholarship at New York Institute of Musical Art	1921
At thirteen gives public concerts and plays over the radio	
At sixteen gives concert of own compositions at New York University	1929
Chorale and Fugue for Jazz (played by Stokowski and Philadelphia Orchestra)	1933
Appointed director of program over W O R	
Later directs Cresta Blanca and Chrysler Hours	1934
First Symphonette (*Second* 1938, *Third* 1939)	1936
Latin-American Symphonette	1940
Spirituals for Orchestra	1941
Lincoln Legend	1942
First Symphony	1943
Second Symphony	1944
Marries Shirley Bank	
Third Symphony	1948
Fall River Legend (ballet)	
Family Album (for band)	1951

The Music of Morton Gould

Chorale and Fugue in Jazz [1]	1933
First Symphonette [2]	1936
Concertette for Piano and Orchestra [2]	1937
Concerto for Piano and Twenty-four Instruments [2]	1937
A Homespun Overture [2]	1938
Second Symphonette [2]	1938
Third Symphonette [2]	1939
Little Symphony [2]	1939
American Caprice	1940
Foster Gallery [2]	1940
Latin American Symphonette [2]	1941
American Salute [2]	1941
Spirituals for Orchestra [2]	1941
Folk Suite [2]	1941
Lincoln Legend [2]	1942
First Symphony [2]	1943
Fanfare for Freedom [2]	1943
New China March [2]	1943
Red Cavalry March [2]	1943
Cowboy Rhapsody [2]	1944
Concertette for Viola and Orchestra [2]	1944
Second Symphony	1944
Concerto for Piano and Orchestra [2]	1944
Concerto for Viola and Orchestra [2]	1944
Concerto for Orchestra [2]	1945
Harvest—for strings [3]	1945
Minstrel Show [3]	1946
Third Symphony [3]	1948
Suite from Fall River Legend [3]	1948
Philharmonic Waltzes [3]	1948
Serenade of Carols—for small orchestra [3]	1949
Big City Blues [3]	1950

433

Modern Music-Makers

MUSIC FOR BAND

Cowboy Rhapsody (for band)	1940
Jericho	1941
Ballad	
Family Album—for band [3]	1951
(and miscellaneous small works for orchestra, band, piano, etc.)	

CHAMBER MUSIC

Suite for Violin and Piano [3]	1945
Guajira—for clarinet and piano	

CHORAL WORKS

Cantata—for chorus and twenty-four instruments	1931
Of Time and the River—a cappella chorus	

STAGE WORKS

Ring of Steel (film)	1941
Interplay (ballet) [2]	1943
Delightfully Dangerous (film)	1944
San Francisco Conference (film)	1945
Billion Dollar Baby (musical comedy) [3]	1945
Fall River Legend (ballet) [3]	1948
Arms and the Girl (musical comedy) [3]	1950

PIANO

Three Piano Sonatas	1930-1936
Sonatina	1939
Boogie Woogie Etude	1943
Prelude and Toccata	1945
Prologue	1945

[1] Carl Fischer Inc.
[2] Mills Music Inc.
[3] G & C (Chappell).

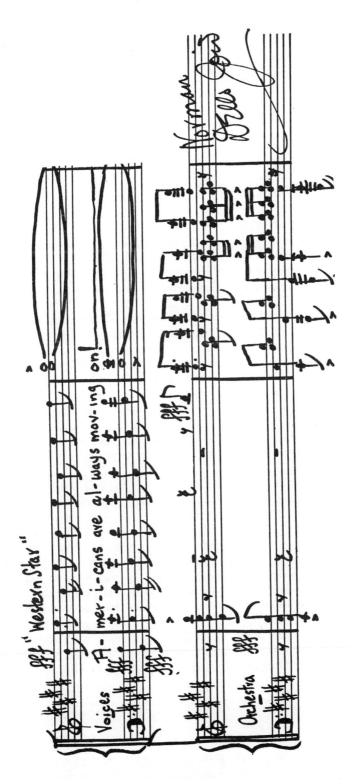

NORMAN DELLO JOIO

NORMAN DELLO JOIO

IN the spring of 1940 Norman Dello Joio saw an announcement in the papers about a summer school of music which was about to open at the Berkshire Music Center, near Lenox, Massachusetts. He immediately applied for a scholarship.

This music school was the dream-come-true of a great conductor and musician. Soon after Koussevitzky took over the direction of the Berkshire Music Festival in 1936, Tanglewood—where Hawthorne is said to have written his famous *Tales*—was presented to the Festival Association as a permanent home. This beautiful estate set in the midst of the gently rolling Berkshire Hills, with a picturesque lake and acres of lawns shaded by fine old elms and maples, was an ideal spot for the summer festivals. The concerts by the Boston Symphony Orchestra were first held in a large tent, but so many people came—from all over the United States—and summer storms proved so disrupting, that finally the present steel shed seating five thousand was erected.

When Tanglewood was donated to the Festival Association, Koussevitzky thought at once what a wonderful place it would make for a music school. Vacation-like surroundings. . . .daily contact with a great orchestra. . . .the best of teachers. . . .what ambitious young musician could ask for a more ideal, more stimulating environment? Four years later the Berkshire Music School became a reality. Serge Koussevitzky's vision and generous encouragement were an enormous influence in furthering the cause of contemporary music in America. From his earliest days in this country he championed our native composers—played their works at his concerts; gave them inspiration and material aid by establishing a music foundation in memory of his wife; and helped to train many of the younger musicians at the Summer School of Music in the Berkshires.

Norman Dello Joio

An interesting group of young musicians attended the school, that first season. Among them were Leonard Bernstein, Harold Shapero, and Lukas Foss. Norman Dello Joio, a thin dark-haired young man with El Greco-like features, was one of the first to enroll. The classes were held in an old boathouse at the edge of the lake. At eleven o'clock the recess bell rang and everyone went for a swim. . . .

Paul Hindemith, whose works Dello Joio admired more than those of any other living composer, had charge of the course in composition. At the beginning Dello Joio found Hindemith cold and reserved, and very difficult to approach. But once the initial barriers were broken down "the picture changed." He turned out to be the most inspiring personality that the young musician had ever had the privilege of knowing. He considers Hindemith "one of the greatest men of the century."

Dello Joio spent two summers at Tanglewood, and during the winter between continued his studies with Hindemith at Yale's School of Music in New Haven. Hindemith, he says, has been the most important musical influence in his life, and has helped him to expand his musical horizons beyond the Italian background that was his original heritage.

Early in the nineteen hundreds, Casimir Dello Ioio (spelled originally with an "I" since the Italian alphabet does not contain the letter "J")—an organist and composer—came over from Italy to settle in the United States. He married an American wife and they made their home in New York City, where Casimiro, who had been an organist in Italy, took on a similar post at the Church of Our Lady of Mt. Carmel. Their son, born January 24, 1913, was given the good old Anglo-Saxon name of Norman.

Most of the elder Dello Joio's friends were musicians, and enthusiastic Italian opera fans. Many were the nights that Verdi's arias rang out until the small hours of the morning. Little Norman would waken from his sleep and creep downstairs, to listen entranced, at the door. Verdi was his first love—and he still puts the Italian master at the head of his musical-favorites list. Before long Norman knew the leading arias by heart, and could pick them out on the piano. His father then started him with regular piano lessons, and was amazed to see how quickly the boy learned.

"Piano-playing has always come easy to me," says Dello Joio. "I have never had to work very hard at it." If it had not been for his still greater interest in composing, he probably would have been a concert artist.

Casimir Dello Joio also taught his son to play the organ. By the time Norman was twelve he had been made assistant to his father at the Church of Our Lady of Mt. Carmel. At fourteen he became organist and choir director in a church of his own, and since then has held several similar positions. His teachers were Pietro Yon—who was his godfather and organist at St. Patrick's Cathedral in New York—and Gaston Déthier.

By way of recreation young Dello Joio wrote music. He composed the way most youngsters play baseball, for the love of it. At that time baseball meant almost as much to him as music. He was extraordinarily good at it. In fact, when he was nineteen he found himself faced with a difficult dilemma. The manager of a professional baseball club made him an alluring offer to join the team. However, he had recently been trying his wings on a first attempt at serious composition—a sonata for violin and piano. When he heard this played by some friends he was so delighted at the way it sounded that he decided to sacrifice the glory of a baseball player's profession for the uncertain, but more inwardly rewarding career of a composer.

Baseball has always remained Norman Dello Joio's chief hobby. Some years later, when he went to Pittsburgh to hear one of his compositions played with the orchestra there, he met the manager of the Pittsburgh Pirates. This man's hobby, curiously enough, was music (he had been writing the program notes for the concerts). He wanted to talk music—Dello Joio wanted to talk baseball. . . . It is not on record which won out.

During those early years, side by side with his professional work as organist, Norman Dello Joio went to All Hallow's School in New York and, following that, to City College. He also attended the Institute of Musical Art, where he studied harmony and music theory, and continued with his composition. While there he won his first award—the Elizabeth Sprague Coolidge prize for a *Piano Trio*. Since then (in 1944 and 1945) he has twice received a Guggenheim Fellowship; the 1943 Town Hall Composition award for his *Magnificat for Orchestra*; and in 1946 a thousand dollar grant from the American Academy of Arts and Letters. He is now head of the

Norman Dello Joio

Music Department at Sarah Lawrence College in Bronxville, N. Y., having succeeded William Schuman when the latter left there in 1945, to go to Juilliard.

Like most of the younger composers, Dello Joio has had firsthand acquaintance with Tin Pan Alley. When he was twenty, to help out expenses, he organized a jazz band that played all over the East. This gave him a good understanding of popular music—though it failed to convert him from his classical heritage. Jazz he considers "a passing phase."

In 1939 Dello Joio won a fellowship to the Juilliard Graduate School, and worked there for three years under Bernard Wagenaar. Two years later the first of his larger works, *Sinfonietta for Orchestra,* was played by the N.B.C. Symphony Orchestra under the direction of Dean Dixon. That was the beginning of his success. When "fan letters" began to come in after this concert, it became apparent that his future as a composer was assured.

He next turned to ballet music. Eugene Loring, director of the Dance Players commissioned him to write two ballets: *Prairie* and *The Duke of Sacramento.* In 1941 Dello Joio was made musical director of the company, and held this position for two years. One of his best known works is his third ballet: *On Stage.* It has toured the United States and England and is now part of the regular repertory of the Ballet Theater—and was for several seasons featured at the Metropolitan.

When Norman Dello Joio read Stephen Vincent Benét's epic poem *Western Star* he immediately thought of it in terms of music. At that time he was looking for a text for a choral work. Two years before as a commission from Robert Shaw, he had written a singularly effective piece for the latter's Collegiate Chorale called *The Mystic Trumpeter* (with French horn obbligato). This had been so successful that Shaw asked him to do another work for his chorus.

As Dello Joio read Benét's book it seemed to him particularly appropriate for the work he had in mind. He began, in fact, to conceive of a series of choral compositions which would cover the entire history of the United States. From Benét's poem he chose the parts that would fit in with the musical form and divided the work into three sections: first, *The Settling of Virginia;* second, *The Settling*

439

Modern Music-Makers

of New England, and third, *Gradual Movement Toward the West* —
a typical expression of America's pioneer spirit:

> Americans are always moving on
> We don't know where we're going
> But we're on our way. . . .

Dello Joio has received many commissions for different types of music. His earlier works include "concertinos" for piano, for flute, and for harmonica, all with orchestra; a *Concerto* for two pianos and orchestra, and one for harp and string orchestra; and *To a Lone Sentry*, commissioned in 1943 by the League of Composers. Among Dello Joio's chamber-music works are: a *Sonata* for violin and piano and *Ite Missa Est* — for the same two instruments; a *Woodwind Quartet;* a *Woodwind Trio* for clarinet, French horn and bassoon, and another for flute, cello and piano; two *Duo Concertantes*, one for two pianos and the other for cello and piano; and a *Sextet for Three Recorders and Three Strings* (or three woodwinds and three strings). He has also written a large number of piano pieces and songs.

The year 1946 proved a banner one for Norman Dello Joio. First, one of his choral works was given at Columbia University's Music Festival in May. *A Jubilant Song,* using lines from Walt Whitman's *A Song of Joys* and commissioned by the G. Schirmer Music Publishing House especially for the occasion, had its initial performance at the festival's concert of contemporary American music for high schools. It was sung by the chorus of the Music and Arts High School, with the composer at the piano. *A Jubilant Song* proved one of the highlights of that program, and received great applause.

A second triumph came several months later when Dello Joio played his *Ricercari for Piano and Orchestra* at a Carnegie Hall concert on December 19, with George Szell conducting the New York Philharmonic-Symphony Orchestra.

This work is based on a very old type of composition, dating back to pre-Bach days. Dello Joio has developed it in modern form; there are three movements in the *Ricercari:* the first in waltz rhythm, the second a slow melodic movement, and the third in a vigorous, syncopated style. The critics praised both the playing and the music.

440

NORMAN DELLO JOIO

Norman Dello Joio

"The solo is glittering throughout, full of virtuoso effects and gratefully balanced against the orchestra" wrote one of them.[1]

Mr. Dello Joio has written a delightful work. Full of brightness and the alertness of youth, the simplicity and the polish of expert craftsmanship, the music reflects the busyness and the surface tension of our times.[2]

Another signal honor came to Norman Dello Joio late in 1946. He was one of three American composers to be represented on a series of concerts in Poland (Aaron Copland and Samuel Barber were the two others), and was invited by the Polish Government to play his *Ricercari* there. Shortly after the December Carnegie Hall concert Dello Joio flew to Poland and appeared with the orchestras of Krakow, Katowice, and Lodz. He was greeted with great enthusiasm and in Krakow had to repeat the entire third movement of his *Ricercari.* After the concert he attended a reception at which officials "expressed Poland's joy over the resumption of cultural contacts with the United States." Then he flew home and again played his *Ricercari* with the Cleveland Symphony.

In 1948 Dello Joio's *Variations, Chaconne and Finale*—based on old Gregorian melodies—won the Music Critics Circle's award for the outstanding work of the season. It was first played by Bruno Walter and the New York Philharmonic-Symphony. Other recent compositions are: *Serenade, Concerto for Clarinet and Orchestra, and New York Profiles* (all orchestral); and A *Psalm of David,* for chorus and orchestra. Two new stage works have been added to his list: a ballet for Martha Graham *Diversion of Angels* (first titled *Wilderness Stair)*—one of the most sensitive of Dello Joio's dance scores—and an opera *The Triumph of St. Joan.* This was originally written for a student production at Sarah Lawrence College, but he is now recasting it into a full-scale three act opera.

It was soon after his appointment as director of the Dance Players, at a concert where some of his own works were played, that Dello Joio met the girl who later became his wife—a dancer named Grayce Baumgold. Their common interest in ballet drew them together, and they were married in June, 1942.

[1] Harold C. Schonberg, *The New York Sun,* Dec. 20, 1946.
[2] Miles Kastendieck, *The New York Journal American,* Dec. 20, 1946.

441

Modern Music-Makers

It was their dream to have a place in the country. Finally, in 1944, they found an English type house built of stone in the wooded section of Chestnut Hill in Wilton. It was not too far from New York and was exactly what they had been looking for. Here they have sectioned off part of their lawn for a ball field. On fine summer days friends gather and Dello Joio goes back to his early love—the sport that almost supplanted music in his life: baseball.

In a picturesque stone-paved studio Dello Joio finds the quiet environment necessary to him for creative work. Here much of his later music has been written—music that reveals "one of the liveliest talents in today's symphonic arenas."[3] Simplicity, tenderness, strength—these, according to Robert Sabin,[4] are the outstanding qualities in Norman Dello Joio's music and in his personality.

[3] Louis Biancolli, *New York World Telegram,* Dec. 20, 1946.
[4] In *Musical America,* Dec. 1, 1950.

Norman Dello Joio

Born January 24, New York City	1913
Attends City College	1930
Attends Institute of Musical Art	1932
Piano Trio (Elizabeth Sprague Coolidge award)	1937
Concertino for Piano and Orchestra	1938
Sonata for Violin and Piano	
Wins Fellowship to Juilliard Graduate School	1939
Woodwind Quartet	
Sinfonietta for Orchestra	1940
Attends first session Berkshire Music School	
Concerto for Two Pianos and Orchestra	1941
The Duke of Sacramento—ballet	
Musical Director of Dance Players	
Magnificat for Orchestra	1942
Duo Concertante for Two Pianos	
Marries Grayce Baumgold	
The Mystic Trumpeter	1943
Concertino for Harmonica and Orchestra	
To a Lone Sentry	
Town Hall Composition Award	
Guggenheim Fellowship (renewed 1945)	1944
Appointed head of Sarah Lawrence Music Department	1945
"On Stage!"—ballet	
Ricercari for piano and orchestra	1946
A Jubilant Song	
Grant from American Academy of Arts and Letters	1946
European tour as composer-pianist	1947
Variations, Chaconne and Finale (New York Critics Circle award)	1948
Diversion of Angels—ballet	1948
Serenade for Orchestra	1948
Concerto for Clarinet and Orchestra	1949
New York Profiles	1949
A Psalm of David	1950
The Triumph of St. Joan—opera	1950

The Music of Norman Dello Joio

444

Norman Dello Joio

Modern Music-Makers

[1] Coleman-Ross.
[2] G. Schirmer.
[3] Weaner-Levany.
[4] C. Fischer.
[5] Hargail.
[6] G. Fischer.

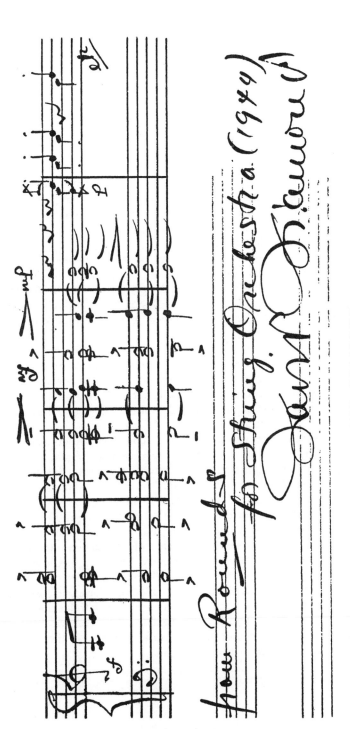

DAVID DIAMOND

DAVID DIAMOND

ONE day in 1944 Serge Koussevitzky looked through the manuscript of a new symphony that had been sent to him by a young composer named David Diamond. He was struck by the originality of the score and stated that he considered it "an important contribution to American musical literature."

Diamond had already written a *First Symphony*, which had been played by Mitropoulos and the New York Philharmonic, and a number of other orchestral works. With the performance of his *Second Symphony* by Koussevitzky and the Boston Symphony Orchestra, he found himself definitely established in the front rank of the younger American composers.

David Diamond's early years were spent in Rochester, New York. He was born there on July 9, 1915, of Austrian-Jewish parents. By profession his father was a carpenter; his mother had been a dressmaker in Lwow before coming to this country, and her greatest love was music—her chief entertainment the theater and opera. To David she passed on a special gift for music. Before he was seven he had learned, without lessons, to play the violin. His parents couldn't afford to buy him an instrument so he borrowed one from a devoted family friend and began setting down original tunes in an ingeniously devised musical notation all his own. This accomplishment so impressed a neighboring Polish boy that David offered to write tunes for him in exchange for doing his school arithmetic problems.

By the time young Diamond was ten the family was in such straightened circumstances that they were obliged to leave Rochester and go to live with relatives who owned a fruit shop in Cleveland. There he came to the attention of André de Ribaupierre, a Swiss musician, and from 1927 to 1929 he attended the Cleveland Institute of Music. At fifteen Diamond returned once more with his family to Rochester and there obtained a scholarship to the Eastman School. Bernard Rogers was one of his teachers at Eastman, in theory and composition, and Effie Knauss in violin.

DAVID DIAMOND

David Diamond

From those earliest days when he rebelled at arithmetic, young Diamond disliked formal training and set tasks. At Eastman instead of practising his violin or studying subsidiary courses, he spent his time writing original pieces or studying scores in the library. The school concerts were his special delight. He played second violin in the orchestra, and sometimes he would be so carried away, listening to the music, that he would forget to play. By temperament he was highly sensitive and emotional. Full of nervous energy which no obstacle could daunt, he had a capacity for work (when the work interested him)which amazed his fellow students and teachers alike.

While at Eastman Diamond wrote his first large orchestral work, a *Symphony in One Movement,* performed there in 1931 at a student's concert. He was, however, dissatisfied with the extra-curricular activities at Eastman, so he applied for a scholarship to the New Music School and Dalcroze Institute in New York and continued his studies with Paul Boepple and Roger Sessions.

Always there was the question of money. The scholarship provided his training, but he still had to eat. At one time he mopped floors to pay for his board. Another time, since he couldn't afford to rent a piano he made friends with a night watchman and elevator boy at the Y.M.H.A. where he was then staying, and persuaded them to let him work at night in an empty practice room. The heat was turned off and it was bitterly cold, but he put on a heavy turtle neck sweater (two sweaters in fact) and went right on working. Once engrossed in his composing he could forget the frigid temperature of the early morning hours.

In the spring of 1935 Paul Whiteman, symphonic-jazz king, established a fellowship in memory of his mother, Elfrida Whiteman, with a $2,500 award for the best orchestral work written by an American and reflecting the American spirit. David Diamond, just turned twenty, won the prize with a composition entitled *Sinfonietta,* based on one of Carl Sandburg's poems in *Good Morning America.* The money he received made it possible for him to continue private study with Roger Sessions. That same summer he received a fellowship to the MacDowell Colony in Peterborough, New Hampshire, and there completed a chamber orchestra piece which he had sketched the previous spring in New York.

In 1936 E. E. Cummings was looking for a composer to write

the music for his ballet scenario called *Tom*.[1] Diamond went to see Cummings and asked him if he could do the score.

Cummings agreed. "It will be best for you to go to Paris and be near Massine, who is to do the choreography," he said, "I'll arrange it through Cary Ross (the financial "Angel") so you can make the trip and stay there until the work is completed."

To appreciate what such an offer meant it would be necessary to have spent a childhood of bitter privation, to have had to struggle every step of the way just to keep going, and finally to have reached a precarious foothold which only sheer determination could maintain. The French school had always appealed to David Diamond more than any other. Now to have an important commission, and on top of that a chance to go to the land of his dreams, was almost too good to be true. He has never forgotten the awe that he felt on arriving in France—the "home of great composers."

That summer turned out to be the first of three spent abroad. During his second year in Paris and Fontainebleau he worked with Nadia Boulanger, thus becoming a member of what Virgil Thomson once called the *"Nadiaboulangerie."* Diamond found Paris exciting and highly stimulating. The city itself was a never ending source of entertainment and inspiration to him. When he visited the Pére Lachaise Cemetery and saw the graves of Oscar Wilde, Sarah Bernhardt and other immortals, he was moved to express his feelings in music, and wrote a *Psalm for Orchestra*. This he dedicated to André Gide, the latter having counseled him to complete the work. Another composition written while in Paris—*Concerto for String Quartet*—he inscribed to Albert Roussel, who had befriended him and introduced him to several musical luminaries.

One memorable day Mlle Boulanger took him with several of her pupils, to meet Stravinsky at the latter's home in the rue St. Honoré. Diamond played for him, with Boulanger, a piano version of his recently composed *Psalm*.

"*Trés intéressant,*" murmured the famous Russian, when they had finished playing. "Of course there are a few weak spots." He turned over the pages of the manuscript. "Here now, something is wrong in the form...."

---

[1] Because of financial and other complications *Tom* was never actually produced. It requires a full evening to perform.

David Diamond

The younger composer was impressed. The passage in question did not satisfy him either. Stravinsky went on to explain: "In an ill-proportioned work you can often find out what's wrong by timing with a stop-watch. Your weak spots are in the shorter sections."

Diamond made the suggested corrections, and his *Psalm for Orchestra* won the 1937 Juilliard Publication Award. One critic called it an "enormously interesting work in the modern idiom of dissonance.... strong music, masculine and declarative,"[2] while another was impressed by its "fine, granitic seriousness, its significant compression of a large idea into a small space, and its spare, telling use of the orchestra."[3] The *Psalm for Orchestra* also helped to gain him a Guggenheim Fellowship in 1938, which enabled him to return to Paris for his third and last year.

David Diamond's ideal among contemporary composers was Maurice Ravel. When the young musician first went to Paris he looked forward with special anticipation to meeting the great French composer. One day he found him at the music publishing house of Durand et Fils, looking through some music, and introduced himself. Ravel was small, shy, "but very charming." That fall Diamond saw him for the last time at a concert where Madeleine Grey sang the *Don Quichotte a Dulcinée* suite. He sat in the front row with a physician (Ravel was then already suffering from the mysterious malady that later took his life). During the intermission, Diamond spoke with him briefly. *"Bonne chance,"* said the little man as they parted. "He had an aloof, far away expression," Diamond says, "as if he were in another world...."

The following December (1937) Ravel died. Diamond felt a sense of personal loss. Two days after his death he composed an *Elegy* in memory of the man whose music had been such an inspiration to him. *Hommage á Satie* was an earlier tribute to another favorite French composer, and his *Aria and Hymn*, to Albert Roussell, still another.

In 1939, when Germany declared war on France, David Diamond was obliged to return to the United States. Then his whole life changed. Gone were the pleasant days of association with artists

---

[2] Isabel Morse Jones, *The Los Angeles Times.*
[3] Albert Frankenstein, *The San Francisco Chronicle.*

who accepted him as a member of their group. In Paris he had had a certain standing, and was considered one of the most gifted of the younger American composers. But in his own country he found himself practically unknown save in New York. Worse still, he had no means of support.

It was a difficult and humiliating period in his career. Once before, after vainly trying all the normal channels open to a musician, he had finally ended up as clerk at a soda counter on the night shift of an upper Broadway drugstore. During the daytime, when he should have been catching up with his sleep, he wrote his *Heroic Piece* for small orchestra. At a later period, when in equally straitened circumstances, Oscar Levant introduced him to Mark Warnow, director of the "Hit Parade" radio program.

"I could get you a job playing violin in our orchestra," Warnow offered.

Diamond was glad of the chance. "But," he confessed, "I haven't touched a violin in years."

"I'll support you while you practice up. Then you can join the Hit Parade." Diamond played with the show for two years, and earned enough to continue with his own work.

Fortunately, soon after his return from Europe, a series of awards helped to tide him over. First he had an opportunity to work at Yaddo, near Saratoga, New York. This luxurious estate, with its fifty-five room Victorian mansion, was formerly the home of Mrs. Spencer Trask (later Mrs. George Foster Peabody). At her death she endowed the place and set it aside as a"residence and retreat for persons actively engaged in artistic and creative work." Each year Mrs. Elizabeth Ames, the executive director, invites a group of artists, writers, and composers to spend a month or more as guests of the estate. In the fall there is usually a Music Festival of Contemporary American music.

At Yaddo, Diamond began his *First Symphony*. A renewal of the Guggenheim Fellowship made it possible for him to finish the symphony and to write his first *String Quartet*. This, with his *Chamber Orchestra Concerto* and *First Symphony* won the 1942 cash prize of the American Academy in Rome. The war, however, prevented him from going to Italy. He remained in New York and completed a *Second Symphony*.

David Diamond

In 1944 a National Academy of Arts and Letters Grant was awarded to David Diamond "in recognition of his outstanding gift among the youngest generation of American composers; and for the high quality of his achievement as demonstrated in orchestral works, chamber music, and songs."

The *Second Symphony* Diamond explains, was written "during days of tense world unrest, and I am quite sure that a certain amount of exterior emotional influence has affected the quality of the symphony." However, it is in no sense a "programmatic" piece. "I have a horror of anything as prosaic as that and since I have never known that method of musical composition, I can only say that the opposite is true. My emotional life and reactions to certain events and situations have worked hand in hand with purely abstract musical conceptions and manipulation of material; and it was always the material that remained foremostly important to me in my working stages."

"His emotion has every evidence of being deep and sincere," wrote one of the Boston critics after the *Second Symphony's* first performance, "and certainly he has the means of conveying it. His themes are not sentimental but they lend themselves to a development whose richness is most expressive."

In 1944 Diamond composed one of his most widely played works: *Rounds for Orchestra*. It was commissioned by Dimitri Mitropoulos and played by him and the Minneapolis Orchestra on November 24 of that same year. Based on the old canonic form (in which the different sections succeed each other, repeating the melody in regular rhythmic periods) with a lyric and expressive adagio movement, *Rounds for Orchestra* won acclaim from audience and critics alike and received the 1946 Music Critics Circle citation. "Diamond's ... *Rounds*... must be rated one of the most musicianly and accomplished scores in the mass of new American works," wrote Hugo Leichtentritt. Olin Downes in reviewing it said:

The felicity of the ideas and their working out is communicative. It is not only sound but youthful writing, full of enthusiasm and imagination in the leading of the parts. There is no strict, regimented succession of

453

Modern Music-Makers

phrase length and intervals, but instead a delightfully free play of rhythm and counterpoint garlanded about the central ideas. The music has a vernal freshness and energy. [4]

David Diamond is one of the most prolific of our contemporary composers. Even in his early days he turned out quantities of music ("mostly juvenalia—not one of which I would care to resurrect, excepting perhaps the *Hommage á Satie*"). Since then he has each year produced a number of important new compositions.

He has written three *String Quartets* (the third of which received the 1947 Music Critics Circle Award); a *Concerto for String Quartet* and a *Piano Quartet;* also a *Concerto for Two Solo Pianos;* a *Flute Quintet* (commissioned by the League of Composers and published by the Society for Publication of American Music); a *Sonata for Cello and Piano;* a *Violin Sonata* (written for and played by Joseph Szigeti) and a *Chaconne for Violin and Piano* (1948). In 1950 he wrote a *Quintet for Clarinet, Two Violas and Two Cellos.*

His long list of orchestral compositions includes four symphonies (the last of these commissioned by the Koussevitzky Music Foundation); *Aria and Hymn;* two concertos for violin, and one for cello; and a *Concerto for Orchestra.* His most recent works are *The Enormous Room, Timon of Athen,* and a *Concerto for Piano and Orchestra.* (1950).

Diamond has done incidental music for a number of plays. His first score was for Margaret Webster's production of *The Tempest* (played on Broadway in 1945) at which he conducted the orchestra. Next came music for Middleton's *The Changeling* and, in 1950, for Tennessee Williams' *The Rose Tattoo.* That same year he composed a completely new score for the Dwight Wiman production of *Romeo and Juliet,* starring Olivia de Haviland. He has also done several film scores: *A Place To Live* (documentary film for the Philadelphia Housing Association); *Strange Victory* (also documentary) and, in 1949, *Anna Lucasta.* So far Diamond has produced only one ballet: *The Dream of Audubon,* which won a Ballet Guild Award.

Diamond himself has a special fondness for his songs, several groups of which have been published. In his own words: "The combination of great and tender texts by Melville, St. Teresa of Avila,

---

[4] *The New York Times,* October 18, 1946.

David Diamond

Joyce, Mansfield, Lovelace, Keats and others, with my particular melodic, polyphonic and harmonic style, makes for the natural continuance of the art song in our century."

David Diamond, like most of the modern composers, has not always been understood. Some critics have called his music "noisy and artificial," "hard and brittle-sec," with "violent color changes." But they all admit that his talent and sincerity have never been doubted by either hearers or critics, and they agree that he has "a highly original style" and "a special gift for orchestration."

Diamond has received a large number of awards, prizes, and commissions, and his works have been played by the leading orchestras throughout the country. With his talent, determination, and immense capacity for work, he will undoubtedly continue to make what Koussevitzky termed "important contributions to American musical literature."

David Diamond

Born July 9, Rochester, New York	1915
Attends Cleveland Institute of Music	1927-1929
Attends Eastman School of Music	1933
Attends Dalcroze Institute, New York	1934-1936
Spends summer at MacDowell Colony	1935
First Concerto for Violin and Orchestra	1936
Sonata for Cello and Piano	
Goes to Paris	
Psalm for Orchestra	
Aria and Hymn for Orchestra	1937
Quintet for Flute, Strings, Piano, commissioned by League of Composers	
Scholarship H. H. Flagler—returns to Paris	
Studies with Boulanger at Fontainebleau, summer	1937
Piano Quartet	1938
Continues studies in Paris with Boulanger	1938
Juilliard Publication Award (*Psalm for Orchestra*)	
Guggenheim Fellowship	
Concerto for Cello and Orchestra	
First String Quartet	1940
First Symphony	1941
The Dream of Audubon (Ballet Guild Award)	
Cash Prize of American Academy in Rome	1942
Paderewski Prize (*Piano Quartet*)	
Guggenheim Fellowship renewal	
Second Symphony	
Grant from National Academy of Arts and Letters	1943
Second String Quartet	
Rounds for String Orchestra (commissioned by Mitropoulos)	1944
Incidental Music for The Tempest	
Third Symphony	1945
Fourth Symphony (commissioned by Koussevitzky Music Foundation)	
Third String Quartet (Music Critics Circle of N.Y.)	1946

David Diamond

Sonata for Violin and Piano	
Ernest Bloch award for *Young Joseph*	
Second Concerto for Violin and Orchestra	1947
Sonata for Piano	
Music for Shakespeare's Romeo and Juliet—concert suite	
Chaconne for Violin and Piano	1948
The Enormous Room—for orchestra	
Lectures on American Music at Salzburg Seminar in American Studies, Schloss Leopoldskron	1949
Conducts the Louisville Orchestra in première performances of *Timon of Athens*	
Concerto for Piano and Orchestra	1950
Clarinet Quintet	1950
Teaches at Metropolitan School of Music in N. Y. C.	1950
Incidental Music for Tennessee Williams' The Rose Tattoo	1951
Incidental Music for Romeo and Juliet starring Olivia de Havilland	1951
Abohah David—Sabbath Eve Service commissioned by Park Avenue Synagogue of N. Y.	1951

457

The Music of David Diamond

ORCHESTRAL WORKS

Hommage à Satie—for chamber orchestra	1934
First Concerto for Violin and Orchestra [1]	1936
Psalm for Orchestra	1936
Suite from the Ballet Tom	1936
Variations for Small Orchestra	1937
Aria and Hymn for Orchestra [2]	1937
Overture for Orchestra [2]	1937
Elegy in Memory of Maurice Ravel [1]	1937
Heroic Piece for Small Orchestra [2]	1938
Concerto for 'Cello and Orchestra	1938
Music for Double String Orchestra, Brass, Tympani	1939
Concert Piece for Orchestra [3]	1939
Concerto for Chamber Orchestra [4]	1940
First Symphony [4]	1941
Second Symphony [3]	1942
Rounds for String Orchestra [5]	1944
Third Symphony [1]	1945
Fourth Symphony [6]	1945
Music for Romeo and Juliet—concert suite [4]	1947
Overture to The Tempest [7]	1947
Second Concerto for Violin and Orchestra	1947
The Enormous Room for orchestra [6]	1948
Timon of Athens a symphonic portrait after Shakespeare, for orchestra [2]	1949
Concerto for Piano and Orchestra [1]	1950

CHAMBER MUSIC WORKS

Partita for Oboe, Bassoon and Piano	1935
Concerto for String Quartet	1936
Trio in G Major for Strings	1937
Quintet for Flute, Strings and Piano [6]	1937
Quartet for Piano and Strings	1938
Sonata for 'Cello and Piano [8]	1938
First String Quartet	1940

David Diamond

Second String Quartet	1943
Third String Quartet [1]	1946
Sonata for Violin and Piano [6]	1946
Canticle and Perpetual Motion for Violin and Piano [5]	1946
Chaconne for Violin and Piano [1]	1948
Quintet for Clarinet, Two Violas, Two 'Cellos	1950

PIANO WORKS

Eight Piano Pieces for Children [6]	1935
Sonatina for Piano [9]	1935
Preludes and Fugues for Piano [2]	1939
Concerto for Two Solo Pianos [1]	1942
Album for the Young for Piano [5]	1946
The Tomb of Melville for Piano [2]	1946
Sonata for Piano [8]	1947

CHORAL WORKS

Four Madrigals for a cappella chorus (from *Chamber Music* by James Joyce) [10]	1937
This Is the Garden for a cappella chorus (E. E. Cummings) [11]	1938
Two Choruses for women's voices a cappella (E. E. Cummings) [1]	1940
Young Joseph for women's voices and string orchestra (text by Thomas Mann)	1944
Chorale for Mixed Chorus a cappella and tenor solo (text by James Agee)	1950
The Martyrs for men's voices a cappella (H. Melville) [1]	1950
Let Us All Take to Singing for men's voices a cappella (H. Melville) [1]	

STAGE WORKS

Tom ballet in four episodes (E. E. Cummings) mixed chorus and large orchestra	1936
The Dream of Audubon ballet (Glenway Wescott)	1941
Incidental Music for the Tempest (Shakespeare) [7]	1944
Incidental Music for The Changeling (Middleton)	1947
Incidental Music for The Rose Tattoo (Tennessee Williams) Cheryl Crawford production	1950
Incidental Music for Romeo and Juliet (Shakespeare) D. Wiman production starring Olivia de Haviland	1950

Modern Music-Makers

FILM

A Place to Live—Documentary film	1941
Strange Victory—Documentary film	1948
Anna Lucasta—film	1949

SONGS

Twelve Songs [5]
Five Songs [3]
Five Songs [1]
Three Songs [12]
Songs from The Tempest [7]
Three Songs [2]
Two Songs [11]
Two Songs [13]

[1] Southern Music Pub.
[2] Leeds Music Corp.
[3] Associated Music Pub.
[4] Boosey & Hawkes.
[5] Elkan-Vogel.
[6] G. Schirmer.
[7] Chappell.
[8] New Music Editions.
[9] Mercury Music Corp.
[10] Edwin F. Kalmus.
[11] Carl Fischer.
[12] Arrow Music Press.
[13] Mercury Music Corp.

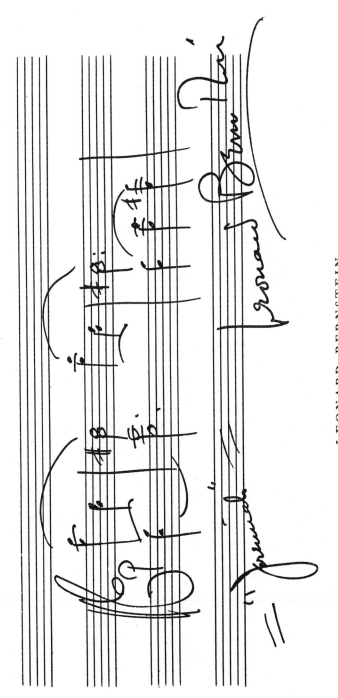

LEONARD BERNSTEIN

LEONARD BERNSTEIN

LEONARD BERNSTEIN insists that his meteoric career has been the result of "accidents, miracles, and coincidences."

These have undoubtedly played an important part in his striking rise to fame; but other factors—such as brilliant musicianship, thorough training, a natural gift for melody, and the enterprise to cpen quickly when opportunity knocks at his door, have also contributed largely to the success of this talented young conductor-composer-pianist—who has been called the "brightest young man in the United States' musical world today."

The most important "miracle" of young Bernstein's career catapulted him into fame on November 14, 1943. By "accident" Bruno Walter, who was to be guest conductor that day, suddenly became too ill to direct the afternoon's concert (it was the first time in fifteen years that such a thing had happened at Carnegie Hall); and by "coincidence" Leonard Bernstein, recently appointed assistant conductor of the orchestra, was the only one available to fill his place.

Without a rehearsal, with only a short visit at Walter's bedside—where the latter obligingly "showed him just how he did it"—the twenty-five-year-old musician led the veteran orchestra players through a difficult and exacting program. This concert made musical history. Koussevitzky wired from Boston: "Listening now. Wonderful." Rodzinski, regular director of the orchestra, drove in from his Stockbridge farm to see how his assistant's debut was coming off. He arrived at intermission time and proudly exclaimed, "This young man has prodigious talent!"

Bernstein was the youngest conductor ever to direct the New York Philharmonic in a regular concert. In spite of the importance of the occasion, that eventful afternoon, and the fact that the concert was being broadcast over a national hook-up, he showed no sign of nervousness. "Advancing to the podium with the unfeigned eager-

Leonard Bernstein

ness and communicative emotion of his years he showed immediately his brilliant musicianship and his capacity to release and control the players. . . ." wrote Olin Downes the following day. "Mr. Bernstein is one of the very few conductors of the rising generation who are indubitably to be reckoned with." All the New York papers joined in glowing tributes to the young conductor. There was even a "success story" editorial about him in *The Times*.

Leonard's parents and his brother Burton sat in a first tier box, that afternoon at Carnegie Hall. If the young conductor cast an occasional glance of triumph in the direction of his father, he could hardly be blamed. Samuel Bernstein had not been at all pleased over Leonard's choice of a career. He was strictly a business man, with no time for what he considered long-haired arts. Russian-Jewish by birth, as was Leonard's mother, he had built up a successful cosmetic business in Boston, Massachusetts, and expected his son, on graduating from Harvard, to come into the firm with him. Leonard, however, had other ideas.

He was born in Lawrence, Massachusetts, August 25, 1918. It was his Aunt Clara who started him—all unwittingly—on what his father would have called the downward path. When he was ten, she moved some of her furniture over to the Bernsteins' home, including an old upright piano. It was a "terribly tinny affair," but the very day of its arrival Lenny lost his heart to it. "We fell in love with each other," he says. From that moment the piano and the boy became inseparable companions.

Almost at once he demanded music lessons. Soon he learned to read music as easily as most boys read the funny papers. He would come home with his arms full of scores, and pound away for hours on end at the old upright.

Leonard next undertook his sister's musical education. Shirley, five years younger, joined him in duets. They sang together interminably—"screamed themselves hoarse. . . ." There was never a minute without music. Father Bernstein rebelled. "Do you want to be one of those wild, struggling musicians?" he would ask, shaking his head. "Believe me, there's no money in music. Now take the cosmetic business. . . ."

Lenny definitely did *not* want to take the cosmetic business. He worked for one month, during a vacation, in the firm's shipping

463

Modern Music-Makers

room—but he "couldn't stick it out." When he was thirteen—a large boy for his years—he played piano with a jazz-orchestra and earned enough pocket-money to be independent. He finds jazz "expansive . . . exciting . . . a great invention. . . ." During the Second World War, although he had by that time become a "serious" musician, Bernstein entertained the soldiers with concerts of boogie-woogie. (It was a great disappointment to him, when he tried to enlist, to be turned down because of chronic asthma.)

During his grammar-school days Leonard went to the Boston Latin School, where he won a musical medal and became Captain of the First Regiment of Boston School Cadets. Between the ages of fourteen and seventeen he studied piano with Helen Coates, assistant to Heinrich Gebhard. Miss Coates has remained in close touch with her brilliant pupil, and since 1944 she has been his private secretary and personal representative.

At Harvard, Bernstein majored in music. He studied composition with Walter Piston and Edward Burlingame Hill, and continued his piano with Heinrich Gebhard. For a Harvard play, Aristophanes' *The Birds,* he wrote his first serious music, and conducted the orchestra in a student performance of it. But he couldn't make up his mind about the future. He played the piano brilliantly, his composing showed unusual talent, and he liked to conduct. Which of these should he choose for his career? He has answered this question, so far, by combining the three.

Shortly before graduating, in 1939, from Harvard, Leonard met Dmitri Mitropoulos, the Greek conductor who had recently arrived in the United States. To him he explained his quandary, and Mitropoulos immediately said, "You should be a conductor!"

Bernstein decided that the Curtis School of Music was the best place to learn conducting. At his audition there he was given some difficult and entirely unfamiliar scores to play at sight. The facility he showed in reading music amazed Fritz Reiner, head of the conducting department. He took the young musician at once into his class, and Leonard remained for the next two years at Curtis, studying conducting with Dr. Reiner, orchestration with Randall Thompson, and piano with Mme Vengerova. He spent the summers of 1940 and 1941 at the Berkshire Music School at Lenox, Massachusetts, (not far from Rodzinski's Stockbridge farm). When he sent in his

464

LEONARD BERNSTEIN

Leonard Bernstein

application for the class in conducting, Koussevitzky, who had already heard of the young man's musical ability said, "Of course I will accept you." During the summer of 1942, he became one of Dr. Koussevitzky's assistants at the Berkshire Music Center.

At twenty-two, Leonard Bernstein was already a conductor of considerable experience, but he found, to his disappointment, that there was no place open to a young orchestra leader in this country— especially if he happened to be American-born. Aside from the weekly concerts given by the students at the Berkshire Music Center there were apparently no opportunities for an ambitious young musician who wanted to conduct.

So he went to Boston and spent a year there teaching, composing and arranging some concerts of contemporary music for the Institute of Modern Art. His first published work, a *Clarinet Sonata*, was performed there on April 21, 1942, by David Glazer with the composer at the piano. He also directed two performances of Aaron Copland's play-opera *The Second Hurricane*. The year following he wrote *Seven Anniversaries*, a group of piano pieces each one dedicated to a special friend. A second set, *Four Anniversaries*, was composed in 1949.

In 1943 Bernstein completed a clever and amusing song-cycle *Five Kid Songs: I Hate Music*. Jennie Tourel gave the first performance of these songs at her Town Hall concert in the fall of that year and since then they have been widely sung. *La Bonne Cuisine*, with words taken from old French recipes, is another diverting song-cycle written in 1950.

After a year in Boston, Leonard Bernstein felt that there was no future for him in that city. He decided to go to New York though he had no prospects there, and no money. He was fortunately able to get a few pupils, played accompaniments for a dollar an hour, and finally got a job making music arrangements for the Harms Music Publishers. All during this time he kept on composing both popular and serious pieces. Before long Harms doubled his salary and offered him a contract for both kinds of music.

Leonard thought that he had settled into a more or less permanent groove when suddenly, "out of the blue," came an offer from Rodzinski (who had heard him conduct at Tanglewood) to become his assistant at the New York Philharmonic. "Miracle number one!" says

Bernstein. Two months later came the second miracle—the momen-
tous concert of November fourteenth, and this was followed by requests to appear as guest-conductor with other symphony orchestras.

Bernstein began his first symphony *Jeremiah* in 1941, while in
Boston, but did not complete it until nearly three years later. He first
conducted it in Pittsburgh, January, 1944, then with the Boston Symphony and the New York Philharmonic. *Jeremiah* was lauded for its
"drive . . . poignancy . . . dramatic strength, and emotional force"—
qualities especially apparent in the third movement *Lamentation*
which contains a soprano solo, (sung originally by Jennie Tourel),
with words in Hebrew from the Biblical text. Bernstein describes the
middle part, in scherzo form, as "a movement about destruction . . .
fitful . . . chaotic . . . brazen . . . seven minutes of wild rhythm. It
couldn't have existed without jazz, though it sounds oriental."

Leonard Bernstein was only twenty-four when he wrote *Jeremiah*,
but this work so impressed the critics, particularly the skill of its
orchestration, that they voted him the 1944 Music Critics Circle
Award.

That same year his first ballet, *Fancy Free* (commissioned by the
Ballet Theater and first performed in April), became the biggest hit
of the 1944 ballet season. It continues to be one of the most popular
works in the repertoire of the Ballet Theater, and has been performed
all over the United States.

Fancy Free depicts the hilarious adventures of three jaunty sailors
on shore leave—exuberant youth rampant. The music is "hard and
New Yorky," Bernstein says, "full of brashness, yet with New York
tenderness too." He didn't think of jazz when he wrote it, but "it
came out jazzy—had to be. . . ." Nor had he any idea of writing "American" music, though *Fancy Free* is of its very essence American.

"Those who try to write music that is deliberately American seldom
succeed," he declares. "Some have used Indian themes, or Puritan
hymns, or Negro tunes, or jazz, but where these are deliberately
'tacked on' they are no more than extraneous tinsel." American music,
Bernstein believes, must be an *unconscious* expression—a compound
of racial experience which will then include all the above styles and
be essentially however indefinably American.

Fancy Free was expanded, that same fall of 1944, into a full-length
musical comedy called *On the Town*. (This was sold to M.G.M. even

Leonard Bernstein

before it went into rehearsal—"the first time in history.") Written in collaboration with Jerome Robbins, who did the choreography, and Betty Comden and Adolph Green, authors of the story, this high-spirited show turned out to be one of the most popular hits on Broadway. Bernstein wrote it at odd moments, between conducting engagements. *On the Town* was in rehearsal, nearly ready for its opening night, before he had finished the final score. He delivered it with the ink scarcely dry. His sister Shirley, inseparable companion since their early childhood, played one of the roles.

Another ballet, also in collaboration with Jerome Robbins, appeared in 1946. *Facsimile* is very different in character from the gay and sparkling *Fancy Free*. The subject matter, an introspective psychological study of "three insecure people" in a stark modernistic setting, is more interesting than appealing. "It is all a little overwrought . . . but is nevertheless an original, admirably sincere and thoroughly to be respected achievement," wrote one critic, who went on to say that Leonard Bernstein's score "is eminently theatrical, making brilliant use of instrumental color contrasts, getting as turbid sometimes in its syncopations as Mr. Robbins' complicated lifts, but containing some beautifully musical passages for all that."[1]

To his ballets and musical comedies, Bernstein brings a fresh and new approach very different from most of the stereotyped patterns in current use. This "long-hair on Broadway," as he has been called, holds basically to popular tradition, but he combines it with a certain amount of symphonic technique. Some critics claim that he sometimes falls between the two, and writes "neither good musical comedy nor first-class symphonic music." But judging by his success in both fields this is not an altogether fair appraisal.

Ever since Bernstein's spectacular debut with the New York Philharmonic, he has been in great demand as a conductor. In 1945 he was appointed Music Director of the New York City Symphony (following Stokowski there). This appointment Bernstein considered a challenge as well as an opportunity; he held auditions for several hundred players and gathered together a fine orchestra (most of the players were young, and a number of them just out of the service),

---

[1] John Martin, *The New York Times*, Nov. 2, 1946.

Modern Music-Makers

conducted it brilliantly,[2] and even appeared on more than one occasion as soloist, directing the orchestra from the keyboard. It was with considerable regret that three years later he was forced to resign from his position with the City Symphony because of the constant requests to appear as guest-conductor with other orchestras.

In the spring of 1946 Bernstein was invited as "representative American conductor" to come to the International Music Festival of Prague, a celebration in honor of the Fiftieth Anniversary of the Czech Philharmonic Symphony. He led the Prague orchestra in two programs of all-American music, including the European première of his own symphony *Jeremiah*. Then he rushed home by plane to conduct two concerts with the NBC Symphony, flew back to London for a four-week's engagement with the London Philharmonic, and got back to the U. S. just in time to rehearse and conduct the American première of Benjamin Britten's new opera *Peter Grimes* at Tanglewood. Each summer, no matter how far his engagements have carried him during the year, Bernstein returns to the Berkshire Music Center, where he is now a member of the music faculty and assistant conductor of the orchestra.

Early in 1948 Bernstein toured Europe again, conducting in Munich, Milan, Budapest, Vienna, Paris, and Holland. That same fall he went to Israel and served for two months as Artistic Director of the newly formed orchestra there. Since then he has returned several times to conduct in Israel. In 1951 when the Israel Orchestra toured the United States, Bernstein shared the conducting with Serge Koussevitzky.

In spite of these many activities Leonard Bernstein managed to write what is so far his most ambitious score—a *Second Symphony*. It was in 1947 that he first read W. H. Auden's Pulitzer Prize winning poem *The Age of Anxiety*. At once he began to "hear the music in his head." But he was very much involved then with a strenuous schedule of public appearances, and it took him nearly two years before he was able to complete his symphony. It was written "everywhere from Tel Aviv to Taos, New Mexico"; most of the orchestration was done on a four weeks tour with the Pittsburgh Symphony, during which he

[2] Bernstein's playing of Marc Blitzstein's new symphony *The Airborne* at the City Center made musical history.

468

Leonard Bernstein

conducted twenty-five concerts in twenty-eight days, and was soloist at twenty-two of the concerts.

The Age of Anxiety is dedicated to Serge Koussevitzky, and was first performed by him and the Boston Symphony Orchestra in April, 1949, with Bernstein playing the solo piano part. Rudolph Elie (in the *Boston Herald*) described the work as "neither a conventional-type symphony nor a conventional-type piano concerto."

It employs the piano, not as a virtuoso now conquering and now conquered by the orchestra, but as a protagonist living, to the full, the events transpiring in the orchestra, which is to say the universe bounded by the poem.

The last movement, following a grotesque dirge, Mr. Elie considers:

one of the most extraordinary symphonic movements in literature, an apotheosis of the jazz spirit. Set for piano and percussion only, it out-bops any contemporary be-bop, and out-boogie's any woogie. Yet it bears no more relation to jazz at Carnegie Hall than Ravel's La Valse bears to the Viennese waltz. It is, in fact, an inspired commentary on jazz, at once sardonic and tender, at once violent and sentimental. . . .

Almost alone of his contemporaries, Mr. Bernstein has written of today for today. His inspiration has come from living and being; he writes here of things he knows and lives. He has taken, as all men of musical genius have done in the past, the musical substances he truly understands.

Following the initial performance in Boston of *The Age of Anxiety,* Bernstein conducted it with the New York Philharmonic-Symphony, Lukas Foss at the piano. He also made the score into music for a ballet of the same name (again with Jerome Robbins as choreographer), and it was presented by the New York City Ballet at the City Center of New York. That same winter of 1949-50 Bernstein composed incidental music for a new Broadway production of *Peter Pan.* Also a set of five pieces (commissioned by the Juilliard Foundation): *Brass Music.* Each of these pieces is dedicated to a dog belonging to one of his friends or relatives. The final number, *Fanfare for Bima* for brass ensemble, is a tribute to Koussevitzky's dog Bima.

Modern Music-Makers

The great facility with which Leonard Bernstein writes music sometimes dismays him. He is inclined to be skeptical of such facility and believes that it might even turn out to be a handicap, if he were to rely on it too much. "Things come to me in a kind of inarticulate flash," he explains, "as if I might have known them in another world." When asked what he likes to do best he says "I am only interested in what I can do well. . . ."

This explains, perhaps, why his activities are so varied, for whatever he undertakes he does well. However, too much success can be an even greater test of character than too little. The career of a successful orchestral conductor (like that of a prima donna who has the world at her feet) presents more allure than the lonely and too often unrewarded path of a creative worker. Can the two be combined?

So far Leonard Bernstein has successfully managed a triple career—though his creative output has been less than one might wish, considering his talent. He himself realizes that continuous public appearances make it difficult if not impossible to do much original work, so he has now decided to take a year or two off and devote himself to composition. He should be able, during that time, to add a number of important new works to the list of his compositions.

Leonard Bernstein

CHRONOLOGICAL CHART OF MAIN EVENTS AND WORKS

Born August 25, Lawrence, Mass.	1918
Graduates from Harvard Academic & Music Courses	1939
Receives scholarship to study conducting with Koussevitzky at	
Berkshire Music Center	1940
Graduates from Curtis Institute	1941
Appointed assistant to Koussevitzky at Tanglewood	1942
Clarinet Sonata	
Appointed assistant conductor of N.Y. Phil.-Symph.	1943
First Symphony Jeremiah	1944
Fancy Free (ballet with Jerome Robbins)	
On the Town (score for music comedy)	
Appointed Music Director of New York City Symphony	1945
Conducts at Prague International Festival	1946
Conducts first American performance of *Peter Grimes*	
Facsimile (ballet with Jerome Robbins)	
Conducts Israel Philharmonic Orchestra in Israel	1947
First European tour as guest conductor	
Resigns from City Symphony after three seasons	1948
Second European season	
Second Symphony The Age of Anxiety	1949
Five Pieces for Brass	1950
Tours Italy—April	
Conducts at Music Festivals of Holland, Edinburgh, Tanglewood,	
and at Amsterdam and Paris	
Guest conductor at Tanglewood Summer Festivals	1946-1950
Tours U. S. and Scandinavia with Israel Orchestra	1951
Retires temporarily from Conducting	
Marries Felicia Montealegre	1951

The Music of Leonard Bernstein

ORCHESTRAL WORKS

First Symphony Jeremiah [1]	1944
Second Symphony The Age of Anxiety—piano and Orchestra	1949
Brass Music	1950

CHAMBER MUSIC

Sonata for Clarinet and Piano [2]	1941-1942

PIANO WORKS

Seven Anniversaries [2]	1942-1943
Four Anniversaries	1948

SONGS

Cycle: Five Kid Songs "I Hate Music" [2]	1943
La Bonne Cuisine—song-cycle	1948

STAGE MUSIC

Fancy Free (with Jerome Robbins)—ballet [1]	1944
On The Town—music-comedy	1944
Facsimile (with Jerome Robbins)—ballet [1]	1946
The Age of Anxiety—ballet	1949
Incidental Music for Peter Pan	1950

CHORAL WORKS

Hashkivenu (text from Friday eve. Synagogue service) mixed chorus, organ	1945

[1] Harms.
[2] Witmark & Sons.

472

HAROLD SHAPERO

HAROLD SHAPERO

AT the outbreak of the Second World War, Nadia Boulanger left France and joined the music faculty of the Longy Conservatory of Music in Cambridge, Massachusetts. Soon after she arrived there a tall, black-haired youth named Harold Shapero brought her the manuscripts of some pieces he had written.

"You are a born composer," she said looking them over. "But—" she added with a shrewd glance at him, "I am not sure that I can teach you!"

Harold hardly knew how to interpret this remark. Could Mlle Boulanger mean that he was too self-assured? (one of his earlier teachers, Krenek, had once remarked, "He enjoys being considered smart"). On the other hand he had studied with some of the world's finest teachers, including Hindemith, Walter Piston, and—briefly—Stravinsky and he knew a good deal about music writing. However there was still much that young Shapero wanted to learn, and he finally persuaded the famous French teacher that he was in earnest. He found Nadia Boulanger the most profound of all the teachers he ever worked with. "She has a way of bringing out the best of which her pupils are capable," he says. "Not through criticism so much as by approving the good parts in their music, and skipping over the others. It's less what she says than what she leaves unsaid!"

Harold Shapero worked with Nadia Boulanger for two years. Then she told him to continue on his own. "Now you should be able to go on by yourself," she insisted. By that time he had acquired "a prodigious technique".

In his early years young Shapero was in no sense a musical prodigy. His parents, of Russian-Jewish birth (like those of Copland), were neither of them musical, and the last thing they would have suspected when Harold was born, April 29, 1920, in Lynn, Massachusetts, was that he would one day become a composer. At seven Harold started with piano lessons, like many another boy of his age. But unlike most of the others, after two years he no longer had to be made to practise. He actually liked it! He decided then and there that he would be a concert pianist.

At fifteen, however, jazz beckoned him into primrose paths. With thousands of other teen-agers he worshiped at the shrine of "name bands," and could imagine nothing more glamorous than to be the leader of one of them. He threw the classics out of the window and proceeded to organize a jazz band of his own. Father Shapero disapproved; but Harold was a headstrong boy and had his own way.

Today, looking back on this interlude, he concludes that it wasn't such a bad experience after all. By the time he was ready to write serious music he had, as he puts it, "gotten jazz out of his system." Composers who discover jazz at a later date in their careers, he says, often become involved for a considerable period before realizing its limitations. Shapero claims that he has always really preferred the classics, and having gone through jazz at an early age, he believes there is little if any of it to be found now in his music.

His Tin Pan Alley period had one important result. When he tried to arrange pieces for his band he discovered—as did William Schuman in like circumstances—that it was not possible to write any kind of music without knowing something of harmony.

Harold was then attending the Newton High School in a suburb of Boston. He went to Nicolas Slonimsky and told him that he wanted to learn how to compose. Slonimsky steered him back to the classics and before long Shapero began to write little pieces of his own. At that time the modern French school appealed to him particularly, and his first piece, he confesses, was "just like Debussy." His teacher didn't think much of those early efforts. "No good!" he would exclaim scornfully. "Just junk. . . ."

Harold's father wanted his son to go to college. To please him— and "to atone for the sins of the jazz band"—young Shapero enrolled at Harvard. His education until then having been considerably interfered with by extra-curricular activities, he wasn't sure that he could pass the entrance examinations. But he had a naturally brilliant mind, when he took the trouble to use it, and he managed to get through without too much difficulty.

At Harvard Shapero majored in music. During his freshman year he saw an advertisement in the paper stating that two scholarships were available for a six months course of study with Ernest Krenek. Harold sat down and hurriedly wrote a piece, then took it and an early piano concerto to the Czech composer.

"This is interesting . . ." said Krenek. To young Shapero's considerable gratification he gave him one of the scholarships. Later Harold learned, somewhat to the chastening of his pride, only two applications had been sent in—one of which was his own.

Ernest Krenek, a leading exponent of atonality, taught mainly in the twelve-tone system, and the difficulties of this higher musical mathematics scared away most of the students. Harold hoped that Krenek would not discover how little he really knew about composition. Learning to write in the twelve-tone system was like plunging into trigonometry before having had elementary algebra. But Shapero set his mind to the task, and soon mastered the fundamentals of atonality. After six months with Krenek, he says, ordinary composition seemed easy in comparison.

Harold Shapero's main work while at Harvard was with Walter Piston. Next in what he calls his "parade of teachers," came Stravinsky. In 1937 Stravinsky arrived at Harvard to take over the chair of Musical Poetics for a year. Young Shapero looked forward to the master's seminar—and to the opportunity of playing some of his compositions for him—as to one of the greatest events in his life. But he found the experience disappointing. Stravinsky spoke only French, and Harold could understand very little of what he said. He gathered, however, that Stravinsky liked his pieces and thought that he had possibilities.

Shapero's next teacher was Hindemith, at the Berkshire Music School. To make up for the years when he played with jazz instead of doing serious work, Harold now spent his summers as well as his winters studying music. From knowing next to nothing about composition, he found that he "suddenly knew a lot."

He graduated from Harvard in 1941, and shortly after was awarded a Naumburg Fellowship. That same year he won the Rome Prize (though he was unable to go to Italy because of the war). For this prize he submitted a *String Quartet* and an orchestral piece which he had originally written for admission to the Berkshire Music School: *Nine Minute Overture* (the title of which he says, "sounds like an egg"). Howard Barlow broadcast the *Overture* with the CBS

Harold Shapero

Orchestra, and was so impressed by the piece's originality that he played it twice on the same program. Young Shapero received considerable publicity, and encouraged by this success wrote a sonata for piano four-hands, and one for violin and piano. The summer of 1943 he spent at Yaddo, and in 1944 went to the MacDowell Colony.

During the two years after leaving Harvard Shapero concentrated on further perfecting what was already an amazing technique. Then he began work on some piano sonatas. He spent a year writing three of them; the first, he says, was finished in a couple of weeks. The second took him six months.

Shapero's next award was a Paine Traveling Scholarship. Since the war was still on and he couldn't go abroad, he went instead to New York. The summer of 1945 proved particularly eventful. He went again to the MacDowell Colony and there met the talented young artist Esther Geller, whose colorful paintings in ultra-modern style have attracted wide attention. The two were married that same fall.

While at the colony Shapero wrote *Serenade in D* which, as he puts it, "struck the jackpot." It brought him the Bearns Prize from Columbia University, the Gershwin Memorial Contest Award, and a Guggenheim Fellowship (renewed in 1947). The first movement of the *Serenade* was played at Carnegie Hall in March, 1946, Leonard Bernstein conducting the Rochester Symphony. The student orchestra at Tanglewood also gave a performance of Shapero's *Serenade*. He recalls that when the players first started to rehearse it they openly rebelled at the difficulties of the score. But after a few days they became so concerned with the music that they took the separate parts home for individual practise, and at the final performance many of them expressed enthusiastic approval.

To complete Shapero's "jackpot," the Koussevitzky Foundation commissioned him to write an orchestral work. *Symphony for Classical Orchestra,* was composed mainly during the following summer when he and his wife went back to the MacDowell Colony for two months of concentrated work—interrupted by several weeks at the Music Festival in the Berkshires. The *Symphony for Classical Orchestra* has been played by George Szell and the Cleveland Orchestra, and the slow movement alone by Leonard Bernstein with the New York Philharmonic and at the 1950 Berkshire Music Festival with the Boston Symphony.

Modern Music-Makers

In 1948 Shapero wrote an overture for orchestra *The Travelers,* also *Variations in C Minor* for piano, and after that *Arioso Variations* (also for piano). He and his wife spent the year 1949-50 at the American Academy in Rome. While there he composed a *Concerto for Orchestra.*

Harold Shapero is noted for his extraordinary command of musical technique. To him the most intricate of modern harmonizations appear simple, and he is surprised when he finds that others consider his music difficult to play. Several of his fellow composers have commented on his fluency. Although he is still at the beginning of his career, he is considered one of the most promising of the young composers.

Harold Shapero

The Music of Harold Shapero

ORCHESTRAL WORKS

Nine-Minute Overture	1940
Serenade (string orchestra)	1945
Symphony for Classical Orchestra	1946-1947
Overture The Travelers	1948
Concerto for Orchestra	1951

CHAMBER MUSIC

Three Pieces For Three Pieces—(flute, clarinet, bassoon)	1939
Trumpet Sonata	1940
Sonata for Violin and Piano	1942

PIANO WORKS

Four-Hand Sonata	1941
Three Amateur Sonatas	1944
Variations in C Minor	1948
Arioso Variations	1949

HAROLD SHAPERO (left rear)
(front) LUKAS FOSS, LOUISE TALMA; (right rear) ARTHUR KOHN

WILLIAM BERGSMA

WILLIAM BERGSMA

WILLIAM BERGSMA, one of the youngest American composers to receive signal honors for his work, was born in Oakland, California, on April 1, 1921. (He says that he has never lived down this "April Fool" date.)

His mother, a gifted and enthusiastic musician who had at one time sung in opera, started young Bill when he was five with piano lessons, and later with the violin. But he detested practising, so eventually "like many another lazy musician" he took up the viola. In this way he was able to enjoy ensemble music with a minimum of practising. From kindergarten on he was always playing in some school orchestra or group of chamber musicians.

When Bill was six, his mother married again, and the family moved to a country estate near Redwood City, forty miles south of San Francisco. Their home became a center where musicians gathered to visit and to play together. Young Bill delighted in these impromptu concerts; before long he, too, was playing with the others.

He began very early to write down snatches of tunes. They were never completed, but setting them down was an absorbing game to him. He ruled his own paper for the purpose—in later years he was surprised to learn that he could buy paper with the staff lines already printed. At that period Elmer Young, of Palto Alto, was his teacher.

Two red-letter days marked William Bergsma's last year at the Burlingame High School. First the Senior Dramatic Society presented a one-act play he had written. The very next night he scored an even greater triumph: his *Scherzo* for full orchestra was given its initial performance by the high school orchestra. In between these two exciting events, and slightly overshadowed by them, his youngest brother was born. Both the play and the music showed outstanding talent. Fifteen-year old Bill Bergsma found himself torn between two choices. Should he decide on a playwright's or a composer's career?

William Bergsma

At that time the two seemed to him equally desirable—but music finally won the day.

Although he had written a number of earlier pieces, the *Scherzo* was his first fully completed composition. Its success so encouraged him that he decided, that summer of 1937, to enroll at the University of Southern California in Los Angeles for a seminar at which Howard Hanson was to give a special course in music theory. As a result of his studies with Hanson, he wrote a ballet.

The story of Paul Bunyan and his legendary exploits had long been one of Bergsma's favorites. Now he composed his ballet with Bunyan as the main character in a succession of incidents both humorous and dramatic. He originally planned the work as a thirty-five minute long ballet with puppets as dancers. Later he arranged a fifteen-minute orchestral suite from the score. The most striking movement is *The Dance of the Blue Ox*—an amazing piece of work for a sixteen-year-old boy. Hanson immediately recognized the talent evident in Bergsma's ballet, and said he would play the suite with the Rochester Orchestra. The first time that Bill Bergsma heard his *Paul Bunyan Suite* (with the exception of a few excerpts by his high school orchestra) was over the radio, when Hanson broadcast it from Rochester.

It had always been understood that Bill would go to college. He was ready to enter Stanford at sixteen, but the family thought him too young and delayed his enrollment until the following year. After two years at Stanford he decided that he had had enough academic training, and since there were few music courses at the university, he transferred in 1940 to the Eastman School of Music in Rochester, New York. There his *Paul Bunyan Suite* had already made him something of a celebrity.

Bergsma spent two years at Eastman's regular school, then two additional winters doing postgraduate work—chiefly with Howard Hanson—and as a teaching fellow. While in Rochester he wrote a number of compositions, and most of them were played by the Eastman Orchestra (some forty performances in four years). These performances of students' works are of inestimable advantage to a young composer. As Bergsma says: "The best education of all is to hear your own things played."

Among the compositions he wrote while in Rochester were a

Modern Music-Makers

Symphony for Chamber Orchestra, a second ballet in a California setting called *Gold and the Señor Commandante* (staged at Eastman in 1942) and, in 1943, an eight-minute orchestral work. The mood of this last is somewhat reminiscent of Samuel Barber's *Adagio for Strings,* though it is written in a very different style. Bergsma calls it *Music on a Quiet Theme* ("with a noisy middle part"). It has been played by several major orchestras, including the New York Philharmonic, the National Symphony, and the Rochester and San Francisco orchestras.

During the same period Bergsma also composed a number of smaller pieces, and two quartets that won considerable acclaim. The *First Quartet* received the Bearns Prize from Columbia University, and was performed by the Gordon Quartet at the 1942 American Music Festival. The *Second Quartet*—commissioned by the Koussevitzky Foundation—had its first playing at the Eastman School Festival of 1944. The next year Bergsma won a grant from the National Institute of Arts and Letters, and in 1946 a Guggenheim Fellowship.

When he came back to California after receiving the National Institute's grant, he was asked to write the musical score for an educational film. It was to be a community undertaking in co-operation with the Palo Alto Children's Theater and the high school orchestra—a film in technicolor called *Titian the Boy Painter.* "We'll be ready to shoot in a week now," they said. "Can you finish the music by then?"

Bergsma agreed before he realized what he had taken on. To write a twenty-five minute orchestra score in eight days is a task that would stagger the most seasoned musician. Fortunately the young composer had an ideal retreat in which to work. Years before he had been offered his choice of a log cabin in a secluded corner of the family's estate, or an upper room whose windows looked out into a grove of redwood trees. He chose the latter. Now, cloistered in the upper room, he worked day and night, with only snatches of sleep in between. When on the eighth day rehearsals began, the orchestral parts were still not all copied. As the rehearsal proceeded, the score was brought out a page at a time from a back room where copyists worked furiously to complete the parts.

That same year of 1945 Bergsma wrote a set of songs to verses by E. E. Cummings, and a chorus for the Collegiate Chorale: *Time for*

William Bergsma

Sleep. Another chorus for the same group appeared in 1946, *On the Beach at Night,* and a third, *Let True Love Among Us Be,* together with a song, *Lullee, Lullay* in 1948.

In the spring of 1946 William Schuman, casting about for fresh young talent for his Juilliard Music School faculty, invited Bergsma to have lunch with him at the Lotos Club in New York.

"How would you like to teach composition at Juilliard this fall?" he asked with characteristic directness.

At first Bergsma hesitated to take on the responsibility, since he was trying to complete a symphony begun two years before. But Schuman assured him that he would have sufficient leisure to do his own work as well as teach, so he accepted the position. That summer he spent as usual in California. Before he left, there was a wedding in the family. . . . When William Bergsma returned to New York to take up his duties at Juilliard, he brought with him his bride, Nancy Nickerson.

A Guggenheim Fellowship made it possible for them to spend the year 1947-8 in the West Indies. There Bergsma wrote, on commission from Carl Fischer, Inc. for the twenty-fifth anniversary of the League of Composers, a piece for string orchestra called *The Fortunate Islands.* At the end of his year in the West Indies he returned to Juilliard and in 1949 completed his *First Symphony.* It was first performed by the Holland Radio in May, 1950, Erich Leinsdorf conducting, and has also been played by the C.B.S. Symphony and at the 1950 Ditson Festival. *Tangents,* a thirty-five minute work for piano, is his most recent work.

Everything, so far, has come to William Bergsma—as he himself admits—"on a silver platter." He has been singularly favored, both in the matter of talent and of advantages, and all of the music that he has written up to this time has been a success. His career seems to refute the old-time belief that difficult conditions and a certain amount of adversity are prerequisites for the development of worthwhile achievement and character. But the testing of the future still lies before him.

William Bergsma

The Music of William Bergsma

ORCHESTRAL WORKS

Paul Bunyan Suite [1]	1937
Dance of the Blue Ox	
Country Dance	
Night—Paul's Work Done	
Siesta and Happy Dance [2]	1941
Music on a Quiet Theme [3]	1943
Four Scenes from The Boy Painter [4]	1945
The Fortunate Islands	1948
First Symphony	1949

CHORAL WORKS

In a Glass of Water	
Time for Sleep (Benét) chorus, piano	1946
On the Beach at Night (Whitman) chorus, a cappella	1946
Black Salt, Black Provender (Bogan) three choruses, two pianos	1946
Let True Love Among Us Be	1948

CHAMBER MUSIC

Suite for Brass Quartet [1]	1940
First Quartet String [5]	1942
Symphony for Chamber Orchestra [2]	1942
Pastorale and Scherzo—recorder, 2 violas [2]	1943
Showpiece—violin and piano [2]	1943
Second String Quartet [2]	1944

STAGE WORKS

Paul Bunyan (ballet)	1937
Gold and the Señor Commandante [6]	1941
Titian—the Boy Painter	1945

Modern Music-Makers

PIANO

Three Fantasies	1943
Tangents	1951

SONGS

Six Songs (E. E. Cummings) [1]	1945
Lullee, Lullay	1948

[1] Carl Fischer, Inc.
[2] Hargail Music Press.
[3] Arrow Press.
[4] G. Schirmer, Inc.
[5] Society for Publication of American Music.
[6] Fleischer Coll.

WILLIAM BERGSMA

PHOTOGRAPH BY DAVID NILSSON

LUKAS FOSS

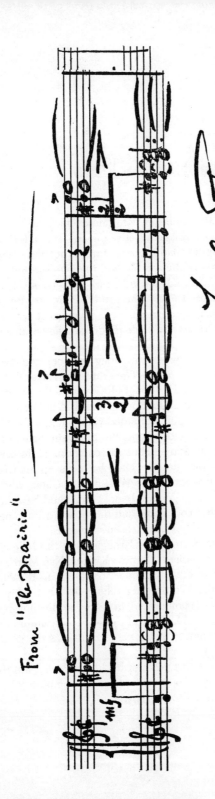

From "The prairie"

LUKAS FOSS

LUKAS FOSS

ARTUR RODZINSKI tuned in, late one evening in 1943, from his farm in Stockbridge, Massachusetts, on an "Invitation to Music" broadcast. The program had already started, but the composition—a cantata with orchestra, Robert Shaw directing—was not familiar to the New York Philharmonic's conductor. "It certainly is *American* music" he said to himself. "But who can the composer be? Not Copland—I'm sure of that. Nor Harris. . . ." Whoever it was, the music impressed him greatly. As the piece progressed he became more and more enthusiastic.

When at the conclusion of the long number the broadcaster announced the name of the piece—*The Prairie,* by Lukas Foss, Rodzinski was still more puzzled. He thought he knew all the American composers, but here was one he had never heard of before. To be sure, Koussevitzky had told him of a talented young man named Foss who had studied conducting with him at the Berkshire School of Music. But he hadn't said anything about his composing. Rodzinski telegraphed CBS for further details. Then he woke up his friend John Finley Williamson, director of the Westminster Choir, who was visiting him but had already gone to bed. "You should have heard that music!" he exclaimed. "Your choir and our New York Orchestra will have to give it at one of our next season's concerts."

The Prairie was performed at Carnegie Hall the following February, 1944, with four soloists—Dorothy Kirsten, Nan Merriman, William Harris, and the negro baritone Tod Duncan—the New York Philharmonic, and the Westminster Choir. The cost of producing this hour-long cantata (comparable, in scope, to Beethoven's *Choral Symphony)* was close to $4,000, and this—the most ambitious American work ever to be put on at Carnegie Hall—was the product of a twenty-one-year-old composer.

Lukas Foss spent the first years of his life in Berlin; but the major part of his training and practically all of his composing have been

Lukas Foss

done in the United States. Unlike most of our distinguished "adopted" composers—such as Stravinsky, Bloch, and Hindemith, who were established composers before coming to America—young Foss was only fifteen when he left Europe, and he was then at the most impressionable period of his life. America had always represented the Promised Land to him; he embraced the customs, language, poetry and music of his chosen country with wholehearted zest. His music is more American in character than that of a number of our native-born composers who were trained abroad.

Lukas' father was a professor of philosophy, and his mother an artist. But neither of them was particularly musical, though one of their relatives, Kurt Schindler, founded the Schola Cantorum in New York. When Lukas was born on August 15, 1922, there was not even a piano in the home. At three years of age his parents gave him a harmonium-accordion for Christmas, and almost at once he began to pick out chords to accompany the old German folk songs that his mother taught him. At seven he began lessons on the piano with Julius Herford. Foss feels particularly indebted to this musician who had a basic influence on his entire approach to music. He learned so rapidly that he could easily have been made into a child prodigy; but fortunately his parents were too farsighted to permit this. Nor was Lukas himself eager for a concert career. "I was always more interested in *music* than in virtuosity," he says.

He was about nine when he heard his first opera—Mozart's *Marriage of Figaro.* This made such an impression on him that he immediately wanted the music, and when his parents gave him the score he proceeded to learn the entire opera, including all the solo parts. He would entertain his family and their friends by giving a full performance of *Figaro,* playing the orchestral accompaniment on the piano and himself singing, with fine dramatic fervor, each of the roles from coloraturo soprano (in falsetto) to basso. This gift for reproducing a work in toto is still one of young Foss's favorite pastimes. To hear him play and sing one of his own choral compositions is a memorable experience.

When Hitler and his Nazi regime came into power, Lukas' father—who is today professor of philosophy at the Quaker College of Haverford—foresaw the future that menaced Germany. In 1933 he left Berlin and took his family to Paris. Lukas, then eleven, attended the

491

Lycée there, and continued his music studies. Lazare Lévy was his teacher in piano, and Noël Gallon in harmony. Later he worked with Felix Wolfes, and attended the Paris Conservatory during his last year in France.

All during their four years in Paris the Fosses talked and dreamed about America. Finally, when their young son was fifteen—"still in knee pants" (French style)—the family moved to New York. Then, as Lukas says, his really serious work began.

He enrolled at the Curtis Institute of Music in Philadelphia, and studied there with Rosario Scalero (composition), Randall Thompson (orchestration), Mme Vengerova (piano), and Fritz Reiner (conducting).

In 1940, when the Berkshire Music School first opened its doors, one of the applicants for Koussevitzky's class in conducting was a slender boy with blue eyes and a shock of curly hair, who looked even less than his eighteen years.

"Aren't you rather young to want to be a conductor?" the Maestro asked the boy.

Lukas Foss didn't think so. "If you would just let me go through the audition . . ." he begged.

Koussevitzky finally agreed, and he was so struck by the boy's talent for all things musical that he not only admitted him to the class in conducting but soon took him under his personal protection. Two years later he appointed him pianist of the Boston Symphony Orchestra.

At the Berkshire Music School young Foss also studied composition with Hindemith, and later continued his work with him at Yale.

During all his spare time Lukas wrote music. Soon after his arrival in the United States Schirmer's published his *Four Two-voiced Inventions* and *Grotesque Dance* for the piano. He had also composed a number of songs, chamber music, and other piano pieces. When he was nineteen a suite for small orchestra to Shakespeare's *Tempest* won him a Pulitzer Scholarship. Since then he has received a number of awards, including the New York Music Critics Circle Citation (for *The Prairie*) and, in 1945, a Guggenheim Fellowship. Foss is the youngest composer ever to have received this honor.

He was about nineteen when he read Carl Sandburg's poem *The Prairie*. This impressed him so profoundly that he immediately

Lukas Foss

wanted to set it to music. Although he had never seen the western prairies, Sandburg's moving words made him feel a part of that vast, open country where *growth* is the keynote of living:

> I am here when the cities are gone.
> I am here before the cities come.
> I nourished the lonely men on horses.
> I will keep the laughing men who ride iron.
> I am dust of men. . . .
>
> I last while old wars are fought, while peace broods
>   mother-like, while new wars arise and the fresh
>   killings of young men. . . .
> I who have seen the red births and the red deaths of
>   sons and daughters, I take peace or war, I say
>   nothing and wait.

In the program notes of *The Prairie's* first performance, Foss wrote,

The attempt to develop an oratorio style based on the American soil and spirit is not new, but Sandburg's epic poem, it seems to me, offers new possibilities in its earthy and almost religious approach. It is a new expression of an old faith drawn from the native soil. The protagonist, simply, is the prairie, but through this poem the prairie grows until it becomes the symbol for the all-embracing principle of *growth* itself.

Foss had already started on *The Prairie* before it occurred to him that he must have permission to use the poem in his cantata. He wrote an imploring letter to Sandburg who replied that it was up to his publisher—but he asked the latter to "give the young man a break." Two years later when Lukas, aged twenty-one, had finally completed the cantata, he presented a copy fresh from the printer to Carl Sandburg at a formal dinner given in honor of the occasion. Sandburg introduced the young musician as "our demon welterweight composer. . . ."

The Prairie was first heard in a short symphonic synthesis played by Koussevitzky and the Boston Symphony Orchestra. This was the first performance by a major symphony of one of Lukas Foss's works.

493

The next May, Robert Shaw and the Collegiate Chorus gave the initial full performance at Town Hall in New York. Then followed the radio presentation, a few weeks later, and the year after that, Rodzinski and the Westminster Choir performed it three times with the New York Philharmonic.

Before beginning *The Prairie*, Foss had started a *Piano Concerto*. He completed this now, that same year of 1943, and conducted the first performance of the work with the C.B.S. Orchestra, Gyorgy Sandor as soloist. The following year Foss himself played the solo part with Arthur Fiedler and the Boston Pops Orchestra. Since then he has performed the concerto with a number of leading orchestras. He has also been guest conductor in Pittsburgh, New York, Los Angeles, and Boston, and his works have been played in Europe and Israel as well as in this country.

His next composition, *Ode for Orchestra*, written during the war and dedicated "To those who will not return," was sketched "in two weeks of uninterrupted labor." In speaking of this work Foss says:

The artist who feels that his art is not an escape from the world, but a direct expression of it. . . .always has the urge to come to grips with the problems of his time and seeks their solution in his particular field of expression. Time can thus become a great incentive. There is, however, no definite program in my *Ode*. . . . I can suggest the general idea. . . . crisis, war, and ultimately "faith." Anything beyond this the music should express better than the words.

Foss's first symphony *(Symphony in G)* was composed at the MacDowell Colony in 1944. He returned to the colony the following summer to work on a ballet. *The Gift of the Magi*—based on O. Henry's story by that name, for the Ballet Theater. This was first produced in Boston, the composer conducting, and later at the Metropolitan in New York.

Two major choral works were written in 1945 and 1946. While these are not actually church music they are both deeply religious in feeling. *Song of Anguish* takes its words from Isaiah and is scored for baritone and orchestra. *Song of Songs,* also with text from the *Bible* and first performed by Koussevitzky and the Boston Symphony in

494

Lukas Foss

March, 1947, was commissioned by the League of Composers for the soprano Ellabelle Davis. Foss finds the negro voice particularly well suited to the type of music that he tries to write. When he heard Gershwin's *Porgy and Bess* he was struck by the rich and vibrant tone of the singers' voices, so different from what he calls the "standardized" tone in singing.

Cyrus Durgin (in *Musical America*[1]) called *Song of Songs* a "remarkable work. . . . A musicianly and emotional setting of verses from the Song of Solomon, rich and colorful."

Song of Songs was played eight times in a single week of March, 1947, by the Boston Symphony Orchestra. During the season 1949-1950 Foss's compositions, according to a survey made, were among the most frequently performed of all American works in this country. His one-act opera, *The Jumping Frog*, taken from Mark Twain's famous story, had four different productions in the year following its completion in 1949.

Two recent honors received by Lukas Foss are the 1949 Award of the Society for the Publication of American Music for his *String Quartet in G*, and in 1950 the most coveted of all prizes—a fellowship to the American Academy of Rome. This last gave him an opportunity to work abroad, so that same year he resigned from his position with the Boston Symphony and went to Italy to become a fellow-in-residence at the academy in Rome. There he began work on a second *Piano Concerto*.

During his brief career young Foss has written quantities of music—"trunksfull," as he puts it—"but not all of it worth printing!" Many of his compositions have been published. His orchestral works, performed by a large number of our leading symphonies, are available on a rental basis.[2] He has also appeared as guest conductor and as piano soloist with several of America's major symphony orchestras, and has recorded with Victor, Decca, Presto and Hargail.

---

[1] March 25, 1947.

[2] To print orchestral scores, requiring countless separate parts for the different instruments, the notes must first be engraved by hand on copper plates, and this is a very costly procedure. But photostatic copies can be produced at a much more reasonable price. A system now exists whereby orchestral works of leading contemporary composers are available to any conductor who may desire to play them.

Modern Music-Makers

Lukas Foss is one of the youngest of our music writers. But he has already established himself as a composer of importance. With high endorsement from Koussevitzky, Rodzinski, Fritz Reiner, Stokowski and others of our musical leaders—with an astonishing record of important works already to his credit and promise of greater still to come, Lukas Foss should be a leading light in the American music of the future.

Lukas Foss

The Music of Lukas Foss

ORCHESTRAL WORKS

Two Symphonic Pieces	1939-1940
Two Pieces for Orchestra: Dance Sketch and Allegro Concertante	1941
The Prairie, symphonic piece [1]	1942
Piano Concerto [1]	1943
Ode for Orchestra [1]	1944
Symphony in G (No. 1) [1]	1944
Pantomime for Orchestra [1]	1945
Second Piano Concerto [2]	1951

CHORAL WORKS

Cantata Dramatica for Orchestra, Solo Tenor, Chorus	1940
We Sing cantata for children	1941
The Prairie—(Cantata for four solo voices, chorus) [1]	1942
Tell This Blood—a cappella chorus [1]	
Song of Anguish (from *Isaiah*) for baritone and orchestra [1]	1945
Song of Songs (second Biblical solo orchestra cantata) for soprano and orchestra [1]	1946

CHAMBER MUSIC

Sonata for Violin and Piano	1937
Four Preludes for Flute, Clarinet and Bassoon	1940
Duo for Cello and Piano [2]	1941
Clarinet Concerto (later turned into piano concerto) [2]	1941-1942
Three Pieces for Violin and Piano [2]	1944
Dedication [2]	1944
Early Song [2]	1944
Composers Holiday [1]	1944
Capriccio for Cello and Piano [1]	1946

SONGS

Three Songs on Goethe Texts	1938
Melodrama and Dramatic song of Michaelangelo for voice and piano	1940

Lukas Foss

PIANO

Four Two-Voiced Invention for Piano [3]	1937
Grotesque Dance [3]	1937
Set of Three Pieces for Two Pianos [3]	1938
March	
Andante	
Concertino	
Sonatina for Piano	1939
Passacaglia for Piano [3]	1940
Fantasy-Rondo for Piano [3]	1944

STAGE WORKS

Incidental Music to the Tempest	1939-1940
Within These Walls—ballet	1944
The Heart Remembers—ballet	1944
Gift of the Magi—ballet	1945
The Jumping Frog—one-act opera	1949

[1] G. Schirmer, on rental.
[2] Hargail, Inc., on rental.
[3] G. Schirmer, Inc.